Principles of Cyberbullying Research

Definitions, Measures, and Methodology

**Edited by
Sheri Bauman
Donna Cross
Jenny Walker**

Routledge
Taylor & Francis Group

LONDON AND NEW YORK

First published 2013
by Routledge
711 Third Avenue, New York, NY 10017

Simultaneously published in the UK
by Routledge
2 Park Square, Milton Park, Abingdon, Oxon OX14 4RN

Routledge is an imprint of the Taylor and Francis Group, an informa business

First issued in paperback 2015

Library of Congress Cataloging-in-Publication Data
Bauman, Sheri.
Principles of cyberbullying research : definitions, measures, and methodology /
Sheri Bauman, Donna Cross, Jenny Walker.
    p. cm.
    Includes bibliographical references and index.
    ISBN 978-0-415-89749-5 (hbk. : alk. paper)   1. Cyberbullying—
Research—Methodology.   2. Bullying—Research—Methodology.
I. Cross, Donna, PhD.   II. Walker, Jenny L.   III. Title.
HV6773.15.C92B38   2013
302.34'302854678—dc23   2012015811

ISBN 978-0-415-89749-5 (hbk)
ISBN 978-1-138-64232-4 (pbk)
ISBN 978-0-203-08460-1 (ebk)

Typeset in Times by Apex CoVantage, LLC

Principles of Cyberbullying Research

In 2010, the International Cyberbullying Think Tank was held in order to discuss questions of definition, measurement, and methodologies related to cyberbullying research. The attendees' goal was to develop a set of guidelines that current and future researchers could use to improve the quality of their research and advance our understanding of cyberbullying and related issues. This book is the product of their meetings, and is the first volume to provide researchers with a clear set of principles to inform their work on cyberbullying. The contributing authors, all participants in the Think Tank, review the existing research and theoretical frameworks of cyberbullying before exploring topics such as questions of methodology, sampling issues, methods employed so far, psychometric issues that must be considered, ethical considerations, and implications for prevention and intervention efforts. Researchers as well as practitioners seeking information to inform their prevention and intervention programs will find this to be a timely and essential resource.

Sheri Bauman, PhD, is a Professor and Director of the School Counseling master's degree program at the University of Arizona, USA.

Donna Cross, EdD, is the Foundation Professor of Child and Adolescent Health in the School of Exercise and Health Sciences, Edith Cowan University in Western Australia.

Jenny Walker, PhD, is President of Cyberbullying Consulting Ltd.

Contents

List of Tables

List of Figures

Preface

Research in the social sciences serves three purposes: acquiring knowledge, translating the findings so they can be applied in practice, and informing policy. Each of these is critical to the field of cyberbullying research. As a new focus of inquiry, the knowledge base on cyberbullying is limited, and the need for solid information is great. Because cyberbullying is a worldwide problem affecting young people, new knowledge has important applications to the development of prevention and intervention programs that are sorely needed. Basing such programs on scientific knowledge increases the possibility that such programs will be effective. Finally, legislation and educational policies are important endeavors that also should be predicated on a dependable empirical knowledge base. As social scientists work toward accumulating knowledge, it is critical that we do so using the most rigorous approaches. This volume is the first to provide guidelines for cyberbullying researchers in order to ensure that high quality practices lead to solid knowledge.

This book is the product of an International Cyberbullying Think Tank held in September 2010 in Tucson, Arizona, and funded by the National Science Foundation. The 20 attendees (who are contributing authors of this volume) came from three continents, eight countries; six states in the United States; and a variety of academic disciplines including psychology, public health, social work, counseling, communications, and education.

The impetus for the meeting was the developing line of inquiry focused on the phenomenon called cyberbullying. As technology became more affordable and available, instances of abuse perpetrated via technology came onto the radar screen of the public, and of researchers. Many scholars, eager to understand this "new" behavior, conducted initial studies using their own definitions of the term, devising measures, and using methods that had been applied to traditional bullying, primarily surveys. Scholars (e.g., Tokunaga, 2010; and Menesini, 2009) recognized that without a standard definition and psychometrically sound measures, the findings of research did not meet the accepted standards of scientific rigor. The goal of the Think Tank was to deliberate upon questions of definition, measurement, and methodologies related to cyberbullying, with the goal of reaching consensus and disseminating the outcomes so that current and future researchers would have guidelines that would improve the quality of research and advance our understanding of cyberbullying and related issues. In addition, the group generated research questions that they hoped would be addressed going forward. We present these in the hope that researchers planning new studies will consider how they might address these questions.

This volume represents the expanded and detailed products that emerged from the meeting. We begin with an introduction that chronicles the extant research and articulates the questions we address in the rest of the book. The next section focuses on the thorny question of the definition of "cyberbullying." Readers will note that there is still some dissent on this issue; researchers need to consider potential alternative conceptualizations and terms, and be clear in their own work about exactly what it is they are studying. We move then to theoretical frameworks, and examine whether theories used to explain traditional bullying are sufficient to explain cyberbullying, or whether a new formulation is called for. One such formulation is presented in this section.

We next address the question of methodology. We open with a discussion of the importance of methodology, and follow with a review of sampling issues as they relate to this field. We present a review of the methods that have been employed so far in cyberbullying research in order to set the stage for our guiding principles, specific recommendations, and then we present a more detailed description of an innovative approach that is particularly suitable for this topic. Finally, given the unique nature of research about technology—and methods that employ that technology, we conclude this section with an overview of ethical issues peculiar to this line of inquiry.

In order to conduct sound research, reliable and valid measures are essential. This section begins with an exposition of the critical importance of measurement. This is followed by a review of psychometric issues that must be considered when conducting cyberbullying research. Then, since researchers around the world are working on this problem, we present the essential processes that are involved in translating measures and determining measurement invariance for different populations. Qualitative studies have much to offer this field, and we include a discussion of those practices next. Finally, we review the content of needed measures, that is, what to measure.

We conclude with two important sections. The Implications section looks at the implications of the topics discussed above for prevention and intervention efforts. How can our principles be translated into practice? What can practitioners take away from this volume? Finally, we consider the way forward. What are the most understudied and needed questions for cyberbullying researchers to address? What areas most need attention?

Michele Ybarra (2011) recently reported the findings from two studies that help us put cyberbullying in context. Although her studies were done in the United States, the findings will be of interest to readers around the globe because they help dispel some conventional wisdom that may not be consistent with the data. In addition, the results also foreshadow many of the issues that will be discussed in this volume. I include her summary of these findings here:

I have recently led two national youth survey efforts: Teen, Health, and Technology, which examines the benefits and risks for lesbian, gay, bisexual, questioning, and transgender youth online (LGBQT), and how this may be similar or different for non-LGBQT youth; and Growing up with Media, which is a longitudinal study of youth to better understand how media is affecting youth behavior.

In Growing up with Media, we included measures of both cyberbullying (i.e., bullying online that is repetitive, over time, and between two actors of differential power) and harassment (e.g., rude and mean comments; threatening or aggressive comments). As we would expect, harassment appears to be a more generalized type of youth victimization than bullying. Based upon cohort data from 2007 and 2008, 24% of youth have been harassed, 13% have been bullied and harassed, and only 1% have been bullied but not harassed online in the past year; the remaining 62% report neither experience. Thus, if youth are being bullied, they're likely being harassed, but the converse does not necessarily follow. From a measurement perspective, this finding suggests that it is important that we as researchers are very clear about what we are measuring: Is it more general aggression that may happen once or multiple times, between youth of equal strength or not; or is it specifically bullying that occurs repeatedly, over time, between people of differential strength? Both victimization experience types are associated with elevated odds of psychosocial challenge and so both should continue to be measured, but given our previous findings that frequency of victimization matters, clarity in measurement is critical.

When we look at Internet harassment rates over time and across age, we see a very clear trend for age: Rates increase steadily from age 10 to age 14, and then plateau thereafter and may even decline a bit by age 17. Across time (i.e., between 2006–2008), rates are quite stable, suggesting that youth are no more likely to be harassed online now than they were earlier. Findings are similar for rates of cyberbullying when we look at data from Growing up with Media data from 2007 and 2008, and Teen Health and Technology data from 2010. Trends for text messaging harassment also suggest an increase by age; across time, things are much less clear however. Text messaging-based bullying rates provide a clearer picture, and suggest that there may have been a slight increase in victimization rates from 2008 to 2010.

We also have reports of distress across time. Some may wonder whether victimization is becoming more upsetting, even if overall rates are stable. Data from our Growing up with Media cohort suggest that distress rates for Internet harassment did not increase from 2006 to 2008, and this is true among younger youth as well as older youth. Thus, harassment does not seem to be getting nastier, more awful, or in some other way more psychologically intense over time.

When comparing different environments, 38% of youth who were bullied at school said they were very or extremely upset by the most serious time they were bullied at school, compared to 15% of youth bullied online. Indeed, youth bullied by phone (33%) and on the way to and from school (39%) also were twice as likely to report being very or extremely upset. It is true that we need to pay attention to the 15% of distressed youth who are bullied online; it also is true that we need to be aware that youth bullied in other environments are even more likely to report distress. No matter where it occurs, bullying can be a traumatic experience.

A concern raised by adolescent health professionals is whether the infusion of technology has created a seemingly inescapable experience for victims. Data from our general cohort of the Teen, Health, and Technology survey suggest that 44% of youth are bullied through at least one mode each year: 39% in-person, 10% by phone, 14% via text messaging, 17% online, and 10% some other way. About half of bullied youth say that they are victimized in one mode only, and the other half report being victimized in two or more modes. Specifically: 11% of all youth are bullied in two modes, 6% in three modes, 3% in four modes, and 3% in all five modes. Together, these data suggest that even with the emergence of Internet and text messaging, in-person is still by far the most common way youth experience bullying. Thus, while it is important to understand how youth are experiencing technology, this should not be done at the expense of attention to the in-person experience. Also, the majority of youth are not bullied; and among those who are, half are bullied through only one mode. Thus, the inescapable experience is not a stereotypical one. Nonetheless, a very concerning 6% of youth report being bullied in 4 or all 5 of the modes that we surveyed. We need to do a better job at identifying and supporting these youth, and ensuring that they are referred into mental health services immediately, if warranted.

Other studies have also surveyed nationally representative samples (Cross, et al., 2009; del Barrio, et al., 2012). In the del Barrio study, 3,000 secondary students in Spain were surveyed, and a limited overlap between traditional bullying and cyberbullying was found, with only 5.5% of traditional targets being also targets of cyberbullying and 5.4% of perpetrators of traditional bullying also engaging in cyberbullying. Only 1.1% of students who were not victimized by traditional bullying were targeted electronically. In the total sample, general bullying was reported by 89.5% of participants, whereas cyberbullying was reported by 10.5%.

The differences in findings across studies, and the differences between the public perception of the prevalence of this problem and the findings of careful research is a reminder that researchers need to work together, establish common language, definitions, methods, and measures so studies can be compared in a meaningful way, and accurate data can be reported.

We use this book as a bully pulpit (pun intended) to encourage the production of high-quality research on the phenomenon of cyberbullying. We write for researchers, both current and future, to present a synthesis of principles that will contribute to more rigorous science. We also address practitioners, who seek guidance from research findings to inform their prevention and intervention programs, and those policy makers who make decisions about policy and legislation. We intend the material contained here to help them select high-quality research that meets the highest standards of the research endeavor.

Sheri Bauman

References

Cross, D., Shaw, T., Hearn, L., Epstein, M., Monks, H., Lester, L., & Thomas, L. 2009. Australian Covert Bullying Prevalence Study (ACBPS). Canberra, Australia: Department of Education, Employment and Workplace Relations.

del Barrio, C., deDios, M. J., Montero, I., Martín, E., Ochaíta, E., Espinosa, . . . Barrios, A. (2011). Cyberbullying among Spanish secondary students: A national survey. *Proceedings of the 15th European Conference on Developmental Psychology* (pp. 369–376). Bologna: Italy: Medimond.

Acknowledgments

The International Cyberbullying Think Tank, at which the idea for this book was developed, was funded by grant 0956790 from the National Science Foundation. The editors and contributors appreciate the support for this important work. For more information on the think tank, go to http://icbtt.arizona.edu/

The editors wish to thank Kurt Marder, M. Ed., senior research associate at the University of Western Sydney in Australia, for his invaluable assistance at the think tank meeting and in the preparation of this book. They also wish to thank the following students for their assistance with preparation of the final document: Sarah Clark, Joanne Cuellar, Connor Eustice, Tessa Hamilton, Mario Kurilo, Carlos Leon, Megan Molina, Macie Myers, and Sarah Seavey.

About the Editors

Sheri Bauman, PhD, is a Professor and Director of the Counseling and Mental Health master's degree program at the University of Arizona. Her research focuses on bullying and cyberbullying. She is the recipient of two grants from the National Science Foundation related to cyberbullying, including one that supported the International Cyberbullying Think Tank, which brought together researchers from around the world to deliberate issues in cyberbullying research. The other grant funded a project to conduct a longitudinal study of the emergence of cyberbullying behaviors from middle childhood through adolescence, which is currently underway. Dr. Bauman has submitted several other proposals for funded research on this issue. She has presented papers and presentations about bullying and cyberbullying in many venues in the United States as well as in Australia, Germany, Austria, Finland, Greece, and Norway. Her book, *Cyberbullying: What Counselors Need to Know* was published in 2011 by the American Counseling Association.

Donna Cross, EdD, is the Foundation Professor of Child and Adolescent Health in the School of Exercise and Health Sciences, Edith Cowan University in Western Australia and Founding Director of the Child Health Promotion Research Centre. She conducts applied multidisciplinary school and family-based research in Australia and internationally. Donna has won over \$8 million in competitive grants to support 48 large intervention and translation research trials to address health issues related to pastoral care including mental health (youth bullying and cyberbullying, violence and aggression prevention, and depression); injury control; and drug use and healthy eating.

Jenny Walker, PhD, is President of Cyberbullying Consulting Ltd. She is the founder of a global blog, www.cyberbullyingnews.com, connecting people and groups to encourage and promote civil communication and behavior in this fast-paced, ever-changing, technology-driven world. Her blog summarizes rapidly changing information on cyberbullying and online safety to help busy researchers, professionals, educators, and parents stay up-to-date. She has taught at the high school and college level, and has served at a residential group home for teens experiencing emotional and behavioral challenges. Born in England, her travels to Europe, Australia, Hong, Kong, Indonesia, the Philippines, and Mexico have added to her global perspective regarding online safety and digital citizenship. She is a published author who offers presentations, training seminars, and workshops on the topics of bullying, cyberbullying, online safety, and digital citizenship.

About the Contributors

Ikuko Aoyama, PhD, is an Assistant Professor in the Department of Psychology at Tokyo University of Social Welfare in Japan. She received her PhD in Educational Psychology from Baylor University in the United States in 2010. Her research interests are cyberbullying, online human behaviors, information moral education, and media literacy.

Marilyn Campbell, PhD, is a Professor in the school of Learning and Professional Studies, Faculty of Education at Queensland University of Technology. She currently lectures in the Masters of Education program preparing teachers for school counseling and in the Masters of Educational and Developmental Psychology preparing psychologists to work in a range of educational and developmental positions. Marilyn has worked as a teacher and psychologist in early childhood, primary, and secondary schools. She has also been a teacher-librarian, school counselor, and supervisor of school counselors. Her research interests are in behavioral and emotional problems in children and adolescents. Her recent work has included research into anxiety prevention and intervention as well as the effects of bullying, especially cyberbullying, in schools. She is the author of the Worrybusters series of books for anxious children.

Noel A. Card, PhD, is Associate Professor in Family Studies and Human Development at the University of Arizona. His research interests include child and adolescent social development and developmental methodology. He has conducted research on various forms and functions of aggression and on the importance of aggressor-victim relationships. His quantitative interests include longitudinal analyses, analysis of interdependent data, and meta-analysis. He was a recipient of the Society for Research in Child Development's Early Career Research Award in 2009, and he is an elected member of the Society for Multivariate Experimental Psychology and fellow of the American Psychological Association.

Rhonda G. Craven, PhD, is Professor and Director of the Centre for Positive Psychology and Education at the University of Western Sydney. Her research focuses on self-concept, maximizing life potential in diverse settings, and educational interventions that make a difference. Her major research interests include bullying measurement and intervention, Aboriginal education, impact of self-concept on academic achievement, and appropriate education for gifted and talented students. Professor Craven has successfully secured over 7 million dollars in nationally competitive funding for 45 large-scale research projects.

Cristina del Barrio, PhD, is Professor, School of Psychology, *Universidad Autónoma de Madrid,* Spain. She participated in TMR project-network EU-funded (Coordinator: PK Smith) and codirected the two national studies of bullying (Ombudsman's-Unicef Reports 2000 & 2007). She conducted research with a developmental approach on *societal cognition* (understanding of nationality, war and peace, children's rights, national identity in immigrant adolescents); and *peer bullying/social exclusion in schools* (incidence, representations, qualitative methods, multi-ethnic schools, programs to improve relationships). Cristina coordinates the research group INEXE focusing on interpersonal processes of inclusion and exclusion in schools. She translated Bartlett, Slobin, Anderson, Lenneberg, Inhelder, Novak, Bradley, Dunn. ISSBD member.

Dorothy L. Espelage, PhD, is a Professor in the Department of Educational Psychology at the University of Illinois, Urbana-Champaign. Her research programs include investigations of bullying, homophobic bullying, dating violence, and sexual harassment among adolescents for almost two decades. She has authored over 90 publications and coedited 4 books. She is principal investigator of a large randomized clinical trial of a school-based bullying prevention program funded by CDC and has funding from NIJ to study adolescent dating violence.

Guadalupe Espinoza is a doctoral candidate in the Psychology Department at the University of California, Los Angeles (UCLA), specializing in Developmental Psychology. Her research interests include student's school climate perceptions and peer relationships (e.g., school bullying, cyberbullying), particularly among adolescents from Latin American backgrounds. She is also interested in better understanding how adolescents use online tools (such as social networking sites) to stay connected with peers.

Margaret F. Gibson has practiced clinical social work in family mental health programs, women's shelters, crisis hotlines, addiction and harm reduction programs, and HIV services. She is currently a doctoral student at the Factor-Inwentash Faculty of Social Work at the University of Toronto where her research focuses on how systems for children with "special needs" shape the experiences of sexual minority parents.

Petra Gradinger, PhD, has studied actuarial mathematics at the Vienna University of Technology and psychology at the University of Vienna in Austria. She received her PhD in psychology from the University of Vienna in 2010. Between

2006 and 2011, she was researcher and lecturer at the University of Vienna. Currently, she is a postdoc researcher at the University of Applied Sciences Upper Austria, School of Health/Social Sciences in Linz. Petra has been familiar with bullying research and bullying prevention for many years and has given presentations at conferences and held seminars for teachers and youth workers on the topic of bullying prevention. Her publications have focused on bullying and cyberbullying, learning and motivation, and methodological issues.

Jaana Juvonen, PhD, is a Professor in Developmental Psychology Program at UCLA. She studies young adolescent peer relationships and school adjustment with her main area of expertise on bullying.

Herbert W. Marsh, PhD, is Distinguished Professor who holds a joint appointment at Oxford University and the Centre for Positive Psychology and Education at the University of Western Sydney. He is widely published (380 articles in 70 journals, 65 chapters, 14 monographs, 370 conference papers) and an ISI highly cited researcher (http://isihighlycited.com/). His major research interests include self-concept and motivation, bullying and peer support, evaluations of teaching effectiveness, developmental psychology, quantitative analysis, value-added and contextual models, sports psychology, peer review processes, and gender differences.

Cheryl Milne, LLB, MSW, is Executive Director of the David Asper Centre for Constitutional Rights at the Faculty of Law, University of Toronto, where she is also the director of the combined JD/MSW program. Previously, she was a legal advocate for children with the legal clinic Justice for Children and Youth where she represented young people in education proceedings, child welfare and family law proceedings, and youth criminal justice. She is vice-chair of the Canadian Coalition for the Rights of Children and teaches constitutional advocacy at the University of Toronto, and Social Work and the Law at Ryerson University.

Faye Mishna, PhD, is Dean and Professor at the Factor-Inwentash Faculty of Social Work, University of Toronto and is cross-appointed to the Department of Psychiatry. Faye holds the Margaret and Wallace McCain Family Chair in Child and Family. Faye's research program is focused on bullying, cyberbullying, and cyber technology in counseling. An integral component of her research entails collaboration with community organizations. Her scholarship is focused on bullying, social work education, and clinical practice. Before joining the faculty, she was Clinical Director of a children's agency. She is a graduate and faculty member of the Toronto Child Psychoanalytic Program. She maintains a private practice in psychotherapy and consultation.

Roberto H. Parada, PhD, is currently a Lecturer in Adolescent Development, Wellbeing, Behaviour and Pedagogical Studies at the University of Western

Sydney. His research interests focus on antibullying interventions, bullying and victimization causes/consequences, positive learning environments, school mental health, child and adolescent self-concept, and the application of cognitive and behavioral interventions in schools. His methodological focus is on factor analysis, structural equation modeling (SEM), and multilevel modeling.

Mrinalini A. Rao is a doctoral candidate in the counseling psychology program in the Department of Educational Psychology at the University of Illinois, Urbana-Champaign. Her research broadly examines the interaction between sociocultural context and development, and their influence on child and adolescent mental health. She is also interested in exploring these transactional processes through advanced developmental methodology. Her dissertation uses longitudinal structural equation modeling to examine the influence of risk and protective factors in family, peer, and school contexts on adolescent substance use and initiation.

Ian Rivers, PhD, is Professor of Human Development within the School of Sport and Education at Brunel University, London. His research focuses on understanding bias-based bullying and the role of bystander in challenging antisocial behavior in schools. He is the author of *Homophobic Bullying: Research and Theoretical Perspectives* (Oxford, 2011), and coeditor of *Bullying: Experiences and Discourses of Sexuality and Gender* (Routledge, 2012).

Peter K. Smith, PhD, is Emeritus Professor of Psychology at the Unit for School and Family Studies, Goldsmiths, University of London, UK. His research interests are in social development, school bullying, and play. He is coauthor of *Understanding Children's Development* (Blackwells, 5th ed. 2011), and author of *Children and Play* (Wiley-Blackwell, 2009). He is coeditor of *Bullying in Schools: How Successful Can Interventions be?* (Cambridge University Press, 2004), *The Nature of Play: Great Apes and Humans* (Guilford Publications, 2005), the *Blackwell Handbook of Childhood Social Development* (Blackwell, 2nd ed. 2011), and *Cyberbullying in the Global Playground: Research from International Perspectives* (Wiley-Blackwell, 2012). He is Chair of COST Action IS0801 on Cyberbullying, which brings together 28 European countries in research networking.

Barbara A. Spears, PhD, is Codirector of the Citizenship and Wellbeing Research Group of the Centre for Research in Education at the University of South Australia. She is a Senior Academic in the School of Education and has contributed to several Australian Research Council projects as Chief Investigator. She is lead researcher in the Safe and Supportive research strand of the Young and Well Cooperative Research Centre (http://www.yawcrc.org.au/research), which is exploring technologies as settings to promote cybersafety and strengthen resilience, mental health, and the well-being of all young people in Australia. She authored the Australian Government report *Behind the Scenes: Insights into the Human Dimension of Covert Bullying* and is coeditor of *The Impact of Technology on*

Relationships in Educational Settings (Routledge, 2012). A qualified and registered teacher, her work has always sought to inform practice.

Dagmar Strohmeier, PhD, has studied psychology, philosophy, and Turkish language and culture at the University of Graz in Austria. She holds a PhD. in psychology from the University of Vienna, Austria. Between 2006 and 2011, she was assistant professor at the University of Vienna. Currently, she is professor for intercultural competence at the University of Applied Sciences Upper Austria, School of Health/Social Sciences in Linz. The main topics in her research involve bullying and victimization; homophily in friendship choices; and the development, implementation, and evaluation of a school-based program to prevent bullying and victimization in youth (ViSC program).

Yuichi Toda, is Professor at Osaka University of Education. He received his BA and MA at University of Tokyo, and then he studied at the doctoral course of University of Tokyo. He was a visiting fellow at Goldsmiths College, University of London, during March 1998–January 1999 and a visiting professor at the University of Vienna during the summers of 2007 to 2010. He has written several English language articles on bullying/ijime (Dixon, Toda, & Abe, 1999; Nicolaides, Toda, & Smith, 2003; Toda, 2005, 2011) and other areas (e.g., Itoh & Toda, 2001).

Robert S. Tokunaga, PhD, is Assistant Professor of Communicology at the University of Hawai'i at Mānoa. His program of research broadly examines the negative psychosocial effects of technology use. His previous research has included studies of cyberbullying, the sexual solicitation of minors over the Internet, and the deficient self-regulation of Internet use. He is currently working on a series of experimental and longitudinal studies investigating the influence of channel factors involved with bullying.

Marion K. Underwood, PhD, is the Ashbel Smith Professor of Psychological Sciences at the University of Texas at Dallas. Her research examines anger, aggression, and gender, with special attention to the development of social aggression. She leads the BlackBerry Project, in which participants were given BlackBerry devices configured to capture the content of text messaging and e-mail to a secure archive. She hopes that this research will illuminate the hidden world of adolescent peer culture, and contribute to the growing body of pioneering research on cyberbullying by moving beyond adolescents' self-reports to examine the actual content of their electronic communication.

Melissa Van Wert, MSW, is a PhD student at the Factor-Inwentash Faculty of Social Work, University of Toronto. Her research interests focus broadly on victimization experiences of children and youth, as well as on strategies for improving the well-being of young people. Her current research focuses more specifically on experiences of maltreatment in childhood and adolescence, and responses of the Canadian child welfare system. She has a keen interest in research design and methods.

Michele Ybarra, PhD, is President and Research Director of the Center for Innovative Public Health Research, a nonprofit research organization centered on understanding the impact on and opportunities for adolescent health represented by new technologies. She is internationally recognized for her work in the field of Internet victimization, including cyberbullying and Internet harassment and unwanted sexual solicitation, and has published extensively on the psychosocial characteristics related to these experiences by youth. She is the Principal Investigator (PI) for Growing up with Media (CDC U49CE000206; R01 CE001543) and the Teen, Health, and Technology Study (R01 HD057191), both of which are national surveys to better understand how new technology affect the health and well-being of young people.

Jina Yoon, PhD, is an Associate Professor in Educational Psychology at Wayne State University (WSU).She received a PhD in School Psychology at Texas A&M University. At WSU, she teaches in the areas of child and adolescent psychopathology and psychotherapy as well as prevention and intervention. Her research interests include childhood aggression/bullying, peer relationships, teacher-student relationships, and school climate. She has published a number of journal articles and book chapters in these areas. Dr. Yoon is a nationally certified school psychologist and a licensed psychologist in the Michigan. She also works with children and adolescents in individual and group therapy at a private practice.

Mike Zeederberg is the Managing Director of Zuni, a digital strategic consultancy that works with clients to implement effective digital strategies. Mike initiated the SOSO campaign and partnership with NAPCAN while he was MD of Profero, and has continued to shape its development at Zuni. He is leading the creative development of the new SOSO campaign for the Young & Well Cooperative Research Centre (http://www.yawcrc.org.au/research).

Part I
Introduction

1 Introduction

*Jenny Walker, Rhonda G. Craven,
and Robert S. Tokunaga*

Cyberbullying is a global concern that many governments and schools are struggling to address (Shariff, 2009). While cyberbullying is a relatively recent development, researchers are beginning to gather a body of scholarly literature addressing this issue.[1] This introduction summarizes key findings from this literature to contextualize the remainder of the book, addresses current challenges in cyberbullying research, and considers the ways forward for research. These key findings include similarities and differences between cyberbullying and non-cyberbullying; overlap between the two forms of bullying; prevalence; age, grade, and developmental differences; gender; motivation; consequences and correlates for perpetrators, targets, and dual perpetrator/targets, including the relationship between cyberbullying and problem behaviors, and cyberbullying and mental and emotional problems; the content and context of cyberbullying messages; and possible adaptive functions of cyberbullying. The section on challenges in current research addresses conceptual and methodological limitations in cyberbullying literature and discusses the importance of theory building on empirical research. The chapter concludes by reviewing what appears to be working in non-cyberbullying research and how that knowledge can inform research on cyberbullying.

KEY FINDINGS IN THE LITERATURE TO DATE

Similarities and Differences between Cyberbullying and Non-Cyberbullying

Some studies suggest a close correlation between cyberbullying and non-cyberbullying (Hinduja & Patchin, 2008, 2009; Ybarra & Mitchell, 2004b), but the "jury is still out" on whether or not cyberbullying is a variation of non-cyberbullying (Bauman, 2011, p. 17 [for an overview of non-cyberbullying versus cyberbullying, see pp. 17–27]). Although some have argued that cyberbullying is similar to non-cyberbullying in a number of significant ways, there are also considerable differences. Researchers (Agatston, Kowalski, & Limber, 2007; Brown, Jackson, & Cassidy, 2006; Kowalski & Limber, 2007; Kowalski, Limber, & Agatston, 2008; McKenna, 2000; McGrath, 2009; Shariff & Hoff, 2007; Slonje & Smith, 2008;

Smith, Mahdavi, Carvalho, Fisher, Russell, & Tippet, 2008) have speculated about some of the key differences between non-cyberbullying and cyberbullying:

- The level of disinhibition involved in cyberbullying;
- The potential anonymity and the resultant lack of accountability facilitating antisocial behavior;
- The unique power and control issues resulting from the "flattening" of the playing field in the virtual world;
- The difficulty of escaping cyberbullying because of the 24/7 connection afforded by technology;
- The potential lesser role for bystanders in cyberbullying;
- The lack of immediate verbal and nonverbal feedback;
- The immediate availability and connectivity of technology allowing for more opportunity to "share" cyberbullying;
- The ability of targets to retaliate more easily via technology;
- The possibility that there may be different age trends in utilizing technology;
- The lesser inclination young people may have to tell an adult about being cyberbullied for fear the adults may overreact or remove access to the technology (this is especially true if families have not discussed cyberbullying ahead of time);
- The lesser awareness adults may have of cyberbullying because it can seem less "visible" to them than non-cyberbullying;
- The increased evidence left behind after cyberbullying—text messages, photos, e-mails, social network pages can all be traced.

Overlap between Cyberbullying and Non-Cyberbullying

Many studies indicate that youth use multiple strategies and platforms to bully others, moving quickly and easily between their online and offline worlds (Hinduja & Patchin, 2009; Maher, 2008; Marsh, McGee, Nada-Raja, & Williams, 2010; Perren, Dooley, Shaw, & Cross, 2010). Some research concludes that non-cyberbullies and victims are most likely to be cyberbullies and cybervictims (Hinduja & Patchin, 2008, 2009; Li, 2007a, 2007b; Raskauskas & Stoltz, 2007). Victims of cyberbullying are likely to experience non-cyberbullying as well (Dempsey, Sulkowski, & Nichols, 2009; Hinduja & Patchin, 2007, 2009; Kowalski & Limber, 2007; Perren et al., 2010; Raskauskas & Stoltz, 2007; Smith et al., 2008; Twyman, Saylor, Taylor, & Comeaux, 2009; Vandebosch & Van Cleemput, 2009; Ybarra, Diener-West, & Leaf, 2007). Although some overlap exists between cyberbullying and non-cyberbullying, studies have found that the majority of youth who are cyberbullied do not also report being bullied at school (Ybarra et al., 2007).

A connection may exist between cyberbullying victimization and later perpetration. A number of studies have found that being victimized by cyberbullying was associated with other forms of victimization and the perpetration of bullying in school (Beran & Li, 2007; Burgess-Proctor, Patchin, & Hinduja, 2009; Kowalski & Limber, 2007; Li, 2007a; Perren et al., 2010; Raskauskas & Stoltz, 2007; Twyman et al., 2009; Vandebosch & Van Cleemput, 2009; Ybarra & Mitchell, 2004a). Other studies (Slonje & Smith, 2008), however, conclude that non-cybervictims are not generally found to be cyberbullies.

Prevalence of Cyberbullying

Research indicates that cyberbullying is not uncommon among youth, but prevalence rates vary significantly based on the age and demographic makeup of those studied, how cyberbullying is defined and measured, the time period in question (previous week, month, year, etc.), and the way the data were collected (Patchin & Hinduja, 2012, p. 15). Patchin and Hinduja (2012) provide two illustrative bar graphs detailing cyberbullying victimization and offending rates across 27 peer-reviewed journals. Victimization rates range from 5.5% to 72%, with an average of 24.4%, while perpetration rates range from 3% to 44.1%, with an average of 18% (p. 17). While it is difficult to identify definitive prevalence rates, research suggests that cyberbullying is the most common risk that minors face online (Palfry, boyd, & Sacco, 2009). Hasebrink, Livingstone, Haddon, and Olafsson (2009) provide prevalence rates for cyberbullying and cybervictimization by European country. The approximate median response for aggressive contact (been bullied/harassed/stalked) is 15%–20%, and the approximate median response for aggressive conduct (sent bullying/harassing messages) is 12%. Tokunaga (2010) cited studies that have found, on average, approximately 20%–40% youths who report being victimized by a cyberbully. McGrath (2009) provides a list of prevalence studies that suggest between 4% and 42% of all young people are cyberbullied. Patchin and Hinduja's (2012) results from seven of their own studies from 2004 to 2010 indicate that, on average, 16.8% of youth reported bullying others (p. 17). Bauman (2011) also provides an Appendix of 38 recent cyberbullying research studies, including prevalence rates, location of the study, sample, findings, and limitations. While prevalence rates are difficult to measure, most studies have found that rates for cyberbullying are lower than for non-cyberbullying (Lenhart, 2007; Li, 2007a; Smith et al., 2008; Williams & Guerra, 2007).

Age, Grade, and Developmental Differences

The majority of research has focused on cyberbullying victimization among minors under the age of 18, although it is worth noting that cyberbullying is not specifically restricted by age (Tokunaga, 2010). Much of the research suggests that cyberbullying (and non-cyberbullying) appears to be most prominent among middle school-aged youth (Cassidy, Jackson, & Brown, 2009; Patchin & Hinduja, 2012; Li, 2007b; Williams & Guerra, 2007). Within that age group, in a study of 3,767 students in grades six through eight, Kowalski and Limber (2007) found that eighth grade students cyberbullied more frequently than sixth or seventh graders, although there were no differences among these grades for cybervictimization. Other studies have found that rates of cyberbullying and victimization are higher for primary school than for secondary school students (Dehue, Bolman, & Vollink, 2008), while still others identify high school students (9th to 12th grade) as more likely to be involved in cyberbullying (Perren et al., 2010; Raskauskas & Stoltz, 2007; Ybarra & Mitchell, 2004). Studies conducted among college age students illustrate that while cyberbullying decreases, it does not diminish entirely among older students (Baldasare, Bauman, Goldman, & Robie, 2012; Kowalski, Giumetti, Schroeder, & Reese, 2012; Smith, Grimm, Lombard, & Wolfe, 2012). The limited data available suggest that the relations between age and cyberbullying follows an inverse U pattern, where rates start out low, increase until about the mid-teenage years, and then begin to decrease over time (Dooley, Cross, Hearn, & Treyvaud, 2009, p. 75).

Gender

Research on gender differences in cyberbullying is "fraught with inconsistent findings" (Tokunaga, 2010, p. 280). Tokunaga's meta-synthesis of research suggests that neither gender is victimized more than the other (p. 280). Some studies, however, find that girls are as likely, if not more likely, than boys to be involved in cyberbullying (Lenhart, 2007; Wolak, Mitchell, & Finkelhor, 2006; Kowalski & Limber, 2007). Hinduja and Patchin's (2011) review of 13 published papers notes that 21.8% of girls and 19.5% of boys reported being victims of cyberbullying (p. 20). These same studies found that 14.1% of girls and 18.5% of boys admitted to cyberbullying others (p. 20). Other studies suggest that girls are more likely to report being cyberbullied (Kowalski & Limber, 2007; Lenhart, 2007; Li, 2007b; Mesch, 2009; Slonje & Smith, 2008; Vandebosch & Van Cleemput, 2009), while others indicate that boys are more likely to be cyberbullies (Aricak et al., 2008; Li, 2006, 2007a; Slonje & Smith, 2008; Vandebosch & Van Cleemput, 2009). Still others have found no significant gender differences in cyberbullying (Li, 2006; Patchin & Hinduja, 2006; Smith et al., 2008; Williams & Guerra, 2007), or that gender differences are uncertain (Gross, 2004; Hinduja & Patchin, 2008).

Some studies indicate that when boys bully with cyber tools, they tend to make more physical threats and more sexually explicit comments, while girls are more likely to resort to name-calling and mocking others for their physical appearance (Beale & Hall, 2007; Burgess-Proctor et al., 2009; Rivers & Noret, 2010). Boys also receive more hate-related messages than girls, while girls are subject to more name-calling than boys (Rivers & Noret, 2010). When specifically examining texting as a form of cyberbullying, some results show that girls are more likely to receive unwanted text messages (Marsh et al., 2010), girls are more likely than boys to be identified as cyberbullies (Raskauskas, 2009), or that there are no gender differences for victims (Raskauskas, 2009).

Motivation

Cyberbullying is often a quick and easy option (Lenhart, 2007) that can satisfy a number of needs: asserting power; gaining satisfaction or prestige; acting out aggressive fantasies online; retaliating after being bullied; gaining attention; looking cool and tough; and satisfying jealousy, all of which can be accomplished with a low chance of getting caught (Kowalski et al., 2008, p. 59). Other motivations include "fun" and to relieve boredom (Cross et al., 2009; Li, 2007; Slonje & Smith, 2008; Varjas, Talley, Meyers, Parris, & Cutts, 2010), or because perpetrators feel humorous, popular, and powerful (Mishna, Cook, Gadella, Daciuk, & Solomon, 2010), or feel good (Cross et al., 2009; Patchin & Hinduja, 2006). Varjas et al. (2010) found that high school students more often identified internally motivated reasons for cyberbullying (for example, redirecting feelings) than externally motivated reasons (no consequences or nonconfrontational). Older youth have identified cyberbullying as a way to negotiate and navigate their relationships (Spears, Slee, Owens, & Johnson, 2009), especially with regard to popularity and sexuality (Guerra, Williams, & Sadek, 2011).

Consequences and Correlates

Research indicates that experience with cyberbullying (both as a target and a perpetrator) can have "a significant effect on the emotional and psychological well-being of adolescents" (Patchin & Hinduja, 2012, p. 24). Some research suggests that the consequences of cyberbullying may be similar to those of non-cyberbullying (Mason, 2008). Others (Raskauskas & Stoltz, 2007) suggest that cyberbullying may have an even greater impact upon the emotional development of youth than non-cyberbullying because of the potential anonymity of cyberbullying and the resulting power imbalance between the perpetrator and the target. Effects can range from trivial levels of distress and frustration to serious psychosocial and life problems (Tokunaga, 2010, p. 281).

Cybervictimization is associated with increased social anxiety (Dempsey et al., 2009); feelings of anger, frustration, and sadness (Patchin & Hinduja, 2006); an inability to concentrate, which negatively affects grades (Beran & Li, 2007); depreciated levels of self-esteem (Didden et al., 2009; Patchin & Hinduja, 2010); fear, and a clear sense of helplessness (Spears et al., 2009); depression (Didden et al., 2009; Patchin & Hinduja, 2006; Perren et al, 2010; Ybarra et al., 2007); and suicidal ideation and behaviors (Hinduja & Patchin, 2010). Other reported academic problems include increased absences and truancy (Katzer, Fetchenhauer, & Belschak, 2009), increased detentions and suspensions, and carrying weapons onto school campuses (Ybarra et al., 2007). Different forms and features of cyberbullying can have differential impact on the victims (Gerson & Rappaport, 2011, p. 68). For example, young people ranked bullying involving photos or video clips as more harmful than bullying over text messages or e-mail (Slonje & Smith, 2008). Additional research is needed to clarify if specific elements of cybervictimization are associated with poorer mental health outcomes for young people (Perren et al., 2010, p. 8).

Youth who perpetrate cyberbullying also are at higher risk (Mishna et al., 2010). They are more likely to concurrently engage in rule breaking, to have problems with aggression (Ybarra & Mitchell, 2007), and to have higher levels of mood disturbance and substance use (Ybarra & Mitchell, 2004). Studies also indicate that perpetrators are at risk for suicidal ideation and behaviors (Bauman, Toomey, & Walker, 2012; Hinduja & Patchin, 2010).

Adaptive Functions of Cyberbullying

Research also is beginning to address the "human dimension" of cyberbullying through analysis of the content of cyberbullying messages (Rivers & Noret, 2010; Spears, et al., 2009). Qualitative studies have found that "relationships are central" (p. 194) to participants' narratives about cyberbullying, with relationship issues ranging from manipulating friendships to issues concerning "sexuality and sexual experiences" (Spears et al., 2009, p. 194). Hoff and Mitchell (2009) also found that relationship/social tensions, such as breakups or ganging up on a person to isolate that person from the group, are central to cyberbullying. Research is also beginning to provide insight into the potential adaptive functions of cyberbullying, including positive consequences of these behaviors, such as entertainment and a way to enhance physical and sexual appeal (Guerra et al., 2011). Finally, research is noting the necessity to include the perspective of youth when considering terms used, definitions employed, and the understanding of the nature of cyberbullying (Baldasare et al., 2011; Mishna et al., 2010; Nocentini et al., 2010).

CHALLENGES IN CYBERBULLYING RESEARCH

Despite more than a half decade since the earliest research on cyberbullying perpetration and victimization was introduced, researchers continue to face a number of conceptual and methodological challenges in studying this phenomenon. The foremost challenge of cyberbullying research is the propagation of inconsistent definitions in scholarly literature and news media. Subsidiary challenges include the dearth of studies that invoke theoretically derived hypotheses. The following section considers conceptual and theoretical issues in cyberbullying research and their influence on the study of cyberbullying. Bringing attention to these shortcomings may provide directions toward which future studies in this area can move.

Conceptual and Methodological Limitations

The term cyberbullying has been defined and characterized in myriad and often conflicting ways in popular press and the growing corpus of literature on this topic. This comes as no surprise given that scholars are unable to arrive at a general consensus on the proper way to spell cyberbullying (cf. cyberbullying, cyber-bullying). Words such as cyberbullying, Internet aggression, and Internet harass-ment have also been used interchangeably, complicating mutual understanding of this phenomenon. In an attempt to reconcile the various names employed to sig-nal cyberbullying and its related conditions, Hertz and David-Ferdon (2008) pro-posed *electronic aggression* as a blanket term to represent the case of aggressive messages communicated through a technology, under which cyberbullying and Internet harassment fall. The definition of electronic aggression, offered by the CDC, acknowledges differences in bullying and harassment; however, the sources of the difference are not made clear. Others have refined the concepts by includ-ing criteria such as willful intent, repetition, and asymmetrical relationships (i.e., power imbalance) as necessary conditions for labeling an event as cyberbullying (e.g., Besley, 2009; Patchin & Hinduja, 2006). Arguments advanced in support of or against the inclusion of any of these criteria have led to the inconsistent defini-tions used in research. Chapter 2 of this volume provides an expanded discussion of definitional issues in cyberbullying related to this limitation.

The way cyberbullying is used in news media further obscures the meaning of the term. Cyberbullying has become an all-encompassing name referring to *any* aggressive interpersonal act communicated through the Internet or mobile tech-nology (Tokunaga, 2010). This broad characterization has precipitated confusion about cyberbullying among the general public and led to events not considered genuine cyberbullying that have been mislabeled as such. The ambiguity of cy-berbullying in popular press, in concert with the lack of understanding about this phenomenon, may also be in part responsible for the reticence among researchers to unite under a common definition.

The inconsistent definitions are endemic in cyberbullying research and pose se-rious problems in measurement (see Part 3 of this volume on measurement issues). The predominant approach employed in studying cyberbullying is global-item measurement wherein a definition of cyberbullying is presented, and respondents are asked how many times and over what period these events happened to them. In instances where cyberbullying is measured as a multidimensional construct (i.e., specific-item measurement), specific subcategories of cyberbullying are pre-sented to respondents who are then asked questions about frequency and duration (e.g., Griezel, Craven, Yeung, & Finger, 2008; Menesini, Nocentini, & Calussi, 2011). In the endeavor to increase content validity of cyberbullying measurement, conceptual definitions closely parallel their operational counterparts. Although agreement between conceptualization and operationalization is indicative of sound methodology, the conflicting definitions of cyberbullying presented to par-ticipants have created obstacles in making cross-study comparisons. Moreover, when considering the body of cyberbullying research as a whole, the mixed find-ings that stem from the inconsistent use of definitions have largely undermined the quality of research on cyberbullying.

The weakness of cyberbullying measurement is not exclusive to the use of inconsistent definitions. Much of the problems lies in the administration of global- and specific-item measures. For instance, some global-item measures of cyberbullying have included paragraph-long definitions of traditional bullying and have asked children and adolescents whether they have encountered analogous behaviors through an electronic or digital technology. This common methodology relies on a child or adolescent's ability to understand the multiple components of traditional bullying (e.g., repetition, power imbalance, intent) and apply it to a different context, something which they may be unable to do (Smith, Cowie, Olafsson, & Liefooghe, 2002; Vaillancourt et al., 2008). Additionally, specific-item measures, while nobly attempting to measure cyberbullying as a multidimensional construct, often avoid or ignore questions that determine whether a legitimate cyberbullying event took place.

In looking at specific behaviors, which generally fall along subdimensions of visual and textual cyberbullying, the direct measurement of perpetration or victimization is lost. The specific-item measures rarely, if ever, ask respondents about the symmetry of power in the interpersonal relationship or perceived intent. Without directly measuring these key components, focus is placed on the smaller details of cyberbullying, which are important, but the broader picture (i.e., whether these events represent genuine cyberbullying experiences) is missing. As such, research has confounded cases of unintentional cyberaggression, genuine cyberaggression, and cyberbullying. Without greater attention to methodological precision, the propagation of high-quality research on cyberbullying and cyberaggression is significantly hampered.

Theory Building in Cyberbullying Research

Although a large proportion of early research on cyberbullying was conducted in the absence of theory, present investigations are beginning to invoke theoretical tenets to inform their empirical hypotheses. Routine activities theory and general strain theory have received recent attention in cyberbullying research and show promise for informing future cyberbullying-specific theory building. In the following section, the two theories are explained, and their application to cyberbullying events is reviewed.

Routine activities theory, proposed by Cohen and Felson (1979), suggests that crime is caused by a chance event in which a motivated offender, suitable target, and a lack of capable guardianship come together. In cyberbullying, the absence of a policing agent on Internet or mobile technologies inhibits adequate protection from a motivated offender. Additionally, suitable targets are characterized as those Internet users who make themselves vulnerable to victimization by participating on various Internet-based technologies, such as chat rooms and social networking websites (Mesch, 2009; Navarro & Jasinski, 2012). The suitable target and lack of guardianship interact to instigate cyberbullying victimization. Advocates of the routine activities approach for cyberbullying contend that electronic and digital technologies, in particular, may be opportune environments for motivated offenders to commit cyberbullying because the lack of supervision over Internet-based and mobile communication lowers the traditional barriers of risk.

General strain theory (Agnew, 1992, 2006) is based on the idea that people experience strain in their lives from an inability to achieve goals, a loss of positively valued stimuli, and the introduction of negative-valued stimuli. From a general strain perspective, strain events have the potential to evoke negative emotional responses such as anger, despair, and frustration (Agnew, 1992). When anger and frustration are incited, particularly when straining events are repeated over time, individuals may become aggressive and are more prone to committing deviant behaviors (Agnew, 1995). General strain theory has been adopted and tested in cyberbullying research. Researchers have theorized that strain can be both the source of and precursor to cyberbullying perpetration (Hinduja & Patchin, 2007; Patchin & Hinduja, 2011; Wallace, Patchin, & May, 2005). This delinquency-strain perspective is supported by consistent findings that show cyberbullying victimization as a contributory cause of cyberbullying perpetration (Patchin & Hinduja, 2011; Yilmaz, 2011). Moreover, strain that stems from experiences with cyberbullying can lead to internalizing deviant behaviors, such as self-harm and suicidal ideation (Hay, Meldrum, & Mann, 2010).

Despite the significant strides made in using theory to ground empirical cyberbullying investigations in the last two years, still more attention must be paid to theory building. It should be acknowledged that it takes time and replication of findings to build good theory, which may explain why cyberbullying research lacks theory. Nevertheless, the cyberbullying literature presently is now well-positioned to begin at least the formative stages of theory building. Something noticeably absent from any attempt to predict cyberbullying and its correlates is a comprehensive discussion about technology's role in instigating perpetration or coping with victimization. As researchers move forward, a better understanding about why individuals use communication technologies as a means to bully must be theorized and tested in future studies. See Part 3 of this volume for a review of relevant theoretical frameworks.

WAYS FORWARD FOR CYBERBULLYING RESEARCH: WHAT IS WORKING IN TRADITIONAL BULLYING RESEARCH?

Ways forward for cyberbullying research can be drawn from what is working in traditional bullying research. The critical interplay of theory, research, and practice has underpinned recent advances in traditional bullying research. Theory, research, and practice are inextricably intertwined, whereby weakness in any one area undermines the others. Definitions of the bullying construct have been proposed in order to identify the nature of the traditional bullying construct and to address within-construct issues (e.g., Elinoff, Chafouleas, & Sassu, 2004). Within-construct studies are a necessary precursor to between-construct studies whereby bullying is related to other constructs. Within-construct studies involve theorizing the nature and structure of bullying; posing theoretical models; devising measurement instruments to test theoretical models; and accepting, rejecting, or revising theory based on empirical research evidence. For example, in operationalizing traditional bullying, there is now wide agreement among researchers that it comprises three forms: verbal, physical, and social (Finkelhor, Ormrod, & Turner, 2007; Mynard & Joseph, 2000, Salmivalli, Kaukiainen, & Lagerspetz, 2000) and that these are direct (e.g., hitting, punching, name-calling; Wolke, Woods, Bloomfield, & Karstadt, 2000) or indirect (e.g., hurtful manipulation of relationships; Crick and Grotpeter, 1995) in nature.

Traditional bullying has also been found to be dynamic and involve multiple participant roles: perpetrators (those who bully others), targets (those who are bullied), bystanders (those who witness bullying), and perpetrators-targets (those who both bully others and are bullied) (e.g., Marsh et al., 2012; Salmivalli, Lappalainen, & Lagerspetz, 1998). Bully and victim factors have been shown to be positively correlated and mutually reinforcing such that prior bullying leads to subsequent victimization, and prior victimization leads to subsequent bullying (Card & Hodges, 2008; Marsh et al., 2004; Marsh, Parada, Yeung, & Healey, 2001; Parada, Marsh, & Craven, 2005). Schuster (1996) also considers that there are four key components in defining school bullying: (1) repetition, (2) enacted by one or more individuals, (3) actions that are deliberately intended to harm the target, and (4) a power imbalance between the person bullying and the person targeted (also see Olweus, 1997; Rigby, 1996; Sutton, Smith, & Swettenham, 1999). These theoretical conceptualizations of the bullying construct have been of great heuristic value in propelling traditional bullying research forward, as defining bullying is fundamental to (a) understanding the nature of the bullying construct; (b) devising appropriate measures and analyses to test theoretical models; and (c) informing interventions to prevent, manage, and address different bullying forms.

Measurement instruments have now been devised to test specific theoretical models, and some have demonstrated sound psychometric properties (e.g., Marsh et al., 2012). The latter is critical in ensuring measures are salient, reliable, and robust for the population samples utilized in primary research studies. The development of valid measures has also enabled investigations that incorporate large sample sizes and representative samples and the application of state-of-the art advances in statistical analyses, strengthening the generalizability and the external validity of findings. Research has supported the theorized forms of traditional bullying and elucidated the dynamic nature of multiple participant roles. Capitalizing on theory and research, anti-bullying interventions have been devised, implemented, and empirically tested with measures that specifically match the intended goals of the intervention, enabling the explication of successful intervention strategies (e.g., whole-school approaches, targeting multiple participant roles). For example, research capitalizing on advances in theory and using robust methodological designs, measurement techniques, and whole-school approaches to preventing bullying has emerged (e.g., Marsh et al., 2004; Parada, 2006; Parada, Craven, & Marsh, 2008; Smith, Pepler, & Rigby, 2004).

With the establishment of sound theory and research, correlates of bullying have also been elucidated, and longitudinal causal modeling studies have begun to be undertaken to identify potent potential constructs that evidence indicates may have a causal influence on reducing bullying. The establishment of a body of literature in traditional bullying research has also enabled the conduct of meta-analyses to explicate the effectiveness of interventions (e.g., Merrell & Isava, 2008; Ttofi & Farrington, 2011; Ttofi, Farrington, & Baldry, 2008). Meta-analyses are primary research investigations that synthesize the results of a number of primary studies to ascertain key findings and new directions in the field under examination. In addition, traditional bullying research has grown to become a truly international endeavor with multiple studies being conducted in varied cultural and substantive contexts to test and extend research findings. The latter has also led to collaborative international research and the establishment of international networks for the exchange of information.

There are many lessons to be learned from the recent advances in traditional bullying research for progressing cyberbullying research and the international body of literature. These include:

1. Ensuring theory, research, and practice are intertwined to advance cyberbullying research;
2. Conceptualizing operational definitions of the cyberbullying construct and theorizing models of the structure of the cyberbullying construct that are amenable to testing to allow revision of theory based on research evidence (see Chapter 6);
3. Developing theoretically grounded cyberbullying measures that reflect conceptualized definitions of the nature of the construct and demonstrating the psychometric properties of these measures for population samples under investigation;
4. Capitalizing on state-of-the-art advances in quantitative and qualitative research methodology (See Chapters 8 and 10 in this volume);
5. Addressing within-construct issues prior to proceeding to between-construct studies;
6. Explicating the relation of cyberbullying to traditional bullying constructs and correlates;
7. Undertaking causal modeling studies and creating longitudinal data sets to identify constructs that seed success in intervening in cyberbullying;
8. Capitalizing on theory and research to develop potentially potent cyberbullying interventions and empirically determining their impact through utilizing measures that specifically match the intended goals of the intervention;
9. Undertaking meta-analyses of the cyberbullying research evidence to synthesize findings and identify new directions; and
10. Drawing upon international efforts to conduct cyberbullying research in different cultural and substantive contexts, undertake cross-cultural research that utilizes common measures, and conduct collaborative studies to extend the generalizability of the evidence base.

Attention to these issues may assist researchers to capitalize on advances in traditional bullying research, avoid previous research pitfalls and limitations, and propel cyberbullying research into a new dawn that results in making a difference.

Note

1 Several journals have devoted special issues to cyberbullying (for example, the *Journal of Adolescent Health*, 2007 [Supplement]; *Journal of Social Sciences*, 2010, 6[4]); key reports, articles, and book chapters include extensive literature reviews (Biegler & boyd, 2010; Dooley, Cross, Hearn, & Treyvaud, 2009; Internet Safety Technical Taskforce, 2008; McGrath, 2009; Patchin & Hinduja, 2012; Tokunaga, 2010); and information on major studies, operational definitions of cyberbullying, and/or annotated findings has been compiled into helpful tables, summaries, and/or figures (Bauman, 2011; Kowalski, Limber, & Agatston, 2008; Patchin & Hinduja, 2012; Rivers & Noret, 2010; Tokunaga, 2010).

References

Agatson, P. W., Kowalski, R., & Limber, S. (2007). Students' perspectives on cyberbullying. *Journal of Adolescent Health, 41*, S59–S60. doi:10.1016/j.jadohealth.2007.08.017

Agnew, R. (1992). Foundation for a general strain theory of crime and delinquency. *Criminology, 30*, 47–87. doi:10.1111/j.1745–9125.1992.tb01093.x

Agnew, R. (1995). The contribution of social-psychological strain theory to the explanation of crime and delinquency. In F. Adler & W. Laufer (Eds.), *The legacy of anomie theory* (pp. 113–137). New Brunswick, NJ: Transaction.

Agnew, R. (2006). Storylines as a neglected cause of crime. *Journal of Research in Crime and Delinquency, 43*, 119–147. doi:10.1177/0022427805280052

Aricak, T. A., Siyahhan, S., Uzenhasanoglu, A., Saribeyoglu, S., Ciplak, S., Yilmaz, N., & Memmedov, C. (2008). Cyberbullying among Turkish adolescents. *Cyberpsychology & Behavior, 11*(3), 253–161. doi:10.1089/cpb.2007.0016

Baldasare, A., Bauman, S., Goldman, L., & Robie, A. (2012). Cyberbullying? Voices of college students. In C. Wankel & L. Wankel (Eds.), *Misbehavior online in higher education* (pp. 127–155). doi:http://dx.doi.org/10.1108/S2044–9968(2012)0000005010

Bauman, S. (2011). *Cyberbullying: What counselors need to know*. Alexandria, VA: American Counseling Association.

Bauman, S., Toomey, R., & Walker, J. (2012). Relations among bullying, cyberbullying, and suicide in high school students. Manuscript submitted for publication.

Beale, A. V., & Hall, K. R. (2008). Cyberbullying: What school administrators (and parents) can do. *Clearing House: A Journal of Educational Strategies, Ideas and Issues, 81*(1), 8–12.

Beran, T., & Li, Q. (2007). The relationship between cyberbullying and school bullying. *Journal of Student Wellbeing, 1*(2), 15–33.

Besley, B. (2009). *Cyberbullying*. Retrieved from http://www.cyberbullying.org/

Biegler, S., & boyd, d. (2010). Risky behaviors and online safety: A 2010 literature review (draft). Retrieved from Harvard University, Berkman Center for Internet and Society website: http://cyber.law.harvard.edu/research/youthandmedia/policy

Brown, K., Jackson, M., & Cassidy, W. (2006). Cyber-bullying: Developing policy to direct responses that are equitable and effective in addressing this special form of bullying. *Canadian Journal of Educational Administration and Policy, 57*, 1–18.

Burgess-Proctor, A., Patchin, J. W., & Hinduja, S. (2009). Cyberbullying and online harassment: Reconceptualizing the victimization of adolescent girls. In V. Garcia & J. Clifford (Eds.), *Female crime victims: Reality reconsidered*. Upper Saddle River, NJ: Prentice Hall.

Card, N. A., & Hodges, E.V.E. (2008). Peer victimization among schoolchildren: Correlations, causes, consequences, and considerations in assessment and intervention. *School Psychology Quarterly, 23*, 451–461. doi:10.1037/a0012769

Cassidy, W., Jackson, M., & Brown, K.N. (2009). Sticks and stones can break my bones, but how can pixels hurt me? *School Psychology International, 30*, 383–402. doi:10.1177/0143034309106948

Cohen, L., & Felson, M. (1979). Social change and crime rate trends: A routine activity approach. *American Sociological Review, 44*, 588–608. doi:10.2307/2094589

Crick, N.R., & Grotpeter, J.K. (1995). Relational aggression, gender, and social-psychological adjustment. *Child Development, 66*, 710–762. doi:10.2307/1131945

Cross, D., Shaw, T., Hearn, L., Epstein, M., Monks, H., Lester, L, & Thomas, L. (2009). Australian Covert Bullying Prevalence Study (ACBPS). Western Australia: Report prepared for the Department of Education, Employment and Workplace Relations (DEEWR).

Dehue, F., Bolman, C., & Vollink, T. (2008). Cyberbullying: Youngsters' experiences and parental perception. *Cyberpsychology and Behavior, 11*, 217–222. doi:10.1089/cpb.2007.0008

Dempsey, A.G., Sulkowski, M.L., & Nichols, R. (2009). Differences between peer victimization in cyber and physical settings and associated psychosocial adjustment in early adolescence. *Psychology in the Schools, 46*(10), 962–972. doi:10.1089/cpb.2007.0008

Didden, R., Scholte, R.H.J., Korzilius, H., de Moor, J.M.H., Vermeulen, A., O'Reilly, M., ... Lancioni, G. E. (2009). Cyberbullying among students with intellectual and developmental disability in special education settings. *Developmental Neurorehabilitation, 12*, 146–151. doi:10.1080/17518420902971356

Dooley, J.J., Cross, D., Hearn, L., & Treyvaud, R. (2009). Review of existing Australian and international cyber-safety research. Child Health Promotion Research Centre, Edith Cowen University, Perth.

Elinoff, M.J., Chafouleas, S.M., & Sassu, K.A. (2004). Bullying: Considerations for defining and intervening in school settings. *Psychology in the Schools, 41*(8), 887–897. doi:10.1002/pits.20045

Finkelhor, D., Ormrod, R.K., & Turner, H.A. (2007). Poly-victimization: A neglected component in child victimization trauma. *Child Abuse & Neglect, 31*, 7–26. doi:10.1016/j.chiabu.2006.06.008

Gerson, R., & Rappaport, N. (2011). Cyber cruelty: Understanding and preventing the new bullying. *Adolescent Psychiatry, 1*, 67–71. doi:10.2174/2210676611101010067

Griezel, L., Craven, R., Yeung, A., & Finger, L. (2008, December). *The development of a multidimensional measure of cyberbullying.* Paper presented at the Australian Association for Research in Education Conference, Brisbane.

Gross, E.F. (2004). Adolescent Internet use: What we expect, what teens report. *Applied Developmental Psychology, 25*, 633–649. doi:10.1016/j.appdev.2004.09.005

Guerra, N.G., Williams, K.R., & Sadek, S. (2011). Understanding bullying and victimization during childhood and adolescence: A mixed-methods study. *Child Development, 82*(1), 295–310. doi:10.1111/j.1467–8624.2010.01556.x

Hasebrink, U., Livingstone, S., Haddon, S., & Olafsson, K. (2009). Comparing children's online opportunities and risks across Europe: Cross-national comparisons for EU kids online. LSE, London: EU Kids Online (Deliverable D3.2, 2nd edition).

Hay, C., Meldrum, R., & Mann, K. (2010). Traditional bullying, cyberbullying, and deviance: A general strain theory approach. *Journal of Contemporary Criminal Justice*, 1–18. doi:10.1177/1043986209359557.

Hertz, M. F., & David-Ferdon, C. (2008). *Electronic media and youth violence: A CDC issue brief for educators and caregivers.* Atlanta, GA: Centers for Disease Control. Retrieved July 23, 2012, from http://www.cdc.gov/violenceprevention/pdf/EA-brief-a.pdf

Hinduja, S., & Patchin, J. W. (2007). Offline consequences of online victimization: School violence and delinquency. *Journal of School Violence, 6*(3), 89–122. doi:10.1300/J202v06n03_06

Hinduja, S., & Patchin, J. W. (2008). Cyberbullying: An exploratory analysis of factors related to offending and victimization. *Deviant Behavior, 29*(2), 1–29. doi:10.1080/01639620701457816

Hinduja, S., & Patchin, J. W. (2009). *Bullying beyond the schoolyard: Preventing and responding to cyberbullying.* Thousand Oaks, CA: Corwin Press.

Hoff, D. L., & Mitchell, S. N. (2009). Cyberbullying: Causes, effects, and remedies. *Journal of Educational Administration, 47*(5), 652–665. doi:10.1108/09578230910981107

Katzer, C., Fetchenhauer, D., & Belschak, F. (2009). Cyberbullying: Who are the victims? A comparison of victimization in Internet chatrooms and victimization in school. *Journal of Media Psychology, 21*, 25–36. doi:10.1027/1864–1105.21.1.25

Kowalski, R. M., Giumetti, G. W., Schroeder, A. N., & Reese H. H. (2012). Cyberbullying among college students: Evidence from multiple domains of college life. In C. Wankel & L. Wankel (Eds.), *Misbehavior online in higher education* (pp. 293–321). doi:10.1108/S2044–9968(2012)0000005016.

Kowalski, R. M., & Limber, S. P. (2007). Electronic bullying among middle school students. *Journal of Adolescent Health, 41*, S22–S30. doi:10.1016/j.jadohealth.2007.08.017

Kowalski, R. M, Limber, S. P., & Agatston, P. W. (2008). *Cyberbullying: Bullying in the digital age.* Malden, MA: Blackwell Publishing. doi:10.1002/9780470694176.ch3

Lenhart, A. (2007, June 27). Cyberbullying and online teens. Pew Internet and American Life Project. Retrieved from the Pew Internet & American Life website: http://www.pewinternet.org/~/media//Files/Reports/2007/PIP%20Cyberbullying%20Memo.pdf.pdf

Li, Q. (2006). Cyberbullying in schools: A research of gender differences [Electronic version]. *School Psychology International, 27*(2), 157–170. doi:10.1177/0143034306064547

Li, Q. (2007a). Bullying in the new playground: Research into cyberbullying and cyber victimization [Electronic version]. *Australian Journal of Educational Technology, 23*(4), 435–454.

Li, Q. (2007b). New bottle but old wine: A research of cyberbullying in schools [Electronic version]. *Computers in Human Behavior, 23*(4), 1777–1791. doi:10.1016/j.chb.2005.10.005

Maher, D. (2008). Cyberbullying: An ethnographic case study of one Australian upper primary school class. *Youth Studies Australia, 27*(4), 50–57.

Marsh, H. W., Parada, R. H., Craven, R. G., & Finger, L. R. (2004). In the looking glass: A reciprocal effects model elucidating the complex nature of bullying, psychological determinants and the central role of self-concept. In C. S. Sanders & G. D. Phye (Eds.), *Bullying: Implications for the classroom* (pp. 63–106). San Diego, CA: Elsevier Academic Press. doi:10.1016/B978–012617955–2/50009–6

Marsh, H. W., Lüdtke, O., Nagengast, B., Trautwein, U., Morin, A.J.S., Abduljabbar, A. S., & Köller, O. (2012). Classroom climate and contextual effects: Conceptual and methodological issues in the evaluation of group-level effects. *Educational Psychologist, 47*(2), 106–124.

Marsh, H. W., Parada, R. H., Yeung, A. S., & Healey, J. (2001). Aggressive school trouble-makers and victims: A longitudinal model examining the pivotal role of self-concept. *Journal of Educational Psychology, 93*, 411–419. doi:10.1037//0022–0663.93.2.411

Marsh, L., McGee, R., Nada-Raja, S., & Williams, S. (2010). Brief report: Text bullying and traditional bullying among New Zealand secondary school students. *Journal of Adolescence, 33*, 237–240. doi:10.1016/j.adolescence.2009.06.001

Mason, K. (2008). Cyberbullying: A preliminary assessment for school personnel. *Psychology in the Schools, 45*, 323–348. doi:10.1002/pits.20301

McGrath, H. (2009). Young people and technology: A review of the current literature (2nd edition). Retrieved from http://www.amf.org.au/Assets/Files/2ndEdition_Youngpeopleandtechnology_LitReview_June202009.pdf

McKenna, K.Y.A. (2000). Plan 9 from cyberspace: The implications of the Internet for personality and social psychology. *Personality & Social Psychology Review, 4*(1), 57–75. doi:10.1207/S15327957PSPR0401_6

Menesini, E., Nocentini, A., & Calussi, P. (2011). The measurement of cyberbullying: Dimensional structure and relative item severity and discrimination. *Cyberpsychology, Behavior, and Social Networking, 14*, 267–274. doi:10.1089/cyber.2010.0002

Merrell, K. W., & Isava, D. M. (2008). How effective are school bullying intervention programs? A meta-analysis of intervention research. *School Psychology Quarterly, 23*(1), 26–42. doi:10.1037/1045–3830.23.1.26

Mesch, G. S. (2009). Parental mediation, online activities, and cyberbullying. *Cyberpsychology and behavior, 12*(4), 387–393. doi:10.1089/cpb.2009.0068

Mishna, F., Cook, C., Gadalla, T., Daciuk, J., & Solomon, S. (2010). Cyberbullying behaviors among middle and high school students. *American Journal of Orthopsychiatry, 80*(3), 362–374. doi:10.1111/j.1939–0025.2010.01040.x

Mynard, H., & Joseph, S. (2000). Development of the Multidimensional Peer Victimization Scale. *Aggressive Behavior, 26*, 169–178. doi:10.1002/(SICI)1098–2337(2000)26:2<169::AID-AB3>3.0.CO;2-A

Navarro, J.N., & Jasinski, J.L. (2012). Going cyber: Using routine activities theory to predict cyberbullying experiences. *Sociological Spectrum, 32*, 81–94. doi:10.1080/02732173.2012.628560

Nocentini, A., Calmaestra, J., Schultze-Krumbholtz, A., Scheithauer, H., Ortega, R., & Menesini, E. (2010). Cyberbullying: Labels, behaviors and definition in three European countries. *Australian Journal of Guidance & Counselling, 20*(2), 129–142. doi:10.1375/ajgc.20.2.129

Olweus, D. (1997). Bully/victim problems in school: Facts and intervention. *European Journal of Psychology of Education, 12*, 495–510. doi:10.1007/BF03172807

Palfry, J. G., boyd, d., & Sacco, D. (2009). *Enhancing child safety and online technologies: Final report of the Internet Safety Technical Task Force.* Durham, NC: Caroline Academic Press.

Parada, R. H. (2006). School bullying: Psychosocial determinants and effective intervention. Unpublished doctoral dissertation, University of Western Sydney, Bankstown.

Parada, R. H., Craven, R. G., & Marsh, H. W. (2008). The Beyond Bullying Secondary Program: An innovative program empowering teachers to counteract bullying in schools. In H.W. Marsh, R. G. Craven, & D. McInerney (Eds.), *International Advances in Self Research:* Vol. 3. Greenwich, CT: Information Age Publishing Inc.

Parada, R. H., Marsh, H. W., & Craven, R. G. (2005). There and back again from bullying to victim and victim to bullying: A reciprocal effects model of bullying behaviours in schools. Paper presented at *the Australian Association for Research in Education International Conference*. Creative Dissent: Constructive Solutions.

Patchin, J. W., & Hinduja, S. (2006). Bullies move beyond the schoolyard: A preliminary look at cyberbullying. *Youth Violence and Juvenile Justice, 4*(2), 148–169. doi:10.1177/1541204006286288

Patchin, J. W., & Hinduja, S. (2010). Cyberbullying and self-esteem. *Journal of School Health, 80*(12), 616–623. doi:10.1111/j.1746–1561.2010.00548.x

Patchin, J., & Hinduja, S. (2011). Traditional and non-traditional bullying among youth: A test of general strain theory. *Youth and Society, 4*, 727–751. doi:10.1177/0044118X10366951

Patchin, J. W., & Hinduja, S. (2012). Cyberbullying: An update and synthesis of the research. In J. W. Patchin & S. Hinduja (Eds.). *Cyberbullying prevention and response: Expert perspectives* (pp. 13–35). New York: Routledge.

Perren, S., Dooley, J., Shaw, T., & Cross, D. (2010). Bullying in school and cyberspace: Associations with depressive symptoms in Swiss and Australian adolescents. *Child and Adolescent Psychiatry and Mental Health, 4*(28), 1–10. doi:10.1186/1753–2000-4-28

Raskauskas, J. (2009). Text-bullying: Associations with traditional bullying and depression among New Zealand adolescents. *Journal of School Violence, 9*(1), 74–97. doi. org/10.1080/15388220903185605

Raskauskas, J., & Stoltz, A.D. (2007). Involvement in traditional and electronic bullying among adolescents [Electronic version]. *Developmental Psychology, 43*(3), 564–575. doi:10.1037/0012–1649.43.3.564

Rigby, K. (1996). *Bullying in schools and what to do about it.* Melbourne: Australian Council for Educational Research. doi:10.1016/0191–8869(96)00105–5

Rivers, I., & Noret, N. (2010). "I h8 u": Findings from a five-year study of text and e-mail bullying. *British Educational Research Journal, 36*(4), 643–671. doi:10.1080/01411920903071918

Salmivalli, C., Kaukiainen, A., & Lagerspetz, K. (2000). Aggression and sociometric status among peers: Do gender and type of aggression matter? *Scandinavian Journal of Psychology, 41*, 17–24. doi:10.1111/1467–9450.00166

Salmivalli, C., Lappalainen, M., & Lagerspetz, K.M.J. (1998). Stability and change of behavior in connection with bullying in schools: A two-year follow-up. *Aggressive Behavior, 24*, 205–218. doi:10.1002/(SICI)1098–2337(1998)24:3<205::AID-AB5>3.0.CO;2-J

Schuster, B. (1996). Rejection, exclusion and harassment at work and in schools: An integration of results from research on mobbing, bullying, and peer rejection. *European Psychologist, 1(4)*, 293–317. doi:10.1027/1016–9040.1.4.293

Shariff, S. (2009). *Confronting cyber-bullying: What schools need to know to control misconduct and avoid legal consequences.* New York: Cambridge University Press. doi:10.1017/CBO9780511551260.002

Shariff, S. & Hoff, D.L. (2007). Cyberbullying: Clarifying legal boundaries for school supervision in cyberspace [Electronic version]. *International Journal of CyberCriminology, 1*(1), 76–118.

Slonje, R., & Smith, P.K. (2008). Cyberbullying: Another main type of bullying? [Electronic version]. *Scandinavian Journal of Psychology, 49*, 147–154. doi:10.1111/j.1467–9450.2007.00611.x

Smith, K. J., Grimm, J., Lombard, A. E., & Wolfe, B. (2012). Cyberbullying: It doesn't stop after high school graduation. In C. Wankel & L. Wankel (Eds.), *Misbehavior online in higher education* (pp. 207–242). doi:10.1108/S2044–9968(2012)0000005013

Smith, P. K., Cowie, H., Olafsson, R. F., & Liefooghe, P. D. (2002). Definitions of bullying: A comparison of terms used, and age and gender differences, in a fourteen-country international comparison. *Child Development, 73*, 1119–1133. doi:10.1111/1467–8624.00461

Smith, P. K., Mahdavi, J., Carvalho, M., Fisher, S., Russell, S., & Tippett, N. (2008). Cyberbullying: Its nature and impact in secondary school pupils [Electronic version]. *Journal of Child Psychology and Psychiatry, 49*(4), 376–385. doi:10.1111/j.1469–7610.2007.01846.x

Smith, P. K., Pepler, D., & Rigby, K. (2004). *Bullying in schools: How successful can interventions be?* Cambridge: Cambridge University Press. doi:10.1017/CBO9780511584466

Spears, B., Slee, P., Owens, L. & Johnson, B. (2009). Behind the scenes and screens: Insights into the human dimension of covert and cyberbullying. *Journal of Psychology, 217*(4), 189–196. doi:10.1027/0044–3409.217.4.189.

Sutton, J., Smith, P. K., & Swettenham, J. (1999). Bullying and "theory of mind": A critique of the "social skills deficit" approach to anti-social behavior. *Social Development, 8*, 117–127. doi:10.1111/1467–9507.00083

Tokunaga, R. S. (2010). Following you home from school: A critical review and synthesis of research on cyberbullying victimization. *Computers in Human Development, 26*, 277–287. doi:10.1016/j.chb.2009.11.014

Ttofi, M. M., & Farrington, D. P. (2011). Effectiveness of school-based programs to reduce bullying: A systematic and meta-analytic review. *Journal of Experimental Criminology, 7*, 27–56. doi:10.1007/s11292–010–9109–1

Ttofi, M. M., Farrington, D. P., & Baldry, C. A. (2008). *Effectiveness of programs to reduce school bullying: a systematic review.* Stockholm: Swedish National Council for Crime Prevention. doi:10.1002/ab.20257

Twyman, K., Saylor, C., Taylor, L. A., & Comeaux, C. (2009). Comparing children and adolescents engaged in cyberbullying to matched peers. *CyberPscyhology and Behavior, 12*, 1–5. doi:10.1089=cpb.2009.0137.

Vaillancourt, T., McDougall, P., Hymel, S., Krygsman, A., Miller, J., Stiver, K., et al. (2008). Bullying: Are researchers and children/youth talking about the same thing? *International Journal of Behavior, 32*, 486–495. doi:10.1177/0165025408095553

Vandebosch, H., & Van Cleemput, K. (2009). Cyberbullying among youngsters: Profiles of bullies and victims. *New Media and Society, 11*(8), 1349–1371. doi:10.1177/1461444809341263.

Varjas, K., Talley, J., Meyers, J., Parris, L., & Cutts, H. (2010). High school students' Perceptions of motivations for cyberbullying: An exploratory study. *Western Journal of Emergency Medicine, 11*(3), 269–273.

Wallace, L. H., Patchin, J. W., & May, J. D. (2005). Reactions of victimized youth: Strain as an explanation of school delinquency. *Western Criminology Review, 6*, 104–116.

Williams, K. R., & Guerra, N. G. (2007). Prevalence and predictors of Internet bullying [Electronic version]. *Journal of Adolescent Health, 41*, S14-S21. doi:10.1016/j.jadohealth.2007.08.018

Wolak, J., Mitchell, K., & Finkelhor, D. (2006). *Online victimization of youth: Five years later.* Retrieved from University of New Hampshire, Crimes Against Children Research Center website: http://www.unh.edu/ccrc/pdf/CV138.pdf

Wolke, D., Woods, S., Bloomfield, L., & Karstadt, L. (2000). The association between direct and relational bullying and behavior problems among primary school children. *Journal of Child Psychology and Psychiatry and Allied Disciplines, 41*, 989–1002. doi:10.1111/1469–7610.00687

Ybarra, M.L., Diener-West, M., & Leaf, P.J. (2007). Examining the overlap in Internet harassment and school bullying: Implications for school interventions *Journal of Adolescent Health, 41*, S42–S50. doi:10.1016/j.jadohealth.2007.09.004

Ybarra, M.L., & Mitchell, J.K. (2004a). Online aggressor/targets, aggressors, and targets: A comparison of associated youth characteristics. *Journal of Child Psychology and Psychiatry, 45*(7), 1308–1316. doi:10.1111/j.1469–7610.2004.00328.x

Ybarra, M.L., & Mitchell, J.K. (2004b). Youth engaging in online harassment: Associations with caregiver-child relationships, Internet use, and personal characteristics. *Journal of Adolescence, 27*(3), 319–336. doi:10.1016/j.adolescence.2004.03.007

Yilmaz, H. (2011). Cyberbullying in Turkish middle schools: An exploratory study. *School Psychology International, 32*, 645–654. doi:10.1177/0143034311410262

Part II

Definitional Questions

2   Why It Matters

Sheri Bauman

The term *cyberbullying* was added to the *Oxford English Dictionary* (OED) in 2010. This respected volume defines the term as "the use of information technology to bully a person by sending or posting text or images of an intimidating or threatening nature" (http://www.oed.com/view/Entry/250879?redirectedFrom= cyberbullying#eid212385852). The OED indicates the first use of the term was in the *Canberra Times* in 1998, but the term was located in an earlier article in the *New York Times* in 1995 (Bauman, 2011). Many scholars and popular writers credit Bill Belsey, a Canadian who launched a cyberbullying website in 2003, with coining the term. His definition is: Cyberbullying involves the use of information and communication technologies to support deliberate, repeated, and hostile behavior by an individual or group that is intended to harm others (www. cyberbullying.ca). Variations on the definition have been used by a number of scholars and writers.

Although these definitions are similar, research requires a precise and accepted definition that all can use. The purpose of a definition is to specify the *essence* of a term (its basic qualities) and to identify the necessary and sufficient conditions for something to be a member of the set being defined. A useful definition is clear and precise. Definitions not only guide the conceptual and theoretical work in a line of inquiry, but also are the basis for the development of measurement instruments that are used in research studies. In some studies, the term and its definition is provided to subjects within the questionnaire. In others, the definition is not explicit but is the basis for the content of items used to assess subjects' experience with this behavior. In both cases, the findings are dependent on the definition used. Thus, it is difficult to generalize findings across studies and to compare findings from different contexts or age groups that use different definitions.

The goal of research is to increase our understanding of a phenomenon, and to build upon the extant literature in a field by investigating new or undiscovered aspects of the topic of interest. When the definition is not agreed upon, the findings do not form a coherent body of accumulating knowledge, but instead form a collection of interesting studies that are loosely linked by a common interest. To advance science, precision is necessary, and the think tank participants propose a definition of cyberbullying in the service of this goal.

The term cyberbullying implies that it is related to, or a variant of, conventional bullying—those bullying behaviors that are perpetrated without the use of technological tools. Whether that is a good marriage is moot at this point because the term is so widely used. The important question is whether the widely accepted components of the definition of traditional bullying accurately describe the phenomenon of cyberbullying. These three components are intentional harm, repetition, and power imbalance such that the victim is unable to respond effectively or successfully defend him- or herself.

Let us consider the first component: intent. First, intent is extremely difficult to determine in someone else. We generally infer intent from the circumstances or outcomes of an action. But with technology, it is possible that a message that appears to have hostile intent was in reality a poor attempt at humor, for example. Without benefit of paralinguistic clues to the meaning of written text, misinterpretation is quite possible. University students in a series of focus groups reported that just such misinterpretation was the cause of considerable distress (Baldasare, Bauman, Goldman, & Robie, 2012). In fact, the students described scenarios in which the misinterpretation was by a third party (not the sender or receiver) who then responded to the text in an inflammatory manner. For example, imagine a friend and I have an inside joke, and I post a comment on his Facebook page whose meaning is contingent on knowing that inside information. The friend gets it but is not offended. However, one of his Facebook friends reads my post, thinks it is in poor taste, and makes a derogatory comment about me on my Facebook wall.

In addition to addressing the issue of intent in the definition of cyberbullying, the question of repetition also requires rethinking. Again, the technological environment allows a message to be "repeated" by reaching a very large audience, whether or not the original sender intended for the image or text to be widely disseminated. Is each person who forwards a message or image "repeating" the offense, or does the sender have to engage in more than one incident directed at the same target for the incident to qualify as bullying?

Finally, we must consider the appropriateness of the power imbalance for a defining attribute of cyberbullying. In conventional bullying, power can be evident in physical power, social status, economic resources, popularity, and so on. Is it necessary for such differences to be present in a technological incident for the incident to be classified as cyberbullying? Is the power differential determined by off-line indicators, or by proficiency with technology? When the power imbalance component is used in the definition of conventional bullying, it is often explicated by saying that the target is unable to defend him- or herself or stop the behavior. In cyberbullying, the harm may be inflicted regardless of the target's response. If a message is posted, and the target is offended, he or she might contact the website and report abuse. Presumably, the website will do so, but the posting could easily have been seen by multiple viewers before removal. Or, a recipient of a cruel text message can block the sender and ensure no further messages will be received, which is an appropriate defense. Does this mean the message does not constitute cyberbullying?

These questions are addressed in the next chapter, which presents the result of the deliberations by participants at the International Cyberbullying Think Tank. An alternative position is offered in the following chapter.

References

Baldasare, A., Bauman, S., Goldman, G., & Robie, A. (2012).Cyberbullying? Voices of college students. In L. A. Wamkel & C. Wankel (Eds.), *Misbehavior online in higher education* (pp. 127–156). Bingley, UK: Emerald Group.

Bauman, S. (2011). *Cyberbullying: What counselors need to know*. Alexandria, VA: American Counseling Association.

Oxford University Press. (2012). *Oxford English Dictionary*. Retrieved from http://www.oed.com

3 Definitions of Bullying and Cyberbullying: How Useful Are the Terms?

Peter K. Smith, Cristina del Barrio, and Robert S. Tokunaga

In this chapter, we consider the definition of bullying and the corresponding definition of cyberbullying. We start by examining the term *bullying* and the defining criteria normally associated with it, namely intent (to harm), repetition, and imbalance of power. We also consider the related term of *harassment*. We then move on to the term *cyberbullying* and a similar term *cyberaggression*. This involves a discussion of how useful the traditional bullying criteria are in the cyber domain. We conclude with some recommendations concerning the understanding and use of the term cyberbullying.

BULLYING AS A SUBSET OF AGGRESSION

In the psychological literature, aggression is generally taken to be a purposeful act intended to cause harm to somebody (or some animate being) who does not wish to be harmed. The somebody is usually somebody else, although of course some people inflict self-harm. The act should be intentional, given that accidental harm is not considered aggressive. For some decades, the literature on aggression focused on direct, in-person kinds of aggression, including direct physical attacks, such as hitting, kicking, punching, and direct verbal attacks, such as threats, taunts, or insults.

But in the early 1990s, the focus was broadened to include other kinds of aggression. Björkqvist, Lagerspetz, and Kaukiainen (1992) introduced the concept of *indirect aggression*, which is aimed at someone but is not perpetrated face to face. It is often accomplished via a third party; for example, spreading nasty rumors about someone. Indirect aggression can also include instances in which a deliberate harmful act took place but the victim was not present during the attack; hiding, stealing or damaging someone's belongings are usually done when the victim is not present and can be considered indirect physical bullying.

Crick and Grotpeter (1995) proposed the term *relational aggression* to refer to aggressive behavior that is intended to damage someone's relationships. This also includes rumor spreading and social exclusion. Although relational aggression is often indirect (e.g., spreading rumors targeting someone's relations and reputation with others; never choosing a mate to work or play with, never talking to him/her), it can be direct, face to face as well ("You can't play with us"). Galen and Underwood (1997) introduced the similar term *social aggression*, referring to aggression intended to damage another's self-esteem or social status. Some evidence suggests that the pain of relational aggression can be more influential than the pain stemming from physical aggression (Chen, Williams, Fitness, & Newton, 2008; Van der Meulen et al., 2003).

It is now generally accepted that aggression should embrace the indirect and relational forms, in addition to the more straightforward hits and insults studied in earlier decades. Especially in adult life, aggression can occur in the workplace, including more sophisticated means such as where someone sets totally unrealistic goals and undermines another's confidence and work satisfaction. And in this century, cyberaggression includes attacks via mobile phones and the Internet.

THE DEFINITION OF BULLYING

Although there is no universally agreed-upon definition, there is an emerging consensus in the Western research tradition that bullying refers to repeated aggressive acts against a specific target (the victim) who cannot easily defend him- or herself (see Olweus, 1999, 2010; Ross, 2002). As Olweus (2010, p.11) describes it, "bullying is a subset of aggression or aggressive behavior . . . with certain special characteristics such as repetitiveness and an asymmetric power relationship." A similar definition, though perhaps with broader connotations, is that bullying is a "systematic abuse of power" (Rigby, 2002; Smith & Sharp, 1994).

Within most of the research literature then, bullying is taken as the following:

- It is an aggressive act.
- It is perpetrated via any of the forms of aggression (e.g., physical, verbal, cyber, direct, or indirect).

but with two further defining criteria:

- There is an imbalance of power between the perpetrator and the target (the victim finds it difficult to defend him/herself).
- It has some element of repetition (these things can happen frequently).

Although the two criteria of power imbalance and repetition are not universally accepted, they are now widely used. In particular, the relative defenselessness of the victim implies an obligation of others to intervene. Olweus (1993) has argued that it is a fundamental democratic right not to be bullied. The increase in international concern about school bullying, which has expanded rapidly over the last 25 years, appears to reflect an increase in concern for human rights issues that was developing throughout the 20th century and continues today (Greene, 2006).

Bullying can happen in many contexts, including the workplace, the home, the armed forces, and prisons. Indeed, topics such as workplace bullying are growing research areas. Nevertheless, the largest focus of bullying research to date has been directed at in-school bullying. In schools, we can think of teacher-teacher, teacher-pupil, pupil-teacher bullying as well as pupil-pupil bullying; although the latter has been the primary area of interest up until now.

BULLYING IN DIFFERENT LANGUAGES

Bullying is basically an Anglo-Saxon or Northern European term. Words for bullying vary in different languages and do not have exactly the same meanings (Smith, Cowie, Olafsson, & Liefooghe, 2002). In Europe, the Latin-based languages lack a term similar to bullying although they have many terms for aggression and violence; however, the English term bullying seems to be readily understood. In Italy, the term *il bullismo* has been introduced into the language (Menesini, 2003). In Spain, the nearest term is *acoso* (harassment), more characteristic of direct, repeated aggression; while *maltrato por abuso de poder* (mistreatment by abuse of power) is used as a more general idiom; plus the word bullying is now sometimes also used (Smith et al., 2002).

In Japan, the term closest to bullying is *ijime*. This focuses more on group processes and the position of the victim in the social network, with more emphasis on social exclusion (Morita, Soeda, Soeda, & Taki, 1999), similar to the Korean term *wang-ta* (Lee, Smith, & Monks, 2011). These differences seem to be related more to the forms and processes of bullying than to the criteria of repetition and power imbalance.

Thus, there is a case to be made that bullying is something of a natural category (Rosch & Mervis, 1975), at least for adults (children tend to use the word bullying in a similar way to aggression, but the importance of the power imbalance criterion is increasingly recognized with age—see Monks and Smith, 2006; Vaillancourt et al., 2008). By a natural category, we mean that if a term very similar to bullying is not present in a lexicon, then the concept is nevertheless readily understood along the lines of the standard definition. The phenomenon appears to exist everywhere; after all, in interpersonal relationships, some people will be tempted to take advantage of others in a more disadvantaged position, for their own benefit. The meaning of terms in different languages do not correspond exactly to each other, but much of this variation refers to type of aggression (physical, verbal, indirect, etc; Smith et al., 2002). Having said this, further research on how relevant terms differ in various languages, and also how well the standard concept of bullying is recognized in all cultures, would certainly be desirable.

We also note, following Rosch and Mervis (1975), that in defining a category, it is preferable to talk of probabilistic characteristics or criteria instead of definitional attributes applying to every example. There can be better and less ideal exemplars of a category, that is, some are more central or prototypical than others (for bullying—hitting vs. ignoring someone). A category can have diffuse borders, widening to embed new exemplars of the concept (for bullying, social exclusion in the past; and cyberbullying more recently).

BULLYING AND CRITERIA FOR BULLYING

We now consider further the three main criteria for bullying, namely, Intent to Harm (shared with aggression), Imbalance of Power, and Repetition (specific to bullying). We do not consider in depth a few further issues, which, while they may be interesting in specific cases or for cross-cultural comparisons, are not central to defining bullying. For instance, bullying can vary in severity. There may be issues around how severe bullying has to be to count as bullying in terms of level of harm. However, such issues apply to aggression generally, and many other concepts, and need not be of concern in the definition. Also, although cross-culturally bullying may vary in how much it is individual based or group based (cf. Japanese "ijime"), we do not regard this as a core feature of the definition. Similarly, arguing that bullying is a relationship issue (Pepler, Craig, Connolly, Yuile, McMaster, & Jiang, 2006) while helpful for practitioners, is already implicit in the concept of intent to harm a specific target.

The Criterion of Intent

Aggression implies an intent to harm a person and a person being harmed (or at least threatened with harm). But how can we decide on intent in actual situations? It is of course necessary that the behavior itself was not just accidental, at least so far as causing harm is concerned. An important criterion here is whether the perpetrator persists in a harmful action even when informed of the harm, rather than desisting and making amends. But given that the behavior itself was intentional, how can we judge that there was actually intent to harm? A common defense of an aggressor or bullying person is that no harm was intended, and "it was just for fun."

We consider that there are three indicative criteria for making a judgment of intent to harm, which correspond to perspectives of the victim, perpetrator, and informed outsider:

1. That the victim did experience harm; this is the most obvious and used criterion, but it is not perfect. Sometimes a victim may be paranoid (Juvonen, Nishina, & Graham, 2001), in the sense of feeling and reporting being threatened or attacked, even when no actual threat or attack seems to be present, or present at a sufficient level to justify calling it aggression or bullying.
2. That the perpetrator intended not only the behavior but the harm; sometimes it is quite clear that the perpetrator meant to harm someone, but they might not succeed if the attack was ineffective or the intended victim did not construe

the attack as particularly threatening or harmful. Thus, this criterion is not perfect either; if the victim does not experience harm, is it aggression or bullying? We also need to bear in mind that some victims may be "deniers," unwilling to accept that someone else means to harm them (Juvonen et al., 2001).

3.   Ultimately, we believe that judgment of intent to harm, while being informed by the views of the victim and the perpetrator, must rest on whether a reasonable person would judge that the action could be foreseen as likely to cause harm to the intended recipient.

The Criterion of Power Imbalance

Imbalance of power appears to be a core criterion for bullying as distinct from aggression. In bullying, it is difficult for the victim to defend him- or herself; thus, a fight between equals (although aggressive) is not bullying. How is "imbalance of power" to be defined? It is clearly multidimensional. But indicative criteria would include the following:

1.   being physically weaker (for example, for physical attacks);
2.   being verbally less fluent (for example, when teased);
3.   lacking confidence or self-esteem;
4.   being outnumbered;
5.   lacking friends or social support;
6.   having a low status or rejected position in the peer group.

In an empirical study, Hunter, Boyle, and Warden (2007) compared questionnaire responses by Scottish 8–13-year-old pupils to items concerning both aggressive behavior and bullying behaviors (where there was a perceived imbalance of power through physical strength, group size, and social popularity). Their study showed that victims of bullying, as opposed to victims of peer aggression more generally, felt less control over the situation and were more depressed.

Another indicator of imbalance of power may be if the victim is in a marginalized group. Here, although at an individual level he or she may be strong or confident, the group to which they identify or to which they are perceived to belong is in a weaker position or is discriminated against. This, of course, varies with societal context but can be defined contextually by ethnicity, race, religion/faith, sex, sexual orientation, or disability. The literature in this area often uses the term harassment as, for example, in racial harassment or sexual harassment. If we take harassment as aggression specifically targeted at someone in a marginalized group from someone outside that group, then there is an imbalance of power, and this can be taken as one kind of bullying. Thus, not all bullying is harassment, but all harassment is bullying.

It is not necessarily any deficit characteristic in the victim that puts him/her in a vulnerable or disadvantaged position. Perhaps it is neutral (being new in a classroom) or a quality that when viewed from a third-party perspective is seen as positive (e.g., being more articulate, having a particular talent) that makes him/her the target of the peer attacks. Imbalance of power very often can be summarized as being different from the majority in the group and thus having less power in the social hierarchy. Sometimes the type of bullying carried out against immigrant people is primarily social exclusion. Del Barrio, Martín, Montero, Guitérrez, Barrios, and de Dios (2008), in a national study of 3,000 Spanish secondary school pupils, found that immigrant students were ignored twice as much as their nonimmigrant peers. This is why bullying can be considered a *situated phenomenon* in Bruner's terms (Bruner, 1990); the specific context determines which characteristics of an individual could make him/her vulnerable.

The Criterion of Repetition

Repetition is often invoked as a defining criterion of bullying. The repetition criterion means that it happens more than just once or twice; thus, a one-off act is not seen as bullying. However, there is not full agreement on the status of repetition as a core criterion.

In the Olweus bullying questionnaire, for example, after giving exemplars of behaviors in the opening definition of bullying, it is stated that "these actions are often repeated," which implies that this is not essential. Some commentators have argued that even one threat or nasty stare can imply a long-term bullying attitude and should be construed as bullying (Guerin & Hennessy, 2002). There are difficulties, too, in deciding what is "just once." A threat such as "I am going to kill you!" even if uttered once, could be regarded as a continuing threat unless it is actually rescinded or apologized for.

Olweus (1999) is explicit that sometimes an interaction is enough to establish a bullying relationship. The consideration of bullying as a kind of relationship helps to understand why one episode (an interaction) can be bullying. Relationships are made of interactions but go beyond them (Hinde, 1987). In bullying—especially in the school setting where pupils share time and place for long periods—an impactful interaction can link the perpetrator and the victim in a relationship inducing (especially in the victim) expectations of future aggressions (Del Barrio, Martín, Almeida, & Barrios, 2003).

To some extent the issue of repetition interacts with intent to harm. Repetition of a harmful action clearly is a very strong indication that the harm is intended by the perpetrator. However, we consider that while an important criterion, repetition is not an essential one for bullying in the way that imbalance of power is central; it is more of a probabilistic indicator.

SUMMARY OF BULLYING AS A CATEGORY

In summary, bullying appears to be a defensible category as regards traditional (i.e., pre-cyberbullying) forms of aggression. It is distinguished by an imbalance of power as a core or central criterion; repetition is a subsidiary criterion, that is, it adds to the recognition of bullying on a probabilistic basis. The distinction of bullying from aggression generally appears to be meaningful, in terms of the impact on victims, and for methods of intervention. The evidence is strongest for victims; for example, the Hunter et al. (2007) study focused on perceptions of victims. More empirical justification for the bullying/aggression distinction would still be useful, especially when taking the perspective of perpetrators. Finkelhor, Turner, and Hamby (2012) have argued that more empirical foundation is needed in this area, and that bullying is only a subcategory of a broader construct of peer victimization.

WHAT ABOUT CYBERBULLYING?

Most studies on cyberbullying over the last six or seven years show a very considerable overlap between pupil involvement in traditional bullying and involvement in cyberbullying, regardless of the exact measurement instruments and definitions employed. This overlap is one of the most well-replicated findings in the relatively new area of cyberbullying (Smith, 2012; Tokunaga, 2010). As usually more pupils are involved in traditional bullying than are involved in cyberbullying, the clearest statement of this overlap is that the majority of those involved online are also involved offline.

It is thus a rather natural step to take the definition of traditional bullying and apply it to the cyber domain. This leads to one well-used definition, namely, that cyberbullying is "an aggressive, intentional act carried out by a group or individual, *using electronic forms of contact*, repeatedly and over time against a victim who cannot easily defend him or herself" (Smith et al., 2008, p. 376).

But how useful is this definition? First, there is an issue about what is meant by "electronic forms of contact." Second, a number of authors have criticized the practice of carrying across the traditional bullying definition to the cyber domain without qualification; these criticisms take two related forms. One is a critique of the two main criteria defining bullying, namely, power imbalance and repetition, when considering cyberbullying. The other unrelated criticism is that it is not feasible to distinguish cyberbullying from a broader concept of cyberaggression or techno-aggression (we use the term cyberaggression from now on). We consider these issues, in turn, in the following sections.

What Is Meant by Electronic Forms of Contact?

The earliest forms of cyberbullying recorded were generally by text message (on mobile phones) or e-mails (on the Internet) (e.g., Rivers & Noret, 2010). Thus, both mobile phones and Internet-based technologies were considered "electronic forms of contact." However, besides texting, mobile phones could be used for nasty phone calls just as could landline phones. There was therefore already an issue as to whether nasty mobile phone calls should be considered a form of cyberbullying. Pragmatically, using landline phones seems to have been a very infrequent form of traditional bullying, whereas the mobile phone has now become an almost indispensable part of young people's lives (Rideout, Foehr, & Roberts, 2010). On this basis, it may make some sense to include all uses of mobile phones, including phone calls, as potentially relevant to cyberbullying.

Ybarra, Boyd, Korchmaros, and Oppenheim (2012) have made distinctions between Internet or online bullying, text message bullying, phone bullying, and "in person" bullying. Two points are to be noted here. First, the advent of smart phones has rendered a simple distinction between Internet and mobile phone use obsolete. The increased possibilities of using the Internet via different technological devices may make it more useful to distinguish among different kinds of communication exchange (sms (text messages), mail, blogs, etc.), rather than among different communication devices (smart phones, computer, etc). Second, "in person" implies face to face, but indirect bullying, such as rumor spreading and some kinds of social exclusion, is not face to face, and indeed can be considered as more similar to the other forms (online, text, phone) in this respect (e.g., Ortega, Elipe, Mora-Merchán, Calmaestra, & Vega, 2009).

Power Imbalance in Relation to Cyberbullying

The "imbalance of power" criterion, if taken in relation to the definition of cyberbullying, states that victims cannot defend themselves easily. But some of the criteria used to assess power imbalance for traditional bullying are not directly relevant to cyberbullying. This is clearly so for being physically weaker, and probably for being verbally less fluent (e.g., when teased), and for being outnumbered (this is obviously so in a physical sense, but being outnumbered in a user sense might still apply to cyberbullying, particularly when considering the third party-type cyberbullying). It is also not immediately obvious that lacking confidence or self-esteem, lacking friends or social support, or being in a low status or rejected position in the peer group apply when the cyberbully can act anonymously. In all such cases, a weaker pupil might feel more able to attack another pupil. And, if cyber victims are actually physically stronger, verbally more fluent or confident, have a larger number of friends, or are more popular, it may have little bearing on how well they can defend themselves. However, the imbalance of power can take a different form (e.g., the number and aggressive nature of actions addressed to the target reducing self-confidence, consequently creating the feeling of powerlessness typical of all types of bullying relationships).

Sometimes in both traditional bullying and cyberbullying, a victim may retaliate or cope to some extent. In traditional bullying, a victim might fight back (and possibly get beaten severely). In cyberbullying, a victim may retaliate digitally (or face to face if the perpetrator is a schoolmate), cope by shrugging it off or dismissing it as "not in real life" (but possibly still suffer ill effects directly or via reputation vis-à-vis others). This does not mean an imbalance of power is absent.

As when making judgments about whether an episode is bullying (see above), imbalance of power should not be inferred solely from the reaction of the victim but should be inferred from the outside perspective as much as possible, using such relevant criteria as discussed below.

So far as cyberbullying is concerned, the relevant criteria for inferring imbalance of power may be rather different from those usually used in traditional bullying. One possible criterion is technological know-how and ICT skills of the perpetrator compared to the victim. While some cyberbullying acts such as sending a nasty text message are easy, other types (such as impersonating someone else on a website) require some technological expertise. Vandebosch and Van Cleemput (2008) found that pupils with more advanced Internet skills were more likely to have experience with deviant Internet and mobile phone activities; and Ybarra and Mitchell (2004) found that cyberbullies rated themselves higher as Internet experts than those who did not cyberbully others.

Vandebosch and Van Cleemput (2008) also argued that anonymity can contribute to a power imbalance. It is more difficult to respond effectively if you do not know the identity of the perpetrator. This is the case for an appreciable proportion of cyberbullying episodes (Smith, 2012; Tokunaga, 2010). Conversely, if a victim does know the perpetrator, then the more conventional criteria of physical/psychological strength and peer group popularity may come back into play (i.e., a victim may be fearful of retaliating against a popular and stronger pupil who may take further revenge offline). This argument is strengthened by the finding that when a victim does know the identity of the perpetrator, it seems that most often it is someone from the same school or someone from his or her vicinity (e.g., Slonje & Smith, 2008; Smith et al., 2008; nevertheless, the lower percentages of observers of cyberbullying among the many observers of traditional bullying confirm the less-open quality of cyberbullying in the school; Del Barrio et al., 2011). Generally, being in a marginalized group position (see above) may then come into play as a criterion for power imbalance.

A further aspect of power imbalance suggested by Dooley, Pyzalski, and Cross (2009) is that since it may be harder to avoid the cyberbullying (that it follows you wherever you are), this in itself can make the victim feel powerless due to not being able to avoid the abuse. The permanent status of the information on display and its multiple potential observers (not always known) expose the victim in a way that makes it very difficult for him/her to defend against it. Here the imbalance of power is not directly related to the characteristics of the perpetrator but is embedded in a situational relationship (Bruner, 1990). For example, a power imbalance is illustrated when someone creates a webpage supplanting a classmate's identity, knowing for sure that others will see this undesired information on the Internet.

Repetition in Relation to Cyberbullying

Issues around repetition are more difficult in cyberbullying as compared to traditional bullying. A single cyberbullying act (e.g., sending a text message or posting

Internet material) may readily snowball beyond the initial control of the perpetrator and be distributed or viewed repeatedly by others based on the technology used. Thus, a single act by a perpetrator may be repeated many times by others and experienced many times by the victim.

If the repetition is not carried out by the perpetrator, is this still cyberbullying? One aspect of this was investigated by Slonje, Smith, and Frisen (2012) by asking what "actively targeted bystanders" (pupils who had been sent or shown information intended to cyberbully someone else) do with the information they saw. Although the majority, 72% of these bystanders, did nothing further to distribute the material, 9% forwarded the material to other friends, and 6% showed or forwarded it to the victim in order to bully him/her further); on a positive note, 13% showed/forwarded the material to the original victim to help him/her.

It should be noted that this aspect of repetition is probably more common in cyber media (e.g., circulation of text messages, repeated visits to websites) but can happen offline too. For example, an initial rumor started by the perpetrator can be repeated many times by others, or an insulting message written on the school wall can be seen repeatedly by others. Thus, repetitious messages are not exclusive to cyberbullying. However, it is arguably more prominent in cyberbullying as the repetition can be very rapid, and the potential audience is much larger online.

As discussed above, we consider the criterion of repetition to be subsidiary, rather than core, in terms of defining bullying. The perspective of the outsider should be the ultimate consideration, relating also to intent to harm. A repeated action is a good indicator of intent to harm, especially if feedback is given by the victim or others to the perpetrator. But in some cases a single act by a perpetrator might reasonably be expected to be repeated by others, and the perpetrator might reasonably be expected to know and even intend this. If you post an offensive comment on a website, you expect many others to see it. If so, then the case for calling this cyberbullying is strengthened.

Is It Useful to Distinguish Cyberbullying from a Broader Concept of Cyberaggression?

It appears possible to defend a conventional definition of cyberbullying, still invoking imbalance of power as a core criterion and repetition as a secondary criterion, in addition to the more general issue of intent to harm as a criterion that also defines cyberaggression. But two pragmatic issues should be noted.

First, there is an issue as to whether children/young people themselves use or recognize the term cyberbullying or indeed what terms they do use to describe this behavior. Grigg (2010), carrying out focus groups with pupils in the United Kingdom, found a variety of terms and argued that cyberaggression was a more useful field of study. Nevertheless, the term cyberbullying is now widely used in the media and by researchers. Just as bullying has come to be a well-understood term across ages and cultures (Smith & Monks, 2008), cyberbullying may come to be understood similarly, even if there is some confusion over the variety of terms at present.

Second, in practice, many studies actually measure cyberaggression or cyber abuse since they do not systematically include measures of imbalance of power or repetition. For example, Law, Shapka, Hymel, Olson, and Waterhouse (2012, Study 2) do not invoke either repetition or imbalance of power as criteria to demarcate cyberbullying, which they also refer to as "Internet victimization." This broader approach is sometimes clearly stated. For example, Law, Shapka, and Olson (2010) explicitly used an "online aggression" scale. Wang, Iannotti, and Nansel (2009) compared different types of bullying, including cyber, and did include imbalance of power in their definition of cyberbullying; but they explicitly examined it only *once or twice or more* because "it is not uncommon in the literature of cyberbullying to count a single incident as an experience of cyberbullying" (p. 370).

These considerations point to the importance of using terms clearly in relation to the definition and measurements used in the study. It is obviously legitimate to carry out studies on cyberaggression! However, we suggest that studies on cyberbullying should pay some consideration to the criteria of power imbalance and repetition. There is also an issue about whether the term *victim* implies "victim of a bully" or simply "recipient of an aggressive act," which we do not consider further in this chapter.

SOME TENTATIVE CONCLUSIONS

In conclusion, we argue that cyberaggression should refer to an intentional harmful behavior against another person using electronic technology (computers, phones, etc.) for communication (text, images). We also argue that cyberbullying should be retained as a concept distinct from cyberaggression. Of course, many researchers wish to study cyberaggression, Internet safety, and other antisocial problems that occur through electronic technologies; however, cyberbullying is another legitimate area of study.

We consider that the concept of cyberbullying embodies three core criteria. The first criterion is intent to harm, which is common to cyberaggression. The second criterion is the existence of a specific target at which the intentionally harmful message is directed. The third criterion is that there is an imbalance of power as a defining characteristic of this subset of cyberaggression. The imbalance of power can be assessed in terms of the differences in technological know-how between the perpetrator and victim, relative anonymity, social status, number of friends, or marginalized group position. Imbalance of power should not be inferred from the reaction of the victim but should be assessed from the outside perspective as much as possible.

Studies on intent to harm that do not include a specific target and imbalance of power should be considered cyberaggression, not cyberbullying, research. These are core criteria for cyberbullying. Concepts are fuzzy, so subsidiary criteria may be helpful (Rosch & Mervis, 1975). Here, we argue that repetition by the perpetrator is not an essential criterion. Repetition in the broader sense, including distribution processes, can be used as subsidiary criterion for cyberbullying. Similarly, the impact on the victim (e.g., whether it causes harm) is a subsidiary criterion. In both cases, their presence can make a stronger judgment that an episode is cyberbullying.

Finally, we note that more research is needed in many of the areas we have discussed. The judgment that bullying is a natural category needs further investigation. Also, the relevance of various criteria for judging imbalance of power in cyberbullying has been little studied until now. For the present, we regard cyberbullying as a viable and defensible concept, but this may change as research develops further, and indeed also as technology develops further and new forms of cyberbullying and cyberaggression emerge. However, we are confident in our call for greater care and precision in research, when using these and related terms.

ACKNOWLEDGMENTS

The material in this chapter was informed by many participants in the International Cyberbullying Think Tank, organized by Sheri Bauman. We are also grateful to Sheri Bauman and David Finkelhor for comments on an earlier version.

References

Björkqvist, K., Lagerspetz, K., & Kaukiainen, A. (1992). Do girls manipulate and boys fight? Developmental trends in regard to direct and indirect aggression. *Aggressive Behavior, 18*, 117–127. doi:10.1002/1098–2337(1992)18:2<117::AID-AB2480180205>3.0.CO;2–3

Bruner, J. S. (1990). *Acts of meaning*. Cambridge, MA: Harvard University Press.

Chen, Z., Williams, K. D., Fitness, J., Newton, N. C. (2008). When hurt will not heal: Exploring the capacity to relive social and physical pain. *Psychological Science, 19*, 789–795.

Crick, N. R., & Grotpeter, J. K. (1995). Relational aggression, gender, and social-psychological adjustment. *Child Development, 66*, 710–722. doi:10.2307/1131945

Del Barrio, C., de Dios, M. J., Montero, I. Martín, E., Ochaíta, E., Espinosa, M. A., Gutiérrez, H., & Barrios, A. (2011). Cyberbullying among Spanish secondary students: A national survey. *Proceedings of the 15th European Conference on Developmental Psychology* (pp. 369–376). Bologna, Italy: Medimond.

Del Barrio, C., Martín, E., Almeida, A., & Barrios, A. (2003). Del maltrato y otros conceptos relacionados con la agresión entre escolares, y su estudio psicológico [On peer maltreatment and other concepts related to aggression, and their psychological study]. *Infancia y Aprendizaje, 26*, 9–24. doi:10.1174/02103700360536400

Del Barrio, C., Martín, E., Montero, I., Gutiérrez, H., Barrios, A., & de Dios, M. J. (2008). Bullying and social exclusion in Spanish secondary schools: National trends from 1999 to 2006. *International Journal of Clinical and Health Psychology, 8*, 657–677.

Dooley, J. J., Pyżalski, J., & Cross, D. (2009). Cyberbullying versus face-to-face bullying: A theoretical and conceptual review. *Zeitschrift für Psychologie/Journal of Psychology, 217*, 182–188. doi:10.1027/0044–3409.217.4.182

Finkelhor, D., Turner, H. A., & Hamby, S. L. (2012). Let's prevent peer victimization, not just bullying. *Child Abuse and Neglect, 36*, 271–274.

Galen, B. R., & Underwood, M. K. (1997). A developmental investigation of social aggression among children. *Developmental Psychology, 33*, 589–600. doi:10.1037//0012–1649.33.4.589

Greene, M. (2006). Bullying in schools: A plea for measure of human rights. *Journal of Social Issues, 62*, 63–79. doi:10.1111/j.1540–4560.2006.00439.x

Grigg, D. (2010). Cyber-aggression: Definition and concept of cyberbullying. *Australian Journal of Guidance and Counselling, 20*, 143–156. doi:10.1375/ajgc.20.2.143

Guerin, S. & Hennessy, E. (2002). Pupils' definitions of bullying. *European Journal of Psychology of Education, 17*, 249–261. doi:10.1007/BF03173535

Hinde, R. A. (1987). *Individuals, relationships and culture.* (Ch. 2: The relationships perspective). Cambridge: Cambridge University Press.

Hunter, S. C., Boyle, J.M.E., & Warden, D. (2007). Perceptions and correlates of peer-victimization and bullying. *British Journal of Educational Psychology, 77*, 797–810. doi:10.1348/000709906X171046

Juvonen, J., Nishina, A., & Graham, S. (2001). Self-views versus peer perceptions of victim status among early adolescents. In J. Juvonen & S. Graham (Eds.), *Peer harassment in school: The plight of the vulnerable and victimized* (pp. 105–124). New York: Guildford.

Law, D. M., Shapka, J. D., Hymel, S., Olson, B. F., & Waterhouise, T. (2012). The changing face of bullying: An empirical comparison between traditional and internet bullying and victimization. *Computers in Human Behavior, 28*, 226–232.

Law, D. M., Shapka, J. D., & Olson, B. F. (2010). To control or not to control? Parenting behaviours and adolescent online aggression. *Computers in Human Behavior, 26*, 1651–1656.

Lee, S-H, Smith, P. K., & Monks, C. (2011). Perception of bullying-like phenomena in South Korea: A qualitative approach from a lifespan perspective. *Journal of Aggression, Conflict and Peace Research, 3*, 210–221. doi:10.1108/17596591111187738

Menesini, E. (2003). *Il bullismo: le azioni efficaci della scuola.* Trento: Erickson Edizione.

Monks, C. P., & Smith, P. K. (2006). Definitions of "bullying": Age differences in understanding of the term, and the role of experience. *British Journal of Developmental Psychology, 24*, 801–821. doi:10.1348/026151005X82352

Morita, Y., Soeda, H., Soeda, K., & Taki, M. (1999). Japan. In P. K. Smith, Y. Morita, J. Junger-Tas, D. Olweus, R. Catalano & P. Slee (Eds.), *The nature of school bullying: A cross-national perspective.* New York: Routledge.

Olweus, D. (1993). *Bullying at school: What we know and what we can do.* Oxford: Blackwell.

Olweus, D. (1999). Sweden. In P. K. Smith, Y. Morita, J. Junger-Tas, D. Olweus, R. Catalano, & P. Slee (Eds.), *The nature of school bullying: A cross-national perspective* (pp. 7–27). London: Routledge.

Olweus, D. (2010). Understanding and researching bullying: Some critical issues. In S. R. Jimerson, S. M. Swearer, & D. L. Espelage (Eds.), *Handbook of bullying in schools: An international perspective* (pp. 9–33). New York: Routledge.

Ortega, R., Elipe, P., Mora-Merchán, J. A., Calmaestra, J., & Vega, E. (2009). The emotional impact on victims of traditional bullying and cyberbullying. A study of Spanish adolescents. *Zeitschrift für Psychologie/Journal of Psychology, 217*, 197–204. doi:10.1027/0044–3409.217.4.197

Pepler, D. J., Craig, W. M., Connolly, J. A., Yuile, A., McMaster, L., & Jiang, D. (2006). A developmental perspective on bullying. *Aggressive Behavior, 32*, 376–384. doi:10.1002/ab.20136

Rideout, V. J., Foehr, U. G., & Roberts, D. F. (2010). *Generation M2. Media in the lives of 8- to 18-year-olds.* Washington, DC: Henry J. Kaiser Foundation. Available online from http://www.kff.org

Rigby, K. (2002). *New perspectives on bullying.* London: Jessica Kingsley.

Rivers, I., & Noret, N. (2010). "I h8 u": Findings from a five-year study of text and email bullying. *British Educational Research Journal, 36*, 643–671. doi:10.1080/01411920903071918

Rosch, E., & Mervis, C .G. (1975). Family resemblances: Studies in the internal structure of categories. *Cognitive Psychology, 7*, 573–605. doi:10.1016/0010–0285(75)90024–9

Ross, D. M. (2002). *Childhood bullying and teasing. What school personnel, other professionals, and parents can do* (2nd ed.). Alexandria, VA: American Counseling Association.

Slonje, R., & Smith, P. K. (2008). Cyberbullying: Another main type of bullying? *Scandinavian Journal of Psychology, 49*, 147–154. doi:10.1111/j.1467–9450.2007.00611.x

Slonje, R., Smith, P. K., & Frisen, A. (2012). Processes of cyberbullying, and feelings of remorse by bullies: A pilot study. *European Journal of Developmental Psychology, 9*, 244–259.

Smith, P. K. (2012). Cyberbullying and cyber aggression. In Shane R. Jimerson, Amanda B. Nickerson, Matthew J. Mayer, & Michael J. Furlong (Eds.), *Handbook of school violence and school safety: International research and practice* (pp. 93–103). New York: Routledge.

Smith, P. K., Cowie, H., Olafsson, R., & Liefooghe, A.P.D. (2002). Definitions of bullying: A comparison of terms used, and age and sex differences, in a 14-country international comparison. *Child Development, 73*, 1119–1133. doi:10.1111/1467–8624.00461

Smith, P. K., Mahdavi, J., Carvalho, M., Fisher, S., Russell, S., & Tippett, N. (2008). Cyberbullying: Its nature and impact in secondary school pupils. *Journal of Child Psychology & Psychiatry, 49*, 376–385. doi:10.1111/j.1469–7610.2007.01846.x

Smith, P. K., & Monks, C. P. (2008). Concepts of bullying: Developmental and cultural aspects. *International Journal of Adolescent Medicine and Health, 20*, 101–112. doi:10.1515/IJAMH.2008.20.2.101

Smith, P. K., & Sharp, S. (Eds.). (1994). *School bullying: Insights and perspectives.* London: Routledge. doi:10.4324/9780203425497

Tokunaga, R. S. (2010). Following you home from school: A critical review and synthesis of research on cyberbullying victimization. *Computers in Human Behavior, 26*, 277–287. doi:10.1016/j.chb.2009.11.014

Vaillancourt, T., McDougall, P., Hymel, S., Krygsman, A., Miller, J., Stiver, K., & Davis, C. (2008). Bullying: Are researchers and children/youth talking about the same thing? *International Journal of Behavioral Development, 32*, 486–495. doi:10.1177/0165025408095553

Vandebosch, H., & Van Cleemput, K. (2008). Defining cyberbullying: A qualitative research into the perceptions of youngsters. *CyberPsychology & Behavior, 11*, 499–503. doi:10.1089/cpb.2007.0042

Van der Meulen, K., Soriano, L., Granizo, L., del Barrio, C., Korn, S., & Schäfer, M. (2003). Recordando el maltrato entre iguales en la escuela: consecuencias e influencia en la actuación del profesorado [Remembering school bullying: consequences and influence on teachers' performance]. *Infancia y Aprendizaje, 26,* 49–62. doi:10.1174/02103700360536428

Wang, J., Iannotti, R. J., & Nansel, T. R. (2009). School bullying among adolescents in the United States: Physical, verbal, relational, and cyber. *Journal of Adolescent Health, 45,* 368–375. doi:10.1016/j.jadohealth.2009.03.021, PMid:19766941, PMCid:2751860

Ybarra, M., Boyd, D., Korchmaros, J., & Oppenheim, J. (2012). Defining and measuring cyberbullying within the larger context of bullying victimization. *Journal of Adolescent Health.*

Ybarra, M. L., & Mitchell, K. J. (2004). Online aggressor/targets, aggressors, and targets: A comparison of associated youth characteristics. *Journal of Child Psychology and Psychiatry, 45,* 1308–1316. doi:10.1111/j.1469–7610.2004.00328.x

4 Definitions: Another Perspective and a Proposal for Beginning with Cyberaggression

Sheri Bauman, Marion K. Underwood, and Noel A. Card

As a relatively new field of scientific inquiry, cyberbullying research has the opportunity to build a substantive body of work that will provide an empirical basis for prevention and intervention program development and evaluation. Because the definition of cyberbullying is the foundation upon which research into the behavior rests, it is essential that consensus be reached on a precise definition. Without agreement, different studies cannot be compared or evidence accumulated in a meaningful way. Without a widely accepted definition, measures of the construct cannot be developed. And, without a definition and reliable and valid measures, research in this field will not advance.

Defining a construct is a challenging endeavor, particularly when, as in this case, the term is also used in colloquial and popular media—nonscientific contexts. Researchers' thinking may be influenced by these informal uses, which can lead to definitions that are not exact enough to allow reliable measurement. An additional dilemma is the tendency to assume that since the construct is labeled as a variant of "bullying," the characteristics should be parallel to those used to define traditional bullying. The think tank attendees struggled to craft a careful definition that would advance the field, and the previous chapter presents the result of deliberations of the work group on definitions. We wish to present another perspective and to suggest that for now, researchers focus on cyberaggression (rather than cyberbullying). With the current evidence available, it appears difficult to reach consensus on the nature of cyberbullying. Focusing on cyberaggression would allow us to continue to study this phenomenon as we wrestle with the complicated issues of what bullying might mean in the context of electronic communication.

> **Cyberaggression**: behavior aimed at harming another person using electronic communications, and perceived as aversive by the target (Schoffstall & Cohen, 2011).

In Chapter 3, our colleagues discuss the question of whether cyberaggression is a more accurate term, given the difficulty of specifying how the standard bullying characteristics (intent, repetition, power imbalance) are manifested in the technological arena. They acknowledge that youth may not use the term *cyberbullying* to describe the behaviors theoretically encompassed by the term. They also consider repetition to be a subsidiary component of cyberbullying that may or may not be present, although they are somewhat equivocal about how repetition should be determined. Smith et al. agree that most studies reported in the literature actually measure cyberaggression because they do not assess the imbalance of power that is seen as a defining attribute. Yet they conclude that cyberbullying is such a widely used term in both scholarly literature and the popular media that it should be retained, and that measures include items to assess the elements of repetition and power imbalance.

Our colleagues propose that all bullying, including cyberbullying, refers to aggressive behavior that is intentional, repetitive, and involves an imbalance of power between the perpetrator and the target such that the target finds it difficult to defend her or himself. They recognize that these criteria may be expressed differently in cyberbullying incidents. One criterion suggested by our colleagues for determining whether intent (which refers to the mental process of the perpetrator) was present is the judgment of a *reasonable person* that the perpetrator should have anticipated the harmful nature of the anticipated action, and that by acting with this knowledge, is demonstrating intent. Our colleagues also suggest that this standard be the ultimate determiner for deciding whether an event includes the power imbalance that is a necessary component of bullying. The *reasonable person* principle has been applied in many legal contexts to determine whether someone has behaved in a manner that the mythical reasonable person would judge to be acceptable. However, the application of this principle has been challenged due to the potential for ambiguity and subjectivity. In the case of cyberbullying, not only is the hypothetical reasonable person not available to weigh in, it is not clear whether that person would be a peer or an adult, whose determinations are likely to vary widely. The reasonable person standard seems just as difficult to apply to cyberaggression as it is to more traditional forms of aggression. Intent to harm is always difficult to observe directly.

In the previous chapter, neither severity of an incident nor the distress of the target were considered to be defining characteristics. Most definitions of aggression include two criteria: the behavior is intended to harm, and the victim feels hurt (Harré & Lamb, 1993). Neither of these is able to be directly observed but can be assessed in other ways, by coding for clear signs of intentionality or distress, or by asking the young people themselves. We propose that as we continue to understand what cyberbullying might mean, we focus for the time being on cyberaggression, assess the extent to which the perpetrator's intent and the victim's distress can be coded, and also use methods that invite youth themselves to share their perceptions of what types of electronic communication seem most intended to harm and are most distressing. It may be the case that those who experience online harassment or cyberbullying are not always distressed by them (e.g., Hinduja and Patchin, 2007, reported that 35% of victims were not bothered by the incident). If an incident (perhaps mean teasing) does not distress the target (perhaps because of contextual and interpersonal information that is not queried in the survey), is it appropriate to characterize the incident as cyberbullying? There is no doubt, however, that the behavior constitutes cyberaggression.

Focusing on cyberaggression for the time being will allow us to continue to assess whether elements or traditional bullying might make sense, and are valuable to retain, in the context of electronic communication, as for example, repetition. We observe that some researchers (e.g., Hinduja & Patchin, 2009; Ybarra (this volume); Ybarra & Mitchell, 2004) distinguish between cyber-harassment (single incidents of electronic aggression) and cyberbullying (repeated incidents). More important for our purposes is the impossibility of measuring the judgment of a reasonable person in researching cyberbullying activity (and in fact, we question whether it is a workable strategy for more traditional forms of aggression, for that matter). If a reasonable person is to be the final arbiter of whether a behavior exhibits the essential components of cyberbullying, then a hypothetical person needs to be involved in the assessment. Finally, we argue that measuring cyberbullying poses great difficulty, given its attributes and the current state of the knowledge base, then researchers should investigate cyberaggression and accurately label the construct, which can be defined and measured with precision.

We follow the lead of other colleagues in this field by defining cyberaggression as did Schoffstall and Cohen (2011, p. 588), "intentional behavior aimed at harming another person or persons through computers, cell phones, and other electronic devices, and perceived as aversive by the victim (Hinduja & Patchin, 2008; Ybarra, Diener-West, & Leaf, 2007; Ybarra & Mitchell, 2004)." We challenge ourselves and our colleagues to develop more precise and valid measures of cyberaggression, which will likely involve systematically studying what youth do and do not perceive to be intentional, hurtful forms of electronic communication. We hope researchers will not be dazzled and distracted by the more unusual forms of cyberbullying that require some technical expertise (such as constructing elaborate, hurtful websites), but focus also on the likely more frequent, garden variety forms of cyberaggression. Most adolescents use text messaging and Facebook daily, so sending nasty text messages or making mean comments on Facebook may be the most frequent forms of cyberaggression.

By studying cyberaggression systematically, we can test the limits of the current definition, but we can also work more systematically toward understanding what bullying might mean in this particular context. Given that most online harassment comes from known peers (Internet Safety Technical Task Force, 2008), assessing a power imbalance for cyberaggression may be possible, as could assessing the repetition. All aggression, whether in electronic form or not, likely occurs at low frequencies but is still intensely distressing. To fully understand what cyberbullying might mean, we suggest first focusing on cyberaggression and taking care at every step to include adolescents' perspectives on what types of electronic communication are intended to harm, distress, and occur most regularly in the different types of media in which they engage daily.

Initially studying the broader construct of cyberaggression also allows researchers to empirically evaluate, rather than assume, whether the features that differentiate cyberbullying from other types of cyberaggression matter. In research on traditional bullying and aggression, there is little or no effort to evaluate empirically whether intentionality, repetition, or power imbalance predicts outcomes for perpetrators or targets. Instead, the importance of these defining characteristics is assumed, with several negative consequences. First, there is a danger that definitional features are misperceived as empirical findings, such as believing that an important finding is that bullying (which laypeople might synonymize with aggression) involves a power differential. Second, this assumption has led to a divide in research traditions, with many bullying researchers dismissing research on "aggression" or "victimization" as irrelevant. Many in our field consider work by Olweus (1978) as the earliest scientific foundation; but it is worth remembering that aggression among youth has been studied for over a century (Burk, 1897). As recently as 2011, Espelage and Swearer perceived an absence of research on bullying in the United States, despite the presence of hundreds of studies on aggression and victimization using U.S. samples. Citing these authors does not reflect a dismissal of the importance of their work; rather, these influential works serve as examples of the common tendency to limit our focus to the specific phenomenon of bullying (versus aggression and victimization) based on definitional assumption lacking empirically tested evidence. A focus within our emerging field on cyberaggression, rather than a restrictive and untested definition of cyberbullying, may allow us to avoid these problems.

CONCLUSIONS

Our recommendation at this stage of the development of the scholarly research is that we focus on—and label—the behavior we are investigating as *cyberaggression*. We have argued above that because measures do not assess the power imbalance that is a defining attribute of cyberbullying, we are not currently studying cyberbullying anyway. It would be more accurate and precise to call this line of inquiry the study of cyberaggression. Doing so would eliminate the requirement that a reasonable person (with the attendant difficulties in locating one of suitable age) be somehow recruited so her or his determination could be incorporated into measures. Furthermore, studying cyberaggression would allow researchers the opportunity to carefully and systematically determine whether the attributes typically included in definitions of cyberbullying have an empirical basis and whether they can be assessed. The many ambiguities surrounding the components of the definition and how they are manifested (or not) in the context of electronic communication should be explored so their inclusion in the definition can be evaluated empirically.

References

Burk, F. L. (1897). Teasing and bullying. *Pedagogical Seminary, 4*, 338–371.
Espelage, D., & Swearer, S. (2011). *Bullying in North American schools* (2nd ed.). New York: Routledge.

Harré, R., & Lamb, R. (1983). *The encyclopedic dictionary of psychology*. Great Britain: Basil Blackwell Publisher Limited.

Hinduja, S., & Patchin, J. W. (2007). Offline consequences of online victimization. *School Violence and Delinquency, 6*(3), 89–112. doi:10.1300/J202v06n03_06

Hinduja, S., & Patchin, J. W. (2008). Cyberbullying: An exploratory analysis of factors related to offending and victimization. *Deviant Behavior, 29*, 129–156. doi:10.1080/01639620701457816

Internet Safety Technical Task Force. (2008). Enhancing child safety & online technologies: Final report to the multi-state working group on social networking of State Attorneys Gender of the United States. Retrieved from http://cyber.law.harvard.edu/sites/cyber.law.harvard.edu/files/ISTTF_Final_Report.pdf

Olweus, D. (1978). *Aggression in the schools: Bullies and whipping boys*. Washington, D.C.: Hemisphere Press (John Wiley).

Schoffstall, C. L., & Cohen, R. (2011). Cyber aggression: The relation between online offenders and offline social competence. *Social Development, 20*, 587–604. doi:10.1111/j.1467–9507.2011.00609.x

Ybarra, M. L., Diener-West, M., & Leaf, P. J. (2007). Examining the overlap in Internet harassment and school bullying: Implications for school intervention. *Journal of Adolescence, 41*, S42–S50. doi:10.1016/jadohealth.2007.09.004

Ybarra, M., & Mitchell, K. J. (2004). Youth engaging in online harassment: Associations with caregiver-child relationships, Internet use, and personal characteristics. *Journal of Adolescence, 27*, 319–336. doi:10.1016/j.adolescence.2004.03.007

Part III

Theoretical Framework

5 Theories of Cyberbullying

*Dorothy L. Espelage, Mrinalini A. Rao,
and Rhonda G. Craven*

Despite the mounting volume of research in the area of traditional forms of bullying (i.e., verbal, physical, relational) that are transmitted face to face, cyberbullying research is only recently beginning to burgeon. To date, the cyberbullying literature has included studies examining the prevalence of cyberbullying among youth, how these prevalence estimates differ across demographic factors (e.g., sex, race), investigating the overlap between face-to-face bullying and cyberbullying, and identifying predictors of cyberbullying involvement. However, discussions of explanatory theories of cyberbullying involvement among youth are sparse and piecemeal, and conclusions have been based largely on cross-sectional studies.

The goals of this chapter are threefold. First, we review numerous theories that have been empirically supported in the aggression, bullying, and general social development literature that might offer some promise in understanding cyberbullying. These theories range from the comprehensive social ecological framework to more specific theories related to communication, social norms, and social learning. Second, a series of longitudinal analyses are presented to evaluate the transactional association between face-to-face bullying perpetration and cyberbullying perpetration, the association between peer victimization and cyberbullying perpetration, and the reciprocal interaction between cyberbullying victimization and perpetration. Third, self-concept theory and research is summarized to highlight how theory could inform prevention efforts.

SECTION 1: REVIEW OF DOMINANT THEORIES

Comprehensive Theory-Social-Ecological Theory

Social ecological theory has been continually applied to school-based bullying and aggression by identifying associated risk and protective factors across all contexts in which youth find themselves.

This theoretical framework posits that children and adolescents' behavior is shaped by a range of nested contextual systems, including family, peers, and school environments (Bronfenbrenner, 1977; Espelage & Horne, 2008).

A child's direct contact with family, peers, and schools comprises the *microsystem*; however, when a child's behavior is influenced by family or school climate, then this interaction is considered the *mesosystem*. Parent-teacher meetings are an example of a mesosystem. The *exosystem* is the social context with which the child does not have direct contact, but which affects her indirectly through the microsystem. The *macrosystem* comprises influences from a child's larger environment such as cultural values, customs, and laws (Berk, 2000). Finally, the dimension of time is included in this framework known as the *chronosystem*. This system exerts itself directly upon the child, through external events (e.g., moving schools) or internal events (e.g., puberty). These events inevitably have a direct impact on the microsystem and mesosystem and impact those systems indirectly through the macrosytsem. Cyberbullying could be an example of the chronosystem's indirect influence on a child's bullying experiences because of the recent increase in social networking sites and the affordability of text messaging.

An example of the application of the social-ecological framework to cyberbullying involvement was recently offered by Low and Espelage (under review), who examined a series of moderated mediation models using longitudinal multiple regression across three time points (each six months apart) to examine predictors of cyberbullying perpetration among 1,023 early adolescents (5th–8th grades). Students completed survey questionnaires assessing cyberbullying perpetration, family conflict, parental monitoring, hostility, depression, empathy, self-esteem, and alcohol and drug use (AOD). Hostility and AOD use were found to be mediators of the association between family conflict and cyberbullying perpetration. This longitudinal study suggests that cyberbullying perpetration can be explained by individual and family characteristics and suggests that the social-ecological theory could offer some direction.

Social Information Processing Theory

One of the most influential models of aggression is the Social Information Processing (SIP) Deficit Model (Dodge & Coie, 1987; Dodge, Pettit, McClaskey, & Brown, 1986), which posits that aggression is largely due to impairment in social problem solving. This complex model has been supported across a multitude of studies and, in general, concludes that aggressive children/adolescents tend to show encoding problems such as hostile attribution error, deficits at the level of representation (e.g., a poor understanding of others' mental states), and a limited repertoire of social problem solutions (Crick & Dodge, 1994). More specifically, the authors found that children who behaved aggressively were more likely to attribute hostility to ambiguous situations and thereby have deficits in interpreting social information. Dodge and Schwartz (1997) further argued that a child's behavior is directly related to his or her mental processing of the situation, and competent social information processing results in adaptive and competent prosocial behavior.

Considerable research supports the applicability of the SIP model to aggression, especially when applied to the reactive aggressive subtype. The thought processes of reactive aggressive children seem to be consistent with the SIP model because these children often show deficits in representation and interpretation (Dodge et al., 1986; Dodge & Coie, 1987; Schwartz, McFadyen-Ketchum, Dodge, Pettit, & Bates, 1998). In contrast to reactive aggression, the SIP model appears to apply differently to proactive aggression. More specifically, proactive aggression has been found to be associated with positive outcome expectations for aggressive behaviors (e.g., Crick & Dodge, 1994; Schwartz et al., 1998). While most of the research mentioned has examined face-to-face interactions, it is likely that there are unique and common dimensions to applying SIP to the study of cyberbullying, especially if cyberbullying is largely proactive in nature. Unique to cyberbullying is the text-based content and the delayed reaction times and rewards associated with it (Dooley, Pyzalski, & Cross, 2009). These are likely to impact how information is processed, what attributions are made, and what behavior emerges from them.

General Strain Theory

General strain theory argues that individuals who experience significant strain will develop anger and frustration in response, which then places them at risk for engaging in deviant behavior (Agnew, 1992). In relation to cyberbullying, youth who have experienced victimization at school might engage in cyberbullying perpetration to release their anger and frustration (Hinduja & Patchin, 2010). We return to this hypothesis in Section 2.

Social Learning and Social Norm Theories

Social learning theory. From a social learning perspective, Bandura (1986) has argued that the external environment contributes, in large part, to the acquisition and maintenance of aggression and other risk behaviors. The development of aggression and other potentially deviant behaviors is posited to be the consequence of exposure to socially deviant role models and inappropriate reinforcement of maladaptive behaviors. For example, a child who bullies other children and receives reinforcement from other students who laugh, join in, or generally offer support to the perpetrator will be likely to continue his/her behavior. What is not clear is whether this reinforcement serves the same type of function in cyberspace. For example, it is plausible that engaging in subtle cyberbullying within social network sites might also provide reinforcement for such behaviors by others "liking" a post, etc.

Social rank or social dominance theory. Social rank or social dominance theory posits that aggression is supported by many societies because aggressive individuals typically have higher rank, status, or power within a group (Blumenfeld, 2005; Hawker & Boulton, 2001). These authors contend that victimizing others serves the function of establishing and maintaining a social hierarchy within a given group. It also serves the purpose of maintaining a distinction between members of the in-group and those of other groups (Blumenfeld, 2005). However, it appears that cyberspace might complicate the application of social rank theory to cyberbullying. Identities are fluid in cyberspace because individuals can decide how they present themselves in these spaces, and they can alter their identities much more easily than in face-to-face interactions (Turkle, 1995). This, coupled with the instant access cyberspace provides to the entire network, provides individuals who are lower in the real-world social hierarchy opportunities to influence and alter the social hierarchies established within cyberspace environments. Another aspect of cyberspace that may embolden lower-rank youth is the potential for anonymity in cyberspace. This may offer victimized youth an avenue to retaliate against perpetrators, or even to take on the perpetrator role and victimize others.

Resource control theory. Resource control theory (RCT) is a theory born out of work by Hawley (1999, 2002), who studied the hierarchical structure of elephants and children's peer groups to determine the strategies used to develop and maintain dominance. Resources are considered the material, social, and informational things that are generally seen as desirable by children. Hawley (1999) has argued that it is likely that the social skills deficit model or a developmental psychopathology model might not account for the adaptive function of bullying and the instrumentality associated with bullying among youth. RCT argues that individual youth have the capacity to employ a wide range of strategies when interacting with their peers to obtain limited resources. More specifically, they use coercive and pro-social strategies to obtain resources, and in doing so foster social dominance. Hawley, Stump, & Ratcliff (2011) have called these bi-strategic controllers within school classrooms, using pro-social (friendly) and coercive (threatening) strategies in combination to obtain resources. Hawley's seminal work is considered one of five key evolutionary insights in an evolutionary model of risky behavior in adolescence (Ellis et al., 2011).

In an attempt to test this theory, our team created competitive and cooperative games and placed bullies on teams with non-bullies in order to assess the strategies that bullies use when playing competitive games to win. Students on teams communicated through an instant messaging mechanism; these messages were coded by independent raters and eventually labeled as pro-social or coercive. Preliminary results with 47 5th-grade students across three classrooms indicate preliminary support for Hawley's resource control theory that bullying would be best described as bi-strategic in nature (Mansilla, Amir, Espelage, & Pu, 2012). As hypothesized, self-reported bullying (name-calling, teasing, exclusion), as assessed on a survey, was associated with the use of both coercive ($r = .49$; aggressive messages to other game players) and pro-social ($r = .34$; friendly messages to other game players), but these strategies were less associated with a measure of pure fighting (physical aggression, $rs = .27, .19$ respectively). As RCT is embedded in evolutionary theories of aggression and bullying, it will be important to continue to expand on its application to cyberbullying.

Social norms theory. The strong influence of peer norms on adolescent behavior has been well-established in real-world adolescent networks. It is likely that similar norms exist for interactions in cyberspace, along with the enforcement of these norms and the penalties associated with breaking them. A common norm in adolescent networks is a code of silence with regard to behaviors that could get peers into trouble. Cyberbullying is particularly hard for adults to monitor, and so reporting of cyberbullying incidents can often be traced back to the victim of cyberbullying. This puts the victim at risk not only for additional bullying and social exclusion, but also increases the chances that the adult will restrict their access to cyberspace in an effort to protect them, thereby denying access to an important medium to interact with friends and peers (Blumenfeld, 2005). This hypothesis is supported by findings from i-SAFE (2004), which found that 58% of respondents chose not to report negative online experiences to adults.

Another application of social norms theory to cyberbullying lies in the inaccurate perception youth have about behaviors their peers are engaging in. Most social norms are implicit, leaving significant room for misinterpretation. Perkins and Bekowitz (1986) refer to this discrepancy between the actual norms and the perceived norm as misperception. This misperception leads youth to engage in deviant behaviors (such as substance use) because they incorrectly believe it to be the norm among their peers or similar age peers (Perkins & Berkowitz, 1986). Adapting this to bullying behaviors, Tershjo and Salmivalli (2003) found that students typically blamed the victim of bullying for violating peer norms and perceived the perpetrators of bullying to serve as enforcers of the peer norms. It is likely that such thinking translates to the cyberbullying context, where rather than viewing cyberbullying as inappropriate aggression, adolescents view it as a tool to enforce social norms (Blumenfeld, 2005).

Finally, in an effort to find acceptance and belonging in peer groups, youth look to and mimic behaviors their peers are engaging in. Thus, if what adults or victims call cyberbullying is seen as an acceptable or positive behavior that demonstrates concordance with peer norms, then adolescents might engage in cyberbullying without thinking of the negative psychological impact it may have on victims.

Online Disinhibition Effect

In some ways, cyberspace provides individuals increased access to their social network. Unlike face-to-face interactions, individuals can engage with a large number of individuals at once. Additionally, interactions in cyberspace can continue around the clock. Thus, adolescents have an increased ability to interact with their peers. At the same time, social interactions through technology lack the immediate, tangible, and emotional feedback that are inherent in face-to-face interactions.

Suler (2004) described a phenomenon called the *online disinhibition effect*, which refers to greatly diminished internal censorship when communicating in cyberspace. He said, "people say and do things in cyberspace they would not ordinarily do in the face-to-face world. They loosen up, feel less restrained and express themselves more openly" (p. 321). This effect can be either benign (encouraging appropriate self-disclosure) or toxic (encouraging mean or cruel attacks on others), and can foster both extensive self-disclosure and acting out behaviors. Suler proposed that six factors inherent in the technology contribute to this effect: dissociative anonymity (which allows one to mentally separate online activity from real life by concealing one's identity); invisibility (inability to see or be seen by those with whom one is communicating); asynchronicity (allowing one to avoid knowing the receiver's immediate reaction to a communication); solipsistic introjections (incorporating an imagined receiver's personality into one's own psyche); dissociative imagination (the belief that the personas one creates in cyber-environments remain in an online world, limiting responsibility for real-world consequences); and minimization of authority (because the usual markers of status are absent in cyberspace). This tendency to exhibit a more narcissistic, aggressive, and uncivil persona in the digital world is also described by Aboujaoude (2011), who proposed that a more dangerous e-personality exists parallel to our non-digital selves.

Additionally, in cyberspace, individuals can choose to interact with others anonymously, and therefore avoid the repercussions that might accompany the bad behavior if they were identifiable. This might encourage adolescents to say or do things online that they are unlikely to do in their face-to-face interactions and to limit their sense of responsibility for these actions (Blumenfeld, 2005). Blumenfeld (2005) found that in investigations of cyberbullying, perpetrators reduced their sense of responsibility for the abusive nature of their online messages using rationalizations centered around offering the targets of their abuse needed and useful information. For example, when identified and asked why they sent abusive messages to others online, perpetrators retorted, "I was only telling the truth. She is ugly, and I felt she had to know it!" Thus, online disinhibition theories offer the field a potential explanation for the cyberbullying involvement.

SECTION 2: TRANSACTIONAL ASSOCIATIONS AMONG SCHOOL BULLYING AND CYBERBULLYING

Much of the writing on cyberbullying equates the behavior to face-to-face bullying behaviors and adapts bullying theories to explain and examine cyberbullying. However, empirical data linking face-to-face bullying and cyberbullying perpetration and victimization are sparse and largely based on cross-sectional studies. Thus, in this next section, a series of longitudinal analyses are presented to evaluate the transactional association between face-to-face bullying perpetration and cyberbullying perpetration, the association between peer victimization and cyberbullying perpetration, and the reciprocal interaction between cyberbullying victimization and perpetration. This dataset tracked 1,132 middle school students from four schools in a Midwestern city over two years in four waves of data collection. Participants included three cohorts of 5th, 6th, and 7th graders.

Bullying Perpetration and Cyberbullying Perpetration

Measures. We first examined the relation between self-reported face-to-face bullying perpetration and cyberbullying perpetration. *Face-to-face bullying perpetration* was measured using the nine-item Illinois Bully Scale (Espelage & Holt, 2001), which assesses the frequency of teasing, name-calling, social exclusion, and rumor spreading. Students are asked how often in the past 30 days they teased other students, upset other students for the fun of it, excluded others from their group of friends, and helped harass other students, etc. Response options include "Never," "1 or 2 times," "3 or 4 times," "5 or 6 times," and "7 or more times." A Cronbach's alpha coefficient of .86 was found for this sample.

Cyberbullying perpetration was assessed with a four-item scale based on the work of Ybarra, Espelage, and Mitchell (2007). Students were asked how often they did the following things in the last year (or since the last survey administration): (1) Made rude comments to anyone online; (2) Spread rumors about someone online, whether they were true or not; (3) Made aggressive or threatening comments to anyone online; and (4) Sent a text message that said rude or mean things. Response options range from Not sure (0), Never (1), to Often (5). A Cronbach's alpha coefficient of .72 was found for this sample at Time 1.

Results. Longitudinal structural equation modeling was used to examine longitudinal associations between face-to-face and cyberbullying perpetration. An item-to-construct balance method was used to develop parcels for both the scales (Little, Cunningham, Shahar, & Widaman, 2002). The measurement model was established, and strong factorial invariance was demonstrated. The structural model that was then imposed provided good fit to the data, $\chi^2_{(219, n = 1132)} = 945.318$; RMSEA $= 0.0542_{(0.0506; 0.0577)}$; NNFI $= .0975$; CFI $= 0.980$. The results of the model tested are shown in Figure 5.1.

These results indicated that higher bullying perpetration at an earlier time point was predictive of increases in cyberbullying perpetration in consecutive time points (after controlling for previous cyberbullying behaviors). Engagement in cyberbullying perpetration did not predict increases in traditional bullying in our data. These results support our hypothesis that bullying perpetration is an antecedent of cyberbullying perpetration in middle school. Findings from this study provide strong support for the link between bullying perpetration and cyberbullying perpetration among a large sample of young adolescents. Bullying perpetration emerged as a precursor to cyberbullying perpetration across two years and four waves of survey data. This study suggests that cyberbullying may be an extension of other bullying behaviors. It is possible that as children get older and increase their engagement with technology, cyberspace becomes another context within which bullying perpetration occurs. Given the substantial predictive power of face-to-face bullying to cyberbullying, bullying prevention programs need to

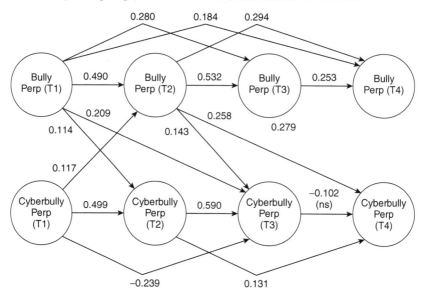

Figure 5.1 Model Fit: $\chi^2_{(219, n=1132)} = 945.318$; RMSEA = 0.0542 $_{(0.0506\,;\,0.0577)}$; NNFI = .0975; CFI = 0.980

consider how face-to-face encounters in school might spill over into cyberspace where adult monitoring and intervention is relatively absent.

Bullying Victimization and Cyberbullying Perpetration

Cyberspace provides perpetrators of bullying an additional venue within which to enforce social norms, assert dominance, and victimize peers. At the same time, electronic communication typically occurs with physical distance between participants and provides valuable time to strategize and plan responses, and often is anonymous. As suggested by the general strain theory, these latter characteristics provide an opportunity to victims of bullying to retaliate against their perpetrators (Agnew, 1992).

However, individuals who engage in cyberbullying also put themselves at risk for face-to-face bullying. Social norms theory suggests that peer victimization serves the purpose of establishing and maintaining a social hierarchy in a group. Any effort to challenge this hierarchy would be met with strong resistance and would likely be met with further victimization.

Thus, associations between peer victimization and cyberbullying were examined in other longitudinal analyses using the same dataset described above.

Measures. Victimization from peers was assessed using the University of Illinois Victimization Scale (UIVS; Espelage & Holt, 2001). Students are asked how often the following things have happened to them in the past 30 days: "Other

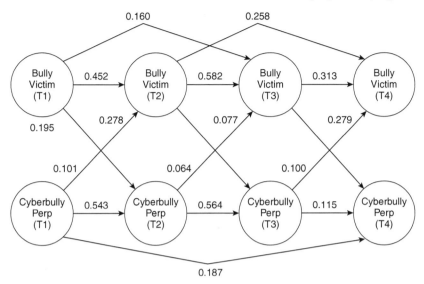

Figure 5.2 Model Fit: $\chi^2_{(222, n=1132)}$ = 854.147; RMSEA = 0.0486 $_{(0.0453; 0.0525)}$; NNFI = .0965; CFI = 0.972

students called me names," "Other students made fun of me," "Other students picked on me," and "I got hit and pushed by other students." Response options include "Never," "1 or 2 times," "3 or 4 times," "5 or 6 times," and "7 or more times." Factor loadings ranged from .55 through .92 for these items, which accounted for 6% of the variance in the factor analysis. Higher scores indicate more self-reported victimization. A Cronbach alpha coefficient of .79 was found in the current sample.

Results. Longitudinal structural equation modeling was conducted. Factorial invariance was established. The structural model that was then imposed provided good fit to the data $\chi^2_{(222, n = 1132)}$ = 854.147; RMSEA = 0.0486$_{(0.0453; 0.0525)}$; NNFI = .0965; CFI = 0.972. Results shown in Figure 5.2 indicate a transactional model, with predictive cross-lagged coefficients across the four waves. This suggests that peer victimization and cyberbullying perpetration operate within a reciprocal influence model. This provides support for both theories, although, initially cyberbullying perpetration predicts peer victimization. It is possible that when youth who do not have status in face-to-face contexts engage in cyberbullying, it puts them at particular risk for peer victimization, which in turn causes them to retaliate in the more removed, safe, cyberspace.

Cyberbullying Victimization and Cyberbullying Perpetration

Taken together, the two sets of analyses support the conventional belief that face-to-face bullying behaviors interact with and cause cyberbullying behaviors and vice versa. In fact, involvement in any sort of bullying behaviors, both as

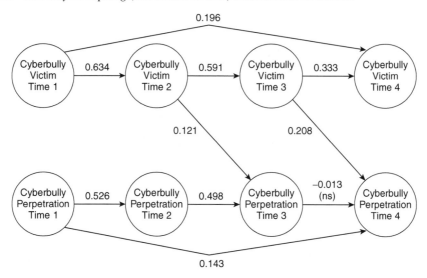

Figure 5.3 Model Fit: $\chi^2_{(225, n=1132)}$ = 1330.890; RMSEA = 0.0640 $_{(0.0606\,;\,0.0674)}$; NNFI = .0942; CFI = 0.953

perpetrator or victim, is predictive of cyberbullying perpetration. So far, we have examined the relation between face-to-face bullying and cyberbullying. It is clear that face-to-face interactions spill over into cyberspace interactions. However, it is also important to examine how interactions in cyberspace impact cyberbullying behaviors beyond the influence of face-to-face encounters. Research on face-to-face bullying has shown that victims of bullying are not always passive, and often respond to being victimized by engaging in perpetration of bullying as well, becoming what are called bully-victims (Holt & Espelage, 2003). Thus, the final analyses tested whether the transactional pattern between victimization and perpetration held in the cyber context. Using the sample described above and the same methodology, the association between cyberbullying victimization and perpetration were examined. Longitudinal structural equation modeling reflected a good fit to the data: $\chi^2_{(225, n = 1132)}$ = 1330.890; RMSEA = 0.0640$_{(0.0606;\,0.0674)}$; NNFI = .0942; CFI = 0.953 (Figure 5.3).

These findings document a predictive relation from cyberbullying victimization to cyberbullying perpetration. This supports the hypothesis that victims of cyberbullying will engage in cyberbullying perpetration and become cyberbully victims.

Summary of Three Sets of Analyses: Back to Theory

Overall, these three sets of analyses indicate that there are causal links between face-to-face victimization and perpetration and involvement in cyberbullying. Taken together, social learning of bullying (Bandura, 1986) appears to be a potential mechanism to explain the overlap between face-to-face bullying and cyberbullying. Although scholars continue to debate whether cyberbullying is similar or different from face-to-face bullying, these findings provide some convincing evidence that they are at least associated longitudinally. The connection between face-to-face perpetration of bullying and cyberbullying perpetration supports a social norms theory of bullying, where bullying is encouraged in school and appears to transfer to the cyber context. Strain theory (Agnew, 1992) is supported with the transactional associations between face-to-face victimization and cybervictimization with cyberbullying perpetration. Future research needs to consider how social information processing might also explain the connection between cybervictimization and cyberbullying perpetration. More specifically, it would be important to determine whether being victimized online or by a text contributes to the development of a hostile attribution bias (Crick & Dodge, 1994) and whether this bias then leads to cyberbullying perpetration. Many of the social development theories of aggression and bullying reviewed in this chapter have not been evaluated within the cyber context. Thus, there is plenty of research that needs to be conducted.

SECTION 3: IMPLICATIONS OF SELF-CONCEPT THEORY AND RESEARCH FOR CYBERBULLYING RESEARCH AND INTERVENTION

The purpose of the following section is to identify the implications of the self-concept construct for cyberbullying research and the development and implementation of effective prevention and intervention approaches. Findings from self-concept research studies in bullying are discussed to explicate important directions in research and development and elucidate the implications of the self-concept construct for cyberbullying research.

Relations among Bullying, Victimization, and Self-Concept

Self-concept has been implicated as central in the bullying and victimization equation, and some recent studies have begun to elucidate why self-concept matters in relation to bullying, victimization, and intervention. Bullies have been hypothesized to engage in bullying behaviors as a means to enhance their self-concepts. For example, Marsh, Parada, Yeung, and Healey (2001) based upon longitudinal structural equation models for students in Grades 8, 10, and 12 found that troublemaker and victim constructs were moderately correlated, suggesting that bipolar categories of being a perpetrator or a target are not useful categorizations, as perpetrators can be both a perpetrator and a target in different incidents. The troublemaker factor was also correlated somewhat negatively with concurrent self-concept, but had small positive effects on subsequent self-concept. These authors argued that low self-concept may trigger troublemaking behavior to enhance self-concept, and that bullies may derive a sense of self-worth from their antisocial activities that is also reinforced by others. These results imply that effective anti-bullying interventions may need to alter the school climate to ensure that cyberbullying is not reinforced by peers reinforcing cyberbullying behaviors.

Marsh et al. (2001) also found that low self-concepts and depression led to being a target, suggesting that interventions could benefit from developing adaptive psychological tools such as enhanced self-concept and resilience. Bullies were found to have low self-concepts on the Honesty/Trustworthiness, Parent Relationships, and School scales; hence, interventions targeting these specific domains of self-concept may be useful for addressing traditional bullying and cyberbullying. Targets also had lower self-concepts than bullies on same-sex and opposite-sex peer-relationship scales, suggesting interventions could benefit from targeting target's social skills. Both bullies and targets were low on anger control, with targets tending to internalize and bullies to externalize. These results imply that interventions could address anger control and foster effective coping strategies.

Marsh et al. (2011), in a longitudinal study, also found that consistent with previous research, target factors were consistently and negatively correlated with multiple domains of self-concept. Similarly, bullying factors were mostly negatively correlated with multiple domains of self-concept. As such, Marsh et al. concluded that neither bullies nor targets have particularly good self-concepts. However, there were some notable distinctions in the patterns of relations, whereby the bully factors were positively correlated with opposite-sex relationships self-concept such that perpetrators consider themselves to be popular with members of the opposite sex. In addition, target factors were most negatively related with same-sex relationships and emotional stability self-concepts. Honesty/trustworthiness self-concept was also negatively related to the bully factors, indicating that perpetrators are aware that bullying is not the right thing to do. As such, both target and bully factors tend to be negatively related to multiple domains of self-concept, implying that enhancing specific domains of self-concept could be a potentially potent intervention strategy to incorporate in intervention. Hence, the results of these longitudinal studies provide important directions for informing intervention and emphasize the centrality of the self-concept construct in relation to this area of research.

Self-Concept and Advances in Bullying Intervention

Jenkin (1996; also see Clayton et al., 2001) argued that perpetrators of bullying are created and trained in school environments that reinforce their behaviors, and targets are often ridiculed due to urban myths that suggest that bullying is just part of "growing up." Anti-bullying interventions that target individuals are largely ineffective, but interventions that target the whole-school community (students, teachers, and parents) in ways that change the school ethos have been demonstrated to be effective. Self-concept theory (e.g., Marsh & Craven, 1997; 2006; Marsh, Parada, Craven, & Finger, 2004) provides a theoretical explanation. It is hypothesized that bullies enhance their sense of power, social self-concept, and

self-esteem by victimizing others. Individuals that watch bullies and do not intervene also provide bullies with social reinforcement by providing them an audience. Therefore, if the school ethos allows bullies to enhance their self-concept
through bullying, interventions that target individuals are not likely to succeed.
In contrast, if the school ethos is altered via a whole-school approach such that
bullying is seen as unacceptable and is no longer condoned by peers, bullying behaviors will no longer contribute to a positive self-concept. Furthermore, once the
school ethos has been addressed, cognitive strategies aimed at individual students
(bullies, targets, and bystanders who reinforce bullying) are likely to be effective.
Therefore, it is important to reinforce the unacceptability of bullying behaviors to
ensure antisocial behaviors cannot result in enhanced self-perceptions. As such,
interventions could benefit from enhancing the self-concepts of targets and redirecting the enhancement of bullies' self-concepts to socially acceptable behaviors. Thus, applying self-concept theory to the problem of bullying has important
practical implications for developing new, potent intervention programs and theoretical implications advancing self-concept theory, anti-bullying research, and
practice.

Reviews of bullying research (e.g., Clayton et al., 2001; Espelage & Horne,
2008; Espelage & Swearer, 2008; Jenkin, 1996; Juvonen & Graham, 2004; Marsh
et al., 2004; Olweus, 1993; Sharp & Smith, 1994) have identified common features
of effective intervention that include (1) employing a whole-school approach that
impacts on school ethos; (2) accounting for bullies, victims, and bystanders;
(3) utilizing intervention strategies at the individual level once school ethos has
been addressed; (4) assisting teachers, parents, and students by providing information about the nature of bullying and effective strategies; (5) including community agencies such as health services; (6) integrating anti-bullying into the school
curriculum; and (7) capitalizing upon cognitive-behavioral strategies to maintain
long-term change.

Parada, Craven, and Marsh (2008) developed the Beyond Bullying Secondary
Program, which capitalizes on advances in anti-bullying research, school ethos,
self-concept, and cognitive psychology. Beyond Bullying takes a multimodal
approach stressing school and teacher empowerment by training school staff in
specific techniques to enhance self-concept, create a positive school ethos, and
intervene in and manage bullying incidents. Beyond Bullying is also designed to
empower secondary students and their parents to contribute to addressing bullying. Resources focus on practical strategies designed to help teachers, students
(bullies, targets, bystanders, other students), and parents to appreciate the rationale
for addressing bullying as a critical social justice issue of our time, understand and
utilize effective practical strategies for preventing and addressing bullying behaviors, and develop a personal commitment to addressing bullying.

In his PhD thesis, Parada (2006; Parada, Craven, & Marsh, 2003) critically evaluated the impact of the Beyond Bullying Secondary Program upon
3,522 secondary students from six Catholic schools in Sydney, Australia, using
a powerful multi-cohort, multi-occasion (Marsh, Craven, & Debus, 1998)

experimental design. In year 1 of the study, baseline data were collected from participants on three occasions. In year 2, at the same time points as for year 1, data were again collected with an intervention being implemented for a period of 10 weeks between Time 1 and Time 2 data collection. Multilevel analysis indicated that the Beyond Bullying Program was able to significantly reduce rates of bullying, being bullied, externalizing anger, pro-bullying attitudes, and avoidant coping strategies (Parada, 2006). In addition, significantly increased rates were reported for students' willingness to advocate for targets of bullying, school support, rule acceptance, school attachment, support seeking, and problem solving. The results also showed that teachers' sense of confidence with their skills and knowledge in relation to intervening and managing bullying were enhanced. In addition, some facets of self-concept were enhanced: Honesty/Trustworthiness self-concept, Verbal, Mathematics, and General School. As such, the intervention was deemed a success adding further support to whole-school intervention strategies and advances in anti-bullying and self-concept theory and research on which the intervention was based. Hence, accounting for advances in self-concept theory and research is helping glean new insights into effective intervention.

FURTHERING CYBERBULLYING RESEARCH AND INTERVENTION

Cyberbullies are hypothesized to engage in cyberbullying as a means to maintain and enhance their self-concepts while deliberately harming the target's self-concepts. Therefore, self-concept is implicated as a central psychosocial construct in the cyberbullying and cybervictimization equation and needs further investigation. In particular, longitudinal studies accounting for the multidimensionality of the self-concept construct (Marsh & Craven, 2006) and multiple cyberbullying roles (bullies, targets, bystanders) testing the causal and reciprocal effects among these latent constructs could assist to elucidate key psychosocial drivers.

Cyberbullying interventions could also benefit from accounting for the role of self-concept in cyberbullying and multiple cyberbullying roles (cyberbully, cyber target, bystanders). For example, interventions could redirect the enhancement of cyberbullies' self-concept to pro-social behaviors and target specific facets of cyberbullies' self-concepts shown to influence cyberbullying (e.g., honesty/trustworthiness, school self-concepts; Marsh et al., 2011); employ strategies to protect and enhance target's self-concepts, coping strategies, and resilience; and educate bystanders to intervene (e.g., training bystanders to not reinforce cyberbullying, help the target, and tell someone who can intervene) to simultaneously reduce self-concept reinforcement by bystanders who encourage cyberbullies online or reinforce their cyberbullying activities in the school environment. Such interventions seem particularly promising given that self-concept has been demonstrated to share a dynamic and reciprocal causal relation with a wide range of outcomes (Marsh & Craven, 1997, 2006) and empirically demonstrated successful traditional bullying interventions have employed self-concept enhancement approaches (e.g., Parada, 2006; Parada et al., 2008).

It also is useful to emphasize that whole-school interventions are potentially potent for cyberbullying intervention, given that reviews of bullying research (e.g., Clayton, Ballif-Spanvill, & Hunsaker, 2001; Espelage & Horne, 2008; Marsh et al., 2004) have identified whole-school interventions as effective. In addition, whole-school bullying interventions accounting for the role of self-concept have also been empirically demonstrated to be effective (Parada et al., 2008). Given it is likely that cyberbulling and traditional bullying forms are related whereby bullying can be enacted in both traditional and cyber forms simultaneously, it is hypothesized that multimodal interventions are promising whereby self-concept, cyberbullying, and traditional bullying are addressed concurrently.

SUMMARY AND CONCLUSIONS

In this chapter, dominant theories of social development and explanatory models of the development of aggression and deviant behavior were reviewed, and attempts were made to extrapolate how these theories might advance the knowledge base about cyberbullying. These theories included the comprehensive social-ecological model that implicates multiple contextual factors in the prediction of engagement in cyberbullying. Additionally, several theories posit the potential powerful impact of social norms and ranking within groups in cyberspace. The question remains whether the unique aspects of cyberspace alters the ways in which peers would normally interact within school peer groups. That is, it is plausible that prestige, dominance, and social standing might play out differently in social network sites or when not all participants are known to one another. Regardless, this chapter demonstrates that many theories of social development could inform future research and practice in the area of cyberbullying.

Longitudinal analyses among a large sample of middle school students indicated that there appears to be causal, transactional relations between school bullying and cyberbullying, suggesting that involvement as a perpetrator of bullying at school is associated with later involvement as a perpetrator in cyberspace. Additionally, being victimized by peers at school was found to be causally linked to cyberbully perpetration, supporting the notion that youth who might hold a lower social rank at school might engage in cyberbullying in attempts to defend or retaliate against in school victimization. A final transactional model supported a causal link between cybervictimization and cyberperpetration, indicating that reporting being victimized was associated with perpetration at a later time point. Given the centrality of cyberspace in the lives of adolescents and the limited parental monitoring in this domain, future research needs to expand these models to include mediators and moderators of these associations and identify points of intervention.

In this chapter, we also discussed how recent advances in self-concept theory and research have important implications for cyberbullying research and intervention. Self-concept is implicated in both traditional bullying and cyberbullying. Perpetrators are hypothesized to bully others to enhance their own self-concepts. Bystander roles also serve to reinforce bullying and thereby the self-concepts of bullies. Being bullied has been shown to adversely impact on targets' self-concepts. Hence, self-concept matters in relation to bullying, victimization, and the role of bystanders such that accounting for self-concept in intervention can be seen as an important goal of future research and intervention.

We also advocate that multimodal interventions are useful to pursue such that self-concept, traditional bullying, and cyberbullying are addressed simultaneously. Whole-school interventions provide a promising vehicle in that according to self-concept theory, if the school ethos is altered such that cyberbullying is no longer reinforced, and cognitive approaches are employed for bullies, targets, and bystanders, cyber and traditional bullying behaviors will no longer contribute to a positive self-concept. Hence, applying self-concept theory to the problem of cyberbullying has important practical implications for advancing self-concept theory, cyberbullying research, and intervention.

References

Aboujaoude, E. (2011). *Virtually you: The dangerous powers of the e-personality.* New York: W.W. Norton & Company.

Agnew, R. (1992). Foundation for a general strain theory of crime and delinquency. *Criminology, 30*(1), 47–87. doi:10.1111/j.1745–9125.1992.tb01093.x

Bandura, A. (1986). *Social foundations of thought and action.* Englewood Cliffs, NJ: Prentice-Hall.

Berk, L. E. (2000). *Child development* (5th ed.). Needham Heights, MS: Allyn & Bacon.

Blumenfeld, W. J. (2005). Cyberbullying: A new variation on an old theme. Paper presented at CHI 2005 Abuse Workshop Portland, OR. Retrieved from http://www.agentabuse.org/papers.htm

Bronfenbrenner, U. (1977). Toward an experimental ecology of human development. *American Psychologist, 32,* 513–531. doi:10.1037/0003–066x.32.7.513

Clayton, C. J., Ballif-Spanvill, B., & Hunsaker, M. D. (2001). Preventing violence and teaching peace: A review of promising and effective antiviolence, conflict-resolution, and peace programs for elementary school children. *Applied and Preventive Psychology, 10*(1), 1–35. doi:10.1016/S0962–1849(05)80030–7

Crick, N. R., & Dodge, K. A. (1994). A review and reformulation of social information-processing mechanisms in children's social adjustment. *Psychological Bulletin, 115,* 74–101. doi:10.1037/0033–2909.115.1.74

Dodge, K. A., & Coie, J. (1987). Social-information-processing factors in reactive and proactive aggression in children's peer groups. *Journal of Personality and Social Psychology, 53,* 1146–1158. doi:10.1037/0022–3514.53.6.1146

Dodge, K. A., Pettit, G. S., McClaskey, C. L., & Brown, M. M. (1986). Social competence in children. *Monographs of the Society for Research in Child Development, 51,* 1–85. doi:10.2307/1165906

Dodge, K. A., & Schwartz, D. (1997). Social information processing mechanisms in aggressive behavior. In D. M. Stoff, J. Breiling, & J. D. Maser (Eds.), *Handbook of antisocial behavior*. (pp. 171–180). New York: John Wiley & Sons. doi:10.1037/0022-3514.53.6.1146

Dooley, J. J., Pyzalski, J., & Cross, D. (2009). Cyberbullying versus face-to-face bullying: A theoretical and conceptual review. *Journal of Psychology, 217*(4), 182–188. doi:10.1027/0044-3409.217.4.182

Ellis, B. J., Del Giudice, M., Dishion, T., Figureredo, A. J., Gray, P., Griskevicius, V., . . . Wilson, D. S. (2011). The evolutionary basis of risky adolescent behavior: Implications for science, policy, and practice. *Developmental Psychology*, epub. doi: 10.1037/a0026220

Espelage, D. L., & Holt, M. K. (2001). Bullying and victimization during early adolescence: Peer influences and psychosocial correlates. *Journal of Emotional Abuse, 2*(2–3), 123–142. doi:10.1300/J135v02n02_08

Espelage, D., & Horne, A. (2008). School violence and bullying prevention: From research based explanations to empirically based solutions. In S. Brown & R. Lent (Eds.), *Handbook of counseling psychology*, 4th ed. (pp. 588–598). Hoboken, NJ: John Wiley and Sons.

Espelage, D. L., & Swearer, S. M. (2008). Current perspectives on linking school bullying research to effective prevention strategies. In T. W. Miller (Ed.), *School violence and primary prevention* (pp. 335–353). New York: Springer. doi:10.1007/978-0-387-77119-9_17

Hawker, D.S.J., & Boulton, M. J. (2001). Subtypes of peer harassment and their correlates: A social dominance perspective. In J. Juvonen and S. Graham (Eds.), *Peer harassment in school: The plight of the vulnerable and victimized*. New York: Guilford Press.

Hawley, P. H. (1999). The ontogenesis of social dominance: A strategy-based evolutionary perspective. *Developmental Review, 19*, 97–132. doi:10.1006/drev.1998.0470

Hawley, P. H. (2002). Social dominance and prosocial and coercive strategies of resource control in preschoolers. *International Journal of Behavioral Development, 26*(2), 167–176. doi:10.1080/01650250042000726

Hawley, P. H., Stump, K. N., & Ratcliff, A. (2011). Sidestepping the jingle fallacy: Bullying, aggression, and the importance of knowing the difference. In D. L. Espelage, & S. Swearer (Eds.), *Bullying in North American schools*. New York: Routledge.

Hinduja, S., & Patchin, J. W. (2010). Bullying, cyberbullying, and suicide. *Archives of Suicide Research, 14*(3), 206–221. doi:10.1080/13811118.2010.494133

Holt, M. K., & Espelage, D. L. (2003). A cluster analytic investigation of victimization among high school students: Are profiles differentially associated with psychological and school belonging? *Journal of Applied School Psychology, 19*(2), 81–98. doi:10.1300/J008v19n02_06

Jenkin, J. (1996). *Resolving violence—An anti-violence curriculum for secondary students*. Melbourne: Australian Council for Educational Research.

Juvonen, J., & Graham, S. (2004). Research-based interventions on bullying. In G. D. Phye & C. S. Sanders (Eds.), *Bullying: Implications for the classroom* (pp. 229–255). San Diego, CA: Elsevier.

Little, T. D., Cunningham, W. A., Shahar, G., &Widaman, K. F. (2002). To parcel or not to parcel: Exploring the question, weighing the merits. *Structural Equation Modeling, 9*, 151–173. doi:10.1207/S15328007SEM0902_1

Low, S., & Espelage, D. L. (Under review). How well can we differentiate electronic bullying from other forms? Examination of commonalities across individual and family predictors in the context of race. *Psychology of Violence*.

Mansilla, J. F., Amir, E., Espelage, D. L., & Pu, W. (2012, April). *A computer-in-the-loop approach for detecting roles in the classroom*. Conference proceedings, International

Conference on Social Computing, Behavioral-Cultural Modeling, & Prediction, College Park, MD.

Marsh, H.W., & Craven, R.G. (2006). Reciprocal effects of self-concept and performance from a multidimensional perspective: Beyond seductive pleasure and unidimensional perspectives. *Perspectives on Psychological Science, 2*, 1314–1336. doi:10.111/j.1745–6916.2006.00010.x

Marsh, H.W., & Craven, R.G. (1997) Academic self-concept: Beyond the dustbowl. In G. Phye (Ed.), *Handbook of classroom assessment: Learning, achievement and adjustment.* San Diego, CA: Academic Press. doi:10.1016/B978–012554255–5/50003-X

Marsh, H.W., Craven, R.G., & Debus, R.L. (1998). Structure, stability and development of young children's self-concepts: A multi-cohort-multi-occasion study. *Child Development, 69*, 1030–1053. doi:10.2307/1132361

Marsh, H. W., Nagengast, B., Morin, A.J.S., Parada, R.H., Craven, R.G., & Hamilton, L.R. (2011). Construct validity of the multidimensional structure of bullying and victimization: An application of exploratory structural equation modeling. *Journal of Educational Psychology, 103*, 701–732. doi: 10.1037/a0024122

Marsh, H.W., Parada, R.H., Craven, R.G., & Finger, L.R. (2004). In the looking glass: A reciprocal effects model elucidating the complex nature of bullying, psychological determinants and the central role of self-concept. In C.S. Sanders & G.D. Phye (Eds.), *Bullying: Implications for the classroom* (pp. 63–106). San Diego, CA: Elsevier Academic Press. doi:10.1016/B978–012617955–2/50009–6

Marsh, H.W., Parada, R.H, Yeung, A.S., & Healey, J. (2001). Aggressive school troublemakers and victims: A longitudinal model examining the pivotal role of self-concept. *Journal of Educational Psychology, 93*(2), 411–419. doi:10:1037/0022–0663.93.2.411

Olweus, D. (1993). *Bullying at school: What we know and what we can do (Understanding Children's Worlds).* Oxford: Blackwell Publishers.

Parada, R.H. (2006). *School bullying: Psychosocial determinants and effective intervention.* Unpublished dissertation manuscript.

Parada, R. H., Craven, R. G., & Marsh, H. W. (2003). The Beyond Bullying Program: An innovative program empowering teachers to counteract bullying in schools. Paper presented at the Joint New Zealand Association for Research in Education and Australian Association for Research in Education Conference, December 1–3, 2003. Auckland, New Zealand.

Parada, R. H., Craven, R. G., & Marsh, H. W. (2008). The beyond bullying secondary program: An innovative program empowering teachers to counteract bullying in schools. *Self-processes, learning, and enabling human potential: Dynamic new approaches* (Vol. 3, pp. 373–426). Charlotte, NC: Information Age.

Perkins, H.W., & Berkowitz, A.D. (1986). Perceiving the community norms of alcohol use among students: Some research implications for campus alcohol education programming. *International Journal of the Addictions, 21*, 961–976.

Schwartz, D., McFadyen-Ketchum, S.A., Dodge, K.A., Pettit, G.S., & Bates, J.E. (1998). Peer group victimization as a predictor of children's behavior problems at home and in school. *Development and Psychopathology, 10*, 87–99. doi:10:1017/S095457949800131X

Sharp, S., & Smith, P.K. (1994). *Tackling bullying in your school: A practical handbook for teachers.* London: Routledge.

Suler, J. (2004). Psychology of cyberspace—The online disinhibition effect. *Cyberpsychology and Behavior, 7* (3), 321–326.

Tershjo, T., & Salmivalli, C. (2003). "She is not actually bullied." The discourse of harassment in student groups. *Aggressive Behavior, 29*, 134–154. doi:10.1089/1094931041291295

Turkle, S. (1995). *Life on the screen: Identity in the age of Internet.* New York: Simon & Schuster.

Ybarra, M., Espelage, D., & Mitchell, K. (2007). The co-occurrence of Internet harassment and unwanted sexual solicitation victimization and perpetration: Associations with psychosocial indicators. *Journal of Adolescent Health, 41*(6), S31–S41. doi:10.1016/j.jadohealth.2007.09.010

6 Potent Ways Forward

New Multidimensional Theoretical
Structural Models of Cyberbullying,
Cyber Targetization, and Bystander
Behaviors and Their Potential
Relations to Traditional Bullying
Constructs

*Rhonda G. Craven, Herbert W. Marsh,
and Roberto H. Parada*

Bullying and cyberbullying are clearly vital international social justice issues of our time. These behaviors have disturbing consequences for the well-being of targets, perpetrators, and communities (Parada, Craven, & Marsh, 2008; Swearer, Espelage, Vaillancourt, & Hymel, 2010). The importance of this topic makes construct validation research vital. A hallmark of academic rigor is that theory, research, and practice are inextricably intertwined; a weakness in any one of these areas undermines the others. In cyberbullying research, in particular, and traditional bullying research, in general, this hallmark is yet to be fully realized. While traditional bullying research has been grounded by seminal advances in theory, research, and practice that have established the key structural components of traditional bullying constructs, these advances have not been fully applied to cyberbullying research in a way that integrates, stimulates new directions in, and extends scholarship. It also appears that cyberbullying research has addressed substantive problems and between-construct issues before within-construct issues such as definition, structure, and measurement have been resolved. The resolution of within-construct concerns should include research that would propose, test, and refine theoretical structural models based on the available empirical evidence. Until these problems have been dealt with, it is likely that integration of advances in the field will be problematic; the generalizability of cyberbullying findings will remain severely limited; findings will be ambiguous; the complexity of the nature and structure of cyberbullying constructs will remain unresolved; and importantly, the relation of cyberbullying constructs to traditional bullying and victimization constructs will remain unclear. New theory-driven approaches are also essential whereby theory is proposed; psychometrically sound measurement instruments devised to test theoretical propositions; and the theory supported, revised, or refuted based on empirical evidence. Such a constructive approach would result in cyberbullying research being theory driven and soundly based on the critical interplay between theory, research, and practice.

In this chapter, it is our thesis that a critical key to advancing cyberbullying research is addressing within-construct issues, whereby the structure of hypothetical cyberbullying constructs and their relation to traditional bullying constructs are theorized and then tested. Testing involves utilizing instrumentation with demonstrated psychometrically sound properties, and then revising theory based on the findings of empirical research to ensure the appropriate scientific interplay between theory and research. In this chapter, hypothesized potential theoretical models of the structure of bullying, cyberbullying constructs (namely, cyberbullying, cyber targetization), and their relation to traditional bullying constructs (bullying, victimization, bystander roles) are theorized, grounded upon recent advances stemming from traditional bullying within-construct research. It is hoped that these proposed models may serve as a potentially edifying theoretical basis from which to further test the place of cyberbullying constructs in relation to traditional bullying constructs. The models might also serve as a basis to begin to integrate traditional bullying and cyberbullying research; stimulate advances in within-construct cyberbullying research, in particular; and provide a theoretical basis for operationalizing bullying constructs as complex, dynamic, and interrelated.

In the first half of this chapter, theoretical models of bullying are posed derived from traditional bullying research. First, a mature structural theoretical model of bullying and victimization constructs is presented stemming from recent empirical findings (Marsh et al., 2011) tackling complex substantive within-construct issues in traditional bullying research. Second, multidimensional theoretical models of bystander roles and their relation to bullying and victimization are proposed. In the second half of this chapter, models of the structure of cyberbullying and cyber targetization are proposed, building upon the theoretical models derived from traditional bullying research. Third, the nature of bystander roles and some hypothetical potential structures that remain to be tested are presented. Finally, a new holistic, hierarchical multidimensional theoretical conceptualization of the structure and relation of cyberbullying and cyber targetization constructs to traditional bullying and victimization constructs is offered. The latter is offered in order to theorize the potential place of cyberbullying constructs within structural models of traditional bullying in an attempt to integrate traditional and cyberbullying within-construct research.

It is also noted that currently, appropriate psychometrically sound measurement tools are not available (at least as a battery) to adequately test the salience of the theoretical proposed models of cyberbullying. Additional mixed methods and qualitative research, in particular, are needed to further elucidate the form, structure, and processes underpinning cyber constructs and the nature, structure, and relations of bystander bullying behaviors to these. This is unfortunate, as without a solid foundation for the development of psychometrically sound measurement tools, it is not possible to test new structural theoretical models proposed or ascertain whether research evidence supports, rejects, or leads to a modification in these theoretical conceptualizations. However, it is vital to boldly conceptualize, configure, and put forth theoretical structural models grounded on the available research evidence, and hopefully in so doing stimulate the critical interplay between theory, research, and practice in this area of investigation. This chapter attempts to stimulate further research by bringing into synergy advances that have elucidated the structure of traditional bullying constructs to theorize the structure of cyberbullying constructs. Through this integration, it locates the place of cyberbullying in a new expanded structural theoretical conceptualization incorporating both traditional and cyberbullying constructs.

RECENT PROGRESS IN TRADITIONAL BULLYING RESEARCH

Some Current Advances and Dilemmas in Traditional Bullying Research

A particularly important starting point for the development of new theoretical conceptualizations of the structure of cyberbullying is beginning with what is known about the structure of traditional bullying. Research in traditional bullying is more established than that of cyberbullying, which is a relatively new area of research that has emerged along with advances in and wide uptake of technology. Progress in traditional bullying research continues to be founded upon advances in theory, research, and practice. These advances have historically involved addressing within-construct issues whereby the nature of bullying has been operationally defined (e.g., as involving intentional harm, repetition, and a power imbalance; Olweus, 1997; Rigby, 1996; Schuster, 1996; Sutton, Smith, & Swettenham, 1999). Traditional bullying involves behaviors that are direct (e.g., hitting and punching; Wolke, Woods, Bloomfield, & Karstadt, 2000) or indirect (e.g., hurtful manipulation of relationships; Crick and Grotpeter, 1995) in nature, and can be further differentiated into at least physical, social, and verbal behaviors (Crick et al., 2001; Finkelhor, Ormrod, & Turner, 2007; Mynard & Joseph, 2000, Salmivalli, Kaukiainen, & Lagerspetz, 2000). Additionally, multiple participant roles (perpetrators, targets, bystanders; e.g., Card & Hodges, 2008; Marsh et al., 2011; Parada, Marsh, & Craven, 2005; Salmivalli, Lappalaninen, & Lagerspetz, 1998) have been described. Research has revealed that the roles are more complex than first thought, as bullying and victimization are positively correlated. It has been proposed that the constructs are mutually reinforcing, so that it is possible to be both be a perpetrator and a target (i.e., bully/victim) (e.g., Harachi, Catalano, & Hawkins, 1999; Marsh et al., 2011; Marsh, Parada, Craven, & Finger, 2004; Parada et al., 2005; Roland & Idsøe, 2001; Salmivalli et al., 1998; Smith et al., 1999; Sullivan, 2000). These key structural components of traditional bullying constructs have been largely validated by a body of research, although they have not as yet been extended to conceptualize and incorporate cyberbullying constructs.

Research in bullying has also been plagued with measurement issues leading Hawker and Boulton (2000) to conclude that available measures have not addressed the complexity of the bullying phenomena. Almost a decade later, researchers (e.g., Gumpel, 2008) have continued to emphasize that progress has been hampered by a lack of psychometrically sound instruments available to test the salience and discriminant validity of theorized roles in bullying. Gumpel (2008) also emphasized the need to assess bullying and victimization simultaneously in order to assess the complex patterns of relations between these domains and subdomains at a single point in time and longitudinally. In addition, Card and Hodges (2008) have lamented that "a well-established, standardized measure of peer victimization does not exist, and commonly used scales accessing broad adjustment contain few items assessing victimization" (p. 452). They also emphasized the need to distinguish between physical, verbal, and social victimization forms.

Recent Advances in Measurement

The theorized structure of bullying and victimization. Recently, progress has been made in testing the salience of at least some aspects of participant roles in relation to bullying and victimization. Rigorous psychometric support has been obtained for the separation of the broad bullying and target domains (e.g., Hussein, 2010). In addition, new advances in measurement have been applied to identify a psychometrically sound measure that can discriminate between bullying and victimization constructs and the subdomains within. Marsh et al. (2011) provided an important example of rigorous construct validation that involved the first application of Exploratory Structural Equation Modeling (ESEM) in relation to a traditional bullying measure designed to measure multiple bullying and victimization factors for adolescents: the Adolescent Peer Relations Instrument (APRI) (Marsh et al., 2004; Parada, 2006; Parada et al., 2008). The APRI includes measures of two domains of bullying (bully and victimization) and three subdomains (verbal, physical, and social) using a total of 36 items (six for each of the three bullying scales and the three victimizations scales). Students respond to statements using a six-point Likert scale (ranging from 1 = *never* to 6 = *every day*) asking them how often in the past year they have engaged in bullying behaviors against other students (bullying) or how often these behaviors had been inflicted upon them (victimization). Participants were a sample of male and female Catholic high school students from Western Sydney who completed the APRI on three occasions over one school year (T1: $n = 3,512$; T2: $n = 3,557$; T3: $n = 3,263$).

Marsh et al.'s (2011) focus was on testing (a) hypothesized multidimensional bullying and victimization constructs for convergent and discriminant validity, (b) measurement invariance and differential item functioning over multiple groups and time, and (c) construct stability over time. They provided a rare traditional bullying within-construct study that also utilized recent advances in ESEM analysis to demonstrate rigorous psychometric support for the a priori factor structure of the APRI in relation to the current standards of goodness of fit; convergent and discriminant construct validation; and tests of differential item functioning related to gender, school year, and longitudinal analysis.

Interestingly, Marsh et al. (2011) also demonstrated that the ESEM approach provided a better fit to the bully and victimization data than a traditional CFA model. ESEM demonstrated that the factor correlations between bullying and victimization (.011–.527) were substantially lower than those based on CFA (.128–.836). While reasonable support for the APRI was found using CFA approaches based on the current standards of goodness of fit indicators, the inflated high correlations among the identified factors undermined the ability to distinguish the subdomains (verbal, social, and physical) for bullying and victimization. The latter is a problem that has plagued traditional bullying research (see Card et al., 2008), and has impeded structural theory development more broadly. Clearly what is important about the Marsh et al. (2011) findings is that (1) these results demonstrate that the bullying and victimization constructs are distinguishable, positively related, and complex; and (2) provide empirical support for three forms of bullying and victimization (physical, social, and verbal), which has important implications for theory development. That is, Marsh et al. provide rigorous research evidence that provides support for a separation of the bullying and victimization constructs, and multidimensional theoretical conceptualization of traditional bullying and victimization constructs and their respective subdomains (i.e., empirical support for the two roles (Bullying, Victimization) and three forms of bullying (Verbal, Social, Physical)—a 2 x 3 factor model).

In addition, consistent with previous research, Marsh et al. (2011) extended their ESEM results to test the causal ordering of bullying and victimization with longitudinal data. Consistent with the indicated positive correlations between bullying and victimization, they found that bullying and victimization are reciprocally related, in that these constructs are mutually reinforcing whereby a person can bully others and also be bullied. These results imply that while bullying and victimization are discrete constructs with demonstrated discriminant validity, they also seem to share a dynamic mutually reinforcing relation whereby being victimized may lead to bullying, and bullying may also lead to victimization. Importantly, Marsh et al. (2011) extended this line of research by demonstrating that that the nature of this relation is domain specific (e.g., physical bullying was more highly correlated with physical victimization than other victimization forms).

While the nature of key traditional bullying constructs has been examined by a body of research, the findings of Marsh et al. (2011) are of great heuristic value by providing sound empirical support for the separation of the three bullying forms (physical, verbal, social) surmised and testing the structure of bullying and victimization and its subdomains in the same model simultaneously. Hence, this study synthesizes and offers new insights about what we know about the structure of traditional bullying constructs. Research findings support bullying and victimization constructs as separate but interrelated constructs. Findings also imply that these constructs are multidimensional in nature comprising at least verbal, physical, and social domains. These findings can form the basis of conceptualizing and posing some initial theoretical multidimensional structural models that are underpinned by research advances. For example, as proposed by Marsh et al. (2011) and Parada (2006), Figure 6.1 depicts a possible representation of a multidimensional model of bullying and victimization constructs whereby traditional bullying and victimization are hypothesized as related latent constructs that each comprises three subdomains.

The structure of bystander roles. The incident of bullying is influenced by both bullies and by the responses of witnesses to bullying behaviors (Sullivan, 2000). Salmivalli, Kaukiainen, Kaistaniemi, and Lagerspetz (Salmivalli, 1999; Salmivalli, Lagerspetz, Bjoerkqvist & Oesterman, 1996) has proposed that bystanders witnessing bullying incidents may react in different participant roles. These include assisting the bullying by joining in or making suggestions as to whom to and how to bully, reinforcing the bullying by looking on or "cheering" the perpetrator, defending the target, or by remaining outside the situation by not doing anything about it. The APRI also measures Participant Roles (Parada, 2000) in relation to bystanders via 24 items measuring bystander reactions to a bullying situation. Students are asked to rate how true these reactions are in relation to what they would do on a six-point Likert scale (1 = *False* to 6 = *True*). These 24 items comprise four scales: Active Reinforcer (behaviors actively encouraging perpetrators); Passive Reinforcer (behaviors passively encouraging perpetrators); Target Advocate (behaviors supporting the target); and Ignore Disregard (behaviors ignoring a bullying incident and doing nothing about it).

Marsh et al. (2011) demonstrated that the four domains of bystander roles were psychometrically sound. They also found that these multidimensional scales shared logical relations with bullying and victimization constructs. Overall, the bully factors were positively related to active and passive reinforcement bystander roles, and negatively related to ignoring and advocating for the perpetrator. The effects also varied for specific subdomains, whereby the bully-physical factor

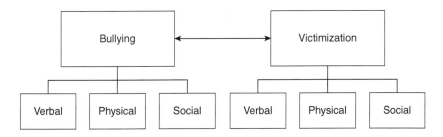

Figure 6.1 A multidimensional structural theoretical conceptualization of bullying and victimization constructs based on traditional bullying research. The model is a two facet model in which the facets are the two roles (bullying and victimization) and the three forms (verbal, physical, social).

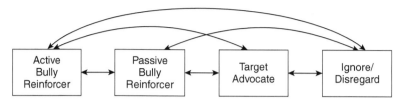

Figure 6.2 A multidimensional and structural theoretical conceptualization of bullying bystander roles

was most strongly associated with the active reinforcing role and the bully-verbal factor more strongly related to passive and victim-advocate factors. The victim factors were positively correlated with actively reinforcing the perpetrator and were essentially unrelated to passively reinforcing, ignoring, or advocating for the victim. Marsh et al. (2011) suggested that these results imply that "victims might identify with bullies more than with other victims, maybe even aspiring to become bullies, or simply willing to reinforce the bullies in an effort to avoid becoming the next victim" (p. 712). These results provide support for a multidimensional theoretical conceptualization of bystander roles that has important implications for theory, research, and practice.

Figure 6.2 depicts a multidimensional model of bystander roles depicting potential behaviors that may ensue as a result of a bystander reacting to a bullying incident. We also emphasize that behavioral responses by bystanders to a bullying incident (or even learning about one from others), may be passive or active in nature. Bystander behaviors are hypothesized to be multidimensional, comprising four subdomains that have been demonstrated to be psychometrically sound as measured by the APRI: Active Bully Reinforcer, Passive Bully Reinforcer, Target Advocate, and Ignore/Disregard. Figure 6.3 provides a between-construct structural model depicting the relation of bullying and victimization multidimensional constructs to multidimensional bystander constructs.

While the Marsh et al. (2011) study provides seminal within-construct and between-construct support for all of these theorized structures, it needs to be emphasized that further research is warranted to continue to test the salience of the proposed multidimensional structural models and further affirm their internal and external construct validity. However, these models do demonstrate that research on traditional bullying and victimization has established much about the multidimensional structure of these constructs, and has elucidated a multidimensional structure for bystander roles. Bystander roles have also been shown to be logically related to multidimensional domains of traditional bullying and victimization. These findings have important implications for theorizing the structure and place of cyberbullying constructs, which are discussed in the next section of this chapter.

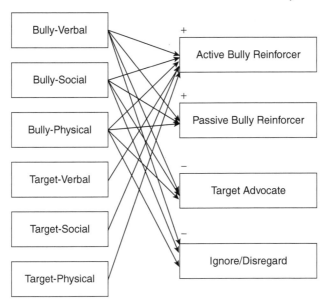

Figure 6.3 A between-construct structural theoretical model of the relations between multiple domains of bullying and victimization and bystander roles

IMPLICATIONS FOR THEORIZING THE STRUCTURE OF CYBERBULLYING CONSTRUCTS AND THEIR RELATION TO TRADITIONAL BULLYING

Advances emanating from traditional bullying research and the proposed structural models presented above provide a potential starting point for possible theoretical representations of the nature of cyberbullying constructs, and their relation to traditional bullying and victimization constructs. Cyberbullying definitions have been discussed elsewhere in this volume. For the purposes of an operational definition, we follow Bauman's (2011, p. 4) definition of cyberbullying as "actions using information and communication technology to harm another person." In this second section of this chapter, we outline some potential theoretical models of the structure and relation of cyberbullying constructs to traditional bullying.

Theorized Structure of the Relation of Cyberbullying to Traditional Bullying Constructs

Although construct validation can be undertaken with an intuitive definition, a mature operational structural construct definition that is formal and explicit allows the construct to be conceptualized clearly, measurable, and therefore testable by empirical research. For example, self-concept research has advanced markedly over recent decades largely founded upon seminal work (Shavelson, Hubner, & Stanton; 1976) advocating the need for within-construct research and providing a potential theoretical model representation and blueprint thereof. Ideally, it is useful to include in a structural definition (1) a within-construct component whereby the observable properties are defined, construct features are linked to each other and to observable attributes of the person; and (2) a between-construct component of the definition whereby its relation to other related and independent constructs is proposed. This is termed a nomological network (Cronbach & Meehl, 1955) approach, whereby a construct is construed conceptually. For example, research pertaining to the structure of bullying and victimization overviewed above implies that these constructs are distinct as well as multifaceted in that three bullying forms have been proposed and are established in the literature (physical, verbal, and social) and recently have been demonstrated by empirical research to be salient (e.g., Marsh et al., 2011). Based on the available body of knowledge, there does not appear to be an overarching (i.e., superordinate) structural bullying factor; the evidence is strong that bullying and victimization are discrete constructs that are dynamically related (see previous discussion). In addition, multiple dynamic participant roles have been proposed (bully, target, bully/target, bystander), and research has begun at least to demonstrate that both bullying and victimization comprise verbal, physical, and social forms. These understandings also suggest that bullying and victimization cannot be understood if the multidimensionality of the constructs is ignored. However, the structure and place of cyberbullying in relation to these research advances is unknown. Cyberbullying constructs have not been included in the development of this body of research because cyberbullying is a relatively new phenomena that is being rapidly enabled through exponential recent advances in digital media and communication technology, which have been embraced by youth around the developed world.

It is theoretically plausible that cyberbullying and cyber targetization are also discrete but related constructs and are multidimensional in nature. Hence, a within-construct portion of a hypothesized structural definition of cyberbullying is that it is a distinct form of bullying. Therefore, we propose that bullying is a multidimensional construct comprising *four* discrete forms (verbal, physical, social, and cyber) and their interrelations. We also hypothesize that cyberbullying and cyber targetization are related but discrete constructs that are distinguishable from each other as they are in traditional bullying (e.g., Marsh et al., 2011). Research has discovered that cyber perpetrators are often also cyber targets (Kowalski & Limber, 2007; Ybarra & Mitchell, 2004). For example, Kowalski and Limber (2007) found a significant correlation between cyberbullying and cyber targetization, and this relation yielded a stronger correlation than traditional bullying and victimization. A possible representation of this theorized structure is depicted in Figure 6.4.

Multidimensional bystander roles have been described related to bullying and victimization. Research has not as yet elucidated the role of bystander roles in

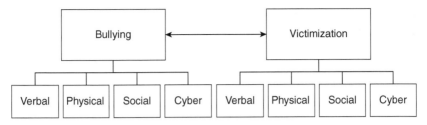

Figure 6.4 A multidimensional structural theoretical conceptualization of bullying and victimization constructs integrating cyberbullying and cyber targetization constructs

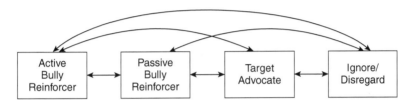

Figures 6.5a A hypothetical domain general structure of bystander roles

relation to cyberbullying, so we do not yet have an empirical basis for theoretical conceptualizations. Qualitative research in this regard is sorely needed to eluci-date theory and inform measurement to establish the underlying constructs. At this time it is not as yet possible to propose a mature theoretical conceptualization. However, given that research has established the salience of bystander roles in relation to traditional bullying and victimization, a number of potential competing hypothetical models are possible to at least outline for testing. As such, we propose some possible competing representations of the structural nature of cyberbully-ing that can be examined by both qualitative and quantitative research. A pos-sible representation is that bystander roles in cyberbullying may be qualitatively similar (i.e., domain general) (i.e., Figure 6.5a, which corresponds to Figure 6.2 above) to the traditional bullying and victimization constructs. Another hypoth-esis is that cyber bystander roles are discrete (i.e., display discriminant validity) from those involved in traditional bullying and comprise four subdomains: Active Cyberbully Reinforcer, Passive Cyberbully Reinforcer, Cyber Target Advocate, and Cyberbullying Ignore/Disregard (Figure 6.5b). The latter possibility is plau-sible because cyberbullying is enacted in the environment of cyberspace, so that the bystander's actions can be made anonymously. It remains to be determined whether or not cyber bystander roles are in fact related to traditional bullying bystander roles. Furthermore, it is possible that bystander roles in of themselves

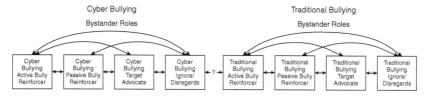

Figure 6.5b A hypothetical model of discrete cyberbullying bystander roles

Figure 6.5c A hypothetical multidimensional model of bystander roles in relation to established forms of bullying

Figure 6.5d A hypothetical multidimensional model of bystander roles in relation to established forms of bullying and incorporating cyberbullying

are multidimensional in the context of established forms of bullying (i.e., Social, Verbal, Physical; Figure 6.5c). While social and verbal forms perhaps may readily translate to the cyberspace environment, the translation of physical forms is less clear, although a student may be physically threatened, and physical forms of bullying are portrayed and disseminated in this environment (e.g., videos of physical bullying). There may also be other forms that are unique to cyberbullying that are yet to be defined (e.g., flaming, sexting, etc.) which would result in a model with four forms (Figure 6.5d).Currently, there is no available measure to test these hypothetical models, and qualitative research has not yet fully elucidated the roles of bystanders in cyberbullying. Hence, the salience of these competing hypothetical models remains to be determined.

We have shown that traditional bullying and victimization are multidimensional constructs that are related to multidimensional bystander constructs (Marsh et al., 2011). Perhaps cyberbullying and cyber targetization are therefore also related to multidimensional bystander constructs in a similar pattern (Bully Cyber will be positively related to Active Cyberbully Reinforcer and Passive Cyberbully Reinforcer and negatively related to Cyber Target Advocate and Cyberbullying Ignore/

Disregard; Cyber Target will be will be positively related to Active Cyberbully) although the exact nature of such a hypothetical relation remains to be described. In an attempt to integrate the relations of traditional bullying, traditional victimization, cyberbullying, cyber targetization, and the relations of bystander roles, we offer a hypothetical integrated structural model (see Figure 6.6).

The between-construct study of these theoretical models will involve relating the constructs to a wide range of important other constructs implicated in bullying and victimization (e.g., self-concept, anxiety, coping, achievement) to ascertain if there are logical relations between discrete constructs. Such relations, if found, will offer further support for the internal and external validity of theoretical conceptualizations. While the models we have proposed build on understandings emanating from traditional bullying research, it needs to be emphasized that extensive further research is required to fully test the salience of the proposed multidimensional structural models and affirm their internal and external construct validity in relation to cyberbullyng. The interplay of theory, research, and practice is vital to achieving these goals. These models have important implications for theorizing the structure and place of cyberbullying and cyber targetization

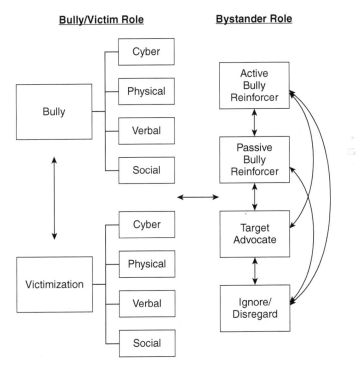

Figure 6.6 A hypothetical integrated multidimensional model of bullying, victimization, and cyberbullying

constructs. As such they provide an important starting point for stimulating advances in cyberbullying theory, research, and practice.

Proposed Structural Definitions of Cyberbullying and Bullying

Following from the theorized models presented above and definitions established in the literature (see Bauman, 2011, for an overview), cyberbullying may be conceived as (a) actions using technology to harm another person that may involve intentional harm, repetition, and/or a power imbalance; (b) a form of bullying that is distinct but related to other bullying forms (i.e., verbal, social, physical), and (d) involving multiple participant roles (perpetrators, targets, bully/targets, bystanders) that are also distinct but related. In broader terms, integrating cyber and traditional forms, we propose that bullying be conceptualized as (a) actions to harm another person that may involve intentional harm, repetition, and/or a power imbalance; (b) multidimensional in nature, being comprised of different direct and indirect forms of bullying that are distinct but related (physical, social, verbal, cyber); and (c) related to multidimensional bystander behaviors that may include actively and passively reinforcing perpetrators, advocating for targets, and ignoring or disregarding bullying behaviors.

Potential Features for Advancing Structural Definition

Seven potential features add precision to the structural definition of the construct. Bullying and victimization may be described as discrete constructs, multidimensional, related, hierarchical, stable, varying with age, and differentiated from other constructs. Each of these seven elements is described below.

An individual's engagement in, subjection to, and being a bystander in bullying situations, whether in a face-to-face or cyber environment, constitute the data on which a person bases her/his perceptions of bullying experiences. A person is likely to reduce the complexity of these experiences by coding and organizing them into categories (e.g., verbal, social, physical, and cyberbullying). These categories correspond to the four forms of bullying and victimization (verbal, social, physical, cyber), and involve multifaceted participant roles (bully, target, bully/target, bystander) that are interrelated (e.g., bullying and being a target are hypothesized to be positively correlated, as are cyberbullying and cyber targetization). Hence, three key features of bullying and victimization are that they are *discrete constructs, multidimensional in nature,* and *related constructs.*

A fourth feature of bullying and victimization is that the constructs may also be *hierarchical* in nature. For example, below a global experience of cyberbullying (as either target or perpetrator) are specific experiences of cyberbullying. These are at the base of the hierarchy to represent specific observable behaviors that are more situation specific (e.g., distributing film material designed to harm a person, writing nasty e-mails designed to harm a person).

A fifth feature is that complex social roles in bullying (perpetrator, target, perpetrator/target, bystander) may be *stable* over time. Perhaps due to the repetitive nature of bullying (in the case of cyberbullying, the repetition may take the form of one act that is widely distributed in cyberspace to a large audience, see Sourander, Helstela, Helenius, & Phia, 2000) or other psychogenic factors that are present or become activated as a result of bullying (e.g., self-concepts, depression, or conduct issues). However, perhaps as the hierarchy is descended, and individual behaviors within singular constructs are examined, bullying and victimization are more and more contextually specific or ecologically dependent. Hence, it may become more amenable to change and therefore less stable. While such a theoretical proposition, if correct, could readily begin to inform intervention—whereby the lower less-stable levels of the hierarchy are targeted—changes at the lower levels may not be powerful enough to transfer to the broader conceptualizations at the higher levels, which may be resistant to change. This would imply and be consistent with the available literature on the need for multimodal intervention strategies that target both lower and higher levels simultaneously. Regardless, the extent of transfer effects in a hierarchical model may be important to explicate, and it is hypothesized that the multidimensional facets of bullying, victimization, and bystander roles in the absence of intervention are stable over time.

A sixth feature is that bullying is hypothesized to vary with age. For example, Marsh et al. (2011) found that for all six factors measured by the APRI, scores were lower in Year 7, increased in Year 8, remained stable over Years 9 and 10, and then declined in Year 11. However, they did report that the structure of bullying, victimization, and role constructs generalized well over adolescent ages even though there were differences in the level of bullying in different year groups. Further research is needed in primary school settings to explicate age trends in this critical period and to learn whether the multiple dimensions of these constructs have similar or different patterns that vary with age.

The seventh feature of victimization and bullying is that their multiple dimensions are *differentiated* from constructs to which they are logically and theoretically related (e.g., self-concept domains, anxiety, coping, achievement) as demonstrated with traditional bullying factors by Marsh et al. (2011). Although for cyberbullying, the between-construct component of the definition and nomological network are beyond the scope and focus of this chapter, it is an important direction for further research.

While the nature of bystander roles and the measurement thereof requires further research in general and, in particular in relation to cyberbullying, bystander research, previous research in traditional bullying provides a starting point to understanding the complexity of the bystander construct. As yet, there are few measurement instruments available to test whether these bystander constructs are salient in the context of a multidimensional conceptualization such as those proposed in this chapter. It is also unknown the extent to which the conceptualization applies to each form of bullying and victimization including cyberbullying and cyber targetization. It also remains to be to be determined empirically whether bystander roles are specific to each form (e.g., Physical Bystander, Social Bystander, Verbal Bystander, Cyber Bystander) and whether the roles may also be further differentiated into multifaceted domain specific bystander constructs (e.g., Cyberbullying Active Reinforcer, Cyberbullying Passive Reinforcer, Cyber Target Advocate, and Cyber Disregard) that are more aligned with conceptualizations of actual behaviors.

Validation of the Theoretical Models Proposed

As emphasized previously, construct validation involves a precise structural definition of the construct, the development of psychometrically sound measurement instruments that are amenable to testing theoretical models, and refining the theory based on empirical research findings. The structural construct definition is fundamental to the theoretically conceptualized structural model and can be utilized to inform both scale and item development. Theorized models can also be seen as a series of hypotheses that must be tested, as do the hypothesized components and relations among them. Findings of such studies may generate counterhypotheses that also need to be tested. Initially, construct validation studies are needed to test the hypothesized structure of the within-construct component of the nomological networks proposed in this chapter. An initial focus on within-construct issues is essential because it is not possible to relate hypothesized latent constructs to other related latent constructs until within-construct issues have been examined and at least some consensus reached about the findings obtained. Once within-construct issues have been resolved, between-construct issues can be pursued to ascertain the empirical evidence for the between-construct component of structural definition of the theoretical model.

Clearly, if the empirical evidence supports proposed theoretical conceptualizations, then the theory is supported. If empirical evidence does not support the theory, then revisions are required, or the entire theoretical model may be refuted. Furthermore, researchers need to be aware that evidence that conflicts with theoretical conceptualizations may also be due to measurement techniques, whereby some aspects of the model cannot be clarified without the development of new measurement techniques (e.g., the advantages that ESEM provides in accessing factor correlations).

SUMMARY

Bullying and cyberbullying are significant international issues. Most studies have examined cyberbullying and traditional bullying constructs in isolation and have focused on relating these constructs to other constructs or examining mean differences in bullying scores in different populations or as a result of intervention. While sound primary studies have provided vital and important insights into the nature of bullying and victimization—and cyberbullying and cyber targetization—as a body of research, this area of research lacks. The focus that would result from agreed-upon structural definitions and theoretical models, demonstrated psychometrically sound measurement instruments that can test proposed theoretical conceptualizations and test within-construct and between-construct issues, a suite of commonly used measurement instruments utilized internationally to aid interpretation and stimulate cross-cultural studies further testing the external validity of findings, and demonstration of the equivalence of many measures currently being utilized so that data collected with an instrument can be related to another existing instrument.

In this chapter, potentially useful theoretical models of the structure of cyberbullying, cyber targetization, and cyberbullying bystander constructs and their theorized relation to traditional bullying research findings have been proposed to draw the findings from significant individual studies and from traditional and cyberbullying literature together into a coherent and integrated theoretical conceptualization that is amenable to testing. Hence, these theoretical conceptualizations may help to draw together traditional bullying research and cyberbullying research and offer directions for future research. It is also hoped that the theoretical models proposed can contribute to stimulating the critical interplay of theory, research, and practice, and help establish more standardization of and agreement in relation to structural definitions, theoretical conceptualizations, utilization of measurement instruments, and interpretations in regard to resolving within-construct issues prior to proceeding to addressing between-construct issues.

References

Bauman, S. (2011). *Cyberbullying: What counselors need to know*. Alexandria, VA: American Counselling Association.

Card, N. A., & Hodges, E. V.E. (2008). Peer victimization among school children: Correlations, causes, consequences, and considerations in assessment and intervention. *School Psychology Quarterly, 23*, 451–461. doi:10.1037/a0012769

Crick, N. R., & Grotpeter, J. K. (1995). Relational aggression, gender, and social psychological adjustment. *Child Development, 66*, 710–722. doi:10.2307/1131945

Crick, N. R., Nelson, D. A., Morales, J. R., Cullerton-Sen, C., Casas, J. F., & Hickman, S. E. (2001). Relational victimization in childhood and adolescence: I hurt you through the grapevine. In J. Juvonen, A. Nishina, & S. Graham (Eds.), *Peer harassment in school: The plight of the vulnerable and victimized* (pp. 196–214). New York: Guilford.

Cronbach, L. J., & Meehl, P. E. (1955). Construct validity in psychological tests. *Psychological Bulletin, 52*, 281–302. doi:10.1037/h0040957

Finkelhor, D., Ormrod, R. K., & Turner, H. A. (2007). Polyvictimization and trauma in a national longitudinal cohort. *Development and Psychopathology, 19*, 149–166. doi:10.1017/S0954579407070083

Gumpel, T. P. (2008). Behavioral disorders in the school participant roles and sub-roles in three types of school violence. *Journal of Emotional and Behavioral Disorders, 16*, 145–162. doi:10.1177/1063426607310846

Harachi, T. W., Catalano, R. F., & Hawkins, D. J. (1999). United States. In P. K. Smith, Y. Morita, J. Junger-Tas, D. Olweus, R. F. Catalano, & P. T. Slee (Eds.), *The nature of school bullying: A cross-national perspective* (pp. 279–295). London: Routledge.

Hawker, D.S.J., & Boulton, M.J. (2000). Twenty years' research on peer victimization and psychosocial maladjustment: A meta-analytic review of cross-sectional studies. *Journal of Child Psychology and Psychiatry,41*, 441–455. doi:10.1111/1469-7610.00629

Hussein, M.H. (2010). The peer interaction in primary school questionnaire: Testing for measurement equivalence and latent mean differences in bullying between gender in Egypt, Saudi Arabia, and the USA. *Social Psychology of Education, 13*, 57–76. doi:10.1007/s11218–009–9098-y

Kowalski, R.M., & Limber, S.P. (2007). Electronic bullying among middle school students. *Journal of Adolescent Health, 41*, 22–30. doi:10.1016/j.jadohealth.2007.08.017

Marsh, H., Nagengast, B., Morin, A.J.S., Parada, R.H., Craven, R.G., & Hamilton, L.R. (2011). Construct validity of the multidimensional structure of bullying and victimization: An application of exploratory structural equation modelling. *Journal of Educational Psychology, 103*, 701–732. doi:10.1037/a0024122

Marsh, H.W., Parada, R.H., Craven, R.G., & Finger, L. (2004). In the looking glass: A reciprocal effect model elucidating the complex nature of bullying, psychological determinants, and the central role of self-concept. In C.E. Sanders & G.D. Phye (Eds.), *Bullying: Implications for the classroom* (pp. 63–109). San Diego, CA: Elsevier. doi:10.1016/B978–012617955–2/50009–6

Mynard, H., & Joseph, S. (2000). Development of the multidimensional peer-victimization scale. *Aggressive Behavior, 26*, 169–178. doi:10.1002/(SICI)1098-2337(2000)26:2_169::AID-AB33.0.CO;2-A

Olweus, D. (1997). Bully/victim problems in school: Facts and intervention. *European Journal of Psychology of Education, 12*, 495–510. doi:10.1007/BF03172807

Parada, R.H. (2000). Adolescent peer relations instrument: A theoretical and empirical basis for the measurement of participant roles in bullying and victimization of adolescence. An interim test manual and a research monograph: A test manual. Penrith, Australia: University of Western Sydney, Self-Concept Enhancement and Learning Facilitation (SELF) Research Centre, Publication Unit.

Parada, R.H. (2006). *School bullying: Psychosocial determinants and effective intervention*. Unpublished doctoral dissertation, University of Western Sydney, Penrith, Australia.

Parada, R.H., Craven, R.G., & Marsh, H.W. (2008). The Beyond Bullying Secondary Program: An innovative program empowering teachers to counteract bullying in schools. In *Self-processes, learning, and enabling human potential: Dynamic new approaches* (Vol. 3, pp. 373–426). Charlotte, NC: Information Age.

Parada, R.H., Marsh, H.W., & Craven, G.R. (2005). *There and back again from bully to victim and victim to bully: A reciprocal effects model of bullying behaviors in schools.* Paper presented at the Australian Association for Research in Education International, Parramatta, Australia.

Rigby, K. (1996). *Bullying in schools—and what to do about it.* Melbourne, Australia: ACER.

Roland, E., & Idsøe, T. (2001). Aggression and bullying. *Aggressive Behavior, 27*, 446–462. doi:10.1002/ab.1029

Salmivalli, C. (1999). Participant role approach to school bullying: Implications for intervention. *Journal of Adolescence, 22*(4), 453–459. doi:10.1006/jado.1999.0239

Salmivalli, C., Lagerspetz, K., Bjoerkqvist, K., & Oesterman, K. (1996). Bullying as a group process: Participant roles and their relations to social status within the group. *Aggressive Behavior, 22*(1), 1–15. doi:10.1002/(SICI)1098–2337(1996)22:1<1::AID-AB1>3.0.CO;2-T

Samlivalli, C., Lappalaninen, M., & Lagerspetz, K. M. (1998). Stablity and change of behavior in connection with bullying in schools: A two-year follow-up. *Aggressive Behavior, 24,* 205–218. doi: 10.1002/(SICI)/1098-2337(1998)24:3<205::AID-AB5>3.0.CO;2-J

Salmivalli, C., Kaukiainen, A., Kaistaniemi, L., & Lagerspetz, K.M.J. (1999). Self-evaluated self-esteem, peer-evaluated self-esteem, and defensive egotism as predictors of adolescents' participation in bullying situations. *Personality & Social Psychology Bulletin, 25*(10), 1268–1278. doi:10.1177/0146167299258008

Salmivalli, C., Kaukiainen, A., & Lagerspetz, K.M.J. (2000). Aggression and sociometric status among peers: Do gender and type of aggression matter? *Scandinavian Journal of Psychology, 41,* 17–24. doi:10.1111/1467–9450.00166

Schuster, B. (1996). Rejection, exclusion, and harassment at work and in schools: An integration of results from research on mobbing, bullying, and peer rejection. *European Psychology, 1,* 293–317. doi:10.1027/1016–9040.1.4.293

Shavelson, R.J., Hubner, J.J., & Stanton, G.C. (1976). Validation of construct interpretations. *Review of Educational Research, 46,* 407–441. doi:10.3102/00346543046003407

Sourander, A., Helstela, L., Helenius, H., & Piha, J. (2000). Persistence of bullying from childhood to adolescence—a longitudinal 8-year follow-up study. *Child Abuse and Neglect, 24,* 873–881. doi:10.1016/S0145–2134(00)00146–0

Smith, P.K., Morita, Y., Junger-Tas, J., Olweus, D., Catalano, R.F., & Slee, P. (Eds.). (1999). *The nature of school bullying: A cross-national perspective.* London, England: Routledge.

Sullivan, K. (2000). *The anti-bullying handbook.* Auckland: New Zealand: Oxford University Press.

Sutton, J., Smith, P.K., & Swettenham, J. (1999). Bullying and "theory of mind": A critique of the "social skills deficit" view of anti-social behavior. *Social Development, 8,* 117–127. doi:10.1111/1467–9507.00083

Swearer, S.M., Espelage, D.L., Vaillancourt, T., & Hymel, S. (2010). What can be done about school bullying? Linking research to educational practice. *Educational Researcher, 39,* 38–47. doi:10.3102/0013189X09357622

Wolke, D., Woods, S., Bloomfield, L., & Karstadt, L. (2000). The association between direct and relational bullying and behavior problems among primary school children. *Journal of Child Psychology and Psychiatry,41,* 989–1002. doi:10.1111/1469-7610.00687

Ybarra, M.L. & Mitchell, K.J. (2004). Online aggressor/targets, aggressors, and targets: a comparison of associated youth characteristics. *Journal of Child Psychology and Psychiatry, 45,* 1308–1316. doi:10.1111/j.1469–7610.2004.00328.x

Part IV
Methods

7 Methodology

Why It Matters

Sheri Bauman

We have established that a clear and precise definition of the construct of *cyber-bullying* is a necessary condition for the pursuit of rigorous research. However, a definition alone is not a sufficient guarantee of high quality research; measures and methods must also be scientifically sound. Entwistle, Tritter, and Calnan (2002) expressed the importance of methodology this way:

> methodological problems compromise the quality and impact of research. The robustness of the methods used is an important determinant of the quality of research, and the perceived robustness of the methods used are [*sic*] important determinants of its credibility. (p. 233)

Applying their observation to cyberbullying research, we must be mindful that our work must be credible to our audience, which includes not only scholars but the larger community (both practitioners and the public at large) that is seeking answers to questions about this problem and how to curtail it. This chapter makes the case for the importance of methodological considerations, which are addressed in the remaining chapters in this section.

We distinguish between research methods and research methodology (Rajasekar, Philominathan, & Chinnathambi, 2006). Methods are the various tools used to gather and analyze data in order to answer research questions. Research methodology refers to a "systematic way to solve a problem" (Rajasekar et al., p. 2) or "a system of principles, practices, and procedures applied to a specific branch of knowledge" (Peffers, Tuuanen, Rothenberger, & Chatterjee, 2007–20088, p. 49). The methodology describes how to select the specific methods and considers the accuracy and efficiency of the methods chosen. Cyberbullying research has not yet developed a unique methodology, but there are certainly methods that are unique to this field that merit close attention as researchers develop new methods and adapt and apply existing methods to this emerging field of inquiry. Before consensus is reached regarding a suitable cyberbullying research methodology, researchers must engage in research and discussion about the merits and demerits of different methods, most important when methods are newly available because of the advances in technology. So we must not only study the problems of cyberbullying, but we must study the methods used in our research to identify those that best contribute to an emerging methodology.

Typically, when discussing methodology, we refer to two traditions: quantitative and qualitative, which are seen as reflecting quite different paradigms. There are also many proponents (e.g., Hanson, Crewswell, Clark, Petska, & Creswell, 2005; Johnson, Onwuegbuzie, & Turner, 2007) of mixed methods research, which borrows from both traditions to provide a more thorough understanding of the problem being studied. In fact, Giddings (2006) suggests that mixed methods research is a new methodological tradition that has been elevated to prominence in the social sciences. Giddings, it should be noted, has reservations about the ways in which the mixed methods methodology has been used.

The question of which methodology is preferable has been addressed by researchers. Schmierbach (2005) conducted an experiment to determine journalists' beliefs about the likelihood of reporting on and publishing findings from social science research provided to them in the form of a press release. Journalists were recruited to respond to a survey seeking journalists' assessment of the accuracy of and newsworthiness of study results. Participants were randomly divided into two groups, with one group receiving a description of findings that were worded to appear to be from a quantitative study and the other receiving the same results written to suggest a qualitative study. The group receiving the quantitative version rated the accuracy and newsworthiness more highly than those with the qualitative version. However, there was no difference between the two groups on the beliefs that the story would be published in respondents' newspapers.

In addition to the broader methodologies, researchers in other disciplines have found it important to study the methods used in their respective fields. In the field of cognitive neuroscience, for example, researchers investigated whether specific methods were associated with the relative impact of publications in one particular decade, the 1990s (Fellows et al., 2005). One method was lesion studies that had been used for many years in the field, and the other was functional imaging methods that had been available more recently. There are advantages and challenges with each method from a scientific perspective. The authors found that functional neuroimaging studies were cited three times as often as lesion studies, which was related to the prestige of the journals in which the neuroimaging studies were published. Further, these researchers examined whether studies using one method cited prior work using the other method; the articles using the neuroimaging method were significantly less likely to cite studies using the lesion method than vice versa. These studies relate to an important purpose of research, which is to disseminate findings, both in scientific journals and in the popular media, so cyberbullying researchers might take several lessons from these studies: (1) methods used may affect how widely the findings are circulated, and (2) as cyberbullying researchers begin to adopt new methods, those should be studied to ensure they are the best to answer the research question and to be well-received by dissemination outlets.

Another study comparing methods used was focused on practical application in the health care context (Gandhi & Bates, 2000). Authors examined several methods by which adverse drug events, potential adverse drug events, and medication errors can be identified. They concluded that one method was most useful for identifying adverse drug events, and another method was more accurate in detecting medication errors. This study has direct applications to patient safety in a hospital setting. In cyberbullying research, there may be some methods that are most useful for basic research while others are more suitable for studies that inform practice. As the field begins to develop prevention and intervention programs, the type of rigorous evaluation studies will become even more important, not least because of the increasing emphasis on evidence-based practice.

If cyberbullying research is to make a significant contribution to the scholarly literature, there is one basic guideline regarding methods: the research question drives the choice of methods and not the other way around (Sackett & Wennberg, 1997). Each available method has unique features that will determine whether it can be applied to answer the research question at hand, and the decision should be based on the ability of the method to provide the "most valid, useful answer" (Sackett & Wennberg, p. 1636). The methods used to answer the question, "What proportion of young people are involved in cyberbullying?" will be different from that used to answer the question, "What is the experience of young people who have been victimized using electronic communication?" or "How effective are classroom lessons on the use of safe use of technology in reducing incidents of cyberbullying?" Researchers need a level of expertise in all methodologies, and when a question points to a methodology that is not as familiar to the researcher, collaboration with other researchers (and other disciplines) can foster the kind of quality research this field must produce.

References

Entwistle, V., Tritter, J. Q., & Calnan, M. (2002). Researching experiences of cancer: The importance of methodology. *European Journal of Cancer Care, 11*, 232–237.

Fellows, L. K., Heberlin, A. S., Morales, D. A., Shivde, G., Waller, S., & Wu, D. H. (2005). Method matters: An empirical study of the impact in cognitive neuroscience. *Journal of Cognitive Neuroscience, 17*, 850–858. doi:10.1162/0898929054021139

Gandhi, T. K., & Bates, D. W. (2000). Methodology matters. Identifying drug safety issues: From research to practice. *International Journal for Quality in Health care, 12*, 69–76. doi:10.1093/intqhc/12.1.69

Giddings, L. S. (2006). Mixed methods research: Positivism dressed in drag? *Journal of Research in Nursing, 11*, 195–203. doi:10.1177.1744987106064635

Hanson, W. E., Creswell, J. W., Clark, V.L.P., Petska, K. S., & Crewwell, J. D. (2005). Mixed methods research designs in counseling psychology. *Journal of Counseling Psychology, 52*, 224–235. doi:10.137/0022–0167.52.2.224

Johnson, R. B., Onwuegbuzie, A. J., & Turner, L. A. (2007). Toward a definition of mixed methods research. *Journal of Mixed Methods Research*, 112–133. doi:10.1177/1558689806298224

Peffers, K., Tuuanen, T., Rothenberger, M. A., & Chatterjee, S. (2007–2008). A design science research methodology for information systems research. *Journal of Management Information systems, 24*(3), 45–77.

Rajasekar, S., Philominathan, P., & Chinnathambi, V. (2006). Research methodology. Retrieved from www.scribd.com/mobile/documents/6949151/download?secret_pass word=wgbtjif)eeq9tb1sdxw

Sackett, D. L., & Wennberg, J. E. (1997). Choosing the best research design for each question: It's time to stop squabbling over the "best" methods. *British Medical Journal, 315*, 1636.

Schmierbach, M. (2005). Method matters: The influence of methodology on journalists' assessment of social science research. *Science Communication, 26*, 269–287. doi:10.1177/1075547004273025

8 Sampling

Sheri Bauman

This chapter focuses on two aspects of sampling. First, the need for researchers to be attentive to sampling strategies in studies they cite and to be judicious about citing those with biased sampling strategies is discussed. Then, considerations that researchers should take into account when making important sampling decisions for their own studies are described.

CITING PREVIOUS RESEARCH

As Kemper, Stringfield, and Teddlie (2002) said, "In research, sampling is destiny" (p. 275). Although selecting a sample is a critical step in any research study, it often gets less attention than necessary. A large proportion of research studies, including those on cyberbullying, utilize convenience samples because of ease of access and efficiency of data collection (Babbie, 2008; Hutch, MacDonald, Hunter, Maitland, & Dixon, 2002; Onweugbuzie & Collins, 2007; Short, Ketchen, & Palmer, 2002). In most cases, the limitations section of an article will point out that the sample was not representative and that generalizations should not be made. However, when those findings are cited in subsequent articles by other researchers, those important pieces of information are often omitted. For example, a 2007 article reporting findings from a study on cyberbullying had been cited more than 184 times as of December 2011. The paper described a study with a sample of 84 high school students who were recruited at special events attended by an unknown percentage of students at two U.S. high schools: one rural and one suburban. Of those attending the first event, one third agreed to participate. For the second event, approximately 45% agreed to participate. So the sample was recruited from a portion of students (those interested in the event) at two high schools in a single geographic area, and only a portion of those participated. Although the authors acknowledged this sampling bias in the limitations section of their article, the findings are cited in other articles without reference to that serious limitation. When researchers cite a study, they imply the findings are valid and that they apply to other populations and contexts. Therefore, researchers need to consider the adequacy of sampling as an important criterion for whether the results should be cited as if they were solid evidence of a finding. Citing such articles, and including a caveat that the study was exploratory and had sampling biases, indicates that the subsequent authors recognize the limitations. If research on cyberbullying is to advance, it is essential that researchers critically review articles they cite. They need to examine closely all aspects of sampling and make a determination about whether we can make any firm conclusions given the sample size and selection practice.

Random selection: A sampling practice in which all possible samples of a given size have the same probability of being selected (Kerlinger, 1986). The sample is then considered to be representative of the population from which it was drawn.

The Effect of Sampling Decisions: An Example

Short, Ketchen, and Palmer (2002) investigated the possibility that sampling practices might explain inconsistent findings across research studies in business management. In their first study, they examined 437 articles published in the top journals in their field over a 20-year period. They discovered that less than 20% of those studies used random selection of samples, and that few mentioned their sampling strategy decisions in the limitations section of the articles. Further, only 10% provided a justification for their sample size decision. Their second study tested a specific relationship (how whether the CEO of the company was also chairperson of the company's board or not [CEO duality] was related to company performance on several indicators) by using four different sampling designs (available or convenience sample, purposive sample, simple random sample, and a stratified sample[1]) with samples of approximately equal size. The *sampling frame* (list of sampling units) was drawn from a large database of company information used by researchers in that field. The size of all samples was large enough to detect small effects with power of .80 and $\alpha = .05$. These researchers found that the relation between CEO duality and performance varied by sampling method, such that in two samples, there was no relation between duality and performance (convenience and simple random sample), while the purposive sample of small firms found higher performance in firms with independent chairpersons, and the stratified random sample found higher performance with duality.

To inform the remainder of the chapter, Table 8.1 provides basic information about the most commonly used sampling strategies; it is not exhaustive but includes those that are most likely to be used in cyberbullying research.

MAKING SAMPLING DECISIONS

Sampling experts (Daniel, 2012; Henry, 2009) provided a useful guide to making sampling decisions that are summarized as follows. The first step relates to the

Table 8.1 Sampling Strategies for Cyberbullying Research

Strategy	Definition	Most often Used in	How accomplished	Cautions	Advantage	Disadvantage
Probability sampling	Based on probability theory, in which each unit in the population has a known probability of being selected.	Quantitative	Taking a sample of individuals who have the same variations that are found in the target populations.	Bias can still be present.	Findings can be generalized to the population.	Requires list of entire population
Simple Random Sampling	Probability-based; Each subject has an equal chance of being in the sample. Researcher decides whether to use sampling with or without replacement; without is more common.	Quantitative	Table of random numbers; drawing names or numbers (lottery method).	Difficult to obtain complete list of population from which to draw sample. May not include enough members of small subgroups.	Can determine population parameters with high degree of precision. High external validity.	Tends to have larger sampling errors than stratified samples of same size.
Stratified Random Sampling	Sampling frame is divided into strata (groups) based on characteristics (e.g., gender, income level, age, race/ethnicity) important to the study. Random sample is then taken from each strata. Sampling can be proportionate or disproportionate.	Quantitative	List of potential members divided into groups first. Then random sampling proceeds. Weighting required if disproportionate sampling is used.	Stratification variables must be related to variables of interest in the study. Sample size should be computed for each stratum.	Sample is representative of population on stratification variables. Protects researcher from getting a non-representative sample.	Requires more prior knowledge of the population than simple random sampling.

(Continued)

Table 8.1 (Continued)

Strategy	Definition	Most often Used in	How accomplished	Cautions	Advantage	Disadvantage
Cluster Sampling	Instead of sampling individuals who are geographically disbursed, clusters (existing groups, such as schools or school districts) are identified.	Quantitative	Instead of attempting to generate a sampling frame of all students in a state, a random sample of school districts can be used. Once districts are selected, a random sample of schools can be selected.	Multi-stage cluster sampling may be needed, which introduces two (or more) sampling errors.	Efficient use of time and resources, especially when large geographic area is involved.	Sampled clusters may not be as representative as simple random sample of = size. Data analysis can be complex.
Systematic Sampling	Selecting units by selecting (using random numbers) every k^{th} person in the sampling frame. K = population/ desired sample size.	Quantitative	Each unit in the sampling frame is given a number. K is calculated. Then a starting number is randomly selected (must be <= sample size), and every k^{th} person after that is selected.	If list of names is ordered in some way, check that the order will not bias selection.	Less cumbersome than simple random sampling, and is useful to select large samples. Ordered list may be more useful than unordered list.	Once first unit is selected, some units will have 0 probability of being selected. Principle of independence is violated.
Purposive Sampling	Selection is based on fit for purpose of study.	Qualitative	Inclusion and exclusion criteria articulated. Participants located.	Specific types (see below) have different requirements.	Internal validity can be high; likely to have less selection bias. Leads to greater depth of information.	Results not generalizable.

Table 8.1 (Continued)

Quota Sampling	Population categories (mutually exclusive) identified, and data are collected from available subjects until pre-determined target number per category is reached.	Quantitative and Qualitative	Quotas may be interlocking or not, proportional or not	Quota samples may be obtained from organization panels (e.g., Harris Interactive) so the sample matches characteristics in the population.	Ensures inclusion of important sub-populations.	Similar to convenience sampling, has selection bias.
Respondent-Assisted Sampling	First, *seeds* are recruited. Then they are asked for referrals.	Qualitative	Variations: snowball sampling, chain-referral sampling, respondent-driven sampling	Contact info is not given to researchers; coupons are given to contacts	Most effective for studying hard-to-reach populations	Non-independence of members of sample; not all respondents are effective recruiters.
Typical Case Sampling	Selection of what researcher considers "typical" or "average" subjects.	Qualitative or Quantitative	Characteristics of "typical" case described, potential participants identified, and persons selected to achieve desired sample size.	Requires current knowledge of population and sites.	Can contribute to theory development. Can provide view of "typical" cases.	Sample may be too homogeneous.

(Continued)

Table 8.1 (Continued)

Strategy	Definition	Most often Used in	How accomplished	Cautions	Advantage	Disadvantage
Deviant Case Sampling (Outlier, unique case, extreme case)	Selection of cases that are at extreme ends of the distribution on a particular characteristic.	Qualitative or quantitative	Participants must be identified via prior testing.		Valuable infortation for theory building and generating hypotheses can be obtained from contrasts.	Information is about cases, not issue.
Mixed Method Strategies	Uses combination of methods, both probability and purposive	Mixed	Concurrent, sequential, or multilevel designs are possible.	In sequential designs, info from first sample required to select second sample. Multilevel designs common in nested situations (e.g., classrooms in schools)	Both numeric and narrative data are gathered.	Researchers must be well-versed in both paradigms.

purpose of the study: is it *exploratory, developmental, descriptive,* or *explanatory*? Different purposes call for different sampling designs. The sampling requirements for an *exploratory* study are the least stringent. Daniel believes that a non-probability small sample is often adequate, while Henry argues that the best strategy is to obtain a purposive sample that is as heterogeneous as possible. Both experts make an assumption that exploratory studies are likely to be constrained by limited resources and time. Much of the published literature on cyberbullying could be called exploratory at this point. Researchers must decide whether a sufficient body of exploratory work now exists so that the more complex studies, with more rigorous sampling practices, can be planned.

Research with a *developmental* purpose is focused on theory building or development of methodology. To date, much of cyberbullying research has focused on adolescents, who are heavy users of technology and developmentally likely to engage in traditional bullying at higher rates than at other developmental points. However, there are a few studies with university students that suggest this behavior is problematic at that level as well. Furthermore, we know that young children are often quite familiar with technology, and that there are opportunities for victimization in online games for children (Bauman & Tatum, 2009). More research, especially via longitudinal studies that examine the developmental trajectories of cyberbullying behaviors, would make a contribution to our understanding of the temporal sequence of this phenomenon. The development of good measures and methods for studying cyberbullying is discussed elsewhere in this volume (see Parts 4 and 5 of this volume); some studies might benefit from using a purposive sample for example, with both high and low levels of the behaviors to investigate whether measures or methods can be used with these groups.

Much research in cyberbullying to date has been *descriptive* in nature, attempting to identify the prevalence of this behavior. Rates of cyberbullying and victimization reported in the literature vary widely, partially due to different measures and methods used in the studies, but also because of the absence of probability sampling. Rigorous sampling practices provide much more precision in their estimates. To date, the most rigorous designs in the United States have been used by the Pew Internet and American Life Project and Internet Solutions for Kids, and in Australia as part of the Australian Covert Bullying Prevalence Study (Cross et al., 2009). While descriptive studies are important, it is not often that researchers seek only to describe the characteristics of the population with respect to this behavior. More often, descriptive information is included in explanatory studies.

The purpose of *explanatory* studies is to investigate differences between groups (including between experimental and control groups in intervention studies), relations among variables, or to understand complex relationships. In combined descriptive and explanatory studies, researchers need to select samples with the goal of attaining precision in estimates and statistical power to detect effects. Henry (2009) observed that in explanatory studies, some researchers may choose to emphasize studying a small sample of participants rather than focusing on external validity or generalizability of the findings. The findings of such studies can provide important but incremental understanding for the field.

The second step is to determine the most important variables in the study. Step three is to identify the target population. The target population can be individuals, schools, school districts, or users of a website, and includes all elements of the population to which the researcher intends findings to generalize. There may also be important subpopulations in which the researcher is interested, such as a particular race or ethnic group. If the subpopulation is not considered when the sampling strategy is designed, it may be that there are too few members of the group in the selected sample to conduct needed analyses. An important subpopulation not often considered in sampling decisions is the group of invited participants who do not provide consent forms to participate in the study. This group may include disproportionate numbers of students who are actively engaging in the problematic behavior, which in this case is cyberbullying.

Next, the researcher should consider the method of data collection. Interviews, surveys, and other methods call for different sampling strategies. Interviews are likely to be conducted with smaller groups and to use non-probability sampling strategies, whereas studies using surveys are more likely to use a form of probability sampling. In cyberbullying research, researchers may want to ensure that focus groups or interview participants have experience as perpetrator or target of cyberbullying, which will affect sampling design decisions. Factors such as geographical disbursement of the population, the time needed to conduct interviews, etc., will influence the choice of sampling design. When working with schools, researchers typically confine data collection to times when school is in session. Survey questions typically ask about experiences in the fairly recent past (e.g., this school term, the past three months, the past two weeks), which may overlook behaviors that occur during holidays.

Finally, Henry (2009) asked the basic question, "Is sampling appropriate?" (p. 95). The researcher has two choices: to conduct a census of the entire population (done every 10 years in the United States and Australia and many other countries, consuming considerable time and governmental resources) or to study a sample of the population. There are some cases in which it may be prudent to study everyone in the population. In a study currently in process, researchers are collecting both qualitative and quantitative data at a small school with a total of 72 students enrolled in four grades. The research team ultimately decided not to sample, but to include all students in the population for two reasons: the school requested the project do so, and high levels or parental consent are typical in this site, and the sample size is feasible in terms of cost and time for data collection. In this case, findings will not generalize to other schools, but disseminating the findings will inform researchers exploring new constructs and trying a new methodology. In most cases, however, studying the entire population is not feasible, and sampling strategies will be necessary. Sampling can provide similar information with less cost, both financial and time. Perhaps more important, appropriate probability sampling allows the researcher to focus on data quality, so that data obtained can more accurately reflect the population. W. E. Deming, who is best known for his management work in Japan in the 1950s, was also a respected statistician. Of sampling, he said, "Sampling is not mere substitution of a partial coverage for a total coverage. Sampling is the science and art of controlling and measuring the reliability of useful statistical information through the theory of probability" (1950, p. 2).

As the field of cyberbullying research advances, studies examining the efficacy of intervention strategies will become more important. Evidence about the risk and protective factors, motivations, and dynamics will inform program development, which must be followed by program evaluation and improvement. This type of research has several unique features that affect sampling. First, the units (typically schools) that are assigned to condition are identifiable, existing groups, which are generally heterogeneous. Although assignment is by group (school), the data will be collected from individual students. So the students are nested within condition (experimental or control) and group (school), and are not independent from one another. Most interventions will focus on the universal level and therefore are designed to be delivered to all students. Therefore, it is schools (matched or unmatched, depending on the study) rather than individual students, that are randomly selected and assigned to condition (Murray, Varnell, & Bittstein, 2004).

An important problem that must be addressed in this type of research design is the expected high intraclass correlations (ICCs) among data from students in the same group[2] (Murray et al., 2004). The ICC statistic shows the variance that is due to group membership, which is in addition to the variance within students. This means that total variance will be increased for group level statistics compared to variance if there had been random assignment to condition. The effect of this is reduced power for statistical tests, larger standard errors, and wider confidence intervals (Donner, Brown, & Brasher, 1990). When there are only a few groups, the reduced degrees of freedom also affect group-level statistics. If these two consequences of using group randomized assignment are not addressed, the Type I error rate will be inflated, by an amount that increases as ICC increases. Donner and colleagues observed that one way to compensate for these problems is to increase either the number of schools in the study or, less desirable, increase the number of students per school. As discussed related to cluster analysis, there are statistical methods to correct for these problems after data have been collected. Murray et al. (2004) described a variety of methods that have been proposed to more accurately determine sample size in group randomized trials; the specifics are beyond the scope of this chapter. The interested reader is referred to the Murray article for an overview of those strategies and references to detailed descriptions. Hsieh (1988) provided a list of formulas to determine sample size in intervention studies. It is important therefore that researchers provide a rationale for their decisions about the number of schools and indicate how those decisions related to the determined sample size (Donner et al., 1990).

> **Sampling error** quantifies the magnitude of error in a sampling design. The formula is based on the parameter, the sample size, and the standard error.
>
> **Sampling bias** means that a sample is not representative of the population from which it was selected. This can be intentional or unintentional and is present to some degree in most studies.

REDUCING SAMPLING ERROR

Even the most careful sampling plan is not perfect, and selected elements (persons) may elect not to participate. Different forms of consent (active versus passive) affect the composition of the sample. In addition, participants may choose to omit parts of the data (decline to answer interview questions, deliberately provide misleading or incorrect responses, skip items on a survey), which is their right as participants. Cyberbullying researchers should also be sure to address the influence of nonparticipation and missing data (see Schlomer, Bauman, & Card, 2010) on the outcome and should consider using weights to compensate for sampling bias (Babbie, 2008).

When making decisions about sampling, it is important to remember that careful attention to sampling strategies can reduce *total error* and thus increase the precision of findings. Total error (the difference between the population value and the sample estimate) has three components: non-sampling bias, sampling bias, and sampling variability (Henry, 2009). Non-sampling bias results from differences between the target population and the study population. For example, a researcher may be interested in assessing the frequency of receiving abusive text messages in a middle school sample; if the study population only includes students in public schools (no private or home school students), sampling bias is introduced. While this type of sampling error can be minimized by careful planning, nonresponse is a factor in almost every study. Some identified participants may choose not to participate, and this introduces bias. In studies with children in schools, for which parental permission is required, there will always be some parents who deny permission. It is likely that the group for whom permission is granted differs in some way from those for whom it is denied, introducing bias. This source of bias is compounded by differences between using active consent and passive consent. Studies comparing respondents and nonrespondents have detected differences between the groups (Lohr, 1999). Cyberbullying researchers should report the percentage of the selected sample that did not participate, so readers are aware of that source of bias.

Sampling bias can be the result of selection bias or estimation bias. Selection bias occurs when not every member of the population has an equal chance of being selected. For example, a list of students from a school may omit students who have recently enrolled, or include students who have recently moved away or are involved in special education and not included in mainstream classes. This kind of bias can be corrected by using appropriate weights, provided the probability of selection is known. Estimation bias is introduced when biased estimates from samples do not equal the population value. Sampling variability is a function of the nature of sampling. Even with random samples from a population, the statistics obtained from several random samples from the same population will vary. That is, it is highly unlikely that a particular sample will produce values identical to the population parameters. The *standard error of the estimate* (Babbie, 2008; Henry, 2009) can be used to estimate the precision of a sample statistic and to calculate and report the confidence interval around that statistic. Precision estimates affect the calculation of the sample size needed to detect effects of a specified size. Many computer programs or online sample size estimates will calculate the sample size for the researcher. However, researchers should keep in mind that these procedures call for prior knowledge (e.g., standard deviations) that may be somewhat difficult to find in a new field of inquiry such as cyberbullying. However, this does not mean that cyberbullying researchers can ignore this step. They can search available prior studies, conduct a small pilot study, or make best estimates using a range of values. An additional option might be to use bootstrapping of a pilot sample as a way to determine sample size for a planned study. This may be particularly useful when non-normal distributions are likely, as they are in cyberbullying research.

To illustrate these concepts using a recent cyberbullying study, the following discussion is based on the Australian Covert Bullying Prevalence Study (ACBPS; Cross, et al., 2009). In any survey, it is essential to have reasonable guidelines on the precision of the estimates obtained. The most common way of representing these is through confidence intervals, since these have the potential to be meaningful even when the rates being estimated are quite low. The confidence interval for a specific statistic is the range of values around the statistic where the "true" (population) statistic can be expected to be located with a given level of certainty. The computation of confidence intervals, where a survey has complex multistage sampling and similarly complex weighting procedures, is best done through the use of the bootstrap (See box below). While this is generally recognized as the best procedure available, the resulting confidence intervals do have some shortcomings:

- Where a stratum has only one sampled element such as a single school, it is not possible to simulate the possible variation. When the estimate includes such a stratum, confidence intervals are too small. This problem cannot be resolved with any available method of calculating confidence intervals.
- While the simulated distribution of the estimates is generally quite realistic, this may be less so when rates that are very low—that is, where relatively few non-zero data records contribute to the estimated value. While the probability value associated with the interval will generally be correct, the confidence intervals may appear to vary in size.

For the ACBPS survey, the 106 schools in the sample were resampled 1,500 times—while matching the stratified sampling design—to construct empirical distributions of the prevalence estimates. Once the distributions had been constructed, the 95% confidence intervals for the prevalence estimates were determined by taking the 2.5th and 97.5th percentiles of the distributions. This method of calculation incorporated the nesting of bullying within schools. The bootstrapping was performed for the prevalence estimates using the R statistical package (Cross et al., 2009). Readers interested in the details of this example can find it at http://www.deewr.gov.au/Schooling/NationalSafeSchools/Pages/research.aspx.

An additional note about sampling errors: the formulae for standard errors are specific for each statistic (e.g., mean, proportions). These can be found in most statistics texts, but the general formulae assume that simple random sampling has been used; there are different modifications for different sampling strategies. Henry (2009) provided the following general guidelines: Stratification results in lower standard errors than simple random sampling. The standard error is greater for cluster sampling than simple random sampling. There are strategies that can be employed to adjust for these general situations. The design effect is one such correction and is described later in this chapter. The most challenging situation for the calculation of standard errors is the multistage sampling design often used in large national studies. Some computer programs (e.g., SAS) have available procedures to estimate sampling errors in complex designs. Henry (1990) provides an alternative strategy that involves repeated sampling. The procedure requires that two primary sampling units (PSUs) be included from each stratum in the design in order to use the formula provided. Recall that in the ACBPS study, not all stratums had the requisite two PSUs.

Bootstrapping is a way to determine the shape of a distribution of a population from which a sample was drawn. Using the original (often pilot) sample data, the computer selects a large number of samples (bootstrapped samples) by taking repeated random samples with replacement (when a unit is selected, it stays in the pool and can be selected again). The parameters of the population are computed on the sample of samples (including those needed to calculate sample size). Since the shape of the distribution is not based on an assumption of underlying normality, the strategy works well when data are not normally distributed.

Sample Size

The size of the sample needed for a particular study is a major consideration. Most commonly, researchers use specialized software or tables that provide guidelines for this decision. Daniel (2012) recommends consideration of the following principles that are not always accounted for in formulae used in software or tables. G*Power 3 (Faul, Erdfelder, Buchner, & Lang, 2009) is free software widely used in sample size calculations:

- As noted above, the objectives of the study have implications for sample size. But so does importance, so that the more important the study, the larger the sample size (see next bullet for caveat) to ensure that sampling error is minimized, and rigorous analyses can be conducted. Important studies are those likely to have policy implications or influence costly decisions, where there will be more detailed analyses, including analyses of subpopulations.

- Daniel (2012) reminds us that research is a burden on participants, and that ethically, researchers have an obligation to reduce that burden as much as possible. Thus, the researcher should not include more participants than are needed to detect a significant effect, and should not include fewer participants than are needed to make practical or clinical decisions. The rule of thumb should be to select the smallest sample to achieve the objectives of the study.

- The nature of the population is also related to decisions about sample size. If the population is highly homogeneous on the variables of interest, a smaller sample is needed. If the sample is heterogeneous, a large sample is required. Since most studies involve multiple variables, the variable on which the population is most heterogeneous and for which the most precision is needed should be the one used in determining sample size.

- The geographic distribution of the sample may have an influence on sample size, as costs may increase as distance increases. In cyberbullying research, researchers may use electronic methods of data collection, which minimize the impact of geographic disbursement. Cluster sampling also is a method for reducing costs associated with large areas, but then a larger number of clusters and larger sample size may be necessary to compensate for higher sampling errors (See Table 8.1).

- The researcher must also consider the availability of resources in deciding on sample size. Increases in numbers of participants are associated with increases in costs, needed personnel, and time. Large sample sizes require more training and support of data collectors to ensure that additional bias is not introduced. If seeking funding, applicants can build these factors into the budget, but where budget limits are predetermined, it makes sense for the researcher to use the smallest sample that will yield needed results.

- In general, quantitative studies need larger samples than do qualitative studies, nonexperimental research calls for larger samples than experimental studies, and longitudinal studies require more participants than do cross-sectional studies.

- The planned data analyses must be considered when determining sample size. For example, cell size is important for some analyses, so this must be considered in addition to overall sample size. In addition, the strength of relationships among variables involved also must be considered because the stronger the expected relationship between variables, the smaller the sample size needed to detect it. In comparative studies, the larger the difference between categories, the smaller the sample size needed to find it.

- In non-probability designs, statistical considerations are not paramount, but careful selection strategies are nevertheless very important. Daniel (2012) identified some "rules of thumb" that apply to the kinds of qualitative designs that are most likely to be used by cyberbullying researchers:

Sequential sampling: Intead of determining sample size at the outset of a study, the researcher creates a "stopping rule" (Daniel, 2012), such as data saturation in non-probability sampling. With a probability sampling design, the researcher adds cases until the targeted margin of error is reached. This strategy typically results in smaller samples than those obtained via a fixed number strategy.

- Case studies: 3–5 participants
- Grounded theory: 15–30 participants
- Focus groups: 3–12 groups; 6–12 participants per group depending on age and other factors
- Phenomenological: 6–10 participants
- Ethnography: 35–50 participants from one cultural group

- In qualitative studies using such designs as snowball sampling, sample size is not predetermined, but sampling continues until saturation is reached. Saturation means that new information is not forthcoming from additional subjects. In quantitative designs such as sequential or adaptive sampling, data collection continues until a target margin of error has been attained.

Adaptive sampling design: Instead of making all sampling decisions in advance of data collection, findings at one stage can be used to adjust assignment of additional participants. Snowball sampling is an example of this approach. In survey designs, the researcher may discover that one area (schools, district, state, etc.) exhibits more cyberbullying behavior than others and may add additional cases from that area. Parameter estimation needs to be adapted for these designs; see Thompson & Collins (2002) for details.

- Finally, sample size must take into account nonresponse, ineligibility, attrition/mortality, finite population correction factors, and design effects.

- Some persons listed in the sampling frame will ultimately be found to be ineligible to participate. Sample size determination should assume this will occur.
- The same is true for nonresponse (persons choosing not to participate) and missing data.
- If the sample size is going to be more than 5% of the population, and probability sampling is being used, there is a correction factor (fpc) that should be used to make the appropriate adjustment. Fpc = square root of (N-n)/(N-1), with N = population size and n = sample size.
- In longitudinal designs, researchers must plan for some selective and differential attrition.
- Design effects (DEFF) apply to probability cluster sampling methods. This statistic indicates the difference in precision between the non-simple random sample design and the simple random design, and shows how many more or fewer cases should be included for the actual sample design compared to the number needed for a simple random sample to obtain the same sampling variance to have the same margin of error. Note: DEFF can also be applied as an adjustment to data values after data collection.

An additional approach to the question of determining appropriate sample size was offered by Parker and Berman (2003). They indicated that standard approaches to calculating sample size are based on assumptions that are often not met: that the amount of variability is known, and if previous values are known, that they apply to the current study. They recommended a new way of thinking about sample size that may be highly applicable to cyberbullying research. They suggest that the question be reframed from "What sample size is needed?" to "What information, with this sample size, will this study provide?" Not all studies test hypotheses; exploratory or pilot studies are attempting to learn whether a concept merits further investigation. Even when statistical analyses are essential, Parker and Berman recommend starting with the available sample size, and then determining the characteristics of the information that can be obtained given the design of the study and the assumptions of the statistical analyses conducted. That might be determining the smallest difference that would be statistically significant given the sample size, and then deciding whether it is reasonable to pursue the study. They concluded with their restated paradigm: rather than thinking, "for a difference *X*, I need sample size *Y*" to "for a sample size *Y*, I get information *Z*" (p. 170). This way of thinking offers cyberbullying researchers a means to utilize small sample sizes in exploratory research and still communicate via publications what information could legitimately be derived from the study.

Non-Normal Distributions

Because much of the data in cyberbullying research is not normally distributed, the standard practices for determining sample size may be difficult to implement.

Bootstrapping methods (described above) may be useful in addressing this problem. Muthén and Muthén (2002) demonstrated how to use Monte Carlo simulations to determine sample size. Another related concern is that when a cluster sampling design is used, there is likely to be more similarity within clusters than between them; Knapp (2007) suggested that the concept of *effective sample size (ESS)* is one way to manage that situation.

Monte Carlo simulation: Using randomly generated data with particular characteristics to simulate outcomes with actual data.

An Example from Australia

An example from a covert bullying research project conducted in Australia (Cross et al., 2009) illustrates many of the concepts described above. The basic design of the quantitative survey was a stratified two-stage probability sample. Schools were selected at the first stage of sampling and classes within the schools at the second stage.

The study aimed to recruit and sample a total of 100 schools (50 primary and 50 secondary schools) across the eight States and Territories. Classes from each of the grades 4 to 9 were randomly sampled. Schools were sampled using a stratified sampling technique. Sufficient students needed to be sampled within each stratum to allow for adequate precision of prevalence estimates. All schools that met the inclusion criteria were stratified by State and then by location (metropolitan or nonmetropolitan/provincial). A total of 25 strata were formed, and the study aimed to recruit two primary and two secondary schools, randomly drawn from each stratum. Schools were therefore not sampled proportionately but such that sufficient students were obtained in each stratum to generate prevalence estimates.

Two to three classes of students were selected randomly per grade level per school to obtain 17–25 completed questionnaires per grade level per school.

An Example from the United States

For a proposed study of cyberbullying among deaf and hard-of-hearing middle school students in the United States (Bauman & Antia, 2011), the population is all middle school students who have a documented hearing loss of any degree. The aim is to obtain a nationally representative sample, but there are challenges because students in various settings (residential schools, day schools for the deaf and hard of hearing, or inclusive public or private schools) vary systematically on such important characteristics as degree of hearing loss, communicate language (ASL or English), and academic achievement. Some schools may have only a very few eligible students. So, our sampling design must represent geographical areas as well as types of educational programs.

We proposed a two-stage sampling design with the first stage involving a probability sample of middle school programs. At the second stage, we will select a random sample of students within each selected program. Sampling weights will later be calculated.

We wish to obtain a sample such that population estimates have a margin of error plus or minus 5 percentage points at a 95% confidence level. If we simply selected a random sample, 400 students would be sufficient. However, since we are using a two-stage design, we estimated a design effect of approximately 1.2 and a response rate of 80% to calculate that we will select a sample of 600 students for the study. To do this, we will select two replicates of 45 programs of 470 in the sampling frame, and to select an average of 13–14 students per program in order to obtain an average of 10 or 11 completed surveys. We will stratify programs by type, with schools for the deaf comprising one stratum, and all others will constitute the other. In each stratum, the sample will be selected using equal probability systematic sampling after sorting the list by state and size. We anticipate that some of the 45 selected programs will not respond to the invitation; a similar program from the second replicate will be selected in that case.

SAMPLING IN VARIOUS RESEARCH PARADIGMS

There are differences in sampling strategies employed in qualitative, quantitative, and mixed methods studies that have yet to be discussed here, although Table 8.1 provides the basic information. This delay is deliberate: many sampling strategies can be useful in all paradigms, and the foregoing considerations are more basic. However, readers might appreciate assistance with some way to organize their thinking about the various sampling techniques, and so the excellent papers by Onwuegbuzie and Collins (2007), Teddlie and Yu (2007), and the chapters by Babbie (2008), Daniel (2012), and Henry (2009) were synthesized to create Table 8.1. Included are several probability sampling techniques, purposive sampling techniques, and mixed methods strategies. In general, probability or random sampling strategies allow the researcher to test hypotheses and estimate population parameters. These techniques greatly reduce bias. Non-probability sampling strategies are used when research is exploratory, seeking to generate hypotheses rather than test them. These strategies are also called purposive sampling because the selection of subjects is based on a specific purpose of the researcher. The researcher is not concerned with accurate description of population parameters, but is interested in depth of understanding. The non-probability strategies are generally less labor intensive to use and are often less expensive. Finally, mixed methods studies have their own sampling requirements; time sequence of the qualitative and quantitative component is an important consideration.

SUMMARY

In this chapter, the importance of sampling decisions has been emphasized. It is strongly recommended that cyberbullying researchers articulate their sampling decisions and their rationale for those decisions (Murray, Varnell, & Bittstein, 2004) so that peer reviewers and other researchers can take those factors into account when making their own decisions about the importance and applicability of the findings. In addition, it is important for cyberbullying researchers to take sampling into account when deciding whether to cite findings in subsequent articles. Exploratory studies are likely to have small and/or biased samples; findings will hopefully encourage other researchers to address the questions with larger more carefully designed sampling strategies. To advance a rigorous research program in cyberbullying, researchers must make sampling decisions—identifying the population, determining the most appropriate sampling design, determining necessary sample size—a more intentional and prominent feature of their work.

Notes

1 These terms, and other sampling strategies, are defined in Table 8.1, page 95.
2 Note that depending on the particular study design, the group might be classes or schools.

References

Babbie, E. (2008). *The basics of social research* (4th ed.). Belmont, CA: Thomson Wadsworth.

Bauman, S., & Antia, S. (2011, September 23). *An overlooked population: Bullying and cyberbullying among deaf and hard-of-hearing middle school students in the U.S.* Proposal submitted to the Institute of Education Sciences, U.S. Department of Education.

Bauman, S., & Tatum, T. (2009). Websites for young children: Gateway to social networking? *Professional School Counseling, 13*, 1–10. doi:10.5330/PSC.n.2010–13.1

Cross, D., Shaw, T., Hearn, L., Epstein, M., Monks, H., Lester, L., & Thomas, L. (2009). Australian Covert Bullying Prevalence Study (ACBPS). Canberra, Australia: Department of Education, Employment and Workplace Relations.

Daniel, J. (2012). *Sampling essentials*. Los Angeles: Sage.

Deming, W. E. (1950). *Some theory of sampling*. New York: Dover. doi:10.2307/1400756

Donner, A., Brown, K. S., & Brasher, P. (1990). A methodological review of non-therapeutic intervention trials employing cluster randomization, 1979–1989. *International Journal of Epidemiology, 19*, 795–800. doi:10.1093/ije/19.4.795

Faul, F., Erdfelder, E., Buchner, A., & Lang, A.-G. (2009). Statistical power analyses using G*Power 3.1: Tests for correlation and regression analyses. *Behavior Research Methods, 41*, 1149–1160. doi:10.3758/BRM.41.4.1149

Henry, G. T. (1990). *Practical sampling*. Newbury Park, CA: Sage.

Henry, G. T. (2009). Practical sampling. In L. Bickman & D. Rog, *The Sage handbook of applied social research methods* (2nd ed.) (pp. 77–105). Thousand Oaks, CA: Sage.

Hsieh, F. Y. (1988). Sample size formulae for intervention studies with the cluster as unit of randomization. *Statistics in Medicine, 7*, 1195–1201. doi:10.1002/sim.4780071113

Hutch, D. F., MacDonald, S.W.S., Hunter, M. A., Maitland, S. B., & Dixon, R. A. (2002). Sampling and generalisability in developmental research: Comparison of random and convenience samples of older adults. *International Journal of Behavioural Development, 26*, 345–359.

Kemper, E. A, Stringfield, S., & Teddlie, C. (2002). Mixed methods sampling strategies in social science research. In A. Tashakkori & C. B. Teddlie, *Handbook of mixed methods social and behavioral research* (pp. 273–296). Thousand Oaks, CA: Sage.

Kerlinger, F. N. (1986). *Foundations of behavioral research* (3rd ed.). New York: Holt Rinehart and Winston.

Knapp. T. R. (2007). Effective sample size: A crucial concept. In S. S. Sawilowsky (Ed.), *Real data analysis* (pp. 21–30). Charlotte, NC: Information Age Publishing.

Lohr, S. L. (1999). *Sampling: Design and analysis*. Pacific Grove, CA: Brooks/Cole.

Murray, D. M., Varnell, Sherri P., & Bittstein, J. L. (2004). Design and analysis of group-randomized trials: A review of recent methodological developments. *American Journal of Public Health, 94*, 423–432. doi:10.2105/AJPH.94.3.423

Muthén, L. K., & Muthén, B. (2002). How to use a Monte Carlo study to decide on sample size and determine power. *Structural Equation Modeling, 4*, 599–620. doi:10.1207/S15328007SEM0904_8

Onweugbuzie, A. J., & Collins, K.M.T. (2007). A typology of mixed method sampling designs in social science research. *The Qualitative Report, 12*, 281–316. doi:10.1177/1558689807299526

Parker, R. A., & Berman, N. G. (2003). Sample size: More than calculations. *The American Statistician, 57*, 166–170. doi:10.1198/0003130031919

Schlomer, G., Bauman, S., & Card, N. A. (2010). Best practice for managing missing data in counseling psychology. *Journal of Counseling Psychology, 57*, 1–10. doi:10.1037/a0018082

Short, J. C., Ketchen, D. J., & Palmer, T. B. (2002). The role of sampling in strategic management research on performance: A two-study analysis. *Journal of Management, 28*, 363–385. doi:10.1177/014920630202800306

Teddlie, C., & Yu, F. (2007). Mixed methods sampling: A typology with examples. *Journal of Mixed Methods Research*. doi:10.1177/2345678906292430

Thompson, S. K., & Collins, L. M. (2002). Adaptive sampling in research on risk-related behaviors. *Drug and Alcohol Dependence, 68*, S57–S67. doi:10.1016/S0376–8716(02)00215–6

9 Methods Used in Cyberbullying Research

Guadalupe Espinoza and Jaana Juvonen

Within less than a decade, a new field of cyberbullying research has emerged. This research is extending from mainly descriptive analyses to examining associations between cyberbullying and various risk and protective factors. Given the relatively early stage of research and need for descriptive data, it is not surprising that currently survey methods dominate the field. In addition to a handful of studies relying on other methods (e.g., interviews or focus groups), some novel methods are emerging as research questions are evolving. The goal of the current chapter is to review the advantages and potential disadvantages of the most utilized cyberbullying research methods to date. Additionally, we review methods that lend themselves well to the study of electronic forms of bullying that are currently underutilized.

When reviewing the methods used to study cyberbullying, it is imperative to keep in mind that as of today, most research assesses cyberbullying experiences (i.e., takes the perspective of the victim). There are only a few studies that investigate cyberbullying perpetration (e.g., Ang & Goh, 2010; Li, 2010; Raskauskas & Stoltz, 2007). When gathering data on experiences of cyberbullying (i.e., incidents encountered online or via text messages), self-reports are indeed suitable because they shed light on the subjective experiences of the targets of cyberbullying. However, to better understand the motives behind the perpetration of cyberbullying or the perceptions and (re)actions by witnesses, methods other than self-reports are needed. For example, interviews and focus groups may be particularly effective in asking about witnessing cyberbullying incidents and about bystander perceptions. Multiple methods are particularly helpful when trying to assess the robustness of findings. When considering the multiple perspectives or roles involved in cyberbullying, method selection is likely to be akin to decision making when conducting research on bullying that takes place outside of the electronic context with a few exceptions.

Compared to school bullying, a unique feature of cyberbullying is the multiple and distinct contexts in which youth are targeted or target others online. Therefore, the online environment in which cyberbullying occurs should also guide selection of methods. For example, methods to study private communication, such as e-mail and text messages, versus public online forums, including social network sites and chat rooms, are likely to vary. Whereas observational methods might lend themselves to the study of chat room interactions (Tynes, Reynolds, & Greenfield, 2004), observations may not be possible to examine cyberbullying in private online contexts. Thus, methods used in studies likely vary depending on *where* cyberbullying occurs.

We start the review of methods by describing the most frequently used quantitative methods. The discussion focuses mainly on web-based surveys and structured phone interviews. The comparisons between these two methods also highlights issues related to methods, such as the potential effects of sampling and consent procedures (see Chapter 8 for more information about sampling in a cyberbullying context). The complementary role of qualitative data obtained through interviews and focus groups is reviewed next. Methods that have been relied on by research on school-based bullying, such as daily assessments and longitudinal assessments, are discussed as ways to enhance the methodological rigor of research on cyberbullying. Additionally, the utility value of various data sources (specifically reliance on peers as informants) is discussed. Finally, novel observational and experimental methods used to study electronic communication are introduced as ways to broaden the methodological scope of research on cyberbullying.

QUANTITATIVE METHODS: SURVEYS

Until this point, cyberbullying research has predominately relied on self-reports. Most self-reports are conducted as surveys that enable investigators to describe cyberbullying in terms of location (text messages, social networking sites), types (e.g., threats, rumors), and rates of incidents. Survey methodology is an efficient method for answering questions about prevalence rates (e.g., In a typical month, how often do middle school students experience cyberbullying incidents?) and group differences (e.g., Are girls more likely to report teasing and name-calling of others online compared to boys?). At times, data are gathered also about perceptions, attitudes, opinions, and/or beliefs about cyberbullying (e.g., Mishna, Cook, Gadalla, Daciuk, & Solomon, 2010; Williams & Guerra, 2007). For example, Mishna and colleagues (2010) assessed the reasons (appearance, race, disability) why victims in middle and high school perceived that they were cyberbullied. Additionally, survey data lend themselves to correlational analyses (e.g., Are students who experience cyberbullying incidents more likely to report social anxiety compared to students with no cyberbullying experiences?). Researchers have not only relied on traditional paper-and-pencil surveys conducted within a classroom setting, but have also used web-based surveys with online and school-based samples (e.g., Hinduja & Patchin, 2008; Juvonen & Gross, 2008; Patchin & Hinduja, 2006; Williams & Guerra, 2007).

Although survey methods can be used to study cyberbullying much the same way they are used to examine other forms of bullying, web-based surveys seem particularly appropriate when studying electronic bullying. Research suggests there is little concern that students will provide different responses to online versus paper-and-pencil surveys. That is, there is little evidence of a mode effect in students' responses to web-based surveys (Denscombe, 2006). However, when surveys specifically ask about online behaviors, experiences, and general computer use, Carini and colleagues (2003) find that web-based surveys may be more appropriate than paper surveys. Moreover, when capitalizing on the electronic communication method and also recruiting samples from online communities, access to computers or other electronic communication devices is a nonissue. Moreover, when data are gathered electronically, they are available for analyses more quickly than paper-and-pencil survey data. The efficiency is particularly important inasmuch as electronic communication among teens changes rapidly (e.g., from Instant Messaging to social networking) and therefore the nature of cyberbullying changes its character (e.g., from private to public settings).

Most often, studies that rely on electronic surveys are conducted through a secure website by recruiting participants through popular websites, and participant responses are stored in electronic databases. A particular strength of online recruitment of participants is that it allows researchers to address specific questions aimed toward a particular demographic group, regardless of the investigators' geographic location. For example, a research team with local access to only predominately Caucasian youth have now the opportunity to study cyberbullying among ethnic minority adolescents by placing survey links on sites known to be frequented by youth from those ethnic groups. But web-based recruitment has also some (unexpected) disadvantages.

Although recruitment of participants through websites can secure high-user (and potentially at-risk) samples across wide geographic areas, the samples for cyberbullying studies are often less balanced than one might expect. For example, Patchin and Hinduja (2006) recruited 9–17-year-old youth for their study through the official website of a popular music artist well-regarded by the target age group, and over 30 percent of participants were over the age of 17 and were not included in the final analytic sample. Web-based recruitment tends to also result in female-dominated samples (e.g., Juvonen & Gross, 2008; Patchin & Hinduja, 2006). Such biases in recruitment likely affect the results and, moreover, the generalizability of the findings. Unbalanced or biased samples may also explain some discrepant findings in cyberbullying research. For example, currently prevalence estimates of cyberbullying victimization vary from about 7% (Smith et al, 2008) to 72% (Juvonen & Gross, 2008). We presume that such discrepant estimates not only reflect different samples, but are specifically related to recruitment methods, and accordingly consent issues of whether passive versus active consent is required. Not surprisingly, telephone surveys with parent consent (Smith et al., 2008) vs. anonymous web-based teen survey among mainly frequent Internet user groups with no parental consent (Juvonen & Gross, 2008) yield vastly different prevalence estimates of cyberbullying.

Divergent findings in the field may also be partly explained by the varying conceptual definitions guiding the measurement of cyberbullying (Tokunga, 2010).

Currently, researchers have not agreed upon one standard definition of cyberbullying, and there are several definitions used which restricts the ability to make cross-study comparisons. Hence, different sampling, consent procedures, recruitment strategies, and measurement tools embedded within particular methods are important issues to discuss in published articles.

Surveys via Telephone Interviews

A handful of cyberbullying studies have been conducted via telephone interviews (Mesch, 2009; Mitchell, Finkelhor, Wolak, Ybarra, & Turner, 2010; Wolak, Mitchell, & Finkelhor, 2007; Ybarra, 2004). One of the earliest studies published on cyberbullying (Ybarra, 2004) used data from the Youth Internet Safety Survey (YISS), a telephone survey of regular Internet users between the ages of 10 and 17 years old. Using a national probability design, the sample of households was identified with a child between the ages of 9 and 18. For families meeting the eligibility criteria (e.g., ages 10–17, used the Internet at least six times in the last six months, English speaking), parents were asked to consent for their child to be interviewed on the phone regarding their involvement in and experiences with what the authors called "Internet harassment." Similar methods have been used to interview youth on the phone about parent strategies to monitor their children's Internet activities (Mesch, 2009). Low response rates for such studies are not surprising and need to be discussed in the context of (the generalizability of) the findings.

One of the strengths of large telephone interviews is the ability to obtain access to a nationally representative sample of households with a particular age youth. Because parental permission is required for the phone interview of the youth, parent demographic data (e.g., household education and income) are available from these studies providing important background information. Moreover, gathering data from parents allows researchers to obtain reliable information about the youth respondents (e.g., gender, ethnicity) compared to anonymous web-based surveys with samples recruited online where personal characteristics (e.g., age, sexual orientation) can be misidentified (Hafner, 2001). Yet the procedure of obtaining parental permission and interviewing youth on the phone may result in samples that are not representative of high frequency Internet youth most at risk for cyberbullying.

In summary, cyberbullying research most commonly relies on anonymous surveys. Although online survey samples are typically much larger, geographically wider, and possibly ethnically more diverse than those that are school based, they are not necessarily balanced in terms of gender or age, and the representativeness of the samples is difficult to assess. In contrast, national telephone surveys yield better age-matched samples. However, the low response rates may reflect the effects of parental consent procedures or a youth's reluctance to respond on the phone. Systematic comparisons across methods are needed to better understand the limitations of different forms of surveys. Moreover, such comparisons can help us resolve discrepant findings (e.g., regarding prevalence rates of cyberbullying).

QUALITATIVE METHODS: INTERVIEWS AND FOCUS GROUPS

In addition to quantitative survey research, cyberbullying research also relies on qualitative methods, primarily interviews and focus groups (e.g., Agaston, Kowalski, & Limber, 2007; Mishna, Saini, & Solomon, 2009; Vandebosch & Van Cleemput, 2008). Qualitative methods are well suited for addressing new topics because these methods give emphasis to the experiences, meanings, and views of participants and allows them to provide comprehensive summaries of particular events. Therefore, these methods are valuable at this point to study cyberbullying. In one illustrative study, Vandebosch and Van Cleemput (2008) conducted 53 focus groups among students from 10 to 18 years old in order to understand their perceptions and definitions of cyberbullying. The data suggest that, for the large part, students used similar criteria to define cyberbullying that has been established for measuring cyberbullying via surveys. Interestingly, the findings also revealed that youth who admitted to targeting others online would target not only those weaker than them, as often assumed, but also those they considered equal in power (e.g., former friends). Thus, data from focus groups allow us not only to validate some survey questions, but also to shed new light on the possible similarities and differences between the power dynamics of offline and online bullying.

As Mishna and colleagues (2009) have highlighted, qualitative studies allow researchers to discover important nuances of cyberbullying that might be more difficult to capture with quantitative data. For example, it is often assumed that cyberbullying incidents do not occur at school, but in focus groups students described how they often send text messages to each other at school by hiding their phones under desks (even though cell phones are not permitted at school) or by using them in bathrooms (Mishna et al., 2009).

Qualitative methods are also ideal in providing an in-depth examination of particular issues. For example, Parris, Varjas, Meyers, and Cutts (2012) conducted semi-structured interviews among 20 high school students to examine the specific ways that students report coping with online incidents and to identify useful coping mechanisms to prevent cyberbullying. These types of questions would be difficult to study with survey questions given that little is known about the strategies used by youth (e.g., deleting online accounts or blocking phone numbers). Chapter 17 provides a more in-depth discussion of the qualitative studies conducted on cyberbullying and the advantages and disadvantages of this methodology.

UNDERUTILIZED METHODS

Given the nascent phase of cyberbullying research, there are several methods that remain either underutilized or all together unused. We expect that such methods may be worth considering, especially in light of influential research on school-based bullying that relied on natural observations or experimental methods (Craig & Pepler, 1998; Nesdale & Scarlett, 2004; Ojala & Nesdale, 2004; Pepler & Craig, 1995). We first review school-based methods that have not been used in cyberbullying research, but that have been informative in research on school bullying. As illustrative examples, we then review pioneering studies on electronic communication highlighting how novel observational and experimental methods may lend themselves to research on cyberbullying.

Methods and Lessons Learned from School-Based Bullying

One of the debated questions regarding cyberbullying is the extent of overlap with school-based bullying (e.g., Juvonen & Gross, 2008; Ybarra, Diener-West, & Leaf, 2007). Related to this substantive research question, we can ask whether we could, and should, rely on the same methods to study cyberbullying as we have utilized to investigate school bullying. In particular, daily diary methods and longitudinal research are particularly applicable. In addition, given the (over) reliance on self-reports in research on cyberbullying, it would be valuable to consider how peers can be used as informants to learn more about electronic forms of bullying.

Daily assessments. Completing repeated assessment of daily events and feelings, researchers can capture life as it is lived (Bolger, Davis, & Rafaeli, 2003). By asking youth to report on specific experiences, feelings, and behaviors on a daily basis, this reduces the time elapsed between the encounter and their account of the experience, providing more reliable and valid estimates than typical survey questions. Also, daily methods allow estimation of the associations between variables of interest at the within-subjects (individual) level. For example, using the average level of depressed mood of a person as a baseline, this method allows us to test whether youth are more likely to report depressive symptoms on the same day when they were bullied online. Thus, daily-level analyses allow researchers to be more confident that associations are not a result of unmeasured individual differences, because responses are compared within individuals over time.

In spite of the strengths of the daily report methodology, it is unutilized in research on cyberbullying and also remains infrequently used in research on school-based bullying. One of the few studies relying on four paper-and-pencil daily reports across five days showed that negative peer experiences at school (e.g., being teased by another kid) were associated with negative changes in mood and self-esteem, which, in turn, were associated with aversive interactions with parents later during the same day (Lehman & Repetti, 2007). Examining both personally experienced and witnessed incidents of bullying, Nishina and Juvonen (2005), in turn, found that on days when youth reported being bullied at school, they reported higher levels of anger and anxiety. Moreover, youth also reported heightened levels of anxiety and school dislike on days when they merely witnessed bullying in school. Although both of these studies utilized paper-and-pencil questionnaires, short daily reports could also be collected via electronic methods such as small, handheld computers (Henker, Whalen, Jamner, & Delfino, 2002) or through cell phone texting. Such electronic methods would be particularly fitting to study the specific incidents of cyberbullying and daily well-being.

Longitudinal methods. Whereas daily diaries can provide critical information about the daily functioning of youth, longer-term longitudinal studies examining the consequences of cyberbullying are also needed. Given the lack of longitudinal data (see Werner, Bumpus, & Rock, 2009, for an exception), we do not know whether youth repeatedly bully others or are bullied online, or whether the online context facilitates more temporary or dynamic roles. Although research on school-based bullying suggests that only a small percentage of students who bully others continue to harass their peers (Olweus, 1993), and only a small proportion of victims continue to get bullied (e.g., Nylund, Bellmore, Nishina, & Graham, 2007), continued involvement in bullying is related with a range of psychosocial difficulties (Olweus, 1993). Because cyberbullying is even more likely to remain undetected than school-based bullying because adults are not privy to online interactions among youth (e.g., Juvonen & Gross, 2008; Li, 2007), victims of electronic forms of bullying are likely to continue to suffer in silence. Hence, besides being able to compare electronic bullying to other forms of peer maltreatment, there are specific reasons and valid concerns to conduct follow-up studies to examine the duration, intensity, and possible long-term consequences of continued electronic bullying.

Methodologically, longer-term longitudinal research on cyberbullying does not necessarily differ from other types of longitudinal studies. Participants need to be assessed repeatedly across a designated period (one or more years). Changing technology and the varying popularity of specific communication technologies, however, pose specific challenges on research on cyberbullying. That is, given the rapid advancements in electronic communication, we do not necessarily know whether in the future, youth will continue to use social networking sites or text via their cell phones. Therefore, studies that target specific types of technologies or online contexts need to be well designed to accommodate changes in communication methods across years.

Reliance on peers as informants. To extend beyond self-reported data, other informants are also needed. Peer data (mainly nominations) have been used extensively in school bullying research (e.g., Dijkstra, Lindenberg, & Veenstra, 2008; Juvonen, Graham, & Schuster, 2003) and have allowed us to reliably identify students who bully and those who are victimized to study the correlates of each. In research on cyberbullying, peers may be particularly important informants in providing insights from the perspective of a bystander. Additionally, data from peers who observe online incidents might be helpful in identifying those who cyberbully others. Thus far, cyberbullies have been identified by self-reports that are prone to social desirability biases resulting in underreporting (e.g., Craig, Pepler, & Atlas, 2000). Thus, the inclusion of data sources other than self-report would provide both methodological rigor as well as enrich our understanding of cyberbullying from multiple perspectives (e.g., that of a witness).

Novel Methods to Study Electronic Communication

In addition to relying on methods proven to be useful in research on school-based bullying, research on cyberbullying can also benefit from methods that have been specifically designed to study electronic communication. Below we review a few illustrative studies on topics relevant to cyberbullying that relied on novel observational and experimental methods.

Observational methods. Observational methods may be particularly well suited for studies that examine incidents of cyberbullying in public online contexts. Although not designed to examine cyberbullying per se, one study of adolescents' racial and ethnic discourse in online chat rooms demonstrated the ways in which negative comments about race or ethnicity were not uncommon experiences (Tynes, Reynolds, & Greenfield, 2004). The authors observed communication of monitored and unmonitored teen chat rooms (for about 30 minutes spanning across the day from 12 to 9 p.m.). The chat room discussions observed were transported into a transcript document, and the qualitative data were then quantified. For example, frequency counts of racial references pertaining to others, including direct negative comments regarding racial or ethnic groups, were calculated. Although this method is limited to public domain, it allows researchers to gain insights into online interactions that can give insights about the nature of public forms of electronic harassment.

Other observational research examining adolescents' and young adults' online interactions and behaviors have analyzed information presented on public profiles available through social networking sites (e.g., Mikami, Szwedo, Allen, Evans, & Hare, 2010; Moreno et al., 2009). To date, only one study has used observational methods to specifically study cyberbullying (Mishna, McLuckie, & Saini, 2009a). Mishna and colleagues (2009a) examined the anonymous posts made to a national phone and web counseling service to understand participants' (ages 6–24 years old) online interactions and experiences with cyber abuse (cyber abuse included bullying, stalking, sexual solicitation, and exposure to pornography). From the original 35,000 posts made to the site, 346 posts were extracted after using computer search functions to identify posts related to online relationships and cyber abuse. The study highlighted how most youth will not disclose to their parents that they have been cyberbullied, even if they are frightened. The authors noted that a large limitation of this method is the lack of participant demographic information such as gender and ethnicity. Consequently, the representativeness of the sample remains unknown.

Recent studies on adolescent use of social networking sites also provide interesting examples of how publicly available data could be used to study issues relevant to cyberbullying. For example, Mikami and colleagues (2010) assessed levels of support received from friends by coding the 20 most recent posts left on the participants' profile page (on Facebook or Myspace). Results showed that adolescents with a greater number of friends on their social network site had more positive friend support (as measured by coding posts). This type of method could be used specifically to examine the role of social support for cyberbullying. By relying on a slightly different approach, Salimkhan, Manago, and Greenfield (2010), in turn, asked young adults to give a "tour" of their Myspace profiles. By relying on this novel interview method guided by their social networking profile, the researchers gained important insights about the construction of online identities. Similar methods could be adopted to study how youth react to mean or rude comments received on their own or other's social networking profiles.

Experimental methods. Experiments have several methodological strengths. For example, experiments not only enable researchers to examine a question under most controlled conditions but also allow testing for causal effects. An experimental study conducted by Smith and Williams (2004) to examine the effects of ostracism via cell phones underscores the potential value of such methods for the study of cyberbullying. After completing a pre-experiment survey, 40 undergraduate students were told they would be interacting via text message with two other participants; the other two participants were confederates. In one of the experiment manipulations, some participants were included in text message exchanges for eight minutes while the participants in the "exclusion" condition did not receive responses to any of their text messages. At the end of the text message conversation, all participants completed a post-experiment survey that assessed a set of fundamental needs such as belonging. Consistent with the predictions, the results showed that ostracized individuals reported lower levels of belonging, control, self-esteem, and meaningful existence. Thus, the brief experimental manipulation revealed that even mere exclusions from text message conversations can inflict psychological harm. This finding is an important one because much of the correlational research linking emotional distress and online experiences can be interpreted in two ways: distressed individuals encounter negative online incidents (maybe because they interpret them more negatively than others) as opposed to online experiences causing distress. Future cyberbullying research that relies on experimental methods that allows researchers to manipulate particular variables to examine causal effects will certainly add methodological rigor to the area of cyberbullying.

CONCLUSIONS

Although thus far the research questions have been largely descriptive and hence suitable for survey methods, the field of cyberbullying research is addressing increasingly challenging questions that require different methods. For example, as the opinions, perspectives, and roles of adults (i.e., parents, school personnel) are increasingly being examined in relation to cyberbullying (e.g., Slovak & Singer, 2011), survey methods may only provide us a limited amount of additional information. Moreover, novel or modified research methods may develop as emerging research focuses on cyberbullying incidents that occur among potential at-risk groups (e.g., children with ADHD or Asperger's Syndrome) that have previously been unexamined (e.g., Kowlaski & Fedina, 2011; Popovic-Citic, Djuric, & Cvetkovic, 2011).

A diverse use of survey methodologies and overall diversity in the cyberbullying methods utilized will be particularly beneficial because research findings stemming from various methods will help us better understand how robust certain findings are. Related to this, due to the short history of the field, no cyberbullying meta-analysis has been conducted. Within any particular area of cyberbullying research, there are not yet enough studies to carry out the appropriate meta-analysis techniques. Thus, far, only a meta-synthesis that summarized the existing literature in cyberbullying victimization research has been conducted (Tokunga, 2010). A total of 25 articles were used in the meta-synthesis based on selection criteria established by the author. The meta-synthesis includes a summary of the existing research of cyberbullying and demographic factors such as prevalence rates, age, gender, and disturbances (e.g., psychosocial problems) associated with victimization. As cyberbullying research continues to develop and grow and more studies are published in academic journals, we are moving closer toward expanding from meta-synthesis to conducting meta-analysis studies. In addition, as more interventions and programs are developed to address cyberbullying, it will become particularly imperative to have a strong body of research and meta-analyses that can inform evidence-based interventions.

Based on the review of the methods used thus far and those that are readily available, it is clear that reliance on a wide range of methods (and informants other than self) will enrich research and the insights that can be gained from studies on cyberbullying. We predict that significant advances in the range of methods use to study cyberbullying will take place within the next few years.

References

Agaston, P. W., Kowalski, R., & Limber, S. (2007). Students' perspectives on cyberbullying. *Journal of Adolescent Health, 41*, 59–60. doi:10.1016/j.jadohealth.2007.09.003

Ang, R. P., & Goh, D. H. (2010). Cyberbullying among adolescents: The role of affective and cognitive empathy, and gender. *Child Psychiatry and Human Development, 41*, 387–397. doi:10.1007/s10578–010–0176–3

Bolger, N., Davis, A., & Rafaeli, E. (2003). Diary methods: Capturing life as it is lived. *Annual Reviews in Psychology, 54*, 579–616. doi:10.1146/annurev.psych.54.101601.145030

Craig, W. M., & Pepler, D. J. (1998). Observations of bullying and victimization in the school yard. *Canadian Journal of School Psychology, 13*(2), 41–59. doi:10.1177/082957359801300205

Craig, W. M., Pepler, D., & Atlas, R. (2000). Observations of bullying in the playground and in the classroom. *School Psychology International, 21*(1), 22–36. doi:10.1177/082957359801300205

Denscombe, M. (2006). Web-based questionnaires and the mode effect: An evaluation based on completion rates and data contents of near-identical questionnaires delivered in different modes. *Social Science Computer Review, 24*(2), 246–254. doi:10.1177/0894439305284522

Dijkstra, J. K., Lindenberg, S., & Veenstra, R. (2008). Beyond the class norm: Bullying behavior of popular adolescents and its relation to peer acceptance and rejection. *Journal of Abnormal Child Psychology, 36*, 1289–1299. doi:10.1007/s10802-008-9251-7

Hafner, K. (2001). *The well: A story of love, death & real life in the seminal online community*. New York: Carrol and Graf.

Henker, B., Whalen, C. K., Jamner, L. D., & Delfino, R. J. (2002). Anxiety, affect, and activity in teenagers: Monitoring daily life with electronic diaries. *Journal of the American Academy of Child and Adolescent Psychiatry, 41*(6), 660–670.

Hinduja, S., & Parchin, J. W. (2008). Cyberbullying: An exploratory analysis of factors related to offending and victimization. *Deviant Behavior, 29*, 129–156. doi:10.1080/01639620701457816

Juvonen, J., Graham, S., & Schuster, M. A. (2003). Bullying among young adolescents: The strong, the weak and the troubled. *Pediatrics, 112*, 1231–1237. doi:10.1542/peds.112.6.1231

Juvonen, J., & Gross, E. F. (2008). Extending the school grounds? Bullying experiences in cyberspace. *Journal of School Health, 78*(9), 496–505. doi:10.1111/j.1746-1561.2008.00335.x

Kowalsi, R. M., & Fedina, C. (2011). Cyberbullying in ADHD and Asperger Syndrome populations. *Research in Autism Spectrum Disorders, 5*(3), 1201–1208. doi:10.1016/j.rasd.2011.01.007

Lehman, B. J., & Repetti, R. L. (2007). Bad days don't end when the school bell rings: The lingering effects of negative school events on children's mood, self-esteem, and perceptions of parent-child interaction. *Social Development, 16*, 596–618. doi:10.1111/j.1467–9507.2007.00398.x

Li, Q. (2007). New bottle but old wine: A research of cyberbullying in schools. *Computers in Human Behavior, 23*, 1777–1791. doi: 10.1016/j.chb.2005.10.00

Li, Q. (2010). Cyberbullying in high schools: A study of students' behaviors and beliefs about this new phenomenon. *Journal of Aggression, Maltreatment and Trauma, 19*, 372–392. doi:10.1080/10926771003788979

Mesch, G. S. (2009). Parental mediation, online activities, and cyberbullying. *CyberPsychology & Behavior, 12*(4), 387–393. doi:10.1089/cpb.2009.0068

Mikami, A. Y., Szwedo, D. E., Allen, J. P., Evans, M. A., & Hare, A. L. (2010). Adolescent peer relationships and behavior problems predict young adults' communication on social networking websites. *Developmental Psychology, 46*(1), 46–56. doi:10.1037/a0017420

Mishna, F., Cook, C., Gadalla, T., Daciuk, J., & Solomon, S. (2010). Cyberbullying behaviors among middle and high school students. *American Journal of Orthopsychiatry, 80*(3), 362–374. doi:10.1111/j.1939–0025.2010.01040.x

Mishna, F., McLuckie, A., & Saini, M. (2009a). Real-world dangers in an online reality: A qualitative study examining online relationships and cyber abuse. *Social Work Research, 33*(2), 107–118.

Mishna, F., Saini, M., & Solomon, S. (2009b). Ongoing and online: Children and youth's perceptions of cyberbullying. *Children and Youth Services Review, 31*(12), 1222–1228. doi:10.1016/j.childyouth.2009.05.004

Mitchell, K. J., Finkelhor, D., Wolak, J., Ybarra, M. L., & Turner, H. (2010). Youth Internet victimization in a broader victimization context. *Journal of Adolescent Health, 42*(2), 128–134. doi:10.1016/j.jadohealth.2010.06.009

Moreno, M. A., VanderStoep, A., Parks, M. R., Zimmerman, F. J., Kurth, A., & Christakis, D. A. (2009). Reducing at-risk adolescents' displays of risk behavior on a social networking web site. *Archives of Pediatrics and Adolescent Medicine, 163*(1), 35–41.

Nesdale, D., & Scarlett, M. (2004). Effects of group and situational factors on pre-adolescent children's attitudes to school bullying. *International Journal of Behavioral Development, 28*(5), 428–434. doi:10.1080/01650250444000144

Nishina, A., & Juvonen, J. (2005). Daily reports of witnessing and experiencing peer harassment in middle school. *Child Development, 76*(2), 435–450. doi:10.1111/j.1467–8624.2005.00855.x

Nylund, K., Bellmore, A., Nishina, A., & Graham, S. (2007). Subtypes, severity, and structural stability of peer victimization: What does latent class analysis say? *Child Development, 78*(6), 1706–1722. doi:10.1111/j.1467–8624.2007.01097.x

Ojala, K., & Nesdale, D. (2004). Bullying and social identity: The effects of group norms and distinctiveness threat on attitudes towards bullying. *British Journal of Developmental Psychology, 22*(1), 19–35. doi:10.1348/026151004772901096

Olweus, D. (1993). *Bullying at school.* Cambridge, MA: Blackwell.

Parris, L., Varjas, K., Meyers, J., & Cutts, H. (2012). High school students' perceptions of coping with cyberbullying. *Youth and Society, 44*(2), 284–306. doi:10.1177/0044118X1139888

Patchin, J. W., & Hinduja, S. (2006). Bullies move beyond the schoolyard: A preliminary look at cyberbullying. *Youth Violence and Juvenile Justice, 4*(2), 148–169. doi:10.1177/1541204006286288

Pepler, D. J., & Craig, W. M. (1995). A peek behind the fence: Naturalistic observations of aggressive children with remote audiovisual recording. *Developmental Psychology, 31*(4), 548–553.

Popovic-Citic, Djuric, & Cvetkovic, V. (2011). The prevalence of cyberbullying among adolescents: A case study of middle schools in Serbia. *School Psychology International,* 1–13. doi:10.1177/0143034311401700

Raskauskas, J., & Stoltz, A. D. (2007). Involvement in traditional and electronic bullying among adolescents. *Developmental Psychology, 43*(3), 564–575. doi:10.1037/0012-1649.43.3.564

Salimkhan, G., Manago, A., & Greenfield, P. (2010). The construction of the virtual self on MySpace. *Cyberpsychology: Journal of Psychosocial Research on Cyberspace, 4*(1), article 1.

Slovak, K., & Singer, J. B. (2011). School social worker's perceptions of cyberbullying. *Children and Schools, 33*(1), 5–16.

Smith, A., & Williams, K. D. (2004). R U there? Ostracism by cell phone text messages. *Group Dynamics: Theory, Research and Practice, 8*(4), 291–301. doi:10.1037/1089-2699.8.4.291

Smith, P. K., Mahdavi, S., Carvalho, M., Fisher, S., Russell, S., & Tippett, N. (2008). Cyberbullying: Its nature and impact in secondary school pupils. *Child Psychology and Psychiatry, 49*(4), 376–385. doi:10.1111/j.1469–7610.2007.01846

Tokunga, R. S. (2010). Following you home from school: A critical review and synthesis of research on cyberbullying victimization. *Computers in Human Behavior, 26*, 277–287. doi:10.1016/j.chb.2009.11.014

Tynes, B., Reynolds, L., & Greenfield, P. M. (2004). Adolescence, race, and ethnicity on the Internet: A comparison of discourse in monitored vs. unmonitored chat rooms. *Applied Developmental Psychology, 25*, 667–684. doi:10.1016/j.appdev.2004.09.003

Vandebosch, H., & Van Cleemput, K. V. (2008). Defining cyberbullying: A qualitative research into the perceptions of youngsters. *CyberPsychology and Behavior, 11*(4), 499–503. doi:10.1089/cpb.2007.0042

Werner, N. E., Bumpus, M. F., & Rock, D. (2010). Involvement in Internet aggression during early adolescence. *Journal of Youth and Adolescence, 39*, 607–619. doi:10.1007/s10964–009–9419–7

Williams, K. R., & Guerra, N. G. (2007). Prevalence and predictors of Internet bullying. *Journal of Adolescent Health, 41*, 14–21. doi:10.1016/j.jadohealth.2007.08.018

Wolak, J., Mitchell, K. J., & Finkelhor, D. (2007). Does online harassment constitute bullying? An exploration of online harassment by known peers and online-only contacts. *Journal of Adolescent Health, 41*, 51–58. doi:10.1016/j.jadohealth.2007.08.019

Ybarra, M. L. (2004). Linkages between depressive symptomatology and Internet harassment among young regular Internet users. *CyberPsychology and Behavior, 7*(2), 247–257. doi:10.1089/109493104323024500

Ybarra, M. L., Diener-West, M., & Leaf, P. J. (2007). Examining the overlap in Internet harassment and school bullying: Implications for school intervention. *Journal of Adolescent Health, 41*, 42–50. doi:10.1016/j.jadohealth.2007.09.00

10 Moving beyond Tradition and Convenience

Suggestions for Useful Methods for Cyberbullying Research

Marion K. Underwood and Noel A. Card

Studying cyberbullying well requires that investigators use both the best data collection and analysis methods from existing research on more traditional bullying, but also be creative in devising new methods to do justice to the complexity of bullying via online communication. In this chapter, we make a series of methodological recommendations for potential best practices for this emerging and rapidly growing field. First, the chapter addresses a central issue regarding data collection. To assess cyberbullying, must we rely so heavily on self-report questionnaires on which youth are asked to report on their own behavior, or could we also use the technology to access electronic communication directly to code the social process as it unfolds? Second, the chapter explores whether cyberbullying should be conceived of as a categorical variable (is a young person a cyberbully or not?) or a continuous variable (to what degree does a young person engage in cyberbullying?). Third, the chapter addresses the value of variable-centered versus person-centered analyses. Fourth, the chapter addresses what the units of analysis could and perhaps should be in cyberbullying research. Last, the chapter explores the potential benefits and challenges in conducting longitudinal research on cyberbullying. Comprehensive reviews of these complex issues are beyond the scope of this chapter. The following sections will analyze specific issues, cite relevant examples, and make suggestions for best practices as this field moves forward. Because several of the methods described have not yet been widely used in cyberbullying research, and thus do not have the wide recognition and acceptance associated with the term "best practice," we use the term in an aspirational sense.

ASSESSING CYBERBULLYING WITH SELF-REPORT SURVEYS VERSUS OBSERVATIONAL METHODS

Most of the major investigations of cyberbullying to date rely on self-report surveys on which youth are asked whether they engage in mean behaviors online or in text messaging (e.g., Hinduja & Patchin, 2009; Kowalski & Limber, 2007; Lenhart, 2007; Lenhart, Ling, Campbell, & Purcell, 2010; Nansel et al., 2001; Ybarra & Mitchell, 2007). Self-report measures of cyberbullying are of some value in that they can be used to measure experiences across multiple contexts and because they capture the perspective of the aggressors or victims themselves, which might be most relevant for some outcomes. Experiences that are neither observable by others nor reported to others, which may be particularly likely in cyberbullying, can be identified by this method. However, self-report measures may be selected by some investigators because they are cost effective, can be administered easily to numerous individuals either in person or online, and yield data that do not require extensive coding. The researcher's choice of methodology should be based on sound scientific principles rather than on convenience. Studies comparing self, peer, and teacher reports of bullying and victimization have found only modest correlations; experts (e.g., Smith, 2004) have urged researchers to include multiple informants to increase data quality. The field of cyberbullying research, in particular, will benefit from careful consideration of methodological options so that innovative and rigorous studies will advance understanding of this phenomenon.

There are reasons to question the validity of self-reports of cyberbullying. Youth may underreport their own cyberbullying behavior out of a desire to present themselves in a positive light, fear of adults taking away their electronic devices, not viewing their negative online behaviors as bullying, or a true lack of awareness of the extent to which they harass others online. Some youth may overreport their cyberbullying behavior to seem cool, tough, and savvy about technology. Few studies to date have examined the relation between self-reports of cyberbullying and any other form of assessment. However, evidence for the validity of self-reports of traditional aggression and bullying may be relevant to this question. Even in these relatively more well-developed research literatures, few investigations have included both self-reports of aggression and other types of assessments. The evidence available does not promote much faith in the validity of self-reports of bullying/cyberbullying behavior.

Researchers studying aggression, both physical and social, have long questioned whether self-reports are valid assessments (Lagerspetz, Björkqvist, & Peltonon, 1988; Little, Brauner, Jones, Nock, & Hawley, 2003; Pakaslahti & Keltikangas-Jarvinen, 2000). In a study with 11–12-year-olds in Finland, correlations between self and peer ratings of aggression were modest for both direct aggression for girls ($r = .29$ for girls but $r = .63$ for boys) and indirect aggression for both genders ($r = .23$ for girls and $r = .24$ for boys); Lagerspetz et al., 1988). Research with 5th–10th graders in Germany also found modest correlations between self-reports and peer nominations for overt ($r = .31$) and relational aggression ($r = .21$, Little et al., 2003). A large study with adolescents in Finland found even lower correlations between self and peer ratings on direct ($r = .15$) and indirect ($r = .10$) aggression (Pakaslahti & Keltikangas-Jarvinen, 2000). Overall, correlations between self and peer assessments of aggression are modest, especially for indirect aggression, which is probably more similar to cyberbullying than physical aggression in that both indirect aggression and cyberbullying are more subtle. The correlations above suggest that self-reports of indirect aggression account for between 1 and 6% of the variance in peer reports.

Evidence for the validity of self-reports of bullying is also weak. Experts have noted that the preponderance of the research evidence on bullying rests on anonymous self-report questionnaires for which validity has not been clearly established (Cornell & Brockenbrough, 2004; Cornell, Sheras, & Cole, 2006). The most widely used questionnaire to assess bullying is the Olweus Bully/Victim Questionnaire (BVQ; Olweus, 1996, 2002). One of the few studies to assess inter-rater agreement on the BVQ found only a weak correlation between self-reported bullying and peer nominations for bullying ($r = .12$; Lee & Cornell, 2010). Pellegrini (2001) used several methods to assess victimization (peer nomination, self-report on rating scales, observations, and diary) and found that although peer reports were significantly correlated with the three other measures (.21 to .32), and self-report and diary entries were also significantly correlated (.34), direct observation was not significantly correlated with either self-report or diary entries. In another study investigating agreement among different reporters of bullying and victimization, Branson and Cornell (2009) found that peer-reported bullying was more strongly related to disciplinary violations (.52) than was self-reported bullying (.28).

One challenge in assessing cyberbullying is that it is not clear what should be the criteria for the validity of self-report measures. By definition, cyberbullying occurs in cyberspace or via text messaging, across different online formats, and with various groups of peers who could be from all over the world. Whereas research on traditional aggression and bullying can examine correspondence between self-reports and reports of peers at school, who the peer group might be for research on cyberbullying is less clear. Still, given that most youth report that they know those who are bullying them online (Hinduja & Patchin, 2009; Internet Safety Technical Task Force, 2008), peer reports may currently be more feasible than we think. And, there may be other options for validating self-report assessments of cyberbullying.

Cyberbullying takes place via mediated communication, either online or via text messaging. Many of these technologies allow direct access to the content of electronic communication. Thus, it should be possible to observe some cyberbullying directly. Only a few studies to date have taken advantage of the technology to observe the content of online communication. One study examined themes of identity presentation and sexual exploration by coding adolescents' communication in monitored and unmonitored chat rooms (Subrahmanyam, Smahel, & Greenfield, 2006). Another study invited 10 college students to give investigators guided tours of their Myspace profile wall and photograph pages and coded the construction of social identity (Salimkhan, Manago, & Greenfield, 2010). In an ongoing longitudinal study of origins and outcomes of social aggression, participants were given BlackBerry devices prior to the 9th grade, configured to capture all of their text messaging and e-mail on the devices (Underwood, Rosen, More, Ehrenreich, & Gentsch, 2012). The content of all electronic communication will be gathered throughout the students' four years of high school. Text messaging is by far the most prevalent form of communication on the devices; over half a million text messages sent to and from 200 participants pour into the archive each month.

Direct observation of cyberbullying using technology to access content poses its own set of challenges. First, care must be taken to assure that adolescents are communicating openly even though they are being observed. The evidence so far is encouraging. In the BlackBerry study, a two-day sample of text messaging had 7% of utterances with sexual themes and 7% with profane language, rates similar to those found in the study of unmonitored chat rooms in which anonymous online communication was measured, and youth had no idea they were being observed (Subrahmanyam et al., 2006). Second, directly observing online communication raises ethical challenges related to informed consent and responding to communication about criminal activity, abuse, and suicidality (for discussions of these, see Chapter 12, this volume, and Underwood et al., 2012). Third, definitional issues are just as challenging in observational as in any other type of study; coding systems must be based on operational definitions of cyberbullying (see Chapters 2, 3, and 4, this volume, for discussion of the complex definitional issues). Still, surmounting these challenges is worthwhile, because studying the actual content of online communication could reveal much about the frequency and social processes by which cyberbullying unfolds. As eloquently stated by Greenfield and Yan (2006), studying the content of electronic communication could provide "a window into the secret world of adolescent peer culture" (p.392).

As research of cyberbullying surges forward, few investigators may have both the financial resources to gather content data and the patience for doing the time-consuming coding. What might be helpful are formative studies that include both self-report and other types of assessments of cyberbullying, to help develop the best questionnaires possible. In the BlackBerry study above, so far, correlations between self-reports and observations of electronic communication are not strong. For example, the correlation is weak between self-reports of the simple frequency of text messaging and actual usage measured by electronic billing records ($r = .14$, Underwood et al., 2012). Examining correlations between self-reports and observational assessments of cyberbullying could guide the development of even better survey instruments (see Section V, this volume). Despite their obvious limitations, self-report instruments have much to offer, and specific strategies can increase their validity. For example, evidence suggests that the validity of survey responses is increased by including items asking youth if they are telling the truth and paying attention, then eliminating those participants who report that they are responding inaccurately (Cornell, Klein, Konold, & Huang, 2011). The principles offered in this volume for resolving definitional issues and developing sound instruments will result in more valid methods for both questionnaire and observational studies.

CYBERBULLYING AS A CATEGORICAL VERSUS CONTINUOUS VARIABLE

Whether data on cyberbullying are assessed by questionnaires or by observations or other types of assessment, one basic issue that must be considered is whether cyberbullying is best considered as a categorical or a continuous variable. This choice may be based on both conceptual and statistical grounds and may be motivated by goals of scholars from different disciplines. For example, experts from the field of public health may be most interested in the prevalence of adolescents who have engaged in cyberbullying with varying frequency, whereas investigators who are developmental psychopathologists may seek to examine the phenomenon more closely, to understand how cyberbullying unfolds, whether the behavior is normative at low levels yet problematic for those who do it at extremely high rates, and how it confers risk for maladjustment on particular individuals. Prevention and intervention scientists may want to understand what types of individual characteristics or relationships predict who will engage in cyberbullying to varying degrees, to prevent some from becoming extreme in their online harassment. The decision to consider cyberbullying to be a categorical variable or a continuous dimension has far-reaching consequences, for the design of research but also for how we conceive of youth who engage in cyberbullying. If we conceive of cyberbullies and cybervictims as types of people, it is all too easy to assume that these are invariant behaviors that cannot be changed. Referring to cyberbullies and cybervictims as types of people rather than discussing the behavior of cyberbullying could also be stigmatizing to youth who may only occasionally engage in negative behaviors online.

If investigators perceive cyberbullying as a personality trait, as a proclivity toward this behavior across contexts and time, then classifying individuals as cyberbullies or not may be more sensible. This approach has often been taken in research on traditional bullying, beginning with the seminal work by Olweus (1978, 1993) in which adolescents were categorized as bullies and whipping boys (i.e., victims) and continuing with later studies. For example, Nansel et al. (2001) used data from the World Health Organization Health Behavior in School-Aged Children survey to classify students as non-involved, bullies only, victims of bullying only, or bullies and victims, and then compared students in these categories on adjustment outcomes. Many early studies treated cyberbullying as a categorical variable, in that participants were classified as cyberbullies or not cyberbullies, typically based on responses to self-report questionnaires, then compared on adjustment variables or other outcomes (e.g., Raskauskas & Stolz, 2007; Ybarra & Mitchell, 2007). Prominent studies of cyberbullying have also treated victimization as a categorical variable; participants are classified as victims or not, then compared on adjustment outcomes (Mitchell, Finkelhor, Wlak, Ybarra, & Turner, 2011; Ybarra, Diener-West, & Leaf, 2007).

Reasons for treating cyberbullying as a categorical variable are rarely explicitly stated. Perhaps cyberbullying is treated as a dichotomous variable because the distribution of self-reports is not normal, but skewed so that most participants report no engagement in cyberbullying, and a few endorse an item or two. As one example, of 1,500 youths who responded to the Second Youth Internet Safety Survey, 71% reported never harassing anyone online, 17% reported limited online harassment, 6% reported occasional online harassment, and 6% reported frequent online harassment (Ybarra & Mitchell, 2007). Similarly, a survey study of youths in the United Kingdom reported, "The distributions of cyberaggression and cybervictimization were heavily skewed, and the variables were dichotomized" (Pornari & Wood, 2011). However, methodologists have advised against dichotomizing variables due to non-normality, instead recommending transformations to reduce skew or analyses that do not assume normal distributions of variables (MacCallum, Zhang, Preacher, & Rucker, 2002).

Another reason why cyberbullying may be treated as a categorical variable could be that it is more straightforward conceptually and statistically. It is sorely tempting to view cyberbullying as a personality trait, and cyberbullies as a type of person, as has often been done in research on traditional bullying and aggression. However, for all forms of aggression and bullying, whether these are invariant personality traits is often assumed but rarely tested (see Underwood, Galen, & Paquette, 2001, for a discussion of this issue in relation to social and physical aggression).

Although this approach of classifying individuals as cyberbullies or not is conceptually straightforward, it may not be empirically justified. To classify an adolescent as a cyberbully or not assumes that cyberbullying is a personality trait, a tendency to engage in electronic aggression across modes of communication and across time. Most studies to date that assess cyberbullying classify adolescents as cyberbullies or not based on general items, such as "Have you ever used the Internet to harass or shame someone with whom you were angry?" (Ybarra & Mitchell, 2004), or "I told lies about some students through email or instant messaging" (Williams & Guerra, 2007). Not surprisingly, studies using these general items yielded prevalence rates for cyberbullying behavior that ranged from 9.4% to 36% (for a review, see Calvete, Orue, Estevez, Villardon, & Padilla, 2010). Cyberbullying includes a wide range of behaviors, from sending threatening or insulting messages by e-mail or cell phones to hacking into others' e-mail or Facebook accounts to send messages that could cause great trouble or social pain, to broadcasting embarrassing sexual images of others (Calvete et al., 2010). Prevalence rates for engaging in the specific behaviors "sometimes" or "often" range from 8.6% for sending sexual images to other people to 20.1% for writing embarrassing comments about a classmate on the Internet and 20.2% for intentionally excluding someone from an online group (Calvete et al., 2010). Little published research examines whether it is the same individuals who are reporting engaging in various forms of cyberbullying. Knowing the answer to this question would be valuable both for basic scientists developing conceptual models of cyberbullying and prevention and intervention scientists seeking to reduce cyberbullying among youths.

Although many pioneering studies have examined cyberbullying as a categorical variable, given adolescents' heavy engagement in electronic communication (Lenhart, 2007; Lenhart et al., 2010), it seems that there might be enough negative online behavior occurring for researchers to treat cyberbullying as a continuous dimension. Treating cyberbullying as a continuous dimension acknowledges some youths may engage in this behavior not at all, some a little, some moderately, and some at extreme levels. Treating cyberbullying as a continuous variable also allows risk factors that predict various degrees of cyberbullying to be examined, and determining adjustment outcomes that may result from different levels of involvement. However, if cyberbullying is to be analyzed as a continuous variable, it is important to consider what the units of analysis should be. We consider appropriate units of analysis for cyberbullying research later in this chapter.

VARIABLE-CENTERED VERSUS PERSON-CENTERED ANALYSES

Related to the decision to treat cyberbullying as a continuous versus categorical variable is the decision to perform variable-centered versus person-centered analyses. Variable-centered analyses focus on how being high or low on one variable (e.g., victimization) is related to being high or low on another variable (e.g., depression). Variable-centered analyses may include multiple variables to evaluate independent relations (e.g., cybervictimization predicting depression controlling for traditional victimization) or interactive relations (e.g., victimization predicts depression differentially depending on the child's level of aggression). Person-centered analyses classify individuals into types, and then compare these types on presumed antecedents or consequences. A common example from traditional bullying research is to classify children as bullies, victims, bully-victims, or not involved, and then to compare these groups of children (see, e.g., Nansel et al., 2001; Olweus, 1978). Similar person-centered approaches include distinctions among tough (aggressive and popular), troubled (aggressive and high maladjustment), and model (pro-social, nonaggressive, well-adjusted) children (Rodkin, Farmer, Pearl, & Van Acker, 2000); distinctions among individuals using antisocial, pro-social, and bi-strategic resource control strategies (Hawley, e.g., 2002, 2003); and efforts to classify individuals into aggressor, assistant, victim, and defender roles (see Salmivalli, 2001). Both variable- and person-centered analyses have advantages and disadvantages, which we consider next.

Variable-centered approaches retain the continuum of the measurement of the variables (see discussion above regarding continuous versus categorical variables) and fit well within well-known data-analytic models (e.g., multiple regression). It is also possible to model multivariate relations (e.g., independent, interactive) within well-known statistical frameworks (e.g., multiple regression, structural equation modeling). However, the results of multivariate models can be difficult to conceptualize; for instance, it would be extremely difficult to conceptualize an interaction of aggression, victimization, and friendships predicting depression, even if such an interaction was found to be statistically significant. Moreover, these multivariate models assume multivariate distributions that may not actually exist; there may exist no child in a dataset with the particular combination of variables (e.g., high aggression, victimization, and many friendships) that is being modeled. Further, variable-centered results are disconnected from the more categorical perspectives of practitioners directly working with children.

Person-centered analyses offer the promise of identifying meaningful "types" of individuals who exist. These analyses also provide easily understandable comparisons between these types, and results from these person-centered approaches may be more intuitive to practitioners. However, person-centered approaches also suffer several limitations. The first limitation is that it is often ambiguous whether the groups differ because of differences on one variable or due to a more holistic difference. For example, if bully-victims have poorer adjustment than either bullies or victims, it is unclear if this difference due to the additive impact of bullying plus victimization, or the holistic combination of both experiences. Second, as we described for the categorization of a single variable, the creation of categories from among multiple variables is most often arbitrary, based on median splits or dichotomizations at one standard deviation above the mean. Statistical methods for identifying nonarbitrary groupings exist, including cluster analysis (Aldenderfer & Blashfield, 1984), mixture modeling (McLachlan & Peel, 2000), and taxometrics (Waller & Meehl, 1998). Researchers studying cyberbullying using person-centered analyses should use these analytic tools to identify more evidence-based groupings of individuals, rather than relying on arbitrary classifications.

Decisions between variable- and person-centered analyses are also relevant to longitudinal research on cyberbullying. Panel models represent a prototypical variable-centered longitudinal analysis. Here, values on the presumed outcome variable are predicted by early values on the presumed causal variable, often with more elaborate controls in an effort to make conclusions approaching causality (see Little, Card, Preacher, & McConnell, 2009). This approach focuses on interindividual (between-person) prediction. In contrast, time series analyses examining whether an individual's experience of an event (e.g., victimization) reliably precedes an outcome (e.g., depression) inform intraindividual (within person) prediction. Importantly, the conclusions of interindividual prediction do not necessarily inform intraindividual prediction, and vice versa (Molenaar, 2004). Growth curve models consider both intraindividual and interindividual change over time, though with no ability to make conclusions approaching causality. These growth curve models estimate various parameters, such as an initial level (intercept) and average change over time (slope), in one or more variables. Adapting a variable-centered approach to growth curve models, researchers would also estimate the interindividual (between-person) variability in these growth parameters, and potentially the covariability in growth between multiple variables (e.g., association between change in victimization and change in depression). Growth curve models can also be subjected to person-centered analyses, with common approaches including those by Nagin (1999) and by Muthén (2001). For example, Nagin and Tremblay (1999) identified groups based on developmental trajectories of physical aggression and other externalizing problems across adolescence. Although it may be appealing to think of certain "types" of trajectories across time, the current analytic tools for identifying these growth trajectories suffer numerous limitations (e.g., difficulties in identifying appropriate numbers of groups, artificial groups based on model misspecification; see, e.g., Bauer & Curran, 2003; Little et al., 2009). Cyberbullying researchers interested in these person-centered analyses need to be aware of these limitations.

In conclusion, both variable- and person-centered analyses offer both advantages and limitations. These relative advantages can be balanced by recognizing that variable- and person-centered analyses represent points along a continuum of conceptual and analytic approaches, rather than mutually exclusive categories (Masyn, Henderson, & Greenbaum, 2010). In our view, both variable- and person-centered analyses will be useful in the emerging field of cyberbullying research.

UNITS OF ANALYSIS FOR RESEARCH ON CYBERBULLYING

Research on traditional forms of aggression has almost exclusively conceptualized the individual as the unit of analysis. From this perspective, individuals vary in enacting more or less aggression (or, from a categorical perspective, as being a perpetrator of bullying or not), and individuals vary in receiving more or less victimization (or, as being a target or not). Research on cyberbullying has thus far adapted this individual-oriented perspective, focusing on individual differences in enacting or in receiving more or less cyberbullying.

A focus on individual differences in aggression and victimization has value. There exists relatively strong interindividual stability in both aggression (see Olweus, 1979) and victimization (e.g., Boivin, Hymel, & Bukowski, 1995; Olweus, 1978). Research from this individual-oriented perspective has also identified personal, interpersonal, and familial correlates of individual differences in both aggression and victimization (see, e.g., Card & Hodges, 2008; Hodges, Card, & Isaacs, 2003; Underwood, 2003). Subsequent longitudinal research has then sought to identify which of these correlates serve as antecedents and/or consequences of aggression and victimization (see, e.g., Card & Hodges, 2008), contributing to our understanding of the factors that place children at risk for aggression and/or victimization as well as the probabilistic outcomes of this involvement. There is also value in cyberbullying research investigating the concurrent and longitudinal correlates of individual differences in cyberaggression and cybervictimization. However, despite the value of an individual-oriented focus, the emerging field of cyberbullying research should not adapt this perspective exclusively.

A dyadic orientation to studying aggression is based on the premise that aggression necessarily involves behavior from one individual directed toward another. In other words, any act of aggression necessarily involves at least one aggressor enacting aggressive behavior toward at least one victim. A dyadic orientation to studying aggression uses specific aggressors-victim pairings as the key unit of analysis.

The first study to treat aggressor-victim dyads as the unit of analysis relied on observations of 6- and 8-year-old boys in laboratory play groups over multiple days (Dodge, Price, Coie, & Christopoulos, 1990). Results indicated that 50% of aggressive acts occurred within just 20% of two-child pairings, and that pairings in which aggression occurred in one play session tended to be the same in which aggression occurred in other play sessions. Subsequent research (Coie et al., 1999) using observations of aggression in boys' laboratory play groups used a statistical approach (the social relational model; Kenny, 1994) to decompose variance in the occurrence of aggression into that due to individual differences among aggressors, individual differences among victims, and stable differences across dyads. Although individual differences in aggression and victimization were found (supporting the value of the individual-oriented perspective), stable aggressor-victim relationships accounted for greater variability in the occurrence of aggression. A later study relying on early adolescents' self-reports of aggressor-victim relationships in the middle school context found that specific aggressor-victim relationships accounted for 70 to 77% (for aggressor and victim reports, respectively) of the variability in the occurrence of aggression (Card & Hodges, 2010). These results indicate that dyads are an important unit of analysis in understanding traditional aggression. Research on traditional forms of aggression has begun to examine the relationship correlates of aggressor-victim dyads. For instance, both affect and social cognitions toward specific peers have been shown to predict aggression toward those specific peers (Card & Hodges, 2007; Hubbard, Dodge, Cillessen, Coie, & Schwartz, 2001; Peets, Hodges, & Salmivalli, 2008, 2011).

Is the dyad also a valuable unit of analysis for studying cyberbullying? Although this is an empirical question that has not yet been investigated, there are conceptual reasons that may suggest this approach has value. First, there is evidence that children and adolescents usually have "real-world" interactions with individuals with whom they interact through technology. Thus, there is likely some degree of transfer of relationship features across contexts. Second, the contexts in which cyberbullying has been considered, including communication devices (e.g., cell phones, instant messaging, e-mail platforms) and online sites (e.g., social networking, multiplayer games), typically identify individuals, whether or not that identity can be connected to a real-world identity or is anonymous. Therefore, there is the opportunity to develop relationship histories through repeated interactions, making it likely that dyad-specific behavioral patterns will quickly emerge and stabilize. Individuals inclined to cyberbully others might be drawn to particular behaviors of particular potential victims. Even if acts of cyberaggression were enacted toward random others, the targets could respond in a variety of ways that would reinforce or discourage the aggressor from repeating the act. These possibilities are speculative but can be empirically investigated. If stable cyberbullying dyads are found, then it will be important to investigate the antecedents (e.g., relationship histories, power differentials within the cybercontext) and consequences (e.g., aggressor-victim relationship escalation versus desistance, outcomes for aggressors and victims) of these dyads.

The dyad represents just one alternative to treating the individual as the default unit of analysis. Larger groups of individuals (e.g., online cliques) and entire cyber contexts (e.g., a networking or gaming site) are also viable foci for studying the correlates of cyberbullying. We do not necessarily view any single unit of analysis as most important. Instead, we encourage the emerging field of cyberbullying research to consider diverse units of analyses rather than uncritically following the individual orientation that has dominated traditional bullying research.

LONGITUDINAL RESEARCH ON CYBERBULLYING

Prospective, longitudinal studies would contribute much to our understanding of how cyberbullying develops, whether cyberbullying is stable over time, and how cyberbullying and cybervictimization relate to adjustment. Perhaps because the phenomenon of cyberbullying is fairly recent, few published longitudinal studies exist. One exception is a small study in which middle schoolers competed self-reports of offline aggression, online aggression, and adjustment at two time points one year apart. Engaging in both online and offline aggression at the second assessment was related to being older, being the victim of Internet aggression, and having beliefs supporting relational aggression (Werner & Bumpas, 2010). The stability and relationships among traditional bullying and victimization and cyberbullying and victimization were studied in 1,700 youths (aged 11–16) for two years (Jose, Kljakovic, Scheib, & Notter, 2012). Traditional victimization was more stable than victimization in the cyber-environment; cyberbullying predicted cybervictimization a year later. Longitudinal studies relying on self-reports of aggression suffer the same problems as concurrent studies; as of now, there is little evidence for the validity of self-reports of cyberbullying, and many results may be due to shared method variance.

One possible strategy for understanding developmental causes and consequences of cyberbullying might be to add measures of cyberbullying to ongoing, prospective, longitudinal studies of other forms of aggression that include multiple informants. The BlackBerry Project described above was the second phase of a long-term longitudinal study of developmental origins and outcomes of social aggression that began in 2003 when the sample was 9 years old and in the third grade; the sample will be followed through their first year of college (Underwood et al., 2012). The first phase of the study included teacher, parent, friend, self, and observational assessments of social aggression. The second phase, when participants were in high school, added the collection of electronic communication by giving participants BlackBerry devices configured so that all electronic communication is captured for later coding. In the last year of high school and the first year of college, all Facebook activity will be captured for later coding, not just on the BlackBerry devices but all activity in participants' Facebook accounts (by using a Facebook application developed in response to new Securities Exchange Commission regulations that require financial corporations to monitor employees' social networking communications for compliance with federal laws). This longitudinal study includes yearly assessments of offline aggression and adjustment completed by teachers, parents, friends, and the participants themselves; and in recent years, questionnaire assessments of cyberbullying and cybervictimization. By adding an electronic communication component to this ongoing longitudinal study, we will be able to examine developmental antecedents of cyberbullying and cybervictimization, stability of cyberbullying as assessed by questionnaire and observed in text messaging and e-mail and Facebook activity, and the extent to which cyberbullying and cybervictimization predict maladjustment for older adolescents. This is likely not the only ongoing longitudinal study of aggression to which measures of cyberbullying are being added, though results have yet to be published. We look forward to learning more about what these ongoing studies find about the origins, stability, and outcomes of cyberbullying.

Pioneers studying Internet communication have argued, "Future research should start with adolescent users and attempt to connect their online and off-line worlds and also identify the factors that influence the extent of connectedness or divergence between the two worlds" (Subrahmanyam et al., 2009, p. 242). Studying both the offline and online social worlds of youths who engage in cyberbullying may be our best hope of developing the best methods to assess cyberbullying and to understand how this complex phenomenon unfolds. Longitudinal studies may also allow us the opportunity to understand why some young people refrain from cyberbullying entirely, so that prevention scientists can develop effective programs to help youth become excellent digital citizens, to use the power of electronic communication for good.

CONCLUSIONS

In this chapter, we have highlighted some of the important methodological questions facing the emerging field of cyberbullying research. We first considered methods of assessing cyberbullying, urging researchers to use observations and other assessment approaches rather than relying on the convenience of self-report instruments. We also considered the question of representing cyberbullying as a continuous versus categorical variable, and the related question of whether variable- or person-centered variables are preferable. We also challenged readers to move beyond an exclusive focus on the individual as the unit of analysis that has dominated research on traditional bullying. Finally, we considered the benefits and challenges of conducting longitudinal research on cyberbullying.

Although we have at times made specific recommendations, our larger goal was not to be prescriptive. Instead, we encourage readers to consider carefully each of these issues, seeking to make the most appropriate choices for the research questions on hand. We do explicitly discourage reliance on methodological practices simply because they have become the norm in research on traditional bullying. As researchers at the forefront of this new understanding of cyberbullying, we have the wisdom of decades of research on aggression and victimization as well as the opportunity to explore a diverse range of methodologies for studying this phenomenon.

References

Aldenderfer, M. S., & Blashfield, R. K. (1984). *Cluster analysis*. Newbury Park, CA: Sage. doi:10.1007/978-1-4613-2665-6_8

Bauer, D. J., & Curran, P. J. (2003). Distributional assumptions of growth mixture models: Implications for overextraction of latent trajectory classes. *Psychological Methods, 8*, 338–363. doi:10.1037/1082-989X.8.3.338

Boivin, M., Hymel, S., & Bukowski, W. M. (1995). The roles of social withdrawal, peer rejection, and victimization by peers in predicting loneliness and depressed mood in childhood. *Development and Psychopathology, 7*, 765–785. doi:10.1017/S0954579400006830

Branson, C. E., & Cornell, D. G. (2009). A comparison of self and peer reports in the assessment of middle school bullying. *Journal of Applied School Psychology, 25*, 5–27.

Calvete, E., Orue, I., Estevez, A., Villardon, L., & Padilla, P. (2010). Cyberbullying in adolescents: Modalities and aggressors profile. *Computers in Human Behavior, 26*, 1128–1135. doi:10.1016/j.chb.2010.03.017

Card, N. A., & Hodges, E.V.E. (2007). Victimization within mutually antipathetic peer relationships. *Social Development, 16*, 479–496. doi:10.1111/j.1467-9507.2007.00394.x

Card, N. A., & Hodges, E.V.E. (2008). Peer victimization among schoolchildren: Correlations, causes, consequences, and considerations in assessment and intervention. *School Psychology Quarterly, 23*, 451–461. doi:10.1037/a0012769

Card, N. A., & Hodges, E.V.E. (2010). It takes two to fight in school too: A social relations model of the psychometric properties and relative variance of dyadic aggression and victimization in middle school. *Social Development, 19*, 447–469. doi:10.1111/j.1467-9507.2009.00562.x

Coie, J. D., Cillessen, A.H.N., Dodge, K. A., Hubbard, J. A., Schwartz, D., Lemerise, E. A., & Bateman, H. (1999). It takes two to fight: A test of relational factors and a method for assessing aggressive dyads. *Developmental Psychology, 35*, 1179–1188. doi:10.1037//0012-1649.35.5.1179

Cornell, D. G., & Brockenbrough, K. (2004). Identification of bullies and victims: A comparison of methods. *Journal of School Violence, 3*, 63–87. doi:10.1300/J202v03n02_05

Cornell, D., Klein, J., Konold, T., & Huang, F. (2011). Effects of validity screening items on adolescent survey data. *Psychological Assessment*, Advance online publication. doi:10.1037/a0024824.

Cornell, D., Sheras, P. L., & Cole, J. C. (2006). Assessment of bullying. In S. R. Jimerson & M. J. Furlong (Eds.), *The handbook of school violence and school safety: From research to practice* (pp. 121–210). Mahwah, NJ: Erlbaum.

Dodge, K. A., Price, J. M., Coie, J. D., & Christopoulos, C. (1990). On the development of aggressive dyadic relationships in boys' peer groups. *Human Development, 33*, 260–270. doi:10.1159/000276523

Greenfield, P., & Yan, Z. (2006). Children, adolescents, and the Internet: A new field of inquiry in developmental psychology. *Developmental Psychology, 2006*, 391–394. doi:10.1037/0012-1649.42.3.391

Hawley, P. H. (2002). Social dominance and prosocial and coercive strategies of resource control in preschoolers. *International Journal of Behavioral Development, 26*, 167–176. doi:10.1080/01650250143000427

Hawley, P. H. (2003). Prosocial and coercive configurations of resource control in early adolescence: A case for the well-adapted Machiavellian. *Merrill-Palmer Quarterly, 49*, 279–309. doi:10.1353/mpq.2003.0013

Hinduja, S. & Patchin, J. W. (2009). *Bullying beyond the schoolyard: Preventing and responding to cyberbullying*. Thousand Oaks, CA: Sage Publications.

Hodges, E. V.E., Card, N. A., & Isaacs, J. (2003). Learning of aggression in the home and the peer group. In W. Heitmeyer & J. Hagan (Eds.), *International handbook of research on violence* (pp. 495–509). New York: Westview Press.

Hubbard, J. A., Dodge, K. A., Cillessen, A.H.N., Coie, J. D., & Schwartz, D. (2001). The dyadic nature of social information processing in boys' reactive and proactive aggression. *Journal of Personality and Social Psychology, 80*, 268–280. doi:10.1037//0022–3514.80.2.268

Internet Safety Technical Task Force. (2008). Enhancing child safety & online technologies: Final report to the multi-state working group on social networking of State Attorneys Gender of the United States. Retrieved from http://cyber.law.harvard.edu/sites/cyber.law.harvard.edu/files/ISTTF_Final_Report.pdf

Jose, P. E., Kljakovic, M., Schieb, E., & Notter, O. (2012). The joint development of traditional bullying and victimization with cyberbullying and victimization in adolescence. *Journal of Research on Adolescence, 22*, 301–309.

Kenny, D. A. (1994). *Interpersonal perception: A social relations analysis*. New York: Guilford. doi:10.1037//0022–3514.67.6.1024

Kowalski, R. M., & Limber, S. P. (2007). Electronic bullying among middle school students. *Journal of Adolescent Health, 41*, 22–30. doi:10.1016/j.jadohealth.2007.08.017

Lagerspetz, K.M.J., Björkqvist, K., & Peltonen, T. (1988). Is indirect aggression typical of females? Gender differences in aggressiveness in 11- to 12-year-old children. *Aggressive Behavior, 14*, 403–414. doi:10.1002/1098–2337(1988)14:6<403::AID-AB2480140602>3.0.CO;2-D

Lee, T., & Cornell, D. (2010). Concurrent validity of the Olweus Bully/Victim Questionnaire. *Journal of School Violence, 9*, 56–73. DOI: 10.180/15388220903185613

Lenhart, A. (2007). Cyberbullying. Retrieved from http://www.pewinternet.org/Reports/2007/Cyberbullying.aspx

Lenhart, A., Ling, R., Campbell, S., & Purcell, K. (2010). *Teens and mobile phones*. Retrieved from http://pewinternetorg/Reports/2010/Teens-and-Mobile-Phones.aspx

Little, T. D., Brauner, J., Jones, S. M., Nock, M. K., & Hawley, P. H. (2003). Rethinking aggression: A typological examination of the functions of aggression. *Merrill-Palmer Quarterly, 49*, 343–369. doi:10.1353/mpq.2003.0014

Little, T. D., Card, N. A., Preacher, K. J., & McConnell, E. (2009). Modeling longitudinal data from research on adolescence. In R. M. Lerner & L. Steinberg (Eds.), *Handbook of adolescent psychology* (3rd ed.) (pp. 15–54). New York: Wiley. doi:10.1002/9780470479193.adlpsy001003

MacCallum, R. C., Zhang, S., Preacher, K. J., & Rucker, D. D. (2002). On the practice of dichotomization of quantitative variables. *Psychological Methods, 7*, 19–40. doi:10.1037//1082–989X.7.1.19

Masyn, K. E., Henderson, C. E., & Greenbaum, P. E. (2010). Exploring the latent structures of psychological constructs in social development using the dimensional-categorical spectrum. *Social Development, 19*, 470–493. doi:10.1111/j.1467–9507.2009.00573.x

McLachlan, G., & Peel, D. (2000). *Finite mixture models*. New York: Wiley.

Mitchell, K. J., Finkelhor, S., Wolak, J. D., Ybarra, M. L., & Turner, H. (2011). Youth Internet victimization in a broader victimization context. *Journal of Adolescent Health, 48*, 128–134. doi:10.1016/j.jadohealth.2010.06.009

Molenaar, P.C.M. (2004). A manifesto on psychology as idiographic science: Bringing the person back into scientific psychology, this time forever. *Measurement, 2*, 201–218. doi:10.1207/s15366359mea0204_1

Muthén, B.O. (2001). Latent variable mixture modeling. In G.A. Marcoulides & R.E. Schumaker (Eds.), *New developments and techniques in structural equation modeling* (pp. 1–33). Mahwah, NJ: Erlbaum.

Nagin, D.S. (1999). Analyzing developmental trajectories: A semi-parametric, group-based approach. *Psychological Methods, 4*, 139–157. doi:10.1037//1082–989X.4.2.139

Nagin, D.S., & Tremblay, R.E. (1999). Trajectories of boys' physical aggression, opposition, and hyperactivity on the path to physically violent and nonviolent juvenile delinquency. *Child Development, 70*, 1181–1196. doi:10.1111/1467–8624.00086

Nansel, T.J., Overpeck, M., Pilla, R.S., Ruan, W.J., Simons-Morton, B., & Scheidt, P. (2001). Bullying behaviors among US youth: Prevalence and associate with psychological adjustment. *Journal of the American Medical Association, 285*, 2094–2100. doi:10.1001/jama.285.16.2094

Olweus, D. (1978). *Aggression in the schools: Bullies and whipping boys.* Washington, DC: Hemisphere Press (Wiley).

Olweus, D. (1979). Stability of aggressive reaction patterns in males: A review. *Psychological Bulletin, 86*, 852–875. doi:10.1037//0033–2909.86.4.852

Olweus, D. (1993). *Bullying in the schools: What we know and what we can do.* Cambridge, MA: Blackwell.

Olweus, D. (1996). *The revised Olweus Bully/Victim Questionnaire.* Bergen, Norway: Mimeo, Research Center for Health Promotion (HEMIL), University of Bergen. doi:10.1007/BF02195509

Olweus, D. (2002). *General information about the revised Olweus Bully/Victim Questionnaire, PC program and teacher handbook* (pp. 1–12). Bergen, Norway: Mimeo, Research Center for Health Promotion (HEMIL), University of Bergen.

Pakaslahti, L., & Keltikangas-Jarvinen, L. (2000). Comparison of peer, teacher, and self-assessments on adolescent direct and indirect aggression. *Educational Psychology, 20*, 177–190. doi:10.1080/713663710

Peets, K., Hodges, E.V.E., & Salmivalli, C. (2008). Affect-congruent social-cognitive evaluations and behaviors. *Child Development, 79*, 170–185. doi:10.1111/j.1467–8624.2007.01118.x

Peets, K., Hodges, E.V.E., & Salmivalli, C. (2011). Actualization of social cognitions into aggressive behavior toward disliked targets. *Social Development, 20*, 232–250. doi:10.1111/j.1467–9507.2010.00581.x

Pellegrini, A.D. (2001). A longitudinal study of heterosexual relationships, aggression, and sexual harassment during the transition from primary school through middle school. *Journal of Applied Developmental Psychology, 22*, 1–15.

Pornari, C.D., & Wood, J. (2010). Peer and cyber aggression in secondary school students: The role of moral disengagement, hostile attribution bias, and outcome expectancies. *Aggressive Behavior, 36*, 81–94. doi:10.1002/ab.20336

Raskauskas, J., & Stolz, A.D. (2007). Involvement in traditional and electronic bullying among adolescents. *Developmental Psychology, 43*, 564–575. DOI: 10.1037/0012–1649.43.3.564

Rodkin, P.C., Farmer, T.W., Pearl, R., & Van Acker, R. (2000). Heterogeneity of popular boys: Antisocial and prosocial configurations. *Developmental Psychology, 36*, 14–24. doi:10.1037//0012–1649.36.1.14

Salimkhan, G., Manago, A.M., Greenfield, P.M. (2010). The construction of the virtual self on MySpace. *Cyberpsychology: Journal of Psychosocial Research on Cyberspace, 4*, 1–18.

Salmivalli, C. (2001). Group view on victimization: Empirical findings and their implications. In J. Juvonen & S. Graham (Eds.), *Peer harassment in school: The plight of the vulnerable and victimized* (pp. 398–419). New York: Guilford.

Smith, P.K. (2004). Bullying: Recent developments. *Child and Adolescent Mental Health, 9*, 98–103. Doi:10.1111/j.1475–3588.2004.00089.x

Subrahmanyam, K., Garcia, E.C.M., Harsono, L.S., Li, J.S., & Lipana, L. (2009). In their words: Connecting on-line weblogs to developmental processes. *British Journal of Developmental Psychology, 27*, 219–245. doi:10.1348/026151008X345979

Subrahmanyam, K., Smahel, D., & Greenfield, P. (2006). Connecting developmental constructions to the Internet: Identity presentation and sexual exploration in online teen chat rooms. *Developmental Psychology, 42*, 395–406. doi:10.1037/0012–1649.42.3.395

Underwood, M.K. (2003). *Social aggression among girls*. New York: Guilford.

Underwood, M.K., Galen, B.R., & Paquette, J.A. (2001). Top ten challenges for understanding aggression and gender: Why can't we all just get along? *Social Development, 10*(2), 248–267. doi:10.1111/1467–9507.00162

Underwood, M.K., Rosen, L.H., More, D., Ehrenreich, S., & Gentsch, J.K. (2012). The BlackBerry Project: Capturing the content of adolescents' electronic communication. *Developmental Psychology, 48*, 295–302.

Waller, N.G., Meehl, P.E. (2008). *Multivariate taxometric procedures: Distinguishing types from continua*. Thousand Oaks, CA, Sage.

Werner, N.E., Bumpas, M.F. (2010). Involvement in Internet aggression during early adolescence. *Journal of Youth and Adolescence, 39*, 607–619.

Williams, K.R., & Guerra, N.G. (2007). Prevalence and predictors of Internet bullying. *Journal of Adolescent Health, 41*, 14–21. doi:10.1016/j.jadohealth.2007.08.018

Ybarra, M.L., Diener-West, M., & Leaf, P.J. (2007). Examining the overlap in Internet harassment and school bullying: Implications for school intervention. *Journal of Adolescent Health, 41*, S42-S50. doi: 10.1016/j.jadohealth.2007.09.004

Ybarra, M.L., & Mitchell, K.J. (2004). Online aggressors/targets, aggressors: A comparison of associated youth characteristics. *Journal of Child Psychology and Psychiatry, 45*, 1308–1316. doi:10.1111/j.1469–7610.2004.00328.x

Ybarra, M., & Mitchell, K.J. (2007). Prevalence and frequency of Internet harassment instigation: Implications for adolescent health. *Journal of Adolescent Health, 41*, 189–195. doi:10.1016/j.jadohealth.2007.03.005

11 Methods

Guiding Principles

Sheri Bauman and Donna Cross

In this chapter, we propose five principles to serve as guidelines for cyberbullying research methods: engaging multidisciplinary teams, using a broad selection of quality methods, understanding the importance of formative research, realizing the value of target audience involvement, and promoting ethical practice in online environments. We do not describe these guidelines as "best practice," as there is insufficient evidence to date that these methods (some of which are unique to measure cyberbullying behavior) produce superior results. Nevertheless, considering what is known about research in general and research on aggression; victimization; and bullying, in particular, we believe these principles are grounded in sound scientific methods and fundamental beliefs about the research enterprise. We are also mindful that scientific inquiry into the use of technology is a relatively new area, and we have taken this into account in our recommendations.

Principle 1. Actively engage multiple disciplinary teams and their methodologies in the design and conduct of cyberbullying research. Cyberbullying is a complex phenomenon, and good research will benefit from the perspectives and methods from a variety of disciplines, particularly during the design stage. Collaboration among researchers from diverse disciplines is likely to generate a more comprehensive approach to a study, and innovation is a desirable outcome (Younglove-Webb, Gray, Abdalla, & Thurow, 1999). Working within a singular discipline limits the range of approaches considered. Working only with those who share the same perspective and background can lead to a narrow focus that may overlook important ideas. Janssen and Goldsworthy (1996) observed that a multidisciplinary approach is particularly useful when a new type of problem first generates interest from researchers, which is the case with cyberbullying. They also noted that the multidisciplinary team is best suited to the examination of problems that vary from one setting to another, which is also the case for cyberbullying.

Researchers investigating cyberbullying will want to enlist ideas from informatics specialists, for example, who are experts in the use of technology to solve complex problems, and who may be able to suggest novel technological methods of gathering nuanced data. Statisticians now have very sophisticated methods of modeling, and they too need to be involved in planning analytic strategies, determining adequate sample size for analyses, and perhaps suggesting new ways to approach the framing of research questions. Depending on the methodology to be used in a study, Information Technology (IT) assistance may be necessary, and knowing what is possible in that domain can add depth to the study. For some data collection and analyses, linguists and ethnographers might provide insight from the lens of those disciplines, both in terms of content and process of an investigation.

Although the advantages of a multidisciplinary team are many, such an approach is not without challenges. Each discipline generally has its own common lexicon that may be unfamiliar to those in other fields. What is common knowledge in one field may be unheard of in another, and it is essential that concepts and theories be clearly explained to ensure the research team has clear understandings of the issues being addressed (Uiterkamp & Vlek, 2007). Different disciplines also have varied professional values and even diverse publication outlets, which may require compromise on the part of team members.

Effective multidisciplinary teams have several characteristics: there is relatively equal representation and contribution from the disciplines to maximize the diversity of expertise, there is a high level of collective team identification (Van der Vegt & Bunderson, 2005), and commitment to the team's goals (separate from each member's individual goals). Team composition should be such that there is sufficient diversity of expertise and perspectives but not so much that interaction is stifled.

An international network of such multidisciplinary teams should be established with the goal of collaborating in a variety of ways. Exchanging research ideas and refining them through dialogue is one obvious benefit. In addition, new research methods developed to address cyberbullying can be both enriched with the infusion of ideas from other groups and validated by use in multiple settings and with diverse cultural groups.

Finally, we encourage the dissemination of findings to a broad range of audiences, including scholars in a variety of disciplines, as well as practitioners for whom the findings may inform policy and practice. The challenge of reaching multiple audiences, including scholars, practitioners, and the general public, was addressed by Crosswaite and Curtice (1994). We endorse their recommendations here. First, dissemination of findings should be discussed and planned at the outset of the project, rather than after completion. The research teams should identify key targets to ensure the presentation of results is geared toward those groups. In addition to scholarly journals and conferences, media outlets, professional organizations, practitioner groups, and other avenues for dissemination should be identified and contacts made. Given that researchers are reluctant to publicize findings via other channels before their papers are peer reviewed and accepted for publication, the influence of a paper on future research—or current policy and practice—is delayed at best due to the lengthy review-publication process. The use of the networks of multidisciplinary teams who are communicating regularly about research can enable the more timely dissemination of findings to other researchers, who can then build on the research, use promising methods and measures, and study the problem in other contexts to determine whether findings are similar.

Principle 2. Use quality methods from traditional bullying and other relevant research as a foundation to study the phenomenon of cyberbullying. Other chapters in this section discuss methods that are uniquely applicable to cyberbullying research. Here we emphasize the importance of including "gray literature" when reviewing prior research. Gray literature is important both to understand findings and to consider novel methods that were used in small or pilot studies. Gray literature includes non-peer reviewed articles, technical reports, policy briefs, working papers, doctoral and master's theses, and other items that are typically not found in standard catalog listings. The challenge for researchers is that such information can be difficult to locate. Readers may find it helpful to search www.science.gov for such material. When this chapter was being written, 179 citations for cyberbullying were found. Although many were journal articles that would appear in other searches, there were several that were not likely to be identified via other search engines and would qualify as "gray literature."

We also encourage researchers interested in cyberbullying to develop a repository of all studies, published or not, so that the various methodological practices can be readily examined. In fact, a literature review, focused not on the content of studies but on the methodologies used, would be a valuable contribution to the field. In addition, a mechanism for sharing submitted papers or progress reports for longitudinal studies would also stimulate thinking about novel methods.

Finally, this principle includes theory testing to enable researchers to effectively apply theoretical frameworks to conceptualize their work (see Chapters 5 and 6 in this book). We advocate a deductive approach, which involves testing existing theories to determine their potential application to cyberbullying behavior. A conceptual paper used Social Information Processing theory to examine the unique features of cyberbullying. This is the kind of theoretical work that is much needed as is the empirical testing of these theories. In addition to the deductive approach, inductive work is also needed to develop new theories to describe and explain cyberbullying behavior.

Principle 3. Develop a set of procedures that is intentionally inclusive of the target population's voice to identify key language, behaviors, and perspectives, to inform cyberbullying research methods. Most researchers work in teams of other professionals to design and carry out their work. However, in the cyberbullying field, it is critical that advice be obtained from reference or advisory groups prior to beginning a study. Because the environments that are the context for cyberbullying are complex and dynamic, informants who participate in those environments can educate the researchers about the normative expectations and the social norms in that environment. This is particularly critical in studies that will use observational techniques to understand a particular context in which cyberbullying may occur. It is also critical for framing questions for interviews, surveys, and focus groups. Researchers can easily alienate their participants if they violate the norms of an environment, or if they word questions in ways that are unintentionally insulting or inappropriate. Informants can assist researchers with word choice, selecting topics about which to inquire, and ways to collect these data effectively.

Since much of the research on cyberbullying has involved children and adolescents as participants, involving youth as advisors and collaborators rather than only as subjects is a recent development. Researchers from Queen's University in Belfast observed that in recent years, youth have been included in all aspects of research processes, including development of research questions, data collection and analysis, and disseminating findings (Fargas-Malet, McSherry, Larkin, & Robinson, 2010). Coad and Evans (2007) describe a number of strategies for involving children in the research process, including having "the adult research team train a group of children to act as a reference or advisory group to consult with and guide the research process and help interpret the findings" (p. 44). Young people can be extremely helpful to cyberbullying researchers in developing surveys, for example, where their ability to choose words and phrases that are comprehensible to the intended participants is invaluable. They may also suggest questions that would not occur to adult researchers. Coan and Evans suggest that in addition to consulting with young people in the initial stages of a study, the young people can also assist in the interpretation of findings and ultimately to develop interventions. Their unique perspective may provide interpretations that may otherwise elude the researchers.

Including the voice of informants involves balancing that voice with the researchers' expertise and theoretical grounding. Researchers who achieve that balance are likely to produce findings that will greatly enhance the cyberbullying research field.

Principle 4. Promote and conduct formative research to ensure that research methodology captures the nuances of studying cyberbullying behavior. Although the term cyberbullying—and consequently research studying it—refers to a negative behavior, it is essential that researchers acknowledge that both positive and negative behaviors must be considered to enhance our understanding of communication technology interactions. The context in which cyberbullying occurs is rarely a purely pernicious one, and the dynamics and subtleties of cyberbullying cannot be thoroughly understood without consideration of the positive behaviors that also occur.

Qualitative studies are particularly useful in the early stages of a line of inquiry. Grounded theory approaches contribute to the development and expansion of theory. In addition, findings from qualitative studies can provide a basis for later quantitative work. At this early stage, pilot studies to test new methodologies and instrumentation are very important, and results should be disseminated even if sample sizes are small and findings not definitive. That is, such studies are also testing new methods that other researchers may want to use or adapt in their own work. At times, studies that are considered pilots and/or with small samples can be more difficult to publish, but journals should understand the role of such studies in advancing the field. A mechanism needs to be established to disseminate formative findings from pilot studies and early qualitative work to make them available to the wider cyberbullying research community.

Principle 5. Adhere to accepted ethical protocol that shows respect and care and considers unique challenges associated with cyberbullying research. Although ethical issues are discussed in Chapter 12 of this volume, there are concerns that relate to specific cyberbullying methods that we mention here. First, since online research methods (including surveys, direct observation, website data access, etc.) are very suitable for the study of cyberbullying, researchers must be sure that information included in the consent and assent process is complete. For example, if the researcher will have access to photos posted online, participants need to be aware that some photos are automatically geo-tagged, which means the precise location of the photo can be obtained, compromising privacy. In order to ensure that participants are provided with all the relevant risks in a form that is comprehensible, the use of video to provide information has been suggested. Limited research has been conducted to determine the effectiveness of such strategies (see Flory & Emanuel, 2004, for a review) and to date there is not robust empirical support. However, the studies to date were conducted with adult samples, often with some difficulties (e.g., low reading comprehension or a specific disorder), and may not be relevant to cyberbullying research with young people.

Eysenbach and Till (2001) discussed the unique ethical dilemmas involved in research conducted with online communities, such as chat rooms, website discussion boards, and listservs, etc. (Note that at the time Eysenbach and Till's article was published, Facebook and Twitter did not exist.) They described three types of analyses used in these settings: passive analyses (observing patterns of interaction in a particular forum, for example); active analysis (researchers participate in the discussions, asking for clarification by asking questions); and "traditional research" where the researchers are known as such to the group and may gather data by interviewing participants, administering a survey, or leading focus groups. Eysenbach and Till observed that researchers who visit these online communities to gather data risk being perceived by members as intruders, which could undermine the trust and possibly change the behaviors of members in the community.

Whether or not informed consent is required for some types of qualitative studies is a question that researchers must consider. Eysenbach and Till (2001) recommend that consent is necessary if the context is considered by users to be private, where observers are not expected. This recommendation may be even more salient with online sites such as Facebook, which are semiprivate. That is, they contain information that is public and information that is private, as determined by the user. Because young people are not always careful about setting their privacy settings appropriately, their data may unintentionally be more public than they realize. Alternatively, if the researcher gains permission to access a student's Facebook page and agrees to collect nonidentifiable data, the student's Facebook news feed may also contain comments from many other individuals (the student's Facebook friends) who have not consented to participate. How does the ethical researcher deal with such a situation?

The use of data passively acquired is unlikely to require consent, but researchers should consider the impact on the community should the findings be published.

This question is likely to arise when researchers are interested in particular online communities. In the situation for which an institutional or scientific review board consent is required, how does the researcher obtain it? An e-mail to the list (if one is available) or a posting in a public area could be used to request consent but could be conceived of as intrusive, and if participants know the discussion is being monitored, free communication may be inhibited, and some members may decide to withdraw from the community to avoid being studied. Eysenbach and Till (2001) consider whether it is feasible to contact participants whose quotes would be used after the fact, and allowing them to decline, but permission post facto may not be ethical.

Ages of participants are another consideration unique to online cyberbullying research, given that many are likely to be minors. Accordingly, parental consent is needed along with minor assent. For example, let us assume that a researcher is planning to administer a survey to high school students across a wide geographical area and will do so online. Also assume that the content of the survey and disclaimer have been approved by appropriate scientific review bodies. How does the researcher obtain parental consent in a way that does not discourage participation or encourage dishonesty? We know that many subscribers to Facebook are under the minimum age and that they falsify their birthdates to enroll. We also know that when children on some websites (e.g. Club Penguin) are asked to provide a parent's e-mail to allow the site to verify parental permission, the site is not able to determine whether the e-mail address really belongs to the subscriber's parent. Some children may give a friend's e-mail, for instance. So researchers may have difficulty devising a system that is workable and ethical. We are aware of studies in which there is a place for a parent to check if they grant permission for the child to participate, but there is no way to keep the child from checking such a box themselves. These challenges are difficult to overcome; researchers may choose to obtain consent and permission from students at school to avoid them.

Scientific review boards may not yet be familiar with the methods and associated challenges of cyberbullying research. It would be prudent for researchers engaged in this work to provide information to those bodies to ensure they have the necessary understanding to make appropriate and informed decisions. They, and researchers, need to engage in continuous monitoring of digital developments and research methods to provide respect and care for participants in cyberbullying research.

SUMMARY

In this chapter, we proposed five guiding principles that could be embraced by cyberbullying researchers so that our work in this growing field would be supported by a solid foundation. We urged researchers to pursue multidisciplinary investigations to gain from the perspectives inherent in different fields. We also recommended that methods from both traditional bullying research and those of related fields be considered and included. The need for formative research and research that examines the methods being used should be evaluated for their usefulness in accumulating a solid scientific knowledge base. Finally, we considered that the new technologies and the new possible tools for cyberbullying research must be carefully considered to ensure that the respect and care for participants is infused throughout the work and in an ethical manner.

References

Coad, J., & Evans, R. (2007). Reflections on practical approaches to involving children and young people in the data analysis process. *Children in Society, 22*, 41–52.

Crosswaite, C., & Curtice, L. (1994). Disseminating research results—The challenge of bridging the gap between health research and health action. *Health Promotion International, 9*, 289–296.

Eysenbach, G., & Till, James E. (2001). Ethical issues in qualitative research on Internet communities. *British Medical Journal, 323*, 1103–1105.

Fargas-Malet, M., McSherry, D., Larkin, E., & Robinson, C. (2010). Research with children: Methodological issues and innovative techniques. *Journal of Early Childhood Research, 8*, 176–192.

Flory, J., & Emanuel, E. (2004). Interventions to improve research participants' understanding in informed consent for research. *JAMA, 292*, 1593–1601. doi:10.1001/jama.292.13.1593

Janssen, W., & Goldsworthy, P. (1996). Multidisciplinary research for national resource management: Conceptual and practical implications. *Agricultural Systems, 51*, 259–279.

Uiterkamp, A.J.M.S., & Vlek, C. (2007). Practices and outcomes of multidisciplinary research for environmental sustainability. *Journal of Social Issues, 63*, 175–197.

Van Der Vegt, G. S., & Bunderson, J. S. (2005). Learning and performance in multidisciplinary teams: The importance of collective team identification. *The Academy of Management Journal, 48*, 532–547.

Younglove-Webb, J., Gray, B., Abdalla, C. W., & Thurow, A. P. (1999). The dynamics of multidisciplinary teams in academic. *The Review of Higher Education, 22*, 425–440.

12 Ethical Issues

Faye Mishna, Marion K. Underwood,
Cheryl Milne, and Margaret F. Gibson

Conducting research with children is never a simple undertaking. The involvement of child participants engages researchers' beliefs about who young people are; what research is for; and how risks, commitments, and responsibilities should be prioritized or balanced. As researchers contemplate and make decisions about such considerations, they inevitably venture into the realm of ethics.

The realm of research ethics is, however, part of the same changing world in which both researchers and participants live, and ethical decision making always takes place in a larger social context, with all of its attendant complexities. Technological innovations can thus influence all those involved in the creation of social science research. As rapid technological shifts such as the advent and social integration of Internet or "cyber" communications have brought new possibilities to both children and to researchers, so too have these shifts raised new questions and issues about what behaviors are considered "safe," "responsible," "appropriate," or even "legal." For children and researchers alike, the existing authorities, whether parents and teachers or professional associations and research ethics boards, usually do not yet have the knowledge to offer complete or satisfying responses. Researchers and young people may both, consequently, feel adrift or "on their own" in making decisions about how to contend with the impact of technology. In instances where there is an immediate possibility of technologically mediated harm, such lack of guidance can add to a rising sense of uncertainty and fear.

In this chapter, we consider some central ethical dilemmas faced by researchers who study cyberbullying among children or adolescents. Based on our experiences and knowledge in this new and rapidly expanding area, we highlight the complexities encountered in this type of research. Rather than presenting new guidelines or set procedures for ethical decision making, we offer examples of how researchers might think about ethics and make decisions based on their particular contexts and priorities. Given our assumption that communication technology will continue to change rapidly and in ways we cannot possibly predict, and that young people's social lives will continue to be affected, any definitive ethical "solutions" are likely to be outdated almost as soon as they are developed. Rather, we hope to initiate discussion about how processes of ethical reflexivity can be incorporated as a crucial component of the new and constantly changing cyberbullying research.

CYBERBULLYING IN A CYBER TECHNOLOGICAL WORLD: AN OVERVIEW

Around the world, young people are using technologically mediated communication in overwhelming numbers. A 2009 study found that 71% of all teenagers in the United States owned a cell phone, increasing to 85% of youth from the ages of 15 to 17 (Pew, 2010). In Europe, the usage is estimated at much higher—with 95% of all 16-year-olds in the EU owning a mobile phone. Canadian statistics suggest lower levels of phone usage. Although a 2005 survey found that 56% of 11th grade students owned a cellular phone (Decima, 2006), research shows that 98% of Canadian youth access the Internet and communication technologies on a daily basis (Cassidy, Jackson, & Brown, 2009; Mishna, Cook, Gadalla, Daciuk, & Solomon, 2010). Similarly, 93% of American youth between the ages of 12 to 17 went online, and nearly two thirds of them (63%) go online daily (Lenhart, Purcell, Smith, & Zickuhr, 2010). Australian statistics are similar, with 79% of teenagers owning or using a cell phone (ACMA, 2007) and 80% of households with teens aged 14 to 17 years having Internet access (ABS, 2007).

The majority of young people report very positive feelings about cyber technology and its impact in their lives (Blais, Craig, Pepler, & Connolly, 2008). Social communication is the primary focus of most young people's online activities, and they deeply value the relationships that they develop and nurture through different forms of cyber communication (Mishna, McLuckie, & Saini, 2009; Subrahmanyam, Reich, Waechter, & Espinoza, 2008; Wolak, Mitchell, & Finkelhor, 2003). As in their "offline" interactions however, many young people also report having encountered significant difficulties in the world of online interactions; these come from a wide range of sources and relative levels of risk: from misunderstandings with friends all the way to cyber stalking or sexual exploitation (Mishna et al., 2010; Mishna, Saini, & Solomon, 2009; Mitchell, Finkelhor, & Wolak, 2001, 2003, 2011). Although young people are generally very knowledgeable about how the technologies operate, and often far more savvy and comfortable with the use of cyber technology than most adults, they often have not developed skills in navigating personal relationships and in anticipating and responding to risky situations (Collins, 2003; Steinberg, 2008; Steinberg & Morris, 2001).

Adults, on the other hand, are often skeptical and not particularly skilled in the use and social integration of the technology itself. Indeed, the "digital divide" between generations often leads to communicative impasses. Young people are extremely unlikely to report problems they are experiencing in the online world to adult authorities, for fear that the adults will try to reduce or remove their access to online communication (Kowalski & Limber, 2007; Mishna et al., 2009). Such technological communication is so important to many young people that they will, essentially, take the additional risk of leaving cyber abuse unreported rather than face the possibility of losing access to the technological communication that is so central to their social world (Mishna et al., 2009). Adults, as a result, may have little idea of either the prevalence or impact of cyberbullying or other forms of cyber abuse in children's lives (Kowalski & Fedina, 2011). In addition, the changing patterns of adolescent dating and friendships, with group activities and networks taking a more prominent role (Collins & Laursen, 2004), may make it difficult for adults to interpret or comprehend the impact of group communications on individual young people.

As adults, researchers are generally "catching up" with both technology and with its role in young people's lives. Only recently have researchers and other adults who work with children become increasingly aware that victimization, abuse, harassment, and other harms are not limited to interactions in "offline," shared, physical space. This awareness has led to the definition and study of the risks and harms that children experience in their online lives, including a research focus on cyberbullying.

The vast new world of online communication provides new challenges and opportunities for researchers. Researchers are forced to grapple with a lack of definitional clarity as to what constitutes cyberbullying (see Chapters 2, 3, and 4 in this volume), which makes it difficult for studies to build on each other and poses challenges when investigators might wish to intervene. Research on online communication also poses challenges for informed consent. Online communication may tempt investigators to gather data from minors without parental consent, because youth can be so easily contacted directly via the Internet. Most investigators studying cyberbullying rely on self-report surveys to assess who is involved in what role in various types of cyberbullying. The technology used for online communication, however, makes it possible to capture the actual content of the communication, and as more investigators investigate the content of electronic communication directly, several new ethical challenges will arise.

With no universally accepted definition for how cyberbullying compares with traditional bullying (Vaillancourt et al., 2008; Vandebosch, & Van Cleemput, 2008), several definitions are used in order to study the phenomenon and can differ quite significantly ranging from fairly specific to broad and inclusive definitions (Patchin & Hinduja, 2012). Similar to traditional bullying, certain elements are considered essential for the behavior to constitute cyberbullying: the use of technology with the intent to bully an individual, the individual who is targeted or victimized is negatively affected, and the behavior is repeated (Patchin & Hinduja, 2012). Occurring in the public domain (Craig, personal communication, February 25, 2009), by its very nature cyberbullying comprises a form of repetition since material such as e-mail or pictures can be viewed far and wide; can be distributed not only by the perpetrator but by anyone with access (Campbell, 2005; Patchin & Hinduja, 2012; Slonje & Smith, 2008); and can be difficult and, indeed, impossible to remove (Wolak, Mitchell, & Finkelhor, 2007).

The ethical responsibilities of the researcher may be complicated by such definitional uncertainty. If both "intent" and "harm" may be difficult to anticipate or even establish, how does the researcher decide if he or she has a legal or moral responsibility to intervene? Given the low rates of disclosure to adults (Mishna et al., 2009), the variable reported effects (Ybarra, Mitchell, Wolak, & Finkelhor,

2006), and the potential invisibility of cyberbullying, researchers may be similarly stymied in their anticipation of young people's level of risk or even in attempts to assess the current impact of cyberbullying victimization for a particular individual. They may also, on a societal level, be at risk of either raising unnecessary alarm or downplaying the significance of cyberbullying and other forms of online risk to young people. Given the interest of many social actors such as journalists, teachers, parents, and representatives of online industries, part of researchers' ethical decision making will likely involve the anticipation and ongoing management of how the findings of their studies will be taken up outside of scholarly circles, and how it may consequently affect the lives of young people and their families.

GENERAL ETHICAL PRINCIPLES, THE LAW, AND CYBERBULLYING RESEARCH

As other writers on children and research ethics have noted, ethical challenges in social science research with children can almost never be neatly disentangled from those which arise in research with people of all ages (Mishna, Antle, & Regehr, 2004). Similarly, the ethical challenges of working in technologically mediated domains of human experience cannot be easily separated out from the ethical challenges of other research with children, or indeed research with human participants more generally. Thus, the general principles of research ethics suggested here may have relevance for multiple situations. In this section, we consider several emerging core principles of ethical research with children. We discuss each with an eye to how cyberbullying research may expand upon or challenge these principles and their everyday application in research practice.

Regulation and Codification of Research Ethics

The foundations of internationally recognized research ethics have evolved from the Nuremburg guidelines, as subsequently codified in international agreements such as the *Declaration of Helsinki* (WMA, 2000). Although the original focus of research guidelines was on medical and biological research, social science research with human participants has been increasingly regulated over the final decades of the 20th century (Gallagher, Haywood, Jones, & Milne, 2009). Research Ethics Board (REB) reviews are required by research institutions throughout Canada, the United States, Australia, New Zealand, and the European Union.

The particular recognition of children as "vulnerable" populations in research has also increased since the 1980s (Mishna et al., 2004) and has been codified in documents such as the UN *Convention on the Rights of the Child* (United Nations, 1998). Most international guides or conventions leave it up to domestic law to determine systems for consent including age requirements, but documents such as the European *Convention on Human Rights and Biomedicine* are consistent with the UN *Convention on the Rights of the Child*'s emphasis on the evolving capacities of children. Jurisdictions differ considerably on the requirements for parental involvement and level of consent and the nature of the risk permitted in respect of research involving children (Alderson, 2007). For example, the Swedish Medical Research Council specifically permits research involving children if the research quality is "sufficient, risks are small, parents consent, and the child agrees to participate" (Alderson, 2007).

Researchers across many disciplines and methodologies have raised concerns about the impact of the increasingly bureaucratic and codified implementation of ethics (Scott & Fonseca, 2010). Although some, such as Haggerty (2004), have argued that "rule fetishization" replaces true ethical considerations in contemporary research practice, others have expressed more equanimity or even support for institutionalized ethical review procedures (e.g., Bosk, 2004; Brierley & Larcher, 2011). Some writers have expressed concerns that research ethics review boards may be overly hesitant to support any research with children (Angell, Biggs, Gahleitner, & Dixon-Woods, 2011). At the same time, most writers on research ethics agree that the scope of research ethics actually under the purview of research ethics boards is quite restricted, and that "ethical" research requires going well beyond what the institutionalized process requires. For example, the ethical review process generally takes place prior to the commencement of the research. Although researchers may try to anticipate and plan for ethical challenges and implications in their work, ethical dilemmas and decisions can, and do, arise throughout the research process, perhaps especially in the ever-changing word of online communication. As a result, having "completed" the ethical review process should not be seen as the end of ethical engagement (Mishna et al., 2004).

Cyberbullying and the Law

In addition to research ethics guidelines, the laws of the country where the research is taking place will also have an impact on the research and the researcher's obligations. While most researchers working with children would be familiar with the existence of mandatory reporting requirements for child protection concerns, the ages and categories for which reporting is required may vary according to jurisdiction. Some jurisdictions may have established legal age requirements for consent, while others have legislation that establishes a competency-based approach discussed in more detail below (Alderson, 2007).

Although some cyberbullying behaviors may be categorized as "illegal" in particular jurisdictions, often the legal system is similarly in flux in defining and regulating activities that occur online (Campbell, Chapter 19, this volume; Powell, 2010). There are also significant definitional issues in relation to online sexual content and its communication to and by children. For example, some jurisdictions would consider sexting between teenagers as illegal (Barry, 2010), while others might exempt some forms of communication of sexually explicit images from the legal definition of child pornography so long as the communication is between the two people depicted (Sharpe, 2001). With the increased public awareness of the negative impacts of cyberbullying on children, calls for law reform and stiffer penalties have become more prevalent (Meredith, 2010; Powell, 2010). These concerns arise in cyberbullying research due to the potential for violence or threats of violence, as well as the possible criminal implications inherent in the behavior being studied.

Privacy laws will also vary from jurisdiction to jurisdiction. If the research involves the soliciting of personal information online, there may be legislation particular to the jurisdiction that applies. In addition, legal rules vary to the extent that third parties can monitor telephone or other electronic communications without the consent of all parties to the communication. This may be particularly relevant when communications from a third party, unaware of the research monitoring, reveal evidence of criminal activity that the researcher believes must be ethically reported.

Therefore, while it is important for the researcher to know as much as possible about any mandated legal responsibilities that affect their work, it is not possible to describe in detail the law that might apply to research in this area, and the law is unlikely to anticipate or fully address many of the dilemmas that emerge. Our focus here is on principles of research that are internationally recognized, rather than on particular locally specific principles, and on situations that do not have obvious legal resolutions. We suggest that researchers consult legal experts in their own jurisdictions for advice on specific scenarios.

Many of the legal issues are subsumed under, or assist in the application of, the general principles that have been identified as essential for ethical research practice involving human subjects: autonomy, beneficence, and justice. When working with the emerging technologies, issues of privacy and the limits of confidentiality must be given careful consideration owing to the nature of the communications as much as the possible application of law. Finally, when children are participants in the research, the principle of autonomy is complicated and informed by rules or laws governing parents' participation, the assessment of competence or capacity, and legal limits on confidentiality.

Informed Consent. One area in which the ongoing negotiation of ethical concerns may be particularly evident is in the definition and ongoing negotiation of informed consent. Many researchers have written about the challenges in determining who is deemed capable to consent, and different jurisdictions have different laws about the age at which researchers must seek informed consent from participants, and which ages require the parent or guardian to provide this consent (e.g., Coyne, 2010; Gallagher et al., 2009; Mishna et al., 2004). Some jurisdictions such as the United States have generally required parental consent for all ages of children, while the United Kingdom has tended to apply a competency approach whereby the child may consent if competent to do so (Alderson, 2007). If children are deemed "too young" or otherwise incapable of providing legally recognized informed consent, ethics guidelines still usually require that researchers obtain "assent," in which the young person is offered the opportunity to participate or withdraw in the study, after the parent or guardian has given legal consent for the child's participation (Coyne, 2010).

Although "informed consent" is often discussed as a task that is completed at the beginning of a participant's interaction with researchers, many writers have described the need for conceptualized consent/assent as an ongoing ethical process that is integrated throughout the research project. Both participants and researchers may change their understandings of the project as time goes on. For young people, in particular, the lived experience of participating in research may "inform" them about the project in ways that the abstractions of initial discussion or a written document could not. In particular, many research approaches allow relationships to develop between researchers and young people, such as longitudinal studies, qualitative interviews, and ethnographic investigations. The young person's initial consent and knowledge of confidentiality is likely to be altered as a relationship of trust develops (Mishna et al., 2004; Swartz, 2011). How can researchers give both advance and ongoing warnings that young people may reveal more information than they originally intended as a result of changing emotional contexts in which they feel listened to and cared about?

For both consent and assent, unavoidable power differentials exist between adult researchers and the child participant. Children's understanding and ability to withdraw, ask questions, or say no in a given relationship and setting can therefore be significantly hindered by fear, confusion, or eagerness to please (Gallagher et al., 2009). For a child to withdraw from a project once it has begun can be a particularly daunting proposition, especially when research has already been approved, and thus supported, by parents and/or teachers or other authorities. There are other power differentials to consider, such as that between parents and children. At times, the process of obtaining informed consent from parents or guardians may put the young person at risk, and a waiver for parental consent may be the most ethical approach. For example, when participation in a research project may reveal the young person's involvement in an activity or identity that may be otherwise unknown to parents, obtaining parental consent may create real dangers for youth participants as well as create a barrier to participating for many young people (Coyne, 2010). An example of such research might include cyberbullying research that focuses on lesbian, gay, bisexual, or transgender youth. Less dramatically, however, researchers may unwittingly create conflict within families when parents and children have different opinions about the research study (e.g., when the parent does not consent to the child's participation and the child wants to participate). In cyberbullying research, the prevalent gap between what parents and children know and believe about technology and its impact on young people's lives can make such intergenerational conflict all the more likely.

Researchers also need to be cognizant of the fact that online communication may tempt us to collect data from youth online without ever having face-to-face interactions, which has both advantages and perils. On the positive side, online data collection could allow youth in marginalized groups to participate in research in private, without having to risk stigma associated with identifying themselves, even to the researcher. The ability to collect data directly from youth online however, without any face-to-face interaction poses some risks for researchers.

Investigators might be tempted to collect data from youth directly, without the parental consent required in many countries, including the United States. Investigators must remain mindful of ethical principles and laws that require parent consent for minors to participate in research and refrain from using the easy methods that the Internet provides to contact youth directly for data collection. Just because we can contact youth directly without their parents' consent does not mean we should. Also, the fact that no face-to-face interaction is involved could raise questions about the true identity of the participants and whether observations are independent, thus seriously compromising the validity of the research. Youth who feel strongly about the research questions could participate online multiple times, perhaps posing as different individuals.

Although local laws and policies may sharply differentiate between research with young people and research with adults, ethical challenges of defining and negotiating consent also occur in research with adult participants. Indeed, although research standards generally assume that adult participants are autonomous, purely rational actors, there is considerable evidence that many research participants, children and adults alike, have understanding of research projects and of their role and rights as participants that diverge sharply from what the researchers themselves believe (Coyne, 2010; Gallagher et al., 2009). Thus, any consideration of research ethics with children points to larger issues of informed consent for research with any and all participants.

Protection and Limits to Confidentiality. The ethical responsibility to protect young people from harm often exists in tension with the ethical responsibility to preserve privacy or confidentiality. Across most jurisdictions, there is a clear legal requirement to protect children from harm through the mandated reporting of child abuse or other exceptions to confidentiality. In such cases, there are often clear guidelines about how researchers should proceed. Researchers nevertheless must clearly communicate and confirm what children and parents/guardians understand confidentiality to mean in order to meet their ethical responsibilities of informing children and guardians as part of the process of consent and assent. It has become standard for most "consent" documents and discussions to contain a section about information obtained during the research process to which confidentiality applies.

In cyberbullying research, confidentiality is likely to be particularly important to potential participants because cyberbullying: (1) is usually concealed from adult authorities such as teachers and parents, (2) is capable of getting somebody "in trouble" with parents or school systems, and (3) often involves the involuntary disclosure of information (both true and false) as a tactic of victimizing others. Additionally, many cases fall into a "gray area" in which children report experiencing some risk or harm that does not meet legal definitions of child maltreatment or immediate danger. Because young people usually do not report such incidents to adults in their lives, it is likely that the researcher may be the only adult who has heard the extent of the child's involvement in cybervictimization or perpetration. The researcher has a responsibility to weigh the risk of harm to the child as he or she considers various forms of action. Cyberbullying researchers must therefore have a clear and ongoing conversation with participants about what does and does not remain "confidential," and how the researchers meet their "protection" responsibilities, including those that may not be legally mandated.

In research studies in which children come to trust researchers, issues of protection, confidentiality, and informed consent can become increasingly tricky to navigate (Gallagher et al., 2009; Swartz, 2011). For example, a young person might feel so comfortable being listened to and responded to during a qualitative interview that he or she reveals that he or she is being victimized online by a particular, known peer (similar concerns would also arise if the young person revealed being a perpetrator of cyberbullying). If the young person is distressed, for example, having nightmares or difficulty concentrating, but is not in immediate danger of harm, there is no legal mandate for the researcher to follow. If, as often happens, the young person is unwilling to disclose the cyberbullying to anyone else in authority and tells the researcher if asked that he or she is okay and "will tell if it gets really bad," the researcher is faced with a dilemma. Specifically, the researcher must decide how much to push the student and ultimately whether he or she should break confidentiality in order to meet the ethical principle of protection (Mishna at al., 2004).

In such a scenario, the researcher needs to wonder about the meaning of the child disclosing the cyberbullying but asking the researcher not to tell anyone and saying that at this point, he or she isn't planning to tell. Given the low likelihood of the child disclosing outside of the research setting, researchers are in a position of having to take any disclosure seriously. Even if the child does not assent to further disclosure, the researcher must consider whether the child is anticipating that the adult will actually "do something" to protect them. The researcher may decide, from interactions with a particular child that the young person is, in fact, telling an adult about the situation because he or she *wants* the adult to intervene, despite the child communicating something altogether different. There is no "risk-free" choice the researcher can make. Disclosing the situation to someone else risks patronizing a child and violating his or her stated request and the principle of confidentiality and self-determination. However, not disclosing risks may mean "dropping the ball" on a child's request (and need) for assistance and protection, however indirectly it might be stated.

An additional ethical concern arises when researchers have "child-friendly" interpersonal skills which they can employ to help children feel comfortable, but also, at times, to overcome a child's initial hesitancy or resistance to revealing information (Gallagher et al., 2009; Swartz, 2011). When researchers also have a background in clinical practice or other professional experience working with young people, such additional skills and roles can both add to and complicate the negotiation of consent and disclosure. If a researcher is able to talk with the young person involved in a way which encourages the child to "decide" to disclose, this ultimately may resolve a protection concern, but such "soft" pressure introduces other ethical concerns about whose decisions are ultimately being respected.

Protection and confidentiality can also be complicated by the administrative settings of cyberbullying studies. Because a large number of cyberbullying studies have taken place in educational settings, (e.g., Bauman, 2010; Mishna et al., 2010; Williams & Guerra, 2007), an important question is whether and how researchers ensure that children's participation is kept confidential from teachers and school administrators. Additionally, educators at research sites might want to know if there are students in need of additional protection, or if certain students are known to pose a risk to others. Indeed, the educators' own ethical codes regarding bullying may come into play. Finally, given students' common assumption that schools do not respond effectively to cyberbullying (Agatston, Kowalski, & Limber, 2007), young people may feel that they either cannot withdraw or cannot be honest about their experiences with cyberbullying if the research is seen as a "school activity" (Gallagher, et al., 2009). Researchers must consider how to balance these various ethical responsibilities as they engage with other systems and authorities, and determine how they can separate their projects from classroom expectations.

Respect for Children's Capacity and Knowledge. "Respect for participants" is another overarching principle of research ethics that can be difficult to codify. In research with young people, such "respect" can be particularly tenuous and difficult to reconcile with the dominant definition of young people through a lens of "vulnerability." There is a long history of viewing children as not capable, not knowledgeable, and as generally passive objects rather than agents in research endeavors (Clavering & McLaughlin, 2010; Mishna et al., 2004). More recently, researchers have begun to investigate ways to involve children in research to a greater extent and to respect their knowledge as distinctive from, but not subordinate to, knowledge held by adults (DePalma, 2011; Munford & Sanders, 2004). Such participatory approaches do not negate the need for researchers to consider how children perceive, experience, and are affected by the research process (Waller & Bitou, 2011). Rather, it is imperative that researchers continue to consider how power operates throughout all stages of the research process.

Such approaches have particular potential in cyberbullying research, given the expertise that young people have with both emerging technologies and their uses in social communication. Researchers can work *with* the technological differences between generations, rather than attempting to impose adult knowledge and values onto young people. There is considerable evidence that many young people hold greater (although not limitless) expertise where technology is concerned, and researchers can involve youth advisory committees or think about other ways to encourage young people's agency within the research enterprise (Mishna et al., 2009). It is important that adult knowledge not be discounted, however, since many young people may have incredible technological savvy in some areas while holding mistaken beliefs about both technology and relationships. For example, many young people continue to believe that items "deleted" from their computers have been expunged from the Internet record (Mishna et al., 2010). Thus, research can also offer an opportunity to expand young people's knowledge and ability to make decisions about relationships and online risks. Additionally, respect for children and recognition of their rights can be translated into advocating for young people's access to both participating in and benefiting from research (Mishna et al., 2004; Modi, 2011). Particular groups of young people might be either over- or under-researched, without necessarily receiving equitable benefits from research enterprises. Researchers should not only strive to minimize harm to young people who participate directly, but also to maximize the benefit to both participants and to young people in the community in which the research takes place.

Ethics and Technological Research Methods. Although many investigators rely on self-report surveys to assess cyberbullying, technology makes it entirely possible to access and study the content of online communication directly, without having to ask youth to report on what they say and do online. The technology itself makes it possible for investigators to access blogs and chat rooms, and with some effort and expense, text messaging and e-mail. Capturing the content of online communication avoids the inevitable biases related to self-report, especially for negative behavior such as cyberbullying. Adolescents may underreport their own online bullying because they are motivated to present themselves in a positive light, because they do not view negative online communication as harmful enough to count as bullying, or because they are truly unaware of their negative behavior. Studying the actual content of adolescents' blogs, online communication in chat rooms, and text messaging allows researchers to observe directly exactly what adolescents say in their electronic communication and with whom they communicate.

Because studying electronic communication provides "a window into the secret world of adolescent peer culture" (Greenfield & Yan, 2006, p. 392), using these methods raises important ethical issues. The following discussion focuses on ethical issues that have arisen in an ongoing longitudinal study in which adolescents were given BlackBerry devices with paid service plans and unlimited text messaging, configured so that the content of all communication using the devices would be captured and saved to a secure online archive for later coding (see the BlackBerry Project, for a detailed description of this method; also see Underwood, Rosen, More, Ehrenreich, & Gentsch, 2012). Similar ethical dilemmas would ensue in studies of online communication in chat rooms, Instant messaging, e-mail, weblogs, or really any other forum for electronic communication.

The first ethical and scientific challenge relates to informed consent. Ethical guidelines mandate that adolescents as well as their parents be informed that electronic communication is being monitored. However, getting this informed consent might lead adolescents to alter their communication and to censor the types of remarks in which researchers and policy makers might be most interested, such as cyberbullying and sexting. Results from a content analysis of text messaging in the BlackBerry Project suggest that youth are communicating frankly and openly despite our monitoring (Underwood et al., 2012). The percentages of sexual utterances (6.6%) and profane messages (7%) were similar to those found in a previous content analysis of adolescents' conversations in unmonitored chat rooms (Subrahmanyam, Smahel, & Greenfield, 2006). Participants in the BlackBerry Project may communicate openly despite the monitoring because they have been participating in the study for many years and understand the policies on confidentiality. In our archive of text messaging, we sometimes see participants discussing how we protect confidentiality. For example, when a friend was openly communicating about selling drugs, our participant reminded the person, "Hey, be careful, the BlackBerry Project people are watching, but don't worry, they won't tell anyone." These data suggest that adolescents may engage in cyberbullying even if they know communication is monitored, but investigators studying cyberbullying by directly examining online communication should take care to convey information about confidentiality in clear and specific terms.

The second ethical challenge also relates to consent. The technology used in the BlackBerry Project captures all messages sent from and received by the BlackBerry device. Although parents and target youth have given consent for us to capture the content of their communication, we do not have consent for those who send messages to youth in our study. Investigators in early studies of online communication have argued convincingly that electronic communication can be observed without consent in some situations because the electronic communication need not be uniquely identifiable, unless individuals choose to use their actual full names as their online user names (see Subrahmanyam et al., 2006; Whitlock, Powers, & Eckenrode, 2006). In studies of cyberbullying using technological methods, investigators could find themselves in the position of perhaps needing to alert authorities about behavior by youth not participating in the research, which raises many practical, logistical challenges.

The third ethical challenge related to using technology to observe online communication directly relates to the fact that participants may engage in extreme cyberbullying or discuss antisocial conduct freely and openly. The long-term goals of the BlackBerry Project include understanding developmental origins of antisocial behavior. Therefore, the researchers cannot intervene every time they see discussions of rule-breaking activities. Because this study is funded by the National Institutes of Health in the United States, the researchers were able to obtain a Federal Certificate of Confidentiality, which allows them to assess antisocial behavior without having to report it to the police (although they are still required to report child or elder abuse, suicidality, or imminent danger of harm to others). The youth assent and parent consent forms clearly convey to participants and parents exactly what we are and are not required to report.

Probably the most serious ethical challenge related to observing online communication directly relates to the researchers' responsibility to monitor the massive volume of online communication in their archive for messages related to child abuse or intent to harm self or others. The archiving technology was developed to allow financial corporations to monitor their employees' electronic communication for compliance with federal laws, so it is configured to do electronic searches. We conduct weekly searches for a lengthy list of words as phrases such as "rape," "want to die," and "older man." Occurrences of these phrases are examined carefully by reading backward and forward in the archive to understand what might be happening. If there is any question, we contact the appropriate authorities and the family to make sure the child is safe. Investigators studying cyberbullying could microcode selected transcripts for bullying episodes, but could also search large volumes of communication using key word searches for specially selected terms. Cyberbullying researchers should be prepared to monitor online content carefully and to intervene when online communication conveys clear intent to harm self or others.

The fifth ethical challenge concerns situations in which parents strongly desire to see the content of the electronic communication we are gathering because they are desperately worried about their child's safety. For example, parents who sense that their child is extremely distressed by cyberbullying may put pressure on investigators to share the content of the electronic communication. Parents in the BlackBerry Project are fully informed that they will not have access to their adolescent children's electronic communication, but they become understandably eager for the information when emergencies arise. For example, several times in our study, adolescent participants have run away from home and taken their BlackBerry devices, and parents have asked us to share their text messaging so they can figure out where their children have gone. In these situations, after consultation with their Institutional Review Board, the researchers contacted the participant via text messaging on the BlackBerry, urged them to contact their parents, offered them help if they needed any kind of help or protection, and reminded the adolescent participant their participation in the study and it paying for their BlackBerry service depends on their parents continuing to give consent. The researchers have been able to resist giving parents access to adolescents' electronic communication by working to get them in touch with their children, and in all cases, the situation was resolved by the child communicating with the parent within a short time. In studies of cyberbullying in which parents are eager to see electronic communication that investigators cannot share, researchers could work with parents and youth to foster communication about cyberbullying so that perhaps the child would be willing to share the content with the parents.

Because observing adolescents' electronic communication provides such a vivid portrait of their social lives, it is difficult to anticipate all of the challenges that can arise. Still, the wealth of information about cyberbullying that could be yielded by examining the content of electronic communication seems well worth the risks. Examining what adolescents actually say online could help to understand how cyberbullying unfolds and whether and how peers intervene or defend one another from cyberbullying. Detailed information about these social processes could be valuable for developing more effective prevention and intervention programs. We believe that it is possible to navigate the challenges of studying the consent of adolescents' online communication with the utmost care and respect for young participants.

CONCLUSION

In this chapter, we reviewed significant ethical dilemmas that can arise in conducting research on cyberbullying among children and adolescents. With each successive generation, communication technology is growing exponentially as a central fixture within our society and is dramatically changing individuals' social interactions, learning strategies, and choice of entertainment. Although regular Internet use typically begins in preadolescence (DeBell, 2005), usage is starting at younger ages (Bumpus & Werner, 2009), and children are increasingly socializing online (Valkenburg, Schouten, & Peter, 2005; Woodard & Gridina, 2000). It is imperative therefore to consider the types of ethical dilemmas that researchers conducting cyberbullying will face. As definitive ethical "solutions" are likely to become outdated almost as soon as they are developed, it is necessary to engage in discussion about the kinds of ethical dilemmas and ways to consider these that emerge in cyberbullying research.

Researchers also have broader ethical responsibilities to disseminate results in ways that increase young people's agency and well-being beyond the confines of research. For example, research that relates directly to prevention strategies that educators, parents, and youth themselves might use can be seen as fulfilling such a broad-based ethical mandate (e.g., Mishna, Cook, Saini, Wu, & MacFadden, 2011). There are also opportunities for researchers to broaden their understanding of ethical practice as they address multiple causes and effects of social inequity, including those that are not legally sanctioned. For example, while many jurisdictions have laws that prohibit certain forms of bias-based bullying (such as victimization based on race or sex), researchers can highlight the prevalence and impact of other, less widely recognized forms of discrimination such as bullying of young people who have developmental or learning disabilities (Kowalski & Fedina, 2011). In advocating for a broader understanding of "bias," researchers can expand the mandate of ethical research practice. Such advocacy work would also reflect the transnational nature of cyberbullying concerns. If the cyber practices affecting young people can so easily cross institutional jurisdictions and state borders, researchers cannot rely on codified policies of what "ethical" research can mean. Rather, we must engage in collaborative, flexible, and continual reexaminations of ethical praxis.

References

Agatston, P. W., Kowalski, R., & Limber, S. (2007). Students' perspectives on cyberbullying. *Journal of Adolescent Health, 41*, S59–S60. doi:10.1016/j.jadohealth.2007.09.003

Alderson, P. (2007). Competent children? Minors' consent to health care treatment and research. *Social Science & Medicine, 65*, 2272–2283. doi:10.1016/j.socscimed.2007.08.005

Angell, E., Biggs, H., Gahleitner, F., & Dixon-Woods, M. (2011). What do research ethics committees say about applications to conduct research involving children? *Archives of Disease in Childhood, 95*, 915–917.

Australian Bureau of Statistics (ABS). (2007). *Household use of information technology in Australia 2006–07.* Cat. No. 8146.0. Canberra: Commonwealth of Australia.

Australian Communications and Media Authority (ACMA). (2007). *Media and communications in Australian families 2007: Report of the media and society research project.* Canberra: Commonwealth of Australia.

Barry, J. L. (2010). The child as victim and perpetrator: Laws punishing juvenile "sexting." *Vanderbilt Journal of Entertainment and Technology Law, 13*(1), 130–153.

Bauman, S. (2010). Cyberbullying in a rural intermediate school: An exploratory study. *Journal of Early Adolescence, 30*(6), 803–833.

Blais, J. J., Craig, W. M., Pepler, D., & Connolly, J. (2008). Adolescents online: The importance of Internet activity choices to salient relationships. *Journal of Youth and Adolescence, 37*(5), 522–536. doi:10.1007/s10964–007–9262–7

Bosk, C. (2004). The ethnography and the IRB: Comment on Kevin D. Haggerty, "Ethics creep: Governing social science research in the name of ethics." *Qualitative Sociology, 27*(4), 417–420. doi:10.1023/B:QUAS.0000049240.88037.51

Brierley, J., & Larcher, V. (2011). Lest we forget . . . research ethics in children: perhaps onerous, yet absolutely necessary. *Archives of Disease in Childhood, 95*(11), 863–866. doi:10.1136/jme.2010.040667

Bumpus, M. F., & Werner, N. E. (2009). Maternal rule-setting for children's Internet use. *Marriage and Family Review, 45*(6), 845–865. doi:10.1080/01494920903224442

Campbell, M. A. (2005). Cyberbullying: An old problem in a new guise? *Australian Journal of Guidance & Counselling, 15*(1), 68–76. doi:10.1375/ajgc.15.1.68

Cassidy, W., Jackson, M., & Brown, K. (2009). Sticks and stones can break my bones, but how can pixels hurt me? Students' experiences with cyber-bullying. *School Psychology International, 30*(4), 383–402. doi:10.1177/0143034309106948

Clavering, E. K., & McLaughlin, J. (2010). Children's participation in health research: From objects to agents? *Child: Care, Health and Development, 36*(5), 603–611. doi: 10.1111/j.1365–2214.2010.01094.x

Collins, W. A. (2003). More than myth: The developmental significance of romantic relationships during adolescence. *Journal of Research on Adolescence, 13*, 1–24. doi: 10.1111/1532–7795.1301001

Collins, W. A., & Laursen, B. (2004). Changing relationships, changing youth: Interpersonal contexts of adolescent development. *Journal of Early Adolescence, 24*(1), 55–62. doi: 10.1177/0272431603260882

Coyne, I. (2010). Research with children and young people: The issue of parental (proxy) consent. *Children & Society, 24*, 227–237.

DeBell, M. (2005). *Rates of computer and Internet use by children in nursery school and students in kindergarten through twelfth grade: 2003* (NCES 2005–111). Washington, DC: U.S. Department of Education, National Center for Education Statistics.

Decima Research. (2006). *Using wireless technologies in Canada.* Prepared for Canadian Wireless Telecommunications Association.

DePalma, R. (2011). Socially just research for social justice: Negotiating consent and safety in a participatory action research project. *International Journal of Research & Method in Education, 33*(3), 215–227.

Gallagher, M. Haywood, S. L., Jones, M. W., & Milne, S. (2009). Negotiating informed consent with children in school-based research: A critical review. *Children & Society, 24*, 471–482.

Greenfield, P., & Yan, Z. (2006). Children, adolescents, and the Internet: A new field of inquiry in developmental psychology. *Developmental Psychology, 42*(3), 391–394. doi: 10.1037/0012–1649.42.3.391

Haggerty, K. D. (2004). Ethics creep: Governing social science research in the name of ethics. *Qualitative Sociology, 27*(4), 391–414. doi:10.1023/B:QUAS.0000049239.15922.a3

Kowalski, R. M., & Fedina, C. (2011). Cyberbullying in ADHD and Asperger Syndrome populations. *Research in Autism Spectrum Disorders, 9*, 1201–1208. doi:10.1016/j.rasd. 2011.01.007

Kowalski, R. M., & Limber, S. P. (2007). Electronic bullying among middle school students. *Journal of Adolescent Health, 41*, S22–S30. doi:10.1016/j.jadohealth.2007.08.017

Lenhart, A., Purcell, K., Smith, A., & Zickuhr, K. (2010). Social media and mobile Internet use among teens and young adults. *Pew Internet and American Life Project.* Retrieved from http://pewinternet.org/Reports/2010/Social-Media-and-Young-Adults.aspx

Meredith, J. P. (2010). Combating cyberbullying: Emphasizing education over criminalization. *Federal Communications Law Journal, 63*, 312–339.

Mishna, F., Antle, B. J., & Regehr, C. (2004). Tapping the perspectives of children. *Qualitative Social Work, 3*(4), 449–467. doi:10.1177/1473325004048025

Mishna, F., Cook, C., Gadalla, T., Daciuk, J., & Solomon, S. (2010). Cyberbullying behaviors among middle and high school students. *American Journal of Orthopsychiatry, 80*(3), 362–374. doi:10.1111/j.1939–0025.2010.01040.x

Mishna, F., Cook, C., Saini, M, Wu, M. J., & MacFadden, R. (2011). Interventions to prevent and reduce cyber abuse of youth: A systematic review. *Research on Social Work Practice, 21*(1), 5–14. doi:10.1177/1049731509351988

Mishna, F., McLuckie, A., & Saini, M. (2009). Real-world dangers in an online reality: A qualitative study examining online relationships and cyber abuse. *Social Work Research, 33*(2), 107–118. doi:10.1093/swr/33.2.107

Mishna, F., Saini, M., & Solomon, S. (2009). Ongoing and online: Children and youth's perceptions of cyberbullying. *Children and Youth Services Review, 31*, 1222–1228. doi:10.1016/j.childyouth.2009.05.004

Mitchell, K. J., Finkelhor, D., & Wolak, J. (2001). Risk factors for and impact of online sexual solicitation of youth. *Journal of the American Medical Association, 285*(23), 3011–3014. doi:10.1001/jama.285.23.3011

Mitchell, K. J., Finkelhor, D., & Wolak, J. (2003). Victimization of youths on the Internet. *Journal of Aggression, Maltreatment, and Trauma, 8*(1/2), 1–39. doi:10.1016/ S0140–1971(02)00114–8

Mitchell, K. J., Finkelhor, D., & Wolak, J. (2011). Youth Internet victimization in a broader victimization context. *Journal of Adolescent Health, 48*, 128–134. doi:10.1016/j. jadohealth.2010.06.009

Modi, N. (2011). Promoting research for children. *Archives of Disease in Childhood, 95*, 941–944. doi:10.1136/archdischild-2011–300721

Munford, R., & Sanders, J. (2004). Recruiting diverse groups of young people to research: Agency and empowerment in the consent process. *Qualitative Social Work, 3*(4), 469–482. doi:10.1177/1473325004048026

Patchin, J. W., & Hinduja, S. (2012). *Cyberbullying prevention and response: Expert perspectives.* New York: Routledge.

Pew Internet & American Life Project. (2010). *Teens and Mobile Phones.* Pew Research Centre. Retrieved from http://pewinternet.org/Reports/2010/Teens-and-Mobile-Phones. aspx

Powell, A. (2010). Configuring consent: Emerging technologies, unauthorized sexual images and sexual assault. *The Australian & New Zealand Journal of Criminology, 43*(1), 76–90. doi:10.1375/acri.43.1.76

R. v. Sharpe, 1 SCR 45 (2001). doi:10.1080/09627250108553168

Scott, C.L., & Fonseca, L. (2010). Overstepping the mark: Ethics procedures, risky research and education researchers. *International Journal of Research & Method in Education, 33*(3), 287–300. doi:10.1080/1743727X.2010.511710

Slonje, R., & Smith, P.K. (2008). Cyberbullying: Another main type of bullying? *Scandinavian Journal of Psychology, 49,* 147–154. doi:10.1111/j.1467–9450.2007.00611.x

Steinberg, L. (2008). A social neuroscience perspective on adolescent risk-taking. *Developmental Review, 28,* 78–106. doi:10.1016/j.dr.2007.08.002

Steinberg, L., & Morris, A.S. (2001). Adolescent development. *Annual Review of Psychology, 52,* 83–110. doi:10.1146/annurev.psych.52.1.83

Subrahmanyam, K., Reich, S.M., Waechter, N., & Espinoza, G. (2008). Online and offline social networks: Use of social networking sites by emerging adults. *Journal of Applied Developmental Psychology, 29,* 420–433. doi:10.1016/j.appdev.2008.07.003

Subrahmanyam, K., Smahel, D., & Greenfield, P. (2006). Connecting developmental constructions to the Internet: Identity presentation and sexual exploration in online teen chat rooms. *Developmental Psychology, 42,* 395–406. doi:10.1037/0012–1649.42.3.395

Swartz, S. (2011). "Going deep" and "giving back": Strategies for exceeding ethical expectations when researching amongst vulnerable youth. *Qualitative Research, 11*(1), 47–68. doi:10.1177/1468794110385885

Underwood, M.K., Rosen, L.H., More, D., Ehrenreich, S., & Gentsch, J.K. (2012). The BlackBerry Project: Capturing the content of adolescents' electronic communication. *Developmental Psychology, 48,* 295–302.

United Nations (1998). UN Convention on the Rights of the Child. Retrieved from http://www.unicef.org/crc/

Vaillancourt, T., McDougall, P., Hymel, S., Krygsman, A., Miller, J., Stiver, J., & Davis, C. (2008). Bullying: Are researchers and children/youth talking about the same thing? *International Journal of Behavioral Development, 32*(6), 486–495. doi:10.1177/0165025408095553

Valkenburg, P., Schouten, A.P., & Peter, J. (2005). Adolescents' identity experiments on the Internet. *New Media & Society, 7*(3), 383–402. doi:10.1177/1461444805052282

Vandebosch, H., & Van Cleemput, K. (2008). Defining cyberbullying: A qualitative research into the perceptions of youngsters. *CyberPsychology & Behavior, 11*(4), 499–503. doi:10.1089/cpb.2007.0042

Waller, T., & Bitou, A. (2011). Research *with* children: three challenges for participatory research in early childhood. *European Early Childhood Education Research Journal, 19*(1), 5–20. doi:10.1080/1350293X.2011.548964

Whitlock, J.L., Powers, J.L., & Eckenrode, J. (2006). The virtual cutting edge: The Internet and adolescent self-injury. *Developmental Psychology, 42,* 407–417. doi:10.1037/0012–1649.42.3.407

Williams, K.R., & Guerra, N.G. (2007). Prevalence and predictors of Internet bullying. *Journal of Adolescent Health, 41,* S14–S21. doi:10.1016/j.jadohealth.2007.08.018

Wolak, J., Mitchell, K.J., & Finkelhor, D. (2003). Escaping or connecting? Characteristics of youth who form close online relationships. *Journal of Adolescence, 26*(1), 105–119. doi:10.1016/S0140–1971(02)00114–8

Wolak, J.D., Mitchell, K.J., & Finkelhor, D. (2007). Does online harassment constitute bullying? An exploration of online harassment by known peers and online-only contacts. *Journal of Adolescent Health, 41,* S51–S58. doi:10.1016/j.jadohealth.2007.08.019

Woodard, E. H., & Gridina, N. (2000). *Media in the home 2000: The fifth annual survey of parents and children*. Philadelphia: Annenberg Public Policy Center of the University of Pennsylvania.

World Medical Association (WMA). (2000). *Declaration of Helsinki: Ethical principles for medical research involving human subjects*. Adopted by the 52nd WMA General Assembly, Edinburgh, Scotland.

Ybarra, M., Mitchell, K., Wolak, J., & Finkelhor, D. (2006). Examining characteristics and associated distress related to Internet harassment: Findings from the second youth Internet safety survey. *Pediatrics, 118*(4), 1169–1177. doi:10.1542/peds.2006–0815

13 Emerging Methodological Strategies to Address Cyberbullying

Online Social Marketing and Young People as Co-Researchers

Barbara A. Spears and Mike Zeederberg

In spite of being the focus of international research for over 35 years, bullying remains a problem for young people in schools. In recent times, the increasingly available and ready access to technology and social media has seen cyberbullying emerge as the latest iteration of this old problem (Belsey, 2006; Campbell, 2005; Hinduja & Patchin, 2007; Patchin & Hinduja, 2006; Smith et al., 2008). With its arrival has come the need to examine how it is defined, measured, reported, and addressed including exploring the principles and motivations that underpin the behaviors associated with it. Not surprisingly, what is being done currently to explore and address cyberbullying in schools has its roots in "traditional" bullying methodologies and interventions (Cross, Monks, Campbell, Spears, & Slee, 2011a), but the question needs to be posed: Are old ways of thinking being used to target new ways of being? This chapter briefly reflects on what is known about bullying, before considering the role of emerging methodological strategies to address cyberbullying, such as the use of online social marketing and engaging young people as co-researchers.

CONSIDERING THE PAST AND PRESENT: BACKGROUND TO THE PROPOSITION

By way of background to the current proposition, a brief examination of what is known about traditional bullying reveals considerable understanding about this form of interpersonal aggression. From the earliest studies in Scandinavia (Olweus, 1978) through to the national intervention programs being undertaken globally (Spiel, Salmivelli & Smith, 2011; Ttofi & Farrington, 2011), research into the prevalence, nature, and correlates of bullying and, more recently, cyberbullying, has been driven by the need to ensure that students are safe at school and can maximize their academic, social, and emotional potential, free from intimidation, peer harassment, and violence.

Research has demonstrated a range of health-related outcomes and impacts on young people in relation to bullying (Hawker & Boulton, 2000), clearly establishing its profound effects on the individual and the broader community: namely, social (Nansel, Overpeck, Pilla, & Ruan, 2001); physical (Landstedt & Gådin, 2011; Wolke, Woods, Bloomfield, & Karstadt, 2001); mental health (Arseneault, Bowes, & Shakoor, 2010; Kaltiala-Heino, Rimpela, Rantanen, & Rimpela, 2000); and suicidal ideation (Skapinakis et al., 2011). With the recent advent of cyberbullying, exploration into the relationship between the traditional forms and online bullying has revealed an overlap, where those who engage offline are likely to be involved online (Beran & Li, 2007; Cross et al., 2009; Hinduja & Patchin, 2008; Raskauskas & Stoltz, 2007; Smith et al., 2008; Vandebosch & Van Cleemput, 2009). This suggests that they are not totally separate or independent behaviors, indicating that approaches to measuring and addressing cyberbullying could be similar to those employed for traditional bullying. However, as cyberbullying employs technology to enact the bullying relationship, it raises the possibility that different methodologies may need to be employed in the quest to understand the phenomenon and its impact more fully.

Traditional methodological approaches commonly employ self, peer, teacher, and parent-report strategies, which are aimed at informing the nature and prevalence of school bullying, by examining any of the following: the individual (bully/victim, high-risk students); peer (group, participant); classroom (curriculum); school (policy, climate, behavior support/management, supervision, and yard improvements); and community (engaging and involving parents, whole-school) aspects of the phenomenon. While each of these aspects can be addressed individually as a strategy, whole-school antibullying interventions that simultaneously target those who bully, are victimized, stand-by, and are members of the broader community, seem to demonstrate the most promising way of managing bullying in schools at the moment (Cross et al, 2011a, 2011b; Michaud, 2009; Smith, Ananiadou, & Cowie, 2003).

However, research has indicated varied success with interventions. In addition to the content involved in antibullying approaches, the process of implementation, the fidelity of the delivery of the initiative/program, and the relevance of the elements presented to those involved, are all areas related to the success or otherwise of the intervention (Cross et al, 2011b; Rigby & Slee, 2008; Rigby & Smith, 2011; Slee et. al., 2009; Smith, Schneider, Smith & Ananiadou, 2004; Ttofi & Farrington, 2011; Vreeman & Carroll, 2007). Adding further to this, the change forces that operate in and around school environments need understanding (Spears, Slee, Campbell, & Cross, 2011) as these can act as either facilitators or barriers to any intervention, of any kind, in any school setting.

Finally, the current focus on the mobilization and translation of research to sustain and promote antibullying promotion, health, and well-being through policy and practice, is an important contemporary development in the effort to reduce bullying in schools and the broader community (Durlak, Weissberg, Dymnicki, Taylor, & Schellinger, 2011; Elias, Zins, Graczyk & Weissberg, 2003; Spears et al., 2011; Spiel et al., 2011) and represents a shift away from addressing the individual, to the system in terms of prevention, promotion, and intervention.

In briefly reflecting on what we know generally about bullying, the advent of cyberbullying poses the question of whether or not this knowledge can be applied directly to the issue of cyberbullying or whether new methodological strategies are needed to address it.

THE CHALLENGES: SETTINGS, SYSTEMS, ONLINE SOCIAL MARKETING, AND YOUNG PEOPLE AS CO-RESEARCHERS

Cyberbullying presents new challenges for researchers in terms of the ways in which it can be defined, identified, measured, and addressed, simply because of the mediums employed and the fact that, while it represents what is known in terms of power imbalances and intent, there remain many unknowns: such as the notions of repetition and anonymity; and the rapid and constant advances in technology, which usher in potentially new ways of bullying (Campbell, Spears, Cross, & Slee, 2010). In addition, adults do not know from firsthand experience what it means to be an adolescent in this social-media driven context.

Also, for the first time, not all school-related bullying occurs in real time, or in the so-called real world of schools. Technology has and will continue to transform the ways in which young people interact socially, and while methodological strategies used in the past to explore and address traditional bullying may inform our understanding of cyberbullying and associated behaviors, they may not be highly relevant or effective for intervening online or with online behaviors. It is pertinent to therefore look to the future: to consider emerging methods and strategies that are relevant to new and emerging media, online behaviors, and the online spaces in which young people congregate.

It is also relevant to consider the role and agency of youth "voice" in directing understanding, anti-cyberbullying strategies and interventions. Adults do not generally have cyber-experiences to call upon, and this represents a significant shift, as, for the first time, researchers in this field are trying to explore a phenomenon that they generally do not know firsthand: bullying occurring via technologies, and what it means to be a young person socializing online. Young people are said to be the experts in their own technologically enhanced lives, and this expertise represents a methodological strategy that must be explored if cyberbullying is to be addressed.

Settings

Schools are settings where young people have traditionally come together from a very young age: to learn, play, socialize, and to grow; and it is in these institutions that bullying regularly occurs and in which interventions have been, and continue to be, most often focused. There are, however, other spaces where young people socialize and congregate: in public domains outside of schools, such as playgrounds in the local community; sporting facilities, and shopping centers and malls.

Through the advent of technology, however, they are also interacting online, in settings outside of school: in "publically networked spaces" (Boyd, 2007,

p. 7, 2008; Boyd & Ellison, 2007; Ito et al., 2009). Young people seamlessly transfer their socializing and aggressing between online and offline environments: at home, at school, or anywhere they have mobile connections. These new publically networked "settings" can therefore be considered potential intervention platforms, distinct from school settings, and where online methodological strategies can be employed.

Systems

According to Bronfenbrenner's Ecological Systems Theory (1977), offline settings, such as schools, parks, and malls operate within and in relation to systems. Conceptually, the Internet can be considered as both a setting and a system (Spears, 2011, p. 16). As a setting, it operates as a virtual entity, separate from what is considered "real": namely, an online environment, distinct from an offline environment. This presents as a two-dimensional model, where young people congregate and socialize, on and offline, moving effortlessly between the two. What is of importance here is that young people do *not* make an "either/or" distinction for themselves and have referred to it as "the same life" (Spears, Kofoed, Bartolo, Palermiti, & Costabile, 2012). As a system, however, the Internet/online environment overlays and surrounds the existing socioecological system, acting as a third dimension: encircling, intersecting, and interacting with individuals, families, schools, and workplaces ("settings" within "systems"). Indeed, Johnson and Puplampu (2008) proposed the notion of an ecological techno-subsystem where digital technologies impact cognition and child development.

These notions of settings and systems also present cyberbullying researchers with new opportunities and methodological challenges to consider. For this generation of technologically involved young people, schools may no longer be the only or most appropriate setting to educate or intervene against cyberbullying practices. First efforts at moving beyond the offline school setting have seen a plethora of online self-help and information web portals evolve for students, their families, and teachers. But are these sites actually reaching young people, and are they evidence based? Portals, largely designed by adults, for young people to "visit" to gain information, are not where young people are congregating or socializing online. It may be time therefore, to move beyond the traditional whole-school environment as the sole system for (cyber)bullying interventions, and move into the publically networked spaces to which Boyd (2007) referred.

Online Social Marketing

Moving *into* the online spaces in which young people socialize and congregate does not simply mean providing more Internet portals or conducting online surveys to access their perceptions and opinions. It means taking youth-led, user-designed, anti-cyberbullying messaging direct to young people, in the networked spaces in which they choose to congregate, such as Facebook and YouTube, as well as the myriad of other socializing and gaming sites they frequent. This represents an emerging, innovative methodological strategy to address cyberbullying, using authentic advocacy and messaging from young people.

Social marketing techniques have been widely used through media campaigns to deliver messages designed for social good to the community: namely, anti-smoking and similar public health campaigns. Online social marketing techniques are now being employed by communities and governments to formally deliver that same messaging throughout the Internet: targeted through social networking sites and through Twitter and other emerging social media (Evans, 2008). The rapid uptake of such mediums as Twitter, where messages are deliberately short and defined by the number of characters allowed, along with the contemporary idiom of public/citizen journalism, where direct action is taken by the public, using mobile technologies to effect change in society, (namely, Arab Spring or Occupy movements) suggests that young people are at ease with these short and public forms of message delivery. Indeed, Thakeray and Hunter (2010) argued for integrating technology with youth advocacy efforts to affect social change and influence social determinants of health.

This chapter argues that online social marketing, an emergent research, implementation, and intervention strategy that makes use of the Internet as a system beyond that of the school setting, to potentially deliver developmentally relevant, authentic, targeted messaging about cyberbullying to young people online, where they are spending time, socializing and playing. In addition, employing social networking sites as platforms for informal online social marketing messaging, from youth—to youth, where they recruit, advocate, and mobilize support, is another emerging methodological strategy available in the quest to address and reduce cyberbullying. Using both traditional research methods, such as observations, surveys, and focus groups, with Internet mediated research techniques, such as content analysis of language used in certain sites, together with web analytics, which actively and passively record visitor traffic and social networking movements when online, ensures that young people's knowledge, attitudes, and online behaviors can not only be influenced by their peers, but ascertained and measured across time.

Youth Voice and Co-Researchers

Young people have long been, and continue to be, powerful contributors to and shapers of social, economic, environmental, and political change (Hesse-Biber & Leavy, 2010). The combination of the advent of the Internet, the rapid adoption of technologies by young people, and the associated power to influence and mobilize others, presents young people with the unique situation where they can take some control over the messages that are constructed about them and their lives, including those associated with defining, measuring, and addressing cyberbullying.

Young people's voices are needed: to guide the development of any social messaging, so that it is relevant, authentic, targeted, and has meaning for them. If the ultimate aim of any cyberbullying intervention is to improve the social and emotional relationship outcomes for individuals and to have safer schools and society, then interventions that are informed by accurate measurement must be implemented. Accurate measurement requires clear definitions and understandings developed by consensus. Providing opportunities for young people to successfully advocate for, participate in, and drive social change, such as involvement in the creation and delivery of anti-cyberbullying messaging, is empowering and assists in reaching that consensus of understanding required for clear definitions. In addition, the gathering of their "voice" via qualitative means ensures that the lived realities and central core themes of young people's experiences and understanding of cyberbullying can provide clear insight into the meaning it holds for them, as distinct from the meaning given to it by adults. This leads to more authentic definitions and measurement that, in turn, inform the development of genuinely relevant intervention practices.

Spears et al. (2011) further argue, however, that young people should not be simply treated as participants and "data providers," but as co-researchers who, instead, "partner with each other [researchers] to deepen the knowledge and experience base of the phenomenon under examination" (p 10). They further note that this co-construction of meaning is particularly relevant for cyberbullying, as it is a domain that adults did not experience as young people themselves. Involving young people as co-researchers, instead of sources of data or respondents, strengthens this relationship and elevates young people to a position of equal power with researchers, challenging the researchers to recognize and value young people's knowledge and experiences. Inviting young people into the role of the teacher, where they can involve adults in understanding their online experiences, is one strategy that enables young people to adopt the role of co-researcher.

THE CHALLENGE OF INVESTIGATING
THE ONLINE ENVIRONMENT

> *If you keep doing what you are doing, you will keep getting what you are getting.*
> —*Anonymous/Unknown*

Social and technological change is ubiquitous, and Hesse-Biber and Leavy (2010) note that "as new problems emerge and existing methodologies fail to adequately meet the research needs presented by them, then "methodological gaps" appear (pp. 1–3).

With the advent of cyberbullying, a methodological "gap" has appeared: researchers have needed to learn about and adapt to the Internet/online environment, while bringing with them their own assumptions about bullying, derived from their experiences in an offline schooling context and a research history from that context that spans nearly four decades.

The online environment, while representing a social medium for both positive and negative relationship interactions, is neither a school setting nor a social institution. It is a setting in that it sits symbiotically with the offline school/home environment, yet it is also a system that operates in concert with the existing socioecological system (Bronfenbrenner, 1977), intersecting with the individual, school, family, and wider community. How researchers personally understand the online environment—either as simply an extension of their social reality; or as that third dimension encircling the child and its environments; or as a new environment/system with different contexts and rules, together with the ever-increasing ways of accessing it—presents fundamental and ongoing challenges that influence the approaches used to explore cyberbullying (Hesse-Biber & Leavy, 2010).

Methodological diversity is needed for exploring new phenomena such as cyberbullying and young people's experiences as they socialize in and across their online/offline social environments. The challenge of investigating the online environment, according to Hesse-Biber and Leavy (2010, p. v) is discovering the knowledge that is "hidden"..."because it has not been part of the dominant culture or discourse" to date. Cyberbullying, while rooted in traditional bullying behaviors, and with much overlap with bullying offline, is clearly an online phenomenon that presents challenges in discovering its unique "hidden knowledge." Engaging young people as co-researchers—as partners in the research process, who have access to that "hidden knowledge," ensures that they are empowered by this methodological strategy.

Using Online Social Marketing as a Methodological Tool and Intervention Strategy

The challenge of investigating online behaviors, beliefs, knowledge, and attitudes presents opportunities for methodological innovation in cyberbullying research. Traditional social marketing, and most recently, online social marketing, is one approach that could be used to its advantage in this domain. It involves the same techniques used by commercial marketers but "sells ideas, attitudes and behaviours, not products" (See Weinreich (n.d.)). It seeks to influence social behaviors, for social good, rather than for financial benefit, and has been used extensively in health campaigns such as antismoking, drug education, heart disease awareness, and organ donation.

Steckler, McLeroy, Goodman, Bird, and McCormick (1992) argued for an integrated social marketing research model, outlining the ways in which the positivist/interpretivist paradigms might be integrated. They proposed that social marketing research should include both paradigms, "equally and in parallel, to cross validate and build on each other's results" at each stage of the process: in formative research, process evaluation, and outcome evaluation (pp.1–8). Traditionally, mixed methodologies have privileged the positivist approaches, using qualitative approaches only as a means of contributing to the development of questionnaires, or as a way to help clarify or explain quantitative findings, rather than being of value in their own right. Social marketers utilize research throughout the life of the project: during planning, development, implementation, and evaluation phases, which can be in contrast to a more traditional evaluation/research model that may undertake a study at the beginning to develop an intervention, and again at the end, to evaluate its effectiveness (Steckler et. al., 1992). The process of continuous development and ongoing testing, of soliciting audience responses, and preferences and reactions to campaigns while they are running, would seem relevant to operating in the rapidly changing online environment, where young people are quick to employ the latest technological medium for positive or negative uses.

Given the myriad of ways in which young people are using the online environment, and that they meet and socialize in "publically networked" spaces (Boyd, 2007), the question remains: In contemporary e-societies, are schools alone the right contexts for all interventions and research? What role does a whole-school antibullying approach now play in an e-society? If an aim of intervention is to promote positive behavior change in relation to bullying and cyberbullying practices, presumably to improve the health and social–emotional outcomes of young people, how can the methodological strategy of using online social marketing tools and techniques be harnessed, by young people to develop, deliver and test user-driven anti-cyberbullying messaging that is relevant and authentic to them? Social marketing undertaken via multiple media channels, such as social networking and gaming sites, for example, is a powerful means of sharing, organizing, and disseminating information directly to young people in the environments in which they socialize: the publically networked spaces of which Boyd wrote (2007). One such project has already employed such methodological strategies— of online social marketing techniques to send youth-led, informed messages about anti-cyberbullying, and it is briefly reported here. A follow-up, longitudinal study is being undertaken in 2012.

The SOSO Project

The Smart Online: Safe Offline (SOSO http://www.soso.org.au/) project was a two-part collaboration between Australia's National Association for the Prevention of Child Abuse and Neglect (NAPCAN) and digital marketing agency Profero, Sydney (www.profero.com.au). Funded by the Australian government in 2007, a consortium was formed (see www.soso.org.au), bringing together NGOs, government and Internet and media leaders, including Cartoon Network, Habbo Hotel, Microsoft, NinMSN, Yahoo!, Miniclip, Neopets, Piczo, Big Pond, Myspace, and Channel Ten to deliver the first online campaign aimed at educating young Internet users about cybersafety in 2008 (http://www.soso.org.au/smart-online-safe-offline-april-2008-media-release.pdf).

The second campaign, launched in 2009, Cyberbullying Affects Real Lives!, aimed to reduce cyberbullying among young teens aged 9–15 years, by focusing on bystanders (Join In And You're the Bully Too!) and was supported by the Telstra Foundation, Google Australia, and the digital media industry (2008–2010).

To challenge the perceptions that cyberbullying is unacceptable, the campaign included a two minute video clip, using YouTube as an educational platform to connect with young people to deliver the key message: "Kid at school gets a pants down—LOL FWD this!!!" (www.youtube.com/watchvCBjiaytbt5Xwk).

Young people could also link to an interactive game called Web Warriors, where they created a personal avatar (www.webwarriors.com.au) and joined others in actively sharing the antibullying messages, through social networks (Media Release, 2009 http://www.soso.org.au/pr/).

Tagged with simple, straightforward youth-led and created messaging such as "Share It, Spread It, Forward It, Join It and You're a Bully Too," this campaign challenged young people to stand up against cyberbullying together, targeting those whose actions and inactions contribute to the ongoing bullying and cyberbullying of others. Underpinned by Australian research on cyberbullying (Campbell, 2005; Cross et al., 2009; Spears, Slee, Owens, & Johnson, 2009), this innovative educative campaign targeted children in the online social networking and gaming environments in which they played and socialized. The campaign "creative," messaging, and language was developed with young people, including creative discussion groups in schools and online polling and contributions via surveys from young people.

METHODOLOGICAL STRATEGIES TO EVALUATE THE CYBERBULLYING CAMPAIGN

Web Analytics: Demographics of Passive and Active Tracking

Standard web analytics were employed to determine the traffic that visited the site/s, for the purpose of reporting only: IP addresses were collected for broad demographics, and cookies were used to track statistical information automatically (http://www.soso.org.au/privacy.html). Between Wave 1 (October 2009) and Wave 2 (Mid/late December 2009), there were: 54,079 visits; 197,437 page views, and a 22.22% "bounce rate,"[1] which is considered low by industry standards. There were 76,000 YouTube views; 9,000 registered members for the game; and 14,192 "explore" visits, with a game completion rate of 49.60%. The reach and activity through the campaign was tracked via Microsoft's ATLAS ad-serving platform: total impressions[2] were 14, 443, 561. The campaign developed over three times the average clickthrough rate[3] for an online display campaign. Clickthrough rates (CTRs) determined that Habbo Hotel (8.11%), Cartoon Network (2.52%), and Miniclip (1.63%) were the online environments where young people aged 9–15 were more likely to view the messaging.

Surveys and Sample

A specialized market-research consultancy was commissioned to undertake an evaluation of the online campaign.[4] Using an in-house online research provider, parents and their children from an existing data panel were approached in accordance with the relevant industry standards and legal requirements to ensure compliance with ethical procedures. The target market for evaluation comprised children from ages 9–15 (M = 40%; F = 50%, N = 1202). Each age group accounted for 14–15% of the total sample, and a stratified random sample was drawn from five capital cities across Australia: Sydney (36%), Melbourne (29%), Brisbane (15%), Perth (12%), and Adelaide (8%). Online surveys were conducted with children as follows: 44% (n = 528) completed the survey unsupervised; 33% (n = 396) were supervised by a parent; 20% (n = 240) of parents helped with some questions; and 2% (n = 24) of parents helped with most/all questions. A pre-test survey was conducted prior to the campaign launch (Wave 1) in late October (2009, N = 326) and a post-test, post campaign, included recognition and reactions to campaign elements, in mid–late December (2009, N = 876).

What Was Learned and Limitations

Based on data derived through Nielsen NetView,[5] over 80% of young Australians online—between the ages of 10–15—had the opportunity to see the SOSO campaign, meaning the online reach was extensive, and in relevant sites where young people of this age were actively playing or visiting. As a methodological strategy to address cyberbullying, it is evident that online social marketing can reach large audiences well beyond the school setting. In addition, approximately 9 out of 10 of those who took notice, as demonstrated through web analytics and a low "bounce rate" (22.22%), thought it had an impact on their awareness and how they felt about cyberbullying, namely, "I now realize passing things on makes me a bully too." Specifically, 10% of respondents had seen any campaign element; 25% had seen more than one; over 50% discussed the YouTube execution with friends after viewing it and with a main takeout message—"You don't have to put up with it: you can report it." Eighty percent of those surveyed were more aware of cyberbullying from watching the YouTube execution.

Clearly, online social marketing is an emerging methodological strategy with reach and impact beyond the school setting, and one which intersects with the online system in a way that merely having a website/portal for students to visit does not. Attitudes had been impacted upon by the educative aspects of the campaign, but a limitation of the study concerned the extent to which any behaviors actually changed as a result. Also, the sites that were available for use may not have been relevant to other age groups. Another limitation concerns the issue that we do not actually know if young people want to be educated through this approach and if the messages complement what has been occurring in school settings. Consequently, the next phase of the project will explore the capacity for online social marketing techniques to bring about behavior and attitudinal change over time. Through the Young and Well Cooperative Research Centre (http://www.yawcrc. org.au/safe-and-supportive/soso), a five-year, multi-messaging online social marketing campaign to promote young people's well-being and safety online, will be developed and tested, and the first trial phase will be reported in 2012.

CONCLUSION

As young people socialize in online communities beyond the school setting, it is imperative that we look beyond (a) the school community as the sole locale for preventative and interventive approaches to the problem of cyberbullying, and (b) beyond the researcher-driven model of inquiry that uses young people only as participants for data. This chapter has proposed using methodological strategies such as online social marketing as a way of engaging the e-setting actively in educative and interventive approaches to reducing cyberbullying and has presented an example of such a campaign, which shows genuine promise in using youth-designed and led messaging about cyberbullying to change attitudes in other online users. This chapter has also proposed that young people have the capacity to make social change, through teaching researchers about what is authentic for them about their cyberbullying experiences: not as participants in studies devised by adults who can only draw upon their own traditional bullying experiences—but in ways where they use their knowledge to teach adults about this social context, thus assuming the role of co-researcher. While much research is conducted qualitatively, and youth voice is considered an important methodological adjunct to quantitative studies, it is the power of young people to effect social change through their voice as co-researchers and advocates that is the emergent methodological strategy relevant to cyberbullying. They are the experts in their own lived reality, and it is time to take cognizance of this and be led by them to an authentic understanding of their experiences. The SOSO project demonstrates, that for the social marketing messages to be effective, relevant, and useful, they must be user led and youth driven and be contextualized to the environment in which they are shown. Furthermore, it demonstrates the willingness of industry providers to contribute to the positive messages young people can receive when online: in games and social networking sites. The Internet has transformed our ways of being, socializing, and communicating. It is time for research strategies, methodological approaches, and interventions concerned with cyberbullying to join the conversation and employ young people as co-researchers and advocates in many environments, and for online social marketing campaigns to perhaps reflect "online social education campaigns" instead.

ACKNOWLEDGMENTS

This chapter gratefully acknowledges Richard Cooke (CEO, NAPCAN); Maree Falkner (Former CEO, NAPCAN); Madelene McGrath (former SOSO Project manager, NAPCAN); Valentina Borbone, (SOSO Account Manager, Profero).

Notes

1   *Bounce rate* is the percentage of single-page visits or visits in which the person left your site from the entrance (landing) page. This metric is used to measure visit quality—a high bounce rate generally indicates that site entrance pages aren't relevant to your visitors.

The more compelling your landing pages, the more visitors will stay on your site and convert. http://www.google.com/support/analytics/bin/answer.py?answer=81986

2 An *impression* (in the context of online advertising) is a measure of the number of times an ad is displayed, whether it is clicked on or not. Each time an ad displays, it is counted as one impression. Counting impressions is the method by which most web advertising is accounted and paid for, and the cost is quoted in cost per thousand impressions (CPM). http://en.wikipedia.org/wiki/Impression_(online_media)

3 *Clickthrough rate* (CTR) is a way of measuring the success of an online advertising campaign. The CTR for an ad is defined as the number of clicks on an ad divided by the number of times the ad is shown (impressions), expressed as a percentage. http://en.wikipedia.org/wiki/Clickthrough_rate

4 Holistic data are from the client presentation report. Analyses are not available.

5 http://www.nielsen.com/us/en/measurement/online-measurement.html

References

Arseneault, L., Bowes, L., & Shakoor, S. (2010). Bullying victimization in youths and mental health problems: "Much ado about nothing"? *Psychological Medicine, 40*, 717–729. doi:10.1017/S0033291709991383

Belsey, B. (2006). Cyberbullying: An emerging threat to the "always on" generation. Retrieved from www.cyberbullying.ca

Beran, T. T., & Li, Q. (2007). The relationship between cyberbullying and school bullying. *Journal of Student Wellbeing, 1*(2), 15–33.

Bronfenbrenner, U. (1977). Towards an experimental ecology of human development. *American Psychologist, 32*, 513–530. doi:10.1037//0003–066X.32.7.513

Boyd, D. (2007). Why youth (heart) social network sites: The role of networked publics in teenage social life. In David Buckingham (Ed.), *MacArthur Foundation Series on Digital Learning—Youth, Identity, and Digital Media Volume.* Cambridge: MA: MIT Press.

Boyd, D. (2008). *Taken Out of Context American Teen Sociality in Networked Publics.* PhD Dissertation. University of California–Berkeley, School of Information.

Boyd, D., & Ellison, M. B (2007). Social network sites: Definition, history and scholarship. *Journal of Computer-Mediated Communication, 13*(1), 210–230. doi:10.1111/j.1083–6101.2007.00393.x

Campbell, M. (2005). Cyberbullying: An old problem in a new guise? *Australian Journal of Guidance and Counselling, 15*(1), 68–76. doi:10.1375/ajgc.15.1.68

Campbell, M., Spears, B. A., Cross, D. & Slee P. T. (2010). Cyberbullying in Australia In Joaquín A. Mora Merchán & T. Jager (Eds). *Cyberbullying: A cross-national comparison* (pp. 232–244). Landau: Verlag Empirische Pädagogik.

Cross, D., Monks, H., Campbell, M., Spears, B., & Slee, P (2011a). School-based strategies to address cyberbullying. *Occasional Papers #119. Centre for Strategic Education.* Melbourne, Victoria.

Cross, D., Monks, H., Hall, M., Shaw, T., Pintabona, Y., Erceg, E., . . . Lester, L. (2011b). Three-year results of the Friendly Schools whole-of-school intervention on children's bullying behavior. *British Educational Research Journal, 37*(1), 105–129. doi:10.1080/01411920903420024

Cross, D., Shaw, T., Hearn, L., Epstein, M., Monks, H., Lester, L., & Thomas, L. (2009). Australian covert bullying prevalence study (ACBPS). Child Health Promotion Research Centre, Edith Cowan University, Perth. http://www.deewr.gov.au/Schooling/NationalSafeSchools/Pages/research.aspx

Durlak, J. A., Weissberg, R. P., Dymnicki, A. B., Taylor, R. D., & Schellinger, K. B. (2011). The impact of enhancing students' social and emotional learning: A meta-analysis of school-based universal interventions. *Child Development, 82*, 405–432. doi:10.1111/j.1467–8624.2010.01564.x

Elias, M. J., Zins, J. E., Graczyk, P. A., & Weissberg, R. P. (2003). Implementation, sustainability, and scaling up of social-emotional and academic innovations in public schools. *School Psychology Review, 32*, 303–319.

Evans, W. D. (2008) Social marketing campaigns and children's media use. *Children and Electronic Media, 18*(1), 181–203.

Hawker, D. S., & Boulton, M. J. (2000). Twenty years' research on peer victimization and psychosocial maladjustment: A meta-analytic review of cross-sectional studies. *Journal of Child Psychology and Psychiatry, 41*, 441–455. doi:10.1111/1469–7610.00629

Hesse-Biber, S. N. & Leavy, P. (Eds.). (2010). *Handbook of emergent methods*. New York: The Guilford Press.

Hinduja, S., & Patchin, J. W. (2007). Offline consequences of online victimization: School violence and delinquency. *Journal of School Violence, 6*(3), 89–112. doi:10.1300/J202v06n03_06

Hinduja, S., & Patchin, J. W. (2008). Cyberbullying: An exploratory analysis of factors related to offending and victimization. *Deviant Behavior, 29*(2), 129–156. doi:10.1080/01639620701457816

Ito, M., Horst, H. A., Bittanti, M., Boyd, D., Herr-Stephenson, B., Lange, Pascoe, C. J., Robinson, L. (2009) *Living and learning with new media: Summary of findings from the Digital Youth Project* (the John D. and Catherine T. MacArthur Foundation Report on Digital Media and Learning). Retrieved from http://mitpress.mit.edu/catalog/item/default.asp?ttype=2&tid=11940

Johnson, G. M., & Puplampu, P. (2008). A conceptual framework for understanding the effect of the Internet on child development: The ecological techno-subsystem. *Canadian Journal of Learning and Technology, 34*, 19–28.

Kaltiala-Heino, R., Rimpela, M., Rantanen, P., & Rimpela, A. (2000). Bullying at school: An indicator of adolescents at risk for mental disorders. *Journal of Adolescence, 23*, 661–674. doi:10.1006/jado.2000.0351

Landstedt, E., & Gådin, K. G. (2011). Deliberate self-harm and associated factors in 17-year-old Swedish students. *Scandinavian Journal of Public Health*, 39, 17–25. doi:10.1177/1403494810382941

Michaud, P. (2009). Bullying: We need to increase our efforts and broaden our focus. *Journal of Adolescent Health, 45*(4), 323–325. doi:10.1016/j.jadohealth.2009.07.006

Nansel, T., Overpeck, M., Pilla, R., & Ruan, J. (2001). Bullying behaviors among US youth: Prevalence and association with psychosocial adjustment. *Journal of the American Medical Association, 285*(16), 2094. doi:10.1001/jama.285.16.2094

Olweus, D. (1978). *Aggression in the schools: Bullies and whipping boys*. Washington, DC: Hemisphere (Wiley).

Patchin, J. W., & Hinduja, S. (2006). Bullies move beyond the schoolyard: A preliminary look at cyberbullying. *Youth Violence and Juvenile Justice, 4*(2), 148–169. doi:10.1177/1541204006286288

Raskauskas, J., & Stoltz, A. D. (2007). Involvement in traditional and electronic bullying among adolescents. *Developmental Psychology, 43*, 564–575. doi:10.1037/0012–1649.43.3.564

Rigby, K, & Slee, P (2008) Interventions to reduce bullying. *International Journal of Adolescent Medicine and Health, 20*(2), 165–183. doi:10.1515/IJAMH.2008.20.2.165

Rigby, K, & Smith, P. K. (2011). Is school bullying really on the rise? *Social Psychology of Education*, 1381–2890. doi:10.1007/s11218–011–9158-y

Skapinakis, P., Bellos, S., Gkatsa, T., Magklara, K., Lewis, G., Araya, R., . . . Mavreas, V. (2011). The association between bullying and early stages of suicidal ideation in late adolescents in Greece. *BMC Psychiatry, 11.* doi:10.1186/1471–244X-11–22

Slee, P. T., Lawson, M. J., Russell, A., Askell-Williams, H., Dix, K. L., Owens, L., Skrzypiec, G., Spears, B. (2009). *KidsMatter Primary Evaluation Final Report.* KidsMatter and the Centre for Analysis of Educational Futures. Adelaide, South Australia.

Smith, J., Schneider, B., Smith, P., & Ananiadou, K. (2004). The effectiveness of whole-school antibullying programs: A synthesis of evaluation research. *School Psychology Review, 33,* 547–560.

Smith, P. K., Ananiadou, K., & Cowie, H. (2003). Interventions to reduce school bullying. *Canadian Journal of Psychiatry, 48,* 591–599.

Smith, P. K., Mahdavi, J., Carvalho, M., Fisher, S., Russell, S., & Tippett, N. (2008). Cyberbullying: Its nature and impact in secondary school pupils. *Journal of Child Psychology and Psychiatry, 49*(4), 376–385. doi:10.1111/j.1469–7610.2007.01846.x

Spears, B. (2011). CyberChat: Using technology to enhance wellbeing. *Education Technology Solutions, 40,* 16.

Spears, B. A., Kofoed, J., Bartolo, M. G., Palermiti, A., & Costabile, A. (2012). Positive uses of social networking sites: Youth voice perspectives. In A. Costabile & B. A. Spears (Eds.), *Positive uses of technology to challenge cyberbullying.* London: Routledge.

Spears, B., Slee, P., Campbell, M., and Cross, D. (2011). *Educational change and youth voice: Informing school action on cyberbullying.* Seminar Series #208, Centre for Strategic Education, Victoria.

Spears, B. A., Slee, P. T., Owens, L. and Johnson, B. (2009). *Behind the Scenes: Insights into the Human Dimension of Covert Bullying.* http://www.deewr.gov.au/Schooling/NationalSafeSchools/Pages/research.aspx

Spiel, C., Salmivalli, C., & Smith, P. (2011). Translational research: National strategies for violence prevention. *International Journal of Behavioral Development, 35*(5), 381–382. doi:10.1177/0165025411407556

Steckler, A., McLeroy, K. R., Goodman, R. M., Bird, S. T., & McCormick, L. (1992). Toward integrating qualitative and quantitative methods: An introduction. *Health Education Quarterly, 19,* 1–8. doi:10.1177/109019819201900101

Thackeray, R. and Hunter, M. (2010). Empowering youth: use of technology in advocacy to affect social change. *Journal of Computer-Mediated Communication, 15,* 575–591. doi:10.1111/j.1083-6101.2009.01503.x

Ttofi, M. M., & Farrington, D. P. (2011). Effectiveness of school-based programs to reduce bullying: A systematic and meta-analytic review. *Journal of Experimental Criminology, 7,* 27–56. doi:10.1007/s11292–010–9109–1

Vandebosch, H., & Van Cleemput, K. (2009). Cyberbullying among youngsters: Profiles of bullies and victims. *New Media and Society, 11,* 1349–1371.

Vreeman, R., & Carroll, A. (2007). A systematic review of school-based interventions to prevent bullying. *Archives of Pediatric Adolescent Medicine, 161*(1), 78–88. doi:10.1001/archpedi.161.1.78

Weinreich, N. K. (n.d.). www.social-marketing.com/Whatis.html

Wolke, D., Woods, S., Bloomfield, L., & Karstadt, L. (2001). Bullying involvement in primary school and common health problems. *Archives of Disease in Childhood, 85*(3), 197–201. doi:10.1136/adc.85.3.197

Part V

Measures

14 Measurement

Why It Matters

Michele Ybarra

Prevalence rates of cyberbullying vary widely across studies, ranging from 6% (Ybarra, Mitchell, Wolak, & Finkelhor, 2006) to 72% (Juvonen & Gross, 2008) per (school) year. This wide variation is often the source of confusion among politicians and the public, and it can lead to distrust in the data. Reasons for the variance in rates are unclear. It seems likely, however, that much can be attributed to differences in measurement and methodology. Data are collected using national random telephone surveys (Finkelhor, Mitchell, & Wolak, 2000; Wolak, Mitchell, & Finkelhor, 2006), online random surveys (Ybarra, Leaf, Diener-West, 2007), on-line self-selected surveys (Patchin & Hinduja, 2006), and offline convenience samples (Juvonen & Gross, 2008; Raskauskas & Stoltz, 2007). Sampling frames vary from national, to international, to local, and from random to convenience (See Chapter 8, this volume). Furthermore, some studies include youth as young as 10 years of age (Dehue, Bolman, & Vollink, 2008; Finkelhor et al., 2000; Ybarra et al., 2007), while others focus on high school (Raskauskas & Stoltz, 2007). Given noted age differences in prevalence rates (Dehue et al., 2008; Kowalski & Limber, 2007; Slonje & Smith, 2008; Ybarra et al., 2007; Ybarra & Mitchell, 2008), this alone would explain some of the variance. Another variation in measurement is the time frame queried: The longer the time frame used, the greater the number of people who will have had the experience in question. For example, if items on the survey inquired whether the respondent had *ever* experienced cyberbullying, we would expect more people to say yes than if the survey asked respondents if they experienced cyberbullying in the past couple of months. In this section, chapters will focus on issues specific to measurement because it is essential to quality research in the field of cyberbullying.

Since cyberbullying is a relatively new phenomenon, there is not yet consensus on how best to measure it. For example, some studies provide a definition of cyberbullying within a questionnaire (Slonje & Smith, 2008; Smith, Mahdavi, & Carvalho, 2008; Ybarra, Mitchell, & Espelage, 2012) others use a list of behavioral items believed to be components of cyberbullying and no definition (Hinduja & Patchin, 2007; Patchin & Hinduja, 2006); and still others provide both (Dehue, Bolman, & Vollink, 2008; Juvonen & Gross, 2008; Raskauskas & Stoltz, 2007). Generally, studies provide a definition based on the one used in the Olweus

Bully/Victim Questionnaire (Olweus, 1994), which indicates that the experience must be repetitive, continue over time, and be between two people of differential strength or power.

Not all researchers agree that this definition sufficiently captures aggressive behaviors manifested online, however. To address this, many include a list of experiences specific to technology. While some continue to describe these collective behaviors as "cyberbullying" (Hinduja & Patchin, 2007; Raskauskas & Stoltz, 2007), others describe this as "harassment" (Wolak, Mitchell, & Finkelhor, 2007; Ybarra et al., 2007). Irrespective of the label ascribed, these behavioral lists cannot be exhaustive, particularly given the rapid rate at which technological innovations emerge, and therefore they are invariably incomplete as well as inconsistent across studies. To examine whether this difference in measurement affects prevalence rates, we can review data from *Growing Up with Media* (growingupwithmedia.com), which included measures of both cyberbullying (i.e., bullying online that is repetitive, over time, and between two actors of differential power) and harassment (e.g., rude and mean comments, threatening or aggressive comments). As expected, given the more broad definition, harassment appears to be a more generalized type of youth victimization than bullying. Based upon cohort data from 2007 and 2008, 24% of youth were harassed, 13% were both bullied and harassed, and only 1% were bullied but not harassed online in the past year; the remaining 62% reported neither experience. Thus, if youth are being bullied, they're likely being harassed, but the converse does not necessarily follow. From a measurement perspective, this finding suggests that it is important that we as researchers are very clear about what we are measuring: Is it more general aggression that may happen once or multiple times, between youth of equal strength or not; or is it specifically bullying that occurs repeatedly, over time, between people of differential strength? Both victimization experience types are associated with elevated odds of psychosocial challenge, and so both should continue to be studied—simply with clear labels and consistent measurement.

As a new field of inquiry, research on cyberbullying and other forms of Internet harassment are struggling to agree on a common definition and consensus about measurement. To help inform the debate, this chapter will first examine the effect that different measurements and methodologies appear to be having on reported prevalence rates; and second, report the results of a split-form survey testing the impact of different measures on self-reported cyberbullying rates.

In our study (Ybarra, Boyd, Korchmaros, & Oppenheim, 2012), we examined the effects of the different measurement types on the resulting prevalence rate. Three different surveys were administered online. The sample of 1,200 youth between ages 6 and 17 were recruited from an online panel of approximately 30,000 members. Response rates for each survey ranged from 32% to 39%; each participant completed the survey only once, and the sample was balanced purposefully by sex and age group. Weighting to match the population of online youth in the United States was applied.

Participants were randomly assigned to one of four forms of the survey: inclusion of a definition including the word bully, definition of the concept without the word, use of the word *bully* in items with no definition, and no definition and no use of the word. The items following one of these formats were a behavioral list including physical, verbal, and relational incidents. Two items related to behaviors that were most likely to be accomplished using technology, but items did not specify that. Rather, if the respondent indicated they had experienced any of the items on the behavioral list, he or she was asked about the mode of communication by which the action was perpetrated (in person, by phone, text message, or online).

Rates of reported victimization were highest for the form that used neither the definition nor the word *bully* and were lowest for the form that used the word *bully* in the instructions. The use of the word *harassment* was included in one survey form to examine whether it provided additional meaning beyond bully, but the addition of the term did not appear to affect rates.

We also tested the influence of three follow-up questions on the positive predictive value (i.e., the ability to identify "true positives" versus "false positives"). The three questions asked youth who reported being bullied whether they had been bullied by someone who had more power or strength than them, if they had been bullied over time, and if they had been bullied repetitively. Interestingly, rates of youth who said "yes" to all three of these questions were similar across all forms of survey questions. Thus, adding these three follow-up questions seems to neutralize differences in the way that bullying was queried. Because surveys are often limited for space, however, we also examined a more parsimonious follow-up method, whereby the follow-up question about differential power was combined with that of the frequency responses in the original question about whether youth had been bullied (i.e., those who were bullied monthly or more often were deemed to be bullied "repetitively" and "over time") to identify "true positives." Using this method, measures that used the word "bully" resulted in higher positive predictive values.

What are the implications of these findings for researchers? Including the word *bully* in the survey question seems to be important and connote meaning to youth that is similar to what researchers are endeavoring to measure. Certainly, this is only possible when the language has a word *bully*. It should be noted that these findings have not been replicated beyond English speakers in the United States. It is possible that different results would emerge from other populations. An important implication across populations and languages, however, is to consider the use of follow-up questions, especially one about differential power, to make the measures more precise.

I also recommend that the concept of bullying, and therefore measures, be framed as having three dimensions: type (physical, relational), communication mode (face to face, online, phone, or text messaging), and environment (school, home, elsewhere). This prevents potential double counting as technology continues to converge, as well as to be accessible throughout our daily lives. For example, if the Internet is seen as an environment similar to school, then youth who are bullied on Facebook while at school may be categorized as being bullied twice. In this conception of bullying, cyberbullying is bullying using specific modes of communication.

With respect to behavioral lists, it would be ideal to have a universal list that applies across communication mode and environment. For example, one could be targeted by "someone spread rumors about me" face to face, by phone, or online. As such, it could be included in a universal list of bullying experiences.

The other chapters in this section will address technical issues related to measurement: sampling, psychometrics, translation, what to measure, and qualitative measurement. The reader will then have recommendations for many critical factors in measurement. I urge researchers to be explicit about their decisions in all aspects of measurement so that readers of their work can make informed decisions about the importance of the findings.

References

Dehue, F., Bolman, C., & Vollink, T. (2008). Cyberbullying: Youngsters' experiences and parental perception. *CyberPsychology & Behavior, 11*(2), 217–223. doi:10.1089/cpb.2007.0008

Finkelhor, D., Mitchell, K.J., & Wolak, J. (2000). *Online victimization: A report on the nation's youth.* Alexandria, VA: National Center for Missing & Exploited Children. Retrieved from http://www.missingkids.com/en_US/publications/NC62.pdf

Juvonen, J., & Gross, E.F. (2008). Extending the school grounds? Bullying experiences in cyberspace. *Journal of School Health, 78*(9), 496–505. doi:10.1111/j.1746-1561.2008.00335.x

Hinduja S., & Patchin, J.W. (2007). Offline consequences of online victimization: School violence and delinquency. *Journal of School Violence, 6*, 89–112.

Kowalski, R.M., & Limber, S.P. (2007). Electronic bullying among middle school students. *Journal of Adolescent Health, 41* (6 Suppl. 1), S22–S30. doi:10.1016/j.jadohealth.2007.08.017

Olweus, D. (1994). Annotation: Bullying at school: Basic facts and effects of a school based intervention program. *Journal of Child Psychology, 35*(7), 1171–1190. doi:10.1111/j.1469-7610.1994.tb01229.x

Patchin, J.W., & Hinduja, S. (2006). Bullies move beyond the schoolyard: A preliminary look at cyberbullying. *Youth Violence and Juvenile Justice, 4*(2),148–169. doi:10.1177/1541204006286288

Raskauskas, J., & Stoltz, A. (2007). Involvement in traditional and electronic bullying among adolescents. *Developmental Psychology, 43*(3), 564–575. doi:10.1037/0012-1649.43.3.564

Slonje, R., & Smith, P.K. (2008). Cyberbullying: Another main type of bullying? *Scandinavian Journal of Psychology, 49*(2), 147–154. doi:10.1111/j.1467-9450.2007.00611.x

Smith P.K., Mahdavi J., & Carvalho, M. (2008). Cyberbullying: Its nature and impact in secondary school pupils. *J Child Psychol Psychiatry, 49*, 376–385.

Wolak, J., Mitchell, K.J., & Finkelhor, D. (2006). *Online victimization of youth: 5 years later.* Alexandria, VA: National Center for Missing & Exploited Children. Retrieved from: http://www.missingkids.com/en_US/publications/NC167.pdf

Wolak, J., Mitchell, K. J., & Finkelhor, D. (2007). Does online harassment constitute bullying? An exploration of online harassment by known peers and online-only contacts. *Journal of Adolescent Health, 41*(6), S51–S58. doi:10.1016/j.jadohealth.2007.08.019

Ybarra, M., Boyd, D., Korchmaros, J., & Oppenheim, K. (2012). Defining and measuring cyberbullying within the larger context of bullying victimization. *Journal of Adolescent Health, 51*, 53–58.

Ybarra, M., Diener-West, M., & Leaf, P. (2007). Examining the overlap in Internet harassment and school bullying: Implications for school intervention. *Journal of Adolescent Health, 41*(6 Suppl. 1), S42–S52. doi:0.1016/j.jadohealth.2007.09.004

Ybarra, M. L., & Mitchell, K. J. (2008). How risky are social networking sites? A comparison of places online where youth sexual solicitation and harassment occurs. *Pediatrics, 121*(2), e350–357. doi:10.1542/peds.2007–0693

Ybarra M., Mitchell K., & Espelage D. (2012). Comparisons of bullying and unwanted sexual experiences online and offline among a national sample of youth. In O. Ozdemir & F. Ovali (Eds.), *Complimentary Pediatrics* (203–216). Retrieved from http://letibit.net/download/56239.57b4aab44c40823fb.198d7716480/9535101550.rar.html

Ybarra, M. L., Mitchell, K. J., Wolak, J., & Finkelhor, D. (2006). Examining characteristics and associated distress related to Internet harassment: Findings from the second youth internet safety survey. *Journal of the American Academy of Pediatrics, 118*(4), 1169–1177. doi:10.1542/peds.2006–0815

15 Psychometric Considerations for Cyberbullying Research

Noel A. Card

The emerging field of cyberbullying research represents an important focus on a newly emerging problem. Scientific investigation of the prevalence, risk factors, outcomes, and effects of intervention efforts of this phenomenon require tools for measuring cyberaggression and cybervictimization. In this chapter, I provide an overview of principles that, when followed, constitute good measurement of these phenomena.

I begin by reviewing the conceptual foundations of measurement, specifically within the domain representation framework. I consider three important criteria for evaluating the quality of measurement: reliability, validity, and measurement invariance. After describing these criteria conceptually, I describe how they can be, and have been, applied within cyberbullying research. Specifically, I provide a brief overview of the data-analytic evaluations of these three criteria and consider these evaluations within existing literature on measures of cyberaggression and cybervictimization. To foreshadow this review, I note the limitations of previous efforts to consider the full range of measurement criteria, as well as the opportunities afforded if a more complete consideration is adapted. I conclude by offering my perspective on where future research on the measurement of cyberaggression and cybervictimization is most needed.

Before proceeding, I want to clarify the focus and approach of this chapter. Psychometric analysis is an extensive field focusing on the development and quantitative evaluation of measurement instruments. The conceptual and data analytic tools within this field become very complex when considered in much depth, and I suspect that most readers do not need or want the complexity that comes with such depth. Instead, I have written this chapter with the goal of providing readers with an accessible introduction that will allow them to think about the principles of psychometrics in their research on cyberbullying. I will provide minimally technical descriptions of the data analyses used to evaluate psychometric criteria, citing other works to which readers can turn for more thorough treatments. Also, I do not offer recommendations regarding the relative advantages and limitations of a particular measurement approach, such as the use of self-reports versus observations (see Underwood & Card, this volume) or specific acts or technology platforms that should be considered when measuring cyberaggression and cybervictimization (see Smith et al. this volume). My focus here on psychometric principles applies across the measurement approaches considered elsewhere in this book.

FOUNDATIONS OF PSYCHOMETRIC CONSIDERATION

The Domain Representation Framework

One useful conceptual framework of considering the psychometric properties of a measure of cyberaggression or cybervictimization is the domain representation framework (see Little, Lindenberger, & Nesselroade, 1999; Nunnally, 1978). This framework conceptualizes measurement within a multidimensional space, with the dimensions defined conceptually as the potential properties of the phenomena. For instance, we might consider whether acts of cyberaggression are anonymous versus identified, and private (e.g., received only by the target) or public (e.g., observable by many others). Figure 15.1 displays this two-dimensional consideration. In reality, there are many other dimensions that should be considered in conceptualizing cyberaggression (and these dimensions would expand the figure into three-dimensional, four-dimensional, etc., space), but this simplistic consideration is adequate for illustrating the principles of the domain representation framework.

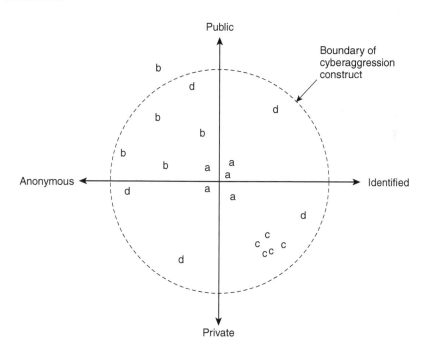

Figure 15.1 Domain representation framework for considering psychometric properties of hypothetical cyberaggression measure

Within this multidimensional space, a boundary is drawn that defines cyber-aggression. Such a boundary is shown as the dashed circle surrounding most of Figure 15.1 (keep in mind that this two-dimensional representation is a gross simplification of the true complexity of defining cyberaggression). This boundary encompasses the "domain" of cyberaggression; if we were to plot any act within the multidimensional space of this figure, those falling within this domain would be considered acts of cyberaggression whereas those acts falling outside of this domain would not be. Although attempting to conceptualize this boundary is a valuable exercise in thinking about the domain (see Smith et al., this volume), it is not absolutely necessary to identify precise boundaries in order to measure cyber-aggression. For cyberaggression, as with many social science phenomena, fuzzy boundaries are adequate for us to proceed in measuring a construct.

Having defined cyberaggression within multidimensional space, whether the boundaries are precise or fuzzy, we now have a domain within which acts are considered cyberaggression and will attempt to measure acts within this boundary. Acts falling within this domain are considered "manifestations" of cyber-aggression (which we will eventually quantify as "manifest variables"). A key tenet of the domain representation framework is that there are an infinite number of manifestations within this domain. Although this tenet may initially seem unreasonable, one only has to start thinking of the ways that cyberaggression could be enacted, and the many ways that each act could be measured, to realize its plausibility. Our task when creating a scale of cyberaggression is to select a limited number of these manifestations that adequately represent the domain of cyberaggression. Three criteria for considering the adequacy of this selection are reliability, validity, and measurement invariance, which are described conceptually next and then considered in detail later in this chapter.

Conceptualizing Reliability

Reliability refers to the repeatability of manifestations of a construct. When measuring cyberaggression, this repeatability can be considered in terms of multiple items on a scale, observations across time, or occurrence of cyberaggression across partners or contexts, to name just some possibilities. In this section, I consider the example of repeatability across multiple items on a scale of cyberaggression, a type of reliability also referred to as internal consistency, as this is the most commonly considered form of reliability in cyberaggression research thus far.

To conceptualize reliability, it is useful to consider again the domain representation framework shown in Figure 15.1. The five "a"s near the center of this figure represent five items (quantifying five manifestations) from a hypothetical scale, A, that is intended to measure cyberaggression. The proximity of any two "a"s represents the strength of the correlation between these items.[1] The close proximity of these five "a" items with each other denotes that the items are strongly correlated. Therefore, the items are repeatable in the sense that they provide overlapping information, and we would consider Scale A reliable.

In contrast, the 5 "b"s scattered around the upper left portion of Figure 15.1 are less close to one another. The greater distances between pairs of "b"s denotes weak correlations between "b" items. This weak correlation implies low repeatability of items on this scale, and we would consider scale B unreliable.

Conceptualizing Validity

Validity refers to the degree that a scale measures what it is intended to measure. It is useful to keep in mind both parts of this definition: (a) what the scale measures, and (b) what the researcher intends it to measure. Validity is the overlap between these two points, and a measurement instrument may therefore be valid for some purposes but not others.

To conceptualize validity, we can again consider the domain representation framework of Figure 15.1. In this figure, what the researcher intends to measure might be the point at which the two-dimensional lines (anonymous versus identified, private versus public) cross. For any set of items, the midpoint among the items represents what this scale measures. The degree to which this center point among items on a scale (what the scale measures) is close to the middle of the figure (what the researcher intends to measure) represents validity.

The scale A, represented by the five "a"s in Figure 15.1, would be a valid measure. The midpoint of these 5 "a"s is very close to the point that the researcher intends to measure. In contrast, the midpoint among the five "b"s lies well left and upward of this center, so scale B is not a valid measure of what the researcher intends to measure.

Figure 15.1 displays two other scales. Scale C consists of the five "c"s in the lower right portion of this figure. These five "c"s are close together, indicating strong correlations among these five items and therefore a highly reliable scale. However, the midpoint among these five "c"s are clearly far from the desired middle of the figure, indicating poor validity of this scale for the researcher's intent. Although the problems with scale C are clear in this picture, the scenario of scale C might be common for two reasons. The first is that researchers might fail to consider the broad domain of the construct and ways of measuring it, and therefore only measure manifestations in a small area of the domain (e.g., only measuring in the lower left quadrant of Figure 15.1). The second reason that this scenario may be common is that researchers may believe the adage that reliability is necessary for validity (which I will show is incorrect later in this chapter). Based on this misconception, a researcher might remove items from a scale in order to achieve high reliability, but this removal biases the validity of the scale. For instance, the researcher using scale C might have originally administered some items falling in the upper left quadrant (and perhaps in the upper right and lower left as well), but found that these items had low correlations with those shown as "c"s in Figure 15.1. The researcher might have therefore removed these other items from scale C in order to improve reliability, but at the expense of reducing validity.

A fourth situation is illustrated by the five "d"s around the boundary of Figure 15.1. The distance between pairs of "d"s indicates that these items would have weak correlations among them, and therefore scale D would have low reliability. However, the midpoint among these five items lies very close to the intended center of this figure, showing that even a scale with low reliability can be valid (Little et al., 1999). There are two ways that researchers can manage this situation of diverse but collectively valid items. First, the researcher can rely on scales that have many items. Reliability is based not only on correlations among items, but also on the number of items in a scale (see below). Therefore, the researcher could include a large number of items from the entire domain in order to obtain a reliable and valid measure of cyberaggression. The second way this situation could be managed is by using latent variable data analytic techniques (i.e., confirmatory factor analysis, structural equation modeling) that can provide results based on the reliable variance among a set of items.

Conceptualizing Measurement Invariance

An important consideration that is too often forgotten is that psychometric properties, including reliability and validity, are properties of the use of a measurement instrument *within a population*, not properties of the measurement instrument itself. Measurement invariance refers to a measure performing in the same way across two or more populations. Within longitudinal studies, measurement invariance can also refer to a measure performing comparably across measurement occasions.

Figure 15.2 displays measurement invariance (2a) and lack of measurement invariance (2b) within the domain representation framework. In this hypothetical scenario, a researcher has measured cyberaggression using three items: (1) aggression in online game environments (e.g., Club Penguin), (2) aggression via hurtful text messages sent to the target, and (3) aggression via circulation of embarrassing pictures. The locations of these three items within the multidimensional space of the cyberaggression domain are shown as points of a triangle, with the middle of the triangle representing the construct centroid. Measurement invariance is evaluated within latent variable models such as confirmatory factor analysis (CFA).[2] The distance between each item and the center point (the construct centroid) represents the strength of each item's factor loading: items closer to the center point have stronger factor loadings, and items further from the center point have weaker factor loadings.[3]

Figure 15.2a displays a hypothetical situation in which measurement invariance of this scale is present across gender within an elementary school sample. For both girls and boys, the first item (aggression in online game environment) is closest to the construct centroid (center of triangle), representing that it has the strongest factor loading on the cyberaggression construct. Also for both genders, the third item (circulating embarrassing pictures) is furthest from the construct centroid, representing that this item has the lowest factor loading. The second

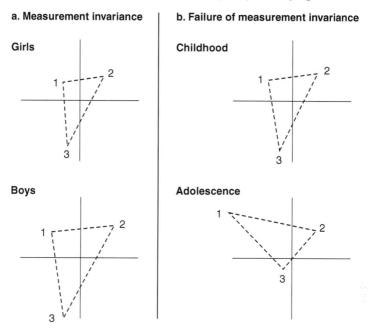

Figure 15.2 Measurement invariance and failure of measurement invariance

item has an intermediate distance, and therefore intermediate factor loading, for both genders. The result in Figure 15.2a is that the shape of the triangles, formed by the three items in the multidimensional cyberaggression domain space, are identical for boys and girls. The triangles do not need to be the same size; in this example, the larger triangle among boys than girls represents lower inter-item correlations, and therefore lower scale reliability, among boys than girls. Nevertheless, measurement invariance is present because items have the same relative strengths of factor loadings across gender: Cyberaggression is strongly indicated by aggression in online environments and weakly indicated by circulation of embarrassing pictures for both genders in this hypothetical example involving elementary school children.

Figure 15.2b displays a hypothetical example in which measurement invariance is not present; in other words, the scale performs differently across populations. In this hypothetical example, the same three-item measure of cyberaggression is administered to elementary school children and to high school adolescents, either through a cohort comparison of different participants in the two ages or through a longitudinal comparison of the same participants at two points in time. The top portion of Figure 15.2b shows a pattern during childhood in which the first item (aggression in online game environment) has the strongest factor loading (closest to the construct centroid), and the third item (circulating embarrassing pictures) has the weakest factor loading (furthest from the construct centroid). In contrast, during adolescence (bottom of Figure 15.2b), a different pattern emerges in this hypothetical example. Here, the third item (circulating embarrassing pictures) now has the strongest factor loading and is displayed closest to the construct, whereas the first item now has a weak loading and is far from the construct centroid. If this hypothetical example were true, it would tell us that cyberaggression is defined by behaviors like circulating embarrassing pictures more so in adolescence than in childhood, whereas childhood cyberaggression is defined by hurtful behaviors on gaming sites more so in childhood than in adolescence. The result of these differences in relative factor loadings across age in Figure 15.2b is that the shape of the triangles defined by these three items differs across age, indicating the failure of measurement invariance across age. This failure of measurement invariance would also mean that the researcher could not conclude that the measure of cyberaggression was assessing the same construct across development. I describe strategies for dealing with the failure of measurement invariance below.

APPLICATIONS IN CYBERBULLYING RESEARCH

Having provided a brief overview of the conceptual foundations of psychometric principles, I next consider the application of these principles in cyberbullying research. I briefly describe the general process of evaluating reliability, validity, and measurement invariance in cyberbullying research. I also review some of the prior cyberbullying research that has considered these psychometric issues; however, previous research has not thoroughly considered these principles. So, I also describe the opportunities that more careful consideration of psychometric principles could offer the emerging field of cyberbullying research. This section is arranged according to considerations of reliability, validity, and measurement invariance.

Reliability

Evaluating the reliabilities of cyberbullying measures with various populations is an important endeavor. Establishing the reliability of measures of cyberaggression and cybervictimization allows researchers to use manifest variable data analyses in their research, as opposed to more complex latent variables analyses to correct for unreliability (though there are additional advantages of more complex analyses). The development of highly reliable instruments is also a key step in using these instruments to identify individuals who may need intervention.

Reliability is typically established by estimating a reliability coefficient among items on a cyberaggression or cybervictimization scale. The most commonly used coefficient is Cronbach's alpha (α), which ranges from 0 to 1.0 and is typically considered "acceptable" at values of .70 or higher and "good" at values of .80 or higher (Devellis, 2003). Cronbach's alpha assumes equal weighting (i.e., equal factor loadings) of items, which is not always a reasonable assumption. Cronbach's alpha is conveniently estimated as a procedure within standard data analysis packages (e.g., SAS, SPSS). Other indices, such as McDonald's omega (ω; McDonald, 1999) relax this assumption and might be better options if the researcher expects that some items are stronger indicators of the construct than other items (i.e., different loadings among items). McDonald's omega is estimated by fitting a single construct model within a CFA (using a software program like EQS, Lisrel, or M-Plus). In addition to evaluating overall reliability, researchers often consider information about individual items, such as the correlations between items and the rest of the scale or factor loading estimates, and may also consider the impact on the reliability estimate if items are removed from the scale.

Reliability, as indexed by Cronbach's alpha, has been evaluated in several studies of cyberbullying using multi-item scales, and the results seem to indicate that reliable multi-item scales can be used (e.g., alpha = .89 in Çetin, Yaman, & Peker, 2011). In research on traditional aggression, a meta-analysis across multiple ways of assessing overt and relational aggression showed that the average Cronbach's alphas are .85 and .82 for measures of overt and relational aggression, respectively (Card, Stucky, Sawalani, & Little, 2008). Therefore, the reliability estimates of measures of cyberaggression are thus far comparable to those found in research on traditional aggression. However, there also exist a number of cyberaggression studies that rely on single items (e.g., Gradinger, Strohmeier, & Spiel, 2009) or do not report reliability estimates (e.g., Kowalski & Limber, 2007; Raskauskas, & Stolz, 2007; Smith et al., 2008; Ybarra & Mitchell, 2004).

Although the generally consistent evaluation of reliability in prior studies is encouraging, two problems are prevalent in the emerging cyberbullying literature. First, conclusions regarding reliability are too often described as aspects of the measurement instrument, rather than as aspects of the measurement instrument with particular population sampled. Researchers should keep in mind that reliability coefficients are population-specific estimates; and an instrument that is reliable with one population might not be reliable with another population. Therefore, researchers should consistently report reliability estimates of their own studies. Second, some studies have given too much emphasis on reliability, removing items to increase reliability without considering the impact this removal has on validity.

Validity

There are numerous approaches to evaluating validity, with no one approach being definitive. Therefore, validity is established as a holistic consideration of a number of aspects. In this section, I consider two aspects of validity: content validity and construct validity.

One aspect of validity, often termed content validity, refers to the degree to which the measurement instrument encompasses the full domain of the construct.

Considering the large circle in Figure 15.1, a measure that samples from all areas within this domain would have strong content validity, whereas a measure that samples from only one section, or that samples from outside this boundary, would have poor content validity. Content validity is a conceptual rather than empirical evaluation, based on careful consideration of the domain space (Figure 15.1) and the content of the items. Definitions of the domain space and manifestations of this space can come from scientists' theoretical/conceptual definitions as well as more open-ended qualitative research with participants (Agatston, Kowalski, & Limber, 2007; Smith et al., 2008).

A second aspect of validity is often called construct validity. This type of validity is established by showing that observed associations of the measure with other constructs are consistent with theoretical expectations. To evaluate construct validity, it is first necessary to articulate expected associations: for instance, a researcher might expect that cyberaggression has a strong positive correlation with traditional aggression, a modest negative correlation with parental monitoring, and negligible correlation with in-school popularity (these are hypothetical associations meant only to illustrate the type of statements that would be made). After specifying these expected associations, the researcher then estimates these correlations from data, comparing the results to the expectations. These correlations can come from simple manifest variable analyses if the scale and the measures of the correlates are highly reliable. An advantage of latent variable CFA is that the correlations of the construct and the correlates will be disattenuated for (not downwardly biased by) unreliability, thus allowing the researcher to evaluate validity even in the context of modest—or even low—reliability (Little et al., 1999). The extent that the observed correlations confirm expectations is evidence for construct validity. A challenge of establishing construct validity is that the failure to confirm expectations could be due either to poor validity of the measurement instrument or to faulty initial expectations. Nevertheless, ongoing theoretical and conceptual refinement of cyberbullying correlates, and accumulating empirical evidence of multiple studies using a variety of measures and correlates will advance the field of cyberbullying research in this direction.

To date, cyberbullying research has considered validity less carefully than reliability (cf. Çetin et al., 2011). This situation is understandable, given the early state of this field. Evaluation of content validity requires detailed articulation of the domain of cyberbullying, cyberaggression, and/or cybervictimization in multidimensional space. Although preliminary efforts to provide formal definitions are ongoing (see Smith et al., this volume), the field should not rush to draw sharp boundaries prematurely. In the research on traditional bullying over the last several decades, formal definitions outpaced evidence of the importance of each dimension of the definitions, and the placement of precise versus fuzzy boundaries resulted in research traditions (bullying versus aggression versus victimization) that were less informed by one another than would have been desirable. Therefore, although clear explications of the multidimensional space of cyberbullying are needed to evaluate content validity, I believe that there is room for multiple domains spaces to coexist in the early stages of this field.

Previous research has given some consideration to construct validity, primarily by evaluating the association of cyberaggression with traditional aggression or cybervictimization with traditional victimization (Gradinger et al., 2009; Kowalski & Limber, 2007; Raskauskas, & Stolz, 2007; Smith et al., 2008; Ybarra & Mitchell, 2004). Depending on conceptual perspective, construct validity might be supported by strong positive correlations (if one conceptualizes cyberbullying and traditional bullying as manifestations of a common tendency) or by modest correlations (if one conceptualizes cyberbullying and traditional bullying as separate phenomena). Alternatively, associations between cyberbullying and traditional bullying might not be conceptualized as informing construct validity, but simply as an interesting empirical question. An alternative approach that has not been used in cyberbullying research is to evaluate associations between different ways of measuring cyberaggression or cybervictimization. This approach would offer some of the most convincing evidence of construct validity. At the same time, even this approach suffers ambiguity in whether these correlations inform validity or are simply empirical questions about inter-informant perceptions. In research on traditional aggression (Card & Casper, under review) and a range of other behaviors and adjustment indices (Achenbach, McConaughy, & Howell, 1987), correlations between different informants has been low. Therefore, finding strong correlations among different reporters' perceptions of cyberaggression and cybervictimization is likely not the sole test of criterion validity. However, the field will need to develop more clearly articulated expectations before better tests of criterion validity can be made.

Measurement Invariance

Measurement invariance is evaluated within confirmatory factor analyses (CFA), a latent variable analysis performed using specialized software such as EQS, Lisrel, or M-Plus. Measurement invariance is evaluated by comparing two models, one in which the factor loadings are freely estimated (i.e., allowed to differ), and a second model in which parallel factor loadings are constrained equally (i.e., forced to have the same estimate) across group or time. Figure 15.3a displays the constraints imposed on the second model when evaluating measurement invariance across groups, and Figure 15.3b displays the constraints imposed on the second model when evaluating measurement invariance across time. The fit of the two models are compared, and if the fit of the second model (constrained factor loadings) is not substantially worse than the fit of the first model (freely estimated factor loadings), then the researcher concludes that measurement invariance holds across these groups or time. If the constraints substantially worsen the fit, then the researcher concludes that measurement invariance does not hold. If measurement invariance fails, the researcher must

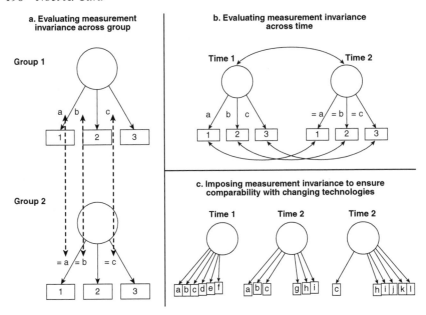

Figure 15.3 Possible applications of measurement invariance in cyberbullying research

relax some of the factor loading equalities to produce a condition called partial invariance (Byrne, Shavelson, & Muthén, 1989), divide the construct into multiple subconstructs for which measurement invariance is found, or else accept that the measure does not perform equivalently, and therefore avoid any comparisons, across groups or time. For details of evaluating measurement invariance, see Card and Little (2006); Cheung and Rensvold (2002); Merredith (1993); Millsap and Cham (2012).

Because measurement invariance can only be evaluated using somewhat advanced data analytic techniques and software, it has received little consideration in traditional aggression research (c.f. Marsh et al., 2011; Vaillancourt, Brendgen, Boivin, & Tremblay, 2003), and I am not aware of any published evaluations of measurement invariance in cyberaggression research. The absence of tests of measurement invariance of cyberaggression measures represents an impediment, because this absence means that we cannot safely make comparisons across gender (or other demographic variables), age (in cohort or longitudinal studies), or pre- versus post-intervention.

The logic of measurement invariance testing also has value in its potential to address a salient challenge of cyberbullying research: managing changing technologies. This challenge applies primarily to longitudinal studies, in which the researcher might assess cyberaggression via specific technologies at one time point, but the potential technologies through which cyberaggression occurs change across the course of the study (new technologies are adopted, old technologies fall out of use). As long as at least some of the technologies can be reasonably measured across successive time points, then it is possible to impose equality of those factor loadings in order to ensure that the same construct is measured across time. This possibility is illustrated in Figure 15.3c. In this hypothetical example, the researcher assesses cyberaggression via six technologies (labeled "a" to "f") at time 1. At time 2, technologies a–c are still used, but technologies d–f are no longer used; instead, new technologies g–i are used. By time 3, technologies c, g, and h are used, as well as technologies j–l. In this scenario, the researcher can impose equality constraints on the factor loadings of technologies that are used (and measured) at successive time points. Doing so allows the researcher to define the underlying construct of cyberaggression equivalently across time, even though old technologies are no longer assessed and new technologies are added.

CONCLUSIONS

In contrast to early work on aggression over a century ago, current cyberbullying researchers are in the fortunate position of having a well-developed conceptual framework and sophisticated data-analytic tools to evaluate and refine the measurement of cyberaggression and cybervictimization. In this chapter, I have described ways of conceptualizing and evaluating the reliability, validity, and measurement invariance of these measures. In order to progress most efficiently, the emerging field of cyberbullying research will need to rely on high-quality measurement, and the time to develop these measurement instruments is now.

Notes

1 The domain representation framework is not only a useful conceptual framework but also a precise geometric representation. Each point in this domain is an endpoint of a vector emanating from a midpoint behind Figure 15.1, and the angle between the vectors reproduces the correlations between variables. Points close together have small angles and strong correlations, points further apart have angles near 90° and are uncorrelated, and points very far apart can have angles greater than 90° and negative correlations.
2 For dichotomous items, Item Response Theory (IRT) models are used, and the term Differential Item Frequency (DIF) testing is commonly used. IRT and DIF are special cases of confirmatory factor analysis and evaluation of measurement invariance that I describe here.
3 In this chapter, I focus only on the type of measurement invariance called "weak" or "loading" invariance. Another type of measurement invariance is "strong" or "intercept" invariance. For descriptions of other types of measurement invariance, see Meredith (1993) or Card and Little (2006).

References

Achenbach, T.M., McConaughy, S.H., & Howell, C. (1987). Child/adolescent behavioral and emotional problems: Implications of cross-informant correlations for situational specificity. *Psychological Bulletin, 101*, 213–232. doi:10.1037/0033–2909.101.2.213

Agatston, P. W., Kowalski, R., & Limber, S. (2007). Students' perspectives on cyber bullying. *Journal of Adolescent Health, 41*, s59–s60. doi:10.1016/j.jadohealth.2007.09.003

Byrne, B. M., Shavelson, R. J., & Muthén, B. (1989). Testing for equivalence of factor covariance and mean structures: The issue of partial measurement invariance. *Psychological Bulletin, 105*, 456–466. doi:10.1037/0033-2909.105.3.456

Card, N. A., & Little, T. D. (2006). Analytic considerations in cross-cultural research on peer relations. In X. Chen, D. C. French, & B. Schneider (Eds.), *Peer relations in cultural context* (pp. 75–95). New York: Cambridge University Press.

Card, N. A., Stucky, B. D., Sawalani, G. M., & Little, T. D. (2008). Direct and indirect aggression during childhood and adolescence: A meta-analytic review of gender differences, intercorrelations, and relations to maladjustment. *Child Development, 79*, 1185–1229. doi:10.1111/j.1467-8624.2008.01184.x

Çetin, B., Yaman, E., & Peker, A. (2011). Cyber victim and bullying scales: A study of validity and reliability. *Computers & Education, 57*, 2261–2271. doi:10.1016/j.compedu.2011.06.014

Cheung, G. W., & Rensvold, R. B. (2002). Evaluating goodness-of-fit indexes for testing measurement invariance. *Structural Equation Modeling, 9*, 233–255. doi:10.1207/S15328007SEM0902_5

DeVellis, R. F. (2003). *Scale development: Theory and applications*. Thousand Oaks, CA: Sage.

Gradinger, P., Strohmeier, D., & Spiel, C. (2009). Traditional bullying and cyberbullying: Identification of risk groups for adjustment problems. *Journal of Psychology, 217*, 205–213.

Kowalski, R. M., & Limber, S. P. (2007). Electronic bullying among middle school students. *Journal of Adolescent Health, 41*, 22–30. doi:10.1016/j.jadohealth.2007.08.017

Little, T. D., Lindenberger, U., & Nesselroade, J. R. (1999). On selecting indicators for multivariate measurement and modeling with latent variables: When "good" indicators are bad and "bad" indicators are good. *Psychological Methods, 4*, 192–211. doi:10.1037/1082-989X.4.2.192

Marsh, H. W., Nagengast, B., Morin, A.J.S., Parada, R. H., Craven, R. G., & Hamilton, L. R. (2011). Construct validity of the multidimensional structure of bullying and victimization: An application of exploratory structural equation modeling. *Journal of Educational Psychology, 103*, 701–732, doi:10.1037/a0024122

McDonald, R. P. (1999). *Test theory: A unified treatment*. Mahwah, NJ: Erlbaum.

Merredith, W. (1993). Measurement invariance, factor analysis and factorial invariance. *Psychometrika, 58*, 525–543. doi:10.1007/BF02294825

Millsap, R. E., & Cham, H. (2012). Investigating factorial invariance in longitudinal data. In B. Laursen, T. D. Little, & N. A. Card (Eds.), *Handbook of developmental research methods* (pp. 109–127). New York: Guilford.

Nunnally, J. C. (1978). *Psychometric theory*. New York: McGraw Hill

Raskauskas, J., & Stolz, A. D. (2007). Involvement in traditional and electronic bullying among adolescents. *Developmental Psychology, 43*, 564–575. doi:10.1037/0012-1649.43.3.564

Smith, P. K., Mahdavi, J., Carvalho, M., Fisher, S., Russell, S., & Tippett, N. (2008). Cyberbullying: Its nature and impact in secondary school pupils. *Journal of Child Psychology and Psychiatry, 49*, 376–385. doi:10.1111/j.1469-7610.2007.01846.x

Vaillancourt, T., Brendgen, M., Boivin, M., & Tremblay, R. E. (2003). A longitudinal confirmatory factor analysis of indirect and physical aggression: Evidence of two factors over time? *Child Development, 74*, 1628–1638. doi:10.1046/j.1467–8624.2003.00628.x

Ybarra, M.L., & Mitchell, K.J. (2004). Youth engaging in online harassment: Associations with caregiver-child relationship, Internet use, and personal characteristics. *Journal of Adolescence, 27*, 319–336. doi:10.1016/j.adolescence.2004.03.007

16 Cybervictimization and Cyberaggression in Eastern and Western Countries

Challenges of Constructing a Cross-Culturally Appropriate Scale

Dagmar Strohmeier, Ikuko Aoyama, Petra Gradinger, and Yuichi Toda

A huge body of evidence shows that substantial numbers of children and youth around the globe are regularly involved in abusive peer relationships in kindergartens and schools. In Western countries, abusive peer relationships that are characterized by an imbalance of power and a certain degree of repetition are usually defined as bullying, while in Japan these behaviors are labeled *ijime*. With the increase of modern forms of communication tools like computers and mobile phones, a new form of bullying emerged that is carried out in cyberspace and called cyberbullying in Western countries (Li, 2006; Slonje & Smith, 2008; Smith et al., 2008) and *net ijime* in Japan. Although bullying and ijime share important characteristics, culture comparative research has also demonstrated that cultural values like individualism or collectivism affect their nature (Kanetsuna & Smith, 2002; Nesdale & Naito, 2005). Therefore, it is necessary to apply a culturally sensitive approach when constructing a cross-culturally valid scale.

The main goals of the present chapter are twofold: First, we demonstrate that bullying and ijime are not fully equivalent concepts in Eastern and Western countries, both on a theoretical level and on the level of terms used in ordinary languages. The richness of these cultural concepts has important implications for the construction of cross-culturally valid scales. Second, a procedure for developing a cross-culturally valid scale and how to establish cross-cultural validity statistically will be described by using data collected in Austria and Japan.

THE NATURE OF BULLYING AND IJIME

Bullying is considered to be a complex relationship issue (e.g., Pepler, 2006) and is classified as a subset of aggressive behavior including (1) intentional harm doing, (2) repetition, and (3) imbalance of power (e.g., Olweus, 1991; Roland,

1989; Sharp & Smith, 1993). Bullying includes a variety of negative acts, which can be delivered face to face, by indirect or relational means (Crick & Grotpeter, 1995), or by using electronic forms of contact (Smith et al., 2008).

In Japan, ijime is considered to be "a type of aggressive behavior by (which) someone who holds a dominant position in *a group-interaction process*, by intentional or collective acts, causes mental and/or physical suffering to another person *inside a group*" (Morita & Kiyonaga, 1986). Similarly, Taki and colleagues (2008) defined ijime as "mean behavior or a negative attitude that has clear intentions to embarrass or humiliate others who occupy weaker positions *in a same group.*"

Taki and colleagues (e.g., Morita, H. Soeda, K. Soeda, & Taki, 1999; Taki, 2003) stress some major differences between the definitions of ijime and bullying: (1) group nature, (2) kind of power situation, and (3) referred forms of behavior.

Group Nature

Ijime was found to be a "within-group" phenomenon that happens between "friends" (Kanetsuna & Smith, 2002; Nesdale & Naito, 2005). In Japan, a group of perpetrators or even the whole class harasses a single target (Akiba, 2004; Kanetsuna & Smith, 2002; Toda, Strohmeier, & Spiel, 2008). In line with these findings, over 90% of Japanese students believed that only group-to-one harassments are ijime, and they clearly distinguished ijime and fighting (Maeda, 1999). The group nature of ijime might be explained by collectivistic values like conformity pressure or group harmony (Treml, 2001). In a collective society where conformity is highly valued, ijime might be considered as a justifiable punishment from the whole group toward an atypical outsider (Akiba, 2004) and might easily be accepted from a silent minority (Toda et al., 2008).

Power Situation

Ijime refers to a kind of collective power that is derived from a group-interaction process. Bullying usually refers to a kind of individual power stemming from either personal characteristics like physical strength (Olweus, 1993) or a power asymmetry within a dyadic relationship, typically including a dominant bullying person and a submissive victimized person (Veenstra et al., 2007).

Referred Forms of Behavior

Similar to bullying, ijime covers a wide range of negative acts that might be overt or indirect. The definition of ijime includes any behavior that is acted out to cause mental or psychological suffering to somebody inside a group (Taki, 2003; Taki et al., 2008). However, some Japanese research (e.g., Morita et al., 1999) showed that verbal and indirect forms of ijime are more frequent than physical forms and speculated that ijime might be more indirect compared with the Western phenomenon of bullying (Taki et al., 2008). This argument is again based on a cultural perspective, because avoiding direct actions is very typical in collectivistic cultures where values like group harmony and face saving are highly valued.

Terms Used for Bullying and Ijime

To accurately translate the term "bullying" into other languages is difficult. This is because the meanings of terms used to describe bullying vary greatly and are not similarly understood by adolescents living in different countries (Smith, Cowie, Olafsson, & Liefooghe, 2002). Based on a stick figure cartoon task, researchers found that the term *ijime*, which mainly refers to verbal direct and indirect behavior, does not fully match any term used in an English- or German-speaking country. Therefore, questionnaires including terms like "bullying," "ijime," or any of the German translations used for "bullying" are not likely to measure the same constructs. Furthermore, in Korea there even exists a term ("wang-ta" or "ta") to refer to a student who is bullied by a group. As for cyberbullying, the equivalent term in Japanese is "net ijime." In China, cyberbullying cases are called "kuso" (Shariff, 2009). Kuso is considered a product of entertainment in China, and researchers consider it as a form of bullying (Shariff, 2009).

CULTURAL COMPARATIVE STUDIES ON CYBERBULLYING

Studies investigating cyberbullying in a cultural comparative way are sparse. Only very few studies compared prevalence rates of cyberbullying and cybervictimization across cultures. A cross-cultural study between Canada and China (Li, 2006) revealed that Chinese students were more likely to be cybervictims but less likely to be cyberbullies, compared with Canadians (Li, 2007). Another study comparing Japan and the United States found that Japanese high school students reported less cyberbullying than their U.S. counterparts (Aoyama, Utsumi, & Hasegawa, 2011). From a cross-cultural perspective, it is possible that depending on the technological development of the respective country, different technological devices are used to carry out cyberbullying. For instance, sending mean text messages is the most frequent form of cyber-harassment in Austria (Gradinger, Strohmeier, & Spiel, 2010). On the other hand, cyberbullying in Japan has attracted more public attention in the form of "unofficial school websites." The government report issued by the Ministry of Education, Culture, Sports, Science, and Technology (MEXT, 2008) found that there were nearly 40,000 unofficial school websites, and half of them contained inappropriate postings. Thus, these kinds of websites were considered the origins of cyberbullying in Japan. Recently, profile sites on mobile phones have been popular, and some of them are inaccessible from a PC in Japan. Importantly, many cyberbullying cases happening on those profile sites in Japan were not recognized by adults.

To summarize, researchers have to be careful about the meanings of terms when conducting a cross-cultural or cross-national study. This is important, because items containing terms like "cyberbullying" or "net ijime" may measure different concepts in Western and Eastern countries. Instead of using such ambiguous terms in questionnaires, it might be advisable for researchers to use very specific behavioral descriptions. Such an approach is similar to cross-national studies on traditional bullying that also avoid specific terms (e.g., Taki et al., 2008).

IMPLICATIONS FOR THE CONSTRUCTION OF A CROSS-CULTURALLY VALID SCALE

First, a culturally sensitive, in-depth content analysis is needed to examine similarities and differences of constructs on a theoretical level. Ideally, qualitative pilot studies like focus group interviews with children, teachers, or other experts should be carried out in the participating countries to find out whether already existing measures cover the full range of behaviors considered forms of bullying (e.g., Lee, Smith, & Monks, 2011). These focus group interviews allow detecting aspects of bullying and cyberbullying that might have been overlooked in previous studies.

Second, it is necessary to avoid biases on the level of the ordinary languages by not using terms that are not fully equivalent. Instead, it is possible to rely on very concrete behavioral descriptions, for example, being called mean or hurtful names as examples for verbal victimization, being pushed or shoved as examples for physical victimization, being left out on purpose from an activity as examples for indirect victimization, or being sent mean text messages via mobile phone as examples for cybervictimization. The obvious advantage of using such very concrete behavioral descriptions is that they are usually much easier translated than terms like "bullying" or "ijime." In addition, subjective definitions and perceptions of the participants might be avoided. It is very likely that bullying perpetrators do not want to admit that they bully others, because bullying or ijime are public concepts, and bullies might be aware that they are undesirable. Thus, more neutral behavioral descriptions presented in form of a behavioral "checklist" may capture more accurate ratings of the incidents of bullying or ijime from the perspective of the perpetrators.

Third, it is nevertheless advisable to consider possible response biases when constructing the rating scales of the items. In some countries, Japan for example, children might avoid the extreme response options and might prefer the middle of a scale for their answers (Chen, Lee, & Stevenson, 1995). To be able to control for such biases later in the analyses, a rating scale consisting of at least four response options should be used.

In many cross-cultural studies, statistical equivalence of scales has not always been examined. Therefore, the validity of many cross-cultural comparisons is questionable. To avoid incorrect comparisons, measurement invariance can be tested within confirmative factor analyses (SEM models).

THE CONSTRUCTION OF A CROSS-CULTURALLY VALID VICTIMIZATION AND AGGRESSION SCALE

The main goal of the empirical study was to develop and to pilot a cross-culturally valid victimization and aggression scale. Based on focus group interviews that were conducted with teachers in both Austria and Japan between January and May 2010, a four-factor structure of the victimization and aggression construct was assumed. Harassment carried out with modern forms of communication tools were considered to be a form of general victimization and aggression and thus measured together with direct physical, direct verbal, and indirect relational forms. To avoid overburdening participating schools and students, the measure needed to be as short as possible. Furthermore, culturally laden terms like "sek-kieren" (one of the Austrian terms used for bullying) or "ijime" (the Japanese term used for bullying) were avoided. Instead, very specific behavioral descriptions were used. To measure relational and physical aspects of victimization and aggression, the peer nomination items developed by Crick and Grotpeter (1995) were changed into self-assessments. These items were used because they showed excellent cross-cultural validity between Japan and the United States (Kawabata, Crick, & Hamaguchi, 2010). In Japan, it is very difficult to conduct peer nomina-tions in schools because of ethical considerations. Therefore, in studies conducted in Japan, peer nomination measures are usually changed into self-assessments (Isobe & Hishinuma, 2007). To broaden the scope of the original scale, three di-rect verbal and three cyber items were included in both the victimization and the aggression scale. Exactly three items for these two new subscales were added to get an ideal just-identifiable measurement structure for each construct when ap-plying structural equation models (Little, 1997; Little, Jones, Henrich, & Hawley, 2003).

Procedure

In Japan, students were recruited from one junior high school situated in a metro-politan area in Japan.[1] To be allowed to collect data in this school, the study had to be accepted by the school principal and teachers. In Japan, to obtain teacher consent is obligatory for data collection. Data were collected in spring 2011. In the school, data collection took place at the same day in all participating classes. Questionnaires were administered by the class teachers and took about one hour. All students present in school on the day of data collection took part in the study. In sum, 96% of all eligible students participated in the study.

In Austria, students were recruited from one academic secondary school situ-ated in the capital city.[2] To be allowed to collect data, the study had to be accepted by the local school council, the school principals, and the parents. Participation in the study was voluntary, and strict confidentiality was guaranteed. After the study was approved by the local school council, the research team informed school principals and teachers about the study, and students were provided with parent consent forms. Before data collection, parent consent forms were collected by the teachers. Data were collected in spring 2011. Data collection was carried out by one trained research assistant during regular lessons and lasted about one hour. In total, 90% of eligible students participated in the study.

Participants

In Japan, 205 adolescents (52% girls) aged 13 to 15 years ($M = 14.32$, $SD = 0.95$); and in Austria, 147 youth (50% girls) aged 12 to 16 years ($M = 13.26$ $SD = 1.16$) participated. The Japanese adolescents were older compared with the Austrian youth, $t(350) = 9.33$, $p < 0.01$. In both countries, the participants were drawn from schools enrolling children from upper middle class families. In Japan, due to privacy considerations, it was not possible to collect information about the education level of the parents. In Austria, 31% of the fathers and 28% of the mothers were university graduates, and 33% of the fathers and 29% of the mothers completed high school.

ITEMS

The items were translated into German and Japanese and back translated from these two languages. Before presenting the behavioral descriptions, a standard explanation was given in the questionnaire: Please think about how often the following incidents happened to you in your class during the last two months.

The following two standard questions were presented after each behavioral description:

(1) How often has this happened to you? (victimization)
(2) How often have you done this to others? (aggression)

Alternative answer options were "never," "one or two times," "once or twice a month," "once or twice a week," and "nearly every day." These options were coded between 0 (never) and 4 (nearly every day).

Five items comprised the relational victimization/aggression scale:

(1) Some kids leave other kids out on purpose when it's time to play or do an activity.
(2) Some kids who are mad at somebody get back at that kid by not letting him or her in his group anymore.
(3) Some kids tell lies about another kid to make other kids not like him/her anymore.
(4) Some kids tell other kids they won't like him/her anymore unless they do what they want.
(5) Some kids keep others from liking a kid by telling mean things about him/her.

Three items comprised the physical victimization/aggression scale:

(1)   Some kids hit other kids.
(2)   Some kids push or shove other kids.
(3)   Some kids kick or pull hair.

Three items comprised the verbal victimization/aggression scale:

(1)   Some kids say mean or hurtful things to other kids.
(2)   Some kids make fun of other kids.
(3)   Some kids call other kids mean and hurtful names.

Three items comprised the cybervictimization/aggression scale:

(1)   Some kids call other kids on the phone to hurt or insult them.
(2)   Some kids send text messages to another kid's mobile phone to hurt or insult him or her.
(3)   Some kids post anonymous messages on webpages to hurt or insult other kids.

Statistical Analyses

Data analyses for the modeling were done using Mplus 5.0 (L. K. Muthén & B. O. Muthén, 2007). We implemented maximum likelihood estimation using the MLR estimator of Mplus, which provides standard errors and test statistics that are robust to non-normality of the data and to nonindependence of observations. Three criteria were used in evaluating the model fit: the chi-square test, the Comparative Fit Index (CFI; Bentler, 1990), and the root mean squared error of approximation (RMSEA; Steiger, 1990). Nonsignificant chi-square values indicate good model fit. However, because the chi-square statistic is known to be sensitive to sample size, we used also CFI and RMSEA. CFI ranges from 0 to 1.00, where a value above 0.95 indicates good fit, and a value above 0.90 indicates adequate fit. RMSEA ranges from 0 to ∞, where a value below 0.05 indicates good fit, and a value below 0.08 indicates adequate fit.

In cross-cultural research, measurement invariance is a critical issue and a precondition to make valid comparisons between groups. In the literature, four levels of measurement invariance are discussed: (1) configural or factor-form invariance, (2) metric or factor loading invariance, (3) scalar or intercept invariance, and (4) invariance of residual variance (Chen, 2008). Measurement invariance was investigated using multiple-group CFA in a stepwise fashion, using increasingly restrictive measurement models.

(1)   Factor-form invariance was estimated by a multiple group model in which the latent means in the Austrian sample were constrained to 0; the latent means in the Japanese sample were freely estimated; and the factor loadings,

intercepts, and residuals were freely estimated and allowed to differ between Austria and Japan.

(2) Factor loading invariance was estimated by a multiple group model in which the latent means in the Austrian sample were constrained to 0, the latent means in the Japanese sample were freely estimated, and the factor loadings were freely estimated but constrained to be equal between the two groups while the intercepts and residuals were allowed to differ between Austria and Japan.

(3) Intercept invariance was estimated by a multiple group model in which the latent means in the Austrian sample were constrained to 0, the latent means in the Japanese sample were freely estimated, and the factor loadings and intercepts were freely estimated but constrained to be equal between the two groups, while the residuals were allowed to differ between Austria and Japan.

(4) Residual invariance was estimated by a multiple group model in which the latent means in the Austrian sample were constrained to 0; the latent means in the Japanese sample were freely estimated; and the factor loadings, intercepts, and residuals were freely estimated but constrained to be equal between the two groups.

Because the χ^2 difference test cannot be used for the MLR estimator, the Satorra-Bentler test (Asparouhov & Muthén, 2010) was applied.

MEANS, STANDARD DEVIATIONS, AND BIVARIATE CORRELATIONS OF THE VICTIMIZATION AND AGGRESSION ITEMS

In the first step, we inspected the data descriptively. We calculated two MANCOVAs with country (Japan vs. Austria) as the independent factor and age as the covariate with all 14 victimization items (see Table 16.1) and all 14 aggression items (see Table 16.2) as dependent variables. For the victimization items, multivariate tests using Pillai Spur indicated that the variable country, F (17, 317) = 3.05, $p < .01$, $\eta = .14$, and the covariate age, F (17, 317) = 3.05, $p < .01$, $\eta^2 = .14$, were significant.

For the aggression items, multivariate tests using Pillai Spur revealed the same results. Again, the variable country, F (14, 316) = 6.23, $p < .01$, $\eta = .22$, and the covariate age, F (14, 316) = 3.63, $p < .01$, $\eta = .14$, were significant.

For the victimization items, follow-up univariate analyses (shown in Table 16.1) indicated that the means of the relational items 1, 2, 3, and 5 were higher in Austria compared with Japan. Striking differences were also found for the three cybervictimization items that were also higher in Austria compared with Japan (see Table 16.1). Only for the physical item 1 (being hit by others) the pattern was reversed, because Japanese students scored higher compared with Austrians. For the aggression items, follow-up univariate analyses (shown in Table 16.2) indicated that the means of the relational items 2, 4, and 5 and the mean of the verbal

Table 16.1 Means, Standard Deviations and Bivariate Correlations of the Victimization Items

Variables	Japan M (SD) N = 198	Austria M (SD) N = 138	F (1, 336)	1.	2.	3.	4.	5.	6.	7.	8.	9.	10.	11.	12.	13.	14.
1. leave other out on purpose (relational 1)	.30 (.89)	1.03 (1.07)	22.56**	–	.79	.59	.53	.66	.19	.19	.21	.41	.41	.33	.31	-.05^{ns}	-.03^{ns}
2. get back by not letting in the group (relational 2)	.25 (.79)	.91 (1.01)	20.89**	.62	–	.54	.59	.65	.17*	.26	.32	.44	.44	.31	.31	-.02^{ns}	-.03^{ns}
3. tell lies to make others not like him/her (relational 3)	.29 (.74)	.91 (1.09)	18.15**	.49	.53	–	.62	.69	.26	.26	.14	.44	.36	.44	.50	.16*	-.04^{ns}
4. tell won't like him/her (relational 4)	.22 (.66)	.46 (.80)	2.71	.57	.41	.36	–	.48	.23	.16	.25	.49	.42	.33	.56	.01^{ns}	.07^{ns}
5. keep others from liking a kid (relational 5)	.30 (.87)	.85 (1.07)	9.45**	.52	.48	.60	.42	–	.20	.24	.22	.53	.36	.42	.40	.03^{ns}	-.03^{ns}
6. hit (physical 1)	1.06 (1.58)	1.03 (1.37)	5.22*	.44	.46	.45	.51	.51	–	.78	.46	.41	.51	.45	.28	.04^{ns}	-.04^{ns}
7. push or shove (physical 2)	.83 (1.45)	1.30 (1.24)	1.25	.45	.39	.37	.47	.45	.67	–	.49	.40	.53	.40	.28	.06^{ns}	-.06^{ns}
8. kick or pull hair (physical 3)	.31 (.91)	.67 (1.05)	1.24	.39	.47	.38	.41	.41	.66	.49	–	.37	.39	.24	.33	.14*	-.03^{ns}
9. say mean or hurtful things (verbal 1)	.79 (1.26)	1.39 (1.21)	7.60**	.49	.41	.46	.36	.51	.60	.59	.48	–	.67	.53	.36	.05^{ns}	-.04^{ns}
10. make fun of others (verbal 2)	1.00 (1.44)	1.28 (1.33)	.34	.54	.48	.58	.49	.52	.66	.60	.54	.66	–	.58	.32	.05^{ns}	-.07^{ns}
11. call other kids mean and hurtful names (verbal 3)	.63 (1.24)	.71 (1.03)	.36	.40	.32	.39	.33	.34	.40	.37	.36	.45	.50	–	.29	.11^{ns}	-.05^{ns}
12. call on the phone to hurt or insult (cyber 1)	.09 (.46)	.39 (.70)	13.16**	.37	.30	.23	.38	.41	.46	.32	.34	.44	.36	.34	–	.01^{ns}	-.02^{ns}
13. send text messages to hurt or insult (cyber 2)	.04 (.30)	.40 (.73)	20.07**	.16^{ns}	.23	.38	.18*	.33	.32	.32	.39	.33	.34	.23	.44	–	-.01^{ns}
14. post anonymous messages on webpages to hurt or insult (cyber 3)	.02 (.16)	.28 (.56)	35.57**	.25	.21	.17*	.20*	.26	.21*	.10^{ns}	.18*	.30	.25	.17*	.34	.25	–

Note. ** $p < 0.01$. * $p < 0.05$, $\eta^2 = .01$–.010. All bivariate correlations were statistically significant at $p < .001$ level, except the ones marked with ^{ns}. Correlations above the diagonal are for Austria, below the diagonal for Japan.

Table 16.2 Means, Standard Deviations and Bivariate Correlations of the Aggression Items

Variables	Japan M (SD) $N = 198$	Austria M (SD) $N = 134$	$F_{(1, 329)}$	1.	2.	3.	4.	5.	6.	7.	8.	9.	10.	11.	12.	13.	14.
1. leave other out on purpose (relational 1)	.32 (.84)	.64 (.83)	2.57	—	.55	.34	.42	.61	.16*	.19	.12^{ns}	.37	.32	.20	.28	.17*	−.03^{ns}
2. get back by not letting in the group (relational 2)	.30 (.75)	.60 (.86)	6.59*	.66	—	.39	.30	.53	.16*	.15*	.28	.25	.21	.13^{ns}	.25	.38	−.03^{ns}
3. tell lies to make others not like him/her (relational 3)	.16 (.52)	.26 (.53)	2.57	.20*	.24	—	.13^{ns}	.28	.17*	.15*	.16*	.19	.27	.18*	.27	.12^{ns}	−.02^{ns}
4. tell won't like him/her (relational 4)	.07 (.29)	.22 (.50)	10.37**	.28	.22	.27	—	.27	.20	.21	.15*	.35	.20	.14*	.47	.08^{ns}	−.02^{ns}
5. keep others from liking a kid (relational 5)	.51 (1.04)	.25 (.66)	9.52**	.38	.26	.31	.25	—	.18*	.14*	.15*	.44	.32	.38	.36	.16*	−.03^{ns}
6. hit (physical 1)	1.10 (1.54)	.72 (1.14)	13.25**	.33	.33	.21*	.25	.30	—	.78	.55	.48	.58	.40	.24	.07^{ns}	−.01^{ns}
7. push or shove (physical 2)	.86 (1.46)	.81 (.95)	1.38	.32	.34	.19*	.24	.35	.62	—	.50	.42	.55	.35	.28	.04^{ns}	−.04^{ns}
8. kick or pull hair (physical 3)	.33 (.96)	.34 (.77)	1.05	.27	.35	.22	.26	.38	.49	.38	—	.43	.43	.31	.21	.10^{ns}	−.02^{ns}

(Continued)

Table 16.2 (Continued)

Variables	Japan M (SD) N = 198	Austria M (SD) N = 134	F (1, 329)	1.	2.	3.	4.	5.	6.	7.	8.	9.	10.	11.	12.	13.	14.
9. say mean or hurtful things (verbal 1)	.77 (1.25)	.80 (.96)	.08	.43	.52	.21*	.32	.25	.47	.45	.34	–	.62	.48	.28	.16*	.01^{ns}
10. make fun of others (verbal 2)	1.09 (1.47)	.90 (1.07)	1.56	.43	.53	.19*	.30	.30	.49	.57	.21	.61	–	.55	.16*	.01^{ns}	–.01^{ns}
11. call other kids mean and hurtful names (verbal 3)	.67 (1.28)	.43 (.74)	6.95**	.38	.40	.25	.22	.26	.39	.40	.19*	.45	.50	–	.17*	.08^{ns}	–.04^{ns}
12. call on the phone to hurt or insult (cyber 1)	.05 (.31)	.22 (.53)	8.63**	.25	.19*	.36	.19*	.25	.34	.25	.33	.26	.16^{ns}	.32	–	.31	–.01^{ns}
13. send text messages to hurt or insult (cyber 2)	.04 (.30)	.24 (.55)	6.69**	26	.18*	.11^{ns}	.14^{ns}	.12^{ns}	.09^{ns}	.03^{ns}	.01^{ns}	.15^{ns}	.16^{ns}	.05^{ns}	.18*	–	–.01^{ns}
14. post anonymous messages on webpages to hurt or insult (cyber 3)	.01 (.07)	.11 (.38)	10.28**	.11^{ns}	.08^{ns}	.24	.16^{ns}	.37	.10^{ns}	.11^{ns}	.29	.22	.03^{ns}	.14^{ns}	.21*	.15^{ns}	–

Note. ** $p < .01$. * $p < .05$, $\eta^2 = .01$–.010. All bivariate correlations were statistically significant at $p < .001$ level, except the ones marked with ^{ns}. Correlations above the diagonal are for Japan, below the diagonal for Austria.

item 3 were higher in Austria compared with Japan. Again, striking differences were also found for the three cybervictimization items that were much higher in Austria compared with Japan (see Table 16.2). Again the pattern was reversed for the physical item 1 (hit others); here Japanese students scored higher compared with Austrians.

In Japan, the means of the cybervictimization and cyberaggression items were extremely low. Out of 202 adolescents who answered the cybervictimization items in Japan, only 8 indicated that they were ever called on the phone, 4 indicated that someone sent text messages to them, and only 2 indicated that someone had posted nasty messages on the Internet about them. This result is consistent with the government research that reports that traditional bullying is a major peer victimization form, whereas the prevalence of cyberbullying is less than 5% of total bullying incidents in Japan (MEXT, 2009).

The descriptive inspection of the bivariate correlations of the items also revealed some interesting patterns for the Japanese and Austrian sample. While for the Japanese sample (shown above the diagonal), the five relational victimization items correlated only weakly with the three physical victimization items, these correlations were moderate in the Austrian sample (shown below the diagonal). Moreover, the three cybervictimization items did not correlate with any of the other victimization items in Japan, but correlated weakly to moderate with the other items in Austria. The same patterns were found for the aggression items (see Table 16.2); however, the cyberaggression items did not correlate with the other items in both the Japanese and Austrian sample. Thus, by only inspecting the means and correlations, differences regarding the factor structure of the scales between Japan and Austria could be expected. Most likely, these differences should appear regarding the cybervictimization and cyberaggression scales.

Measurement Models

The measurement models were calculated separately for the victimization and the aggression scales (see Figures 16.1–16.4). In the first step, a four-factor model for victimization was tested for the whole sample (see Figure 16.1). This model showed a very good model fit, χ^2 (71) = 124.19, $p < 0.01$, CFI = 0.96, RMSEA = 0.046. An alternative three-factor model with direct victimization (both verbal and physical), relational victimization and cybervictimization as factors revealed a much worse fit, χ^2 (74) = 188.47, p < 0.01, CFI = 0.91, RMSEA = 0.066. Therefore, a multiple group model (Austria vs. Japan) was calculated for the four-factor model to check for factor-form invariance between the two countries. Although this model showed an acceptable fit, χ^2 (142) = 204.04, $p < 0.01$, CFI = 0.93, RMSEA = 0.063, the latent factor cybervictimization was problematic in the Japanese sample. In line with the inspection of the correlation matrix (see Table 16.1), the three cyber items did not form a latent factor in the Japanese sample. Furthermore, a non-positive definite covariance matrix for this latent construct was detected by the Mplus program. Therefore, it was not possible to further include the latent factor cybervictimization in any of the multiple group analyses.

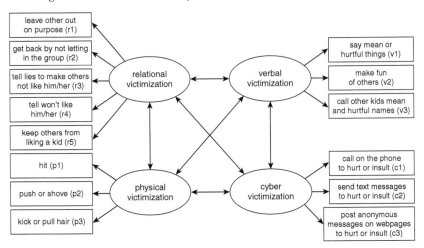

Figure 16.1 Theoretical factor structure of the victimization items

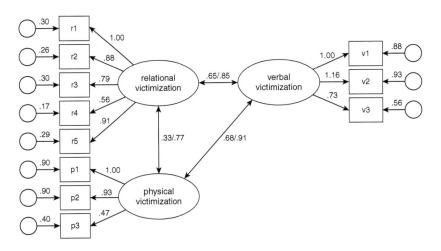

Figure 16.2 Victimization level 3 model: Factor-form, factor-loadings and intercepts constrained. For factor loadings and intercepts (freely estimated but constraint to be equal between Japan and Austria) the unstandardized regression weights are displayed only. For the associations between relational victimization, verbal victimization and physical victimization the standardized regression weights are displayed only. Associations are reported in the following order: Japan / Austria.

In the second step, a four-factor model for aggression was tested for the whole sample (see Figure 16.3). This model showed a very good model fit, χ^2 (71) = 85.93, $p = 0.11$, CFI = 0.98, RMSEA = 0.025. An alternative three-factor model with direct aggression (both verbal and physical), relational aggression, and cyberaggression as factors was a worse fit, χ^2 (74) = 194.34, $p < 0.01$, CFI = 0.83, RMSEA = 0.077. Therefore, a multiple group model (Austria vs. Japan) was calculated for the four-factor model to check for factor-form invariance between the

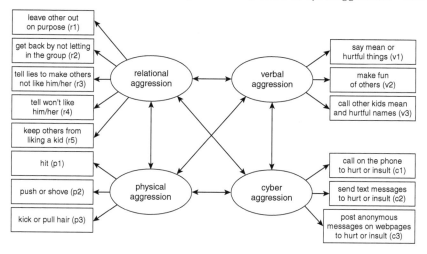

Figure 16.3 Theoretical factor structure of the aggression items

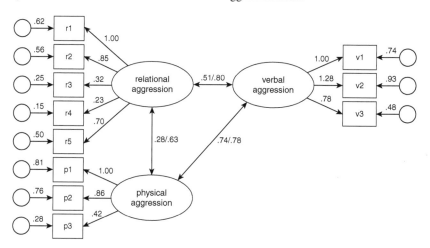

Figure 16.4 Aggression level 3 model: Factor-form, factor-loadings and intercepts constrained. For factor loadings and intercepts (freely estimated but constraint to be equal between Japan and Austria) the unstandardized regression weights are displayed only. For the associations between relational victimization, verbal victimization and physical victimization the standardized regression weights are displayed only. Associations are reported in the following order: Japan / Austria.

two countries. Although this model showed an acceptable fit, 240.88, p < 0.01, CFI = 0.93, RMSEA = 0.050, the latent factor cyberaggression was again problematic in the Japanese sample. In line with the inspection of the correlation matrix (see Table 16.2), the three cyber items did not form a latent factor in the Japanese sample. Furthermore, a non-positive definite covariance matrix for this latent construct was detected by the Mplus program. Therefore, it was not possible to further include the latent factor cyberaggression in any of the multiple group analyses.

Measurement Invariance Tests

Measurement invariance was investigated for a three-factor model for both victimization and aggression using multiple-group CFA in a stepwise fashion, using increasingly restrictive measurement models (see Tables 16.2 and 16.3). Altogether, four models were analyzed: (1) the factor-form invariance model, (2) the factor loading invariance model, (3) the intercept invariance model, and (4) the residual invariance model. For victimization, factor loading invariance could be achieved between Austria and Japan (shown in Table 16.2). Both intercepts and residuals were not invariant between the two countries. For aggression, factor-form invariance could be achieved between Austria and Japan, whereas some of the factor loadings, intercepts, and residuals differed between the two countries (see Table 16.3).

Table 16.3 Models for the Victimization Scales

Model	EQC	df	χ^2	CFI	RMSEA	BIC	ΔModel	Δdf	$\Delta\chi^2$
1	Factor-form invariance	82	137.73**	.95	.06	9824.47			
2	Factor-loading invariance	90	151.89**	.94	.06	9804.44	2–1	8	14.05ns
3	Intercept invariance	98	191.63**	.91	.07	9814.26	3–2	8	51.56*
4	Residual invariance	109	237.54**	.88	.08	9875.97	4–3	11	33.16*

Note. EQC = Equality constraints across groups (Japan/Austria).
*$p < .05$

Table 16.4 Models for the Aggression Scales

Model	EQC	df	χ^2	CFI	RMSEA	BIC	ΔModel	Δdf	$\Delta\chi^2$
1	Factor-form invariance	82	91.76ns	.99	.03	8904.55			
2	Factor-loading invariance	90	112.10ns	.97	.04	8898.55	2–1	8	18.21*
3	Intercept invariance	98	143.34**	.93	.05	8900.42	3–2	8	43.06*
4	Residual invariance	109	193.36	.88	.07	8958.62	4–3	11	34.81*

Note. EQC = Equality constraints across groups (Japan/Austria).
*$p < .05$

DISCUSSION

The present research highlights the manifold challenges when conducting cross-cultural comparative studies on victimization and aggression. To begin with, it was demonstrated that bullying and ijime are similar but not identical constructs in Western and Eastern countries. When considering important cultural dimensions like individualism and collectivism (Hofstede, 2001), these two constructs already differ on a theoretical level. In collectivistic countries like Japan, ijime is considered to be a whole-group phenomenon characterized by an abuse of collective power that is carried out by rather indirect means. In individualistic countries like Austria, bullying is considered to be a problem of dyads or smaller peer groups characterized by an abuse of individual power that is acted out by both direct and indirect means. To further complicate the issue, finding terms to accurately translate these constructs into different languages is difficult or even impossible. As an attempt to overcome these problems, very specific behavioral descriptions were used in the present study. The choice of the items was made based on previous studies (Kawabata et al., 2010) and on focus groups conducted with teachers in both Japan and Austria. Based on these grounds, in both Japan and Austria a four-factor structure for both victimization and aggression was assumed and rigorously tested by using multiple group structural equation models (Chen, 2008). Harassment carried out with modern forms of communication tools was considered to be a form of general victimization and aggression, and thus measured together with direct physical, direct verbal and indirect relational subforms. From a cross-cultural perspective, it was assumed that depending on the technological development in Japan and Austria, different technological devices might be used to harass others with modern forms of communication tools. For instance, sending mean text messages was found to be the most frequent form of cyber-harassment in Austria (Gradinger et al., 2010), while nasty postings on "unofficial school websites" were considered the origins of net ijime in Japan (MEXT, 2008). Therefore, these particular cyber forms were included in the newly developed measure. Unexpectedly, extremely low frequencies of cybervictimization and cyberaggression in Japan made measurement invariance tests of the four-factor structure models impossible. In Japan, hardly any students reported to be actively or passively involved in cyber-harassment. Therefore, we applied multiple group invariance tests for the remaining three-factor solutions. From a statistical point of view, the four levels of invariance are a precondition to make valid cross-cultural comparisons. However, it turned out to be difficult (or maybe even impossible) to achieve invariance in the strongest statistical sense (e.g., residual invariance) between the two countries Japan and Austria. When just inspecting the fit statistics (shown in Tables 16.2 and 16.3), for both the victimization and aggression scales, the intercept invariant model was acceptable. This is important when using latent means and covariance structures (e.g., when comparing latent means in a multiple group model in which intercept invariance is a precondition).

To conclude, the present approach was not successful in establishing a cross-culturally valid scale from a very strict statistical point of view. Nevertheless, this research highlights some interesting cross-national differences when just inspecting the means and correlations of the single items. Contrary to the expectations, Austrian youth scored higher in most of the relational forms of victimization and aggression compared with Japanese, while Japanese students reported to hit others more often and to be hit more often by others compared with the Austrians. This result is in line with another cross-cultural study conducted in Japan and Austria (Toda, Strohmeier, Lampert, & Spiel, 2007). Furthermore, the inter-correlations between physical and relational forms of victimization and aggression were much higher in the Austrian sample compared with the Japanese sample.

Future Studies

Measuring cyber forms of victimization and aggression in Japan appeared to be most challenging. When using self-assessments, hardly any Japanese students reported being actively or passively involved in these kinds of negative peer behaviors. This leads to the fundamental question whether the Western-oriented approach of asking students *directly* about their involvement in any kind of specific negative peer behavior is culturally appropriate. Assuming that cultural values interfere with the answers, it might be worthwhile to creatively think about more *indirect* ways of asking Japanese students about their experiences with victimization and aggression. For instance, in addition to asking Japanese students very straightforward and direct questions like "How often has this happened to *you*?" or "How often have *you* done this to others?," it could be worthwhile to think about more indirect questions like "How often has this happen in *your group*?" or "How many students in *your group* have done this to others?" or "How often has this happen to one of *your friends* in class?," etc. Such an approach is potentially more appropriate for people with an interdependent view of the self (Markus & Kitayama, 1991) who have difficulty thinking about themselves separated from others.

To conclude, after failing to establish cross-cultural validity with the Western-oriented approach of asking questions, a more indirect way of asking questions is strongly suggested for further studies.

Notes

1 In Japan, compulsory schooling starts with a child's sixth birthday and lasts nine school years. Elementary school comprises grades 1 to 6, and junior high school comprises grades 7 to 9.
2 In Austria, compulsory schooling starts with a child's sixth birthday and lasts nine school years. Elementary school comprises grades 1 to 4. After primary school, students can either attend a general secondary school (grades 5 to 8) or an academic secondary school (grades 5 to 12).

References

Akiba, M. (2004). Nature and correlates of ijime [bullying] in Japanese middle schools. *International Journal of Educational Research, 41*, 216–236. doi:10.1016/j.ijer.2005.07.002

Aoyama, I., Utsumi, S., & Hasegawa, M. (2011). Cyberbullying in Japan: Cases, government reports, adolescent relational aggression and parental monitoring roles. In Q. Li, D. Cross, & P. K. Smith (Eds.), *Bullying goes to the global village: Research on cyberbullying from an international perspective.* Oxford, UK: Wiley Blackwell.

Asparouhov, T., & Muthén, B. (2010). Computing the strictly positive Satorra-Bentler chi-square test in Mplus. Retrieved from http://www.statmodel.com

Bentler, P. (1990). Comparative fit indexes in structural models. *Psychological Bulletin, 107*, 238–246. doi:10.1037/0033-2909.107.2.238

Chen, C., Lee, S., & Stevenson, H. W. (1995). Response style and cross cultural comparisons of rating scales among East Asian and North American students. *Psychological Science*, 170–175.

Chen, F. F. (2008). What happens if we compare chopsticks with forks? The impact of making inappropriate comparisons in cross-cultural research. *Journal of Personality and Social Psychology, 95*(5), 1005–1018. doi:10.1037/a0013193

Crick, N. R., & Grotpeter, J. K. (1995). Relational aggression, gender, and social-psychological adjustment. *Child Development, 66*(3), 710–722. doi:10.2307/1131945

Gradinger, P., Strohmeier, D., & Spiel, C. (2010). Definition and measurement of cyberbullying. *Cyberpsychology: Journal of psychosocial research on cyberspace, 4*(2), article 1.

Hofstede, G. (2001). *Culture's consequences: Comparing values, behaviours, institutions, and organizations across nations.* Thousand Oaks, CA: Sage.

Isobe, M., & Hishinuma, Y. (2007). Overt and relational aggression and impression formation in Japanese university students. *Japanese Journal of Personality, 15*(3), 290–300.

Kanetsuna, T., & Smith, P. K. (2002). Pupil insights into bullying, and coping with bullying: A bi-national study in Japan and England. *Journal of School Violence, 1*(3), 5–29. doi:10.1300/J202v01n03_02

Kawabata, Y., Crick, N. R., & Hamaguchi, Y. (2010). The role of culture in relational aggression: Associations with social-psychological adjustment problems in Japanese and US school-aged children. *International Journal of Behavioral Development, 34*(4), 354–362. doi:10.1177/0165025409339151

Lee, S., Smith, P. K., & Monks, C. P. (2011). Perceptions of bullying-like phenomena in South Korea: A qualitative approach from a life span perspective. *Journal of Aggression, Conflict and Peace Research, 3*, 210–221. doi:10.1108/17596591111187738

Li, Q. (2006). Cyberbullying in schools. A research of gender differences. *School Psychology International, 27*(2), 157–170. doi:10.1177/0143034306064547

Little, T. D. (1997). Mean and covariance structures (MACS) analyses of cross-cultural data: Practical and theoretical issues. *Multivariate Behavioural Research, 32*(1), 53–76. doi:10.1207/s15327906mbr3201_3

Little, T. D., Jones, S. M., Henrich, C. C., & Hawley, P. H. (2003). Disentangling the "whys" from the "whats" of aggressive behavior. *International Journal of Behavioral Development, 27*, 122–133. doi:10.1080/01650250244000128

Maeda, R. (1999). Ijime: An exploratory study of a collective form of bullying among Japanese students. (ERIC Document Reproduction Service No. ED438015) Retrieved from ERIC database.

Ministry of Education, Culture, Sports, Science, and Technology. (2008). Seisyonen ga riyo suru gakko hikousiki site nado ni kansuru cyousa (Gaiyo) [Research on adolescents' use of unofficial school websites and other websites] (in Japanese). Retrieved from www.mext.go.jp/b_menu/houdou/20/04/08041805/001.htm

Ministry of Education, Culture, Sports, Science, and Technology. (2009). Heisei 20 nendo jidouseito no mondai koudou nado seitosido jo no syomondai ni kansuru cyousa [Research on problematic behaviors and related problems among adolescents] (in Japanese). Retrieved from www.mext.go.jp/b_menu/houdou/21/11/__icsFiles/afieldfile/2009/11/30/1287227_1_1.pdf

Markus, H.R., & Kitayama, S. (1991). Culture and self: Implications for cognition, emotion, and motivation. *Psychological Review, 98*(2), 224–253. doi:10.1037/0033–295X.98.2.224

Morita, Y., & Kiyonaga, K. (1986). *Ijime: Pathology in classroom.* Tokyo, Japan: Kanekoshobo.

Morita, Y., Soeda, H., Soeda, K., & Taki, M. (1999). Japan. In P.K. Smith, Y. Morita, J. Junger-Tas, D. Olweus, R.F. Catalano, & P. Slee (Eds.), *The nature of bullying: A cross-national perspective* (pp. 309–323). New York: Routledge.

Muthén, L.K., & Muthén, B.O. (2007). *Mplus User's guide* (5th ed.). Los Angeles: Muthén & Muthén.

Nesdale, D., & Naito, M. (2005). Individualism-Collectivism and the attitudes to school bullying of Japanese and Australian students. *Journal of Cross-Cultural-Psychology, 36*(5), 537–556.

Olweus, D. (1991). Bully/victim problems among schoolchildren: Basic facts and effects of a school based intervention program. In D.J. Pepler & K.H. Rubin (Eds.), *The development and treatment of childhood aggression* (pp. 411–448). Hillsdale, NJ: Erlbaum.

Olweus, D. (1993). *Bullying at school: What we know and what we can do.* Oxford, UK: Blackwell.

Pepler, D. (2006). Bullying Interventions: A binocular perspective. *Journal of the Canadian Academy of Child and Adolescent Psychiatry, 15*(1), 16–20.

Roland, E. (1989). A system oriented strategy against bullying. In E. Roland & E. Munthe (Eds.), *Bullying: An international perspective.* London: David Fulton.

Shariff, S. (2009). *Confronting cyber-bullying. What schools need to know to control misconduct and avoid legal consequences.* New York: Cambridge University Press. doi:10.1017/CBO9780511551260

Sharp, S., & Smith, P.K. (1993). Tackling bullying: The Sheffield project. In D. Tattum (Ed.), *Understanding and managing bullying* (pp. 45–56). Oxford, UK: Heinemann.

Slonje, R., & Smith, P.K. (2008). Cyberbullying: Another main type of bullying? *Scandinavian Journal of Psychology, 49*, 147–154. doi:10.1111/j.1467–9450.2007.00611.x

Smith, P.K., Cowie, H., Olafsson, R.F., & Liefooghe, A.P.D. (2002). Definitions of bullying: A comparison of terms used, and age and gender differences, in a fourteen-country international comparison. *Child Development, 73*(4), 1119–1133. doi:10.1111/1467–8624.00461

Smith, P.K., Madhavi, J., Carvalho, M., Fisher, S., Russell, S., & Tippett, N. (2008). Cyberbullying: Its nature and impact in secondary school pupils. *Journal of Child Psychology & Psychiatry, 49*(4), 376–385. doi:10.1111/j.1469–7610.2007.01846.x

Steiger, J. (1990). Structural model evaluation and modification: An interval estimation approach. *Multivariate Behavioral Research, 25*, 173–180. doi:10.1207/s15327906 mbr2502_4

Taki, M. (2003). Ijime bullying: Characteristic, causality and intervention. *Oxford Kobe Seminar: Bullying in schools*. Kobe, Japan: Kobe Institute.

Taki, M., Slee, P., Hymel, S., Pepler, D., Sim, H., & Swearer, S. (2008). A new definition and scales for indirect aggression in schools: Results from the longitudinal comparative survey among five countries. *International Journal of Violence and School, 7*, 3–19.

Toda, Y., Strohmeier, D., & Spiel, C. (2008). Process model of bullying. In T. Katoh & H. Taniguchi (Eds.), *Dark side of interpersonal relationships*. Kyoto: Kitaohji-Shobo.

Toda, Y., Strohmeier, D., Lampert, A., & Spiel, C. (2007). A cross cultural study on aggressive behaviour in Japanese and Austrian pupils. *ECDP—European Conference on Developmental Psychology*. Jena, Germany.

Treml, J. (2001). Bullying as a social malady in contemporary Japan. *International Social Work, 44*, 107–117. doi:10.1177/0020872800104400109

Veenstra, R., Lindenberg, S., Zijlstra, B.J.H., De Winter, A.F., Verhulst, F.C., & Ormel, J. (2007). The dyadic nature of bullying and victimization: Testing a dual-perspective theory. *Child Development, 78*(6), 1843–1854. doi:10.1111/j.1467–8624.2007.01102.x

17 What to Measure?

Ian Rivers

In this chapter, rationales are presented for the types of data that would allow researchers to advance our collective understanding of the phenomenon of cyberbullying. While other authors in this book have considered the ways in which we define the behavior we now describe as "cyberbullying," these definitions are not used uniformly by those who research the field. To date, reports of the incidence of cyberbullying have varied dramatically from 4% (Ybarra & Mitchell, 2004) to 36% among girls (Hinduja & Patchin, 2008) and higher. Researchers have also presumed that they are measuring the same phenomenon across studies as well as longitudinally. For example, Williams and Guerra (2007) studied "Internet bullying" while Li (2005) focused on e-mail, Internet chat room communication, and cell/mobile phone usage. In a review of studies conducted by 18 different individual researchers or groups, Rivers and Noret (2010) noted that there was a great deal of inconsistency in the ways in which bullying via electronic media was operationalized. While the majority of researchers included SMS/text and e-mail bullying, others, but not all, included blogs, instant messages, website comments and uploads, Internet chat rooms, newsgroups, and the sending of pictures and video clips to others. Consequently, researchers have differed substantially in their estimates of frequency or prevalence. Kowalski and Witte (2006) asked students if they had *ever* been cyberbullied, whereas Smith, Mahdavi, Carvalho, Fisher, Russell, and Tippett (2008) used *two or three times* in the past *couple of months* as the marker. Hinduja and Patchin (2008) asked students to report on *repeated* experiences *in the last year*, and Li (2006) asked her participants about cyberbullying taking place *during school*.

Of course, some of the methodological issues highlighted above (particularly issues of prevalence) are a result of the devices and online environments that were available to the general public, and especially children and young people, at the time the studies were conducted. Rivers and Noret (2010) noted in their five-year study of text and e-mail bullying that a rise in the receipt of "nasty or threatening text messages and e-mail" was positively associated with a similar rise in household uptake of cell/mobile phone ownership and Internet connectivity ($r = .88–.96$). Thus, social class, family income, and other environmental factors are likely to play a significant role in establishing baseline statistics, particularly where there remains growth in technology-based markets.

Given the various ways in which cyberbullying has been operationalized, and the fact that there has been very little published about the psychometric properties of some of the questionnaires currently in use, in the following pages a set of guiding principles are suggested to underpin the measurement of this phenomenon. In addition, some illustrative survey questions are provided in the appendix to this chapter.

THE CHALLENGE OF MEASURING BULLYING

The mathematician and cosmologist Sir Hermann Bondi (1964) wrote, "We find no sense in talking about something unless we specify how we measure it; a definition by the method of measuring a quantity is the one sure way of avoiding talking nonsense." His argument is simple: The method of measurement will in and of itself result in a definition that is clear to all. For the last decade or so, the media (and many scholars) have talked about cyberbullying as if it is clearly understood and clearly delineated behavior that meets all the currently understood criteria we ascribe to other forms of bullying. Currently, we define bullying as a *repeated* behavior where there is an *imbalance of power* between the perpetrator and target. This imbalance of power can be physical but also emotional and/or social, and the behavior on the part of the perpetrator must be *deliberate* and *meant to inflict pain or suffering* (physical and/or emotional). Yet, in the case of cyberbullying, can all of these criteria be met? If the perpetrator's identity is hidden, can we safely assume that the behavior is repeated? That is, if the target receives multiple defamatory messages, all anonymous, it is not clear whether the messages all come from the same person (i.e., are repeated) and thus meet the criterion. For the target it may seem to be so, but is it so for the perpetrator?

Current definitions of bullying imply that a relationship exists between the target and the perpetrator (often in the form of a power imbalance) or, at the very least, that those involved have sufficient knowledge to draw inferences or make assumptions about one another. Furthermore, if bullying is objectively defined in terms of a deliberate act meant to inflict pain or suffering, is it appropriate to measure this from the perspective of the target rather than that of the perpetrator? The majority of studies currently available use one definition for both perpetrators or targets without necessarily considering the "way" in which the definition is written (e.g., can a target always discern a deliberate act?). Additionally, can we always assume intentionality when we rarely observe interactions between perpetrators and targets? While there are many instances where intentionality is evident from the way in which the target is humiliated or threatened, there are also times when interactions via electronic communication devices are misinterpreted or sent without premeditation (the hastily written e-mail is one such example). If we believe that these criteria are essential components of the definition, our measures must therefore inquire about the relationship between the involved parties.

Demographics

Usually demographic data are collected in order to show the representativeness or lack thereof of the sample. Variables such as sex/gender, age or grade in school, race or ethnicity, and faith or belief are often used to describe the group under investigation. However, in the case of cyberbullying, the question arises: Which of these characteristics are most pertinent? Certainly sex/gender, age, or grade in school are helpful in providing readers with the demographic characteristics of targets and perpetrators of cyberbullying separately. However, unless the researcher is able to link one or more perpetrators to one or more targets, these variables only offer a very superficial level analysis of the dynamics of cyberbullying. So how might demographic information assist us in understanding cyberbullying? Asking perpetrators to provide demographic and biographical data for their *most recent* target may be one way of exploring the dynamics of this phenomenon. Similarly, asking targets to provide demographic and biographical data of their *actual or presumed* perpetrator or primary perpetrator (if there is more than one) will provide the researcher with a greater understanding of the imbalance of power (other than anonymity) that underlies cyberbullying. We should also inquire about social status within the peer group. Concomitantly, such information can provide additional, confirmatory evidence of the nature of more traditional forms of bullying (physical, verbal, indirect, or relational), which invariably correlates with bullying via electronic devices (Williams & Guerra, 2007).

Defining Cyberbullying through Measurement

The challenge for many researchers studying cyberbullying is to operationalize definitions that do not always capture the dynamic and sometimes subtle nature of this phenomenon, or indeed its evolution. For example, Smith et al. (2008) defined cyberbullying as "an aggressive, intentional act carried out by a group or individual, using electronic forms of contact, repeatedly and over time against a victim who cannot easily defend him or herself" (p. 376). In terms of construct validity, such a definition is useful in that it allows for continuing developments in communication technology and includes the basic definitional criteria most often ascribed to bullying behavior. However, in terms of content validity, problems arise. As noted previously, from the target's perspective, the repeated receipt of unpleasant SMS/text messages suggests bullying; but is it the same perpetrator or group of perpetrators? If each perpetrator sends one unpleasant SMS/text message, does that constitute bullying? On closer reading, Smith et al.'s definition is not constructed from the perspective of the target but from that of the perpetrator—"an aggressive, intentional act carried out by a group or individual using electronic forms of contact, repeatedly and over time against a victim." In this case, the measurement of cyberbullying focuses on the intentionality and persistence of the perpetrator(s), rather than the reactions and responses of intended targets. Thus, additional questions such as, "Why did you . . . ?," "How often did you . . . ,?" and "Were others involved?" are appropriate. However, such questions cannot, by their nature, provide a general estimate of the prevalence of cyberbullying. Rather, they relate to a series of electronic communications where a particular relationship dynamic is or was in play, and we are left with the question, "How do we measure this relationship effectively?"

An alternative definition that has been suggested by various researchers is one that relates to "cyberaggression" rather than cyberbullying. Here cyberaggression is defined as "intentional behavior aimed at harming another person or persons through computers, cell phones, and other electronic devices, and perceived as aversive by the victim" (see Schoffstall & Cohen, 2011, p. 588). This definition could be simplified to say "intentional actions target perpetrated using electronic forms of contact that cause pain and suffering in the target." In this definition, intentionality on the part of the perpetrator and a negative response on the part of the target are clearly expected, but the issue of repetition is not present. However, the relationship dynamic remains: the "intentional behavior" on the part of the perpetrator is perceived as "aversive" by the target. In effect, most researchers who have studied cyberbullying, particularly via anonymous survey instruments, have collected data on two related but separate phenomena: (a) "intentional behaviors" on the part of perpetrators against unidentified targets; and (b) the negative reactions of targets, in many cases, as a result of the behaviors of unidentified perpetrators. In other words, we assume that the self-identified perpetrators and targets are reporting on behaviors and responses to each others' actions, and that their worlds are closed to relationships and interactions with others beyond the remit of the survey instrument (e.g., at school).

As has been noted in previous chapters, researchers are divided on the usefulness of a definition of bullying and, by extension, the concepts of cyberbullying or cyberaggression. It seems likely that the proposed definition (see Chapter 10) is helpful for those who observe (such as teacher or parents) or are privy to such behavior—*the reasonable person*—rather than for establishing perpetrator or target status for the purpose of research. For perpetrators, questions that specify *repeated* and *focused* attempts to intimidate the same target or group of targets over time would provide one measure of prevalence. For targets, questions that illustrate the repeated intimidation by one or more known (or presumed) perpetrators offers an alternative (and perhaps more usual) measure of prevalence. Thus, for both perpetrators and targets, it is important to ensure that their reports not only show the degree of repetition (e.g., *0 = never, 1 = once, 2 = twice, 3 = three times, 4 = four or more times*) within a specific timescale (*past week, past month, last three months, last term, ever*) but that it involved (for perpetrators) or was believed to involve (for targets) the same person or group of people. Here, thresholds for repetition are a matter of judgment for the researcher, however, *0 = never* and *once*, and *1 = twice* to *four or more times* are recommended as a minimum.

Timescale

Linked with the point above, the issue of timescale is one that has consistently confounded researchers trying to establish baseline statistics on all forms of bullying, including cyberbullying. Kowalski and Witte (2006) asked students if they had *ever* been cyberbullied, Smith et al. (2008) asked if it had occurred *two or three times* in the past *couple of months*, Hinduja and Patchin (2008) focused on *repeated* experiences *in the last year*, Li (2006) asked about cyberbullying taking place *during school*, and Rivers and Noret (2010) asked about text and e-mail bullying *this term* (anywhere from the past three to nine weeks). In addition to inconsistency across studies, Bovaird (2010) argued that reliance upon the accuracy of autobiographical memory presents numerous problems for the bullying researcher. He suggested that autobiographical memory is not only constructive (i.e., we do not always remember experiences exactly), but it is also subject to distortions that are affected by the passing of time and by the stories we have heard, or the assumptions we make as details fade. Bovaird (2010) acknowledged, however, that people do tend to better remember those events that have personal significance for them, and it is likely that targets will better remember particularly unpleasant experiences. Yet, it seems unlikely that such memories will be representative of day-to-day events and, as yet, we do not know if perpetrators are likely to remember or single out particular episodes of bullying as do targets.

Given the limitations of memory suggested by Bovaird (2010), it would seem appropriate to reduce the timescale for measuring cyberbullying to one where distortions of memory are unlikey to have an effect. While there is some evidence to suggest that, at least in retrospective studies conducted with adult former victims of bullying, memories tend to remain stable (see Rivers, 2001), the degree of distortion prior to data collection is unknown. Thus, two approaches are recommended. First, an approach using data gathered daily (e.g., daily diaries) on random days across one or two weeks can be beneficial in providing an accurate index of current levels of bullying and cyberbullying in a school (see Nishina & Juvonen, 2005). Alternatively, a "snap shot" approach asking respondents to report on their experiences over the last five days or week is also likely to yield an accurate estimate of perpetrator and target prevalence. Notwithstanding a "global" measure of bullying duration is also useful in determining the chronic nature of such behavior. Question such as, "How old were you when the bullying started?," or "How old were you when you started bullying others?" provide a framework to explore other contextual factors such as whether bullying started when a student transitioned from one school to another (e.g., elementary to middle or junior high school). Similarly, questions asking students to estimate the length of time they have been targets or perpetrators of cyberbullying also allows researchers to map such experiences and behavior against market uptake of new technologies (see Rivers & Noret, 2010).

Types of Cyberbullying

As technology advances, so too do the ways in which perpetrators can intimidate their targets. Rivers and Noret (2010) suggested that the ways in which researchers operationalized cyberbullying has been inconsistent and have been limited by the time in which the study took place and the technology available to children and young people at that particular time. In light of this, two options are open to the researcher: (a) to use a definition in the question that does not specify a particular mode or medium of communication such as "electronic forms of contact"; or (b) to specify each mode or medium in which an individual can perpetrate or be a target of cyberbullying (cell/mobile phone call, SMS/text message, e-mail message, video message or upload, picture distribution or upload, Facebook entry, webpage entry including Bebo and Myspace, blog entry, message via an app, instant messaging, "flaming," "flooding," or "kicking" in online environments, including newsgroups and games; see Rivers, Chesney, & Coyne, 2011). While the former is recommended, as the specific medium may change over time—often quite rapidly—other methods can be used though they might easily omit modes of cyberbullying from a list, giving a biased estimate of prevalence.

Estimates of prevalence are perhaps best served by the use of a question or item referring to a global construct such as cyberbullying or cyberaggression, or one that encompasses the deliberate sending or posting of messages or images electronically or intimidating behavior online. However, such a question or item would require clarification, either by priming participants with a more extensive definition (used in many of the early studies of bullying behavior) or, as some researchers have opted to do, by providing examples of such behavior. Such an approach would allow researchers to categorize students has having been bullied or bullied others (see Solberg & Olweus, 2003).

To obtain an understanding of the different forms of cyberbullying and its correlates, researchers often find it necessary to explore each mode or medium in turn. While there is likely to be a considerable degree of repetition in the form of the questions asked (particularly if the hypothesis suggests that certain forms of cyberbullying will be more frequent, more severe, or impact upon the target more than others), such information can also help target resources and interventions in schools. Alternatively, researchers can ask open-ended questions to allow participants to supply the form by which the harm was perpetrated.

One way this has been attempted is in a study of cyberbullying among college students (Bauman, Baldasare, Goldman, & Barre, 2012). Following survey items inquiring about the frequency of specific experiences (e.g., How often has someone changed a picture of you in a negative way and posted it electronically), using the Cyberbullying Experiences Survey (Doane, Kelley, & Padilla, 2011), participants were queried further on those items for which their response was any option other than "*never.*" The follow-up items were "How upset were you by this experience?," "Was the perpetrator anonymous or known to you?," and "Which medium was used in the most serious incident?" (Facebook, the website "The Dirty," through text messaging, through tweeting, through e-mail, on a social networking site other than Facebook, on a blog [Which one?—Text box for answer], in a chat room [Which one?—Text box for answer], through an online gaming site [Which one?—Text box for answer], other [text box for response]). Because this survey was administered electronically, the follow-up items were only presented when the response to the main item was positive.

Determining Severity and Impact Upon Targets

The issue of severity is one that has always been inferred in bullying research rather than explored directly. Most often, severity is assumed to be correlated with frequency: the more a target is bullied, the more severe the bullying (Menesini, Nocentini, & Calussi, 2011). Yet, we also know that there is a hierarchy when it comes to assumed severity with picture/video clip bullying have the greatest impact upon targets. Mobile/cell and landline phone calls, SMS/text messages, and posts to websites have been found to have a neutral impact relative to other forms of bullying in some studies. Finally, bullying perpetrated by e-mail, in chatrooms, or via instant messages is perceived by victims to be less hurtful (see Smith et al., 2008).

In Menesini et al.'s (2011) study, item response theory (IRT) modeling was used to determine which forms of cyberbullying were the most "severe" in terms of frequency. Two thresholds were set for the study: threshold 1 where 0 = *never* and 1 = *from only once or twice* to *always*; and threshold 2 where 0 = *never* or *only once or twice* and 1 = *two or three times a month* to *always*). For males in their study, silent/prank phone calls and insults via instant messaging had the lowest severity parameter using thresholds 1 and 2. Those items with the highest severity parameters at threshold 1 were found to be insults on blogs, nasty text messages, and unpleasant pictures/photos on web sites. At threshold 2, it was nasty text messages, phone pictures/photos/video of violent scenes and unpleasant pictures/photos on websites. For females, a similar profile emerged for low severity parameters at thresholds 1 and 2. However, those items with the highest severity parameters at threshold 1 were found to be phone pictures/photos/video of violent scenes, phone pictures/photos/video of intimate scenes, and unpleasant pictures/photos on websites. Those items with the highest severity parameters at threshold 2 were found to be phone pictures/photos/video of intimate scenes, insults in chat rooms, and unpleasant pictures/photos on websites. While this research confirms that there is a hierarchy of severity drawn from incidence rates, the term "severity" should be viewed as much as a subjective assessment by the target as it is a supposed objective measure of frequency. Thus, one devastating incident can be more traumatic than a series of very frequent minor incidents. The Bauman et al. (2012) study attempted to address this issue.

Taking a more clinical or health-focused approach to the concept of severity, a very different set of criteria emerge for establishing whether an act or outcome can be classified as "severe." Gustafson and Holloway (1975) considered the measurement of severity in burns patients and created a severity index model that required the consideration of six interrelated factors:

- The presence of a quantitative variable;
- The presence of a qualitative (experiential) variable;
- The estimate of relative weight or importance of each variable;
- The extent to which the quantitative variable is present;
- The severity function of the quantitative variable;
- The extent to which the qualitative variable is present.

Here, severity is as much a judgment call by the participant and the researcher as it is an objective measure. The quantitative variable can be characterized by questions such as, "How much . . . ?," "How many . . . ?," or "How often . . . ?" The qualitative variable may be represented by a question such as, how upset were you? (It can itself be a scale, e.g., *0 = not at all—4 = extremely*).The researcher must then decide the relative weight she or he gives to these two variables. In terms of establishing a severity function, weighting might be applied if the perpetrator is older than the target, physically bigger than the target, if there is more than one perpetrator, if the perpetrator has some socially or culturally avowed dominance over the target, or if the medium used (visual *versus* text) is presumed to have a greater impact upon target. Mishna (2006) suggested that additional markers of severity could include whether the bullying was physical or nonphysical (in the case of cyberbullying, this equates with whether or not it involved a threat to physical safety), whether an adult was informed (teacher or parent), and whether the target had a group of friends from whom she or he could receive support. Such information may be obtained from the demographic and biographical information collected about perpetrators and targets, or alternatively a separate scale can be created where each aspect of the severity function is scored *0 = not present or 1 = present*, and then summed. An index of the severity function could be calculated by multiplying the number of factors that can impact upon severity by the response to the question "How upset were you?" Alternatively, using previous researchers' assessments of severity in bullying (see Menesini et al., 2011; Mishna, 2006; Smith et al., 2008), it is also possible to apply differential weightings to the factors that might impact upon severity, but those weightings would require support—both empirical and theoretical. Finally, the scale of the response to the qualitative variable will determine whether or not the threshold for cyberbullying has been met. If a target is not upset by the intentionally negative actions of one or more others, then such attempts to intimidate her or him cannot meet the criteria for cyberbullying because of the failure to elicit an emotional response.

Severity should thus be a composite score, based upon the relative weightings given to particular items in a survey instrument or questionnaire, and an assessment of whether or not a baseline or threshold has been reached—quantitatively ("How often . . . ?") and qualitatively ("How much were you upset?").

The qualitative aspect of severity could also be measured according to an expert (researcher) assessment of distress, either by using standardized instruments to measure target distress, and/or by setting threshold levels. For example, Alwash and McCarthy (1988) developed a very simple scale for measuring the severity of injuries to children in the home. In their study of 402 children, the expert (i.e., doctor) assessed severity using the following three-threshold criteria: mild, moderate, and severe. Here "mild" required no intervention, "moderate" required routine intervention, and "severe" required hospitalization. In the case of assessing the impact of cyberbullying, the degree to which a student is upset by one or more experiences can be categorized as follows:

How much did this upset you?

- 0 = not at all, or 1 = a little (Mild)
- 2 = moderately or (3) quite a bit (Moderate)
- 4 = extremely (Severe)

Regardless of the way in which one measures the qualitative impact of cyberbullying, a single measure such as frequency is unlikely to be sufficient to provide a reliable estimate of severity and thus, as suggested earlier; it would seem advisable to explore the potential of creating a composite measure.

STABILITY OF PERPETRATOR AND TARGET ROLES

If bullying is a dynamic experience and subject to the changing nature of human relationships, then, by extension, we have to accept that there will be some fluidity in participant roles. However, studies that have explored the stability of bullying roles over time suggest that while being a target in primary/elementary school does not predict being a target in secondary school (although there is an increased likelihood), being a perpetrator in primary/elementary school does predict being a perpetrator in secondary school (Schäfer, Korn, Brodbeck, Wolke, & Schulz, 2005). For anonymous self-report surveys, the measurement of stability in bullying roles over time does present significant challenges, however, Monks, Smith, and Swettenham (2003) have shown that there is a great degree of consistency in peer- and self-reports of bullying roles, which suggests that while details relating to the nature and prevalence of cyberbulling could be obtained via self-reports, stability of participant roles may be better established over time by asking peers to nominate perpetrators and targets of recent incidents.

Assessing Bystander Status

Studying bystanders presents a series of methodological issues for the researcher that cannot be easily overcome. Estimates of prevalence from the perspective of the bystander can be confounded by the fact that several bystanders may have witnessed and reported on one event or a series of events that involve two particular protagonists. Thus, including bystander reports of cyberbullying is more likely to inflate estimates of prevalence. Second, there is the issue of defining bystander status. Salmivalli, Lagerspetz, Björkqvist, Österman, and Kaukiainen (1996) identified four very different types of bystander—the assistant, reinforcer, defender, and the outsider. Whereas Twemlow, Fonagy, and Sacco (2004) identifed seven—the bully bystander, puppet-master variant of the bully bystander, victim bystander, avoidant bystander, abdicating bystander, sham bystander, and the helpful bystander. Finally, Rivers, Poteat, Noret, and Ashurst (2009) identified four behavioral categories of bystander—bully-witness, victim-witness, witness, and bully-victim-witness. In a more recent article focusing on the issues relating to the concept and clinical significance of bystander status in bullying research, Rivers (2012), argued that there are three overarching types of bystander: the co-victim or co-target, perpetrator's confederate, and isolate. As the name implies, the co-victim or co-target is affected by what she or he sees, the confederate supports the perpetrator, and the isolate tries to remove her- or himself from the bullying situation. However, the isolate is very different from the individual who is not involved in any form of bullying, and thus should be considered as a separate category of respondent. Thus, a series of questions that assess whether students have seen or heard about one incident or a series of incidents, participated in the victimization of the target, and the degree to which they were upset by the incidents they have witnessed would allow for a discrete analysis of all three roles: the co-victim, confederate, and isolate.

Antecedents, Moderators, and Mediators

Attempting to elicit the reason why someone has been a target of cyberbullying or has perpetrated cyberbullying might not be as difficult as it first seems, and quite often those antecedents can be specific to the demographic characteristics of a class, a school, or a geographic region. Thus measures of biased-based and unbiased-based bullying are useful to determine whether specific person-centered characteristics are related to reports of cyberbullying, or whether other factors come into play. In an anonymous survey, it is often difficult to assess these issues without asking respondents to report on a specific incident. Asking respondents to comment on the most recent incident they experienced, perpetrated, or witnessed is likely to yield rich data to help formulate interventions. Bias-based bullying may relate to a person's race or ethnicity, immigration status, socioeconomic status, sexual orientation or perceived sexual orientation, weight, size or body shape, special needs, and/or disability. Non-biased bullying may relate to being good or not so good at schoolwork, good or not so good at sports, possessions, friendship networks, or brand of clothing worn. In one recent study of perpetrators of bullying, Rivers, Poteat, Noret, & Ashurst (2011) found that self-reported rates of hostility among perpetrators were significantly related to targets who were not good at sports ($r_{pb} = .23$), not good at schoolwork ($r_{pb} = .22$), owned items the perpetrator wanted ($r_{pb} = .19$), who had bullied others ($r_{pb} = .19$), had special needs ($r_{pb} = .16$), and were or were perceived to be lesbian or gay ($r_{pb} = .16$). Asking these or similar questions would allow researchers to determine the motivations that lie behind cyberbullying.

In terms of moderating and mediating factors, an assessment of active support networks (including friends and family), school support networks (peers, teachers, and other staff), recreational interests, and social skills offer opportunities to better understand the social context in which cyberbullying takes place. For example, students with more friends, better social networks, and supportive families may be less likely to be the targets of bullying than those who are isolates and perhaps struggle to develop relationships with peers (Pepler & Craig, 1995). Again, we must ask these questions specifically with respect to cyberbullying rather than assume that the findings from traditional bullying studies will apply to this new context.

Risk and Protective Factors

Linked to the study of moderating and mediating effects on cyberbullying is the exploration of risk and protective factors. The conceptualization of risk, in measurement terms, is difficult, as risk changes according to the context in which the study takes place. For cyberbullying, risk may be conceptualized in terms of unrestricted access to the Internet or unsupervised engagement with online "friends." Risk can also be conceptualized in terms of adults' lack of understanding of children's and young peoples' technology-mediated lives. Do parents or teachers understand what a social network is and what it can do? Questions or items that ask respondents to answer simply *yes* or *no* about adult involvement in their technological lives will provide a baseline assessment of potential risk ("no") and protection ("yes"). Additional risk and protective factors that should be considered relate to adults' and young peoples' awareness of tactics to combat cyberbullying and reporting mechanism to Internet service providers (ISPs), website administrators, or cell/mobile phone service providers. For both adults and young people, scenarios or directed questions (e.g., "What would you do if . . . ?") that offer an opportunity to answer using multiple-choice responses provide an effective means of assessing both knowledge of reporting mechanisms and potential risk—especially where they fail to choose an appropriate response. Bauman and

Card (2012) have included such items on their survey of youth, and also directly surveyed teachers and parents to check whether student perceptions match adult self-reports regarding proficiency with technology, types of recommendations they would make to students, etc.

CONCLUDING COMMENTS

There are significant challenges for the researcher in measuring the prevalence, nature, and dynamics of cyberbullying. In this chapter, suggestions have been offered based upon an assessment of the data that is currently available and the degree to which such data has yet to adequately capture the relationship of the perpetrator and the target. It is suggested that a composite approach to establishing perpetrator and target status is likely to yield a more accurate assessment of prevalence in a given context (elementary or high school, college or university); however, such data will not provide an understanding of the relationship between perpetators and targets unless other methods of data collection such as peer and teacher nominations are used to triangulate self-report data. It is recognized that some of the data items presented in the appendix will not lend themselves easily to studies involving elementary school students, and it is also acknowledged that a single uniform definition of cyberbullying has not been suggested, though other authors have commented on the utility of general and specific definitions. Cyberbullying is an evolving phenomenon, and as it evolves so too must the way in which we measure it. Each study of cyberbullying is limited by the time in which it is conducted and the technology that is available. As new technologies emerge, so too will new ways of bullying others; and for researchers, this means that we need to be ready to develop ever-more sophisticated scales of measurement.

References

Alwash, R., & McCarthy, M. (1988). Measuring severity of injuries to children from home accidents. *Archives of Disease in Childhood, 63*, 635–638. doi:10.1136/adc.63.6.635

Bauman, S., Baldasare, A., Goldman, L., & Barre, A. (2012). *Cyberbullying in older adolescents: A survey of university students in the U.S.* Poster presented at the Conférence Internationale sur Le Cyberharcèlement, Paris, France.

Bondi, H. (1964). *Relativity and common sense: A new approach to Einstein.* Toronto: General Publishing Company.

Bovaird, J.A. (2010). Scales and surveys: The problem with assessing bullying behaviors. In S.R. Jimerson, S.M. Swearer, & D.L. Espelage (Eds.). *The handbook of bullying in schools: An international perspective* (pp. 277–292). New York: Routledge.

Doane, M., Kelley, M. L., & Padilla, M. A. (2011, April). Development of the Cyberbullying Experiences Survey. *Society for Research on Child Development*, Montreal, Canada.

Gustafson, D.H., & Holloway, D.C. (1975). A decision theory approach to measuring severity in illness. *Health Services Research, 10*, 97–106.

Hinduja, S., & Patchin, J.W. (2008). Cyberbullying: An exploratory analysis of factors related to offending and victimization. *Deviant Behavior, 29,*129–156. doi:10.1080/01639620701457816

Kowalski, R.M., & Witte, J. (2006). *Youth Internet survey.* Unpublished manuscript, Clemson University.

Li, Q. (2005, April). *Cyberbullying in schools: Nature and extent of adolescents' experiences.* Paper presented at a meeting of the American Educational Research Association, Montreal, Canada.

Li, Q. (2006). Cyberbullying in schools: A research of gender differences. *School Psychology International, 27,* 157–170. doi:10.1177/0143034306064547

Menesini, E., Nocentini, A., & Calussi, P. (2011). The measurement of cyberbullying: Dimensional structure and relative item severity and discrimination. *Cyberpsychology, Behavior, and Social Networking, 5,* 267–274.

Monks, C.P., Smith, P.K., & Swettenham, J. (2003). Bullying in infant classes: Roles taken, stability and relationship to sociometric status. *Merrill Palmer Quarterly, 49,* 453–469.

Pepler, D.J., & Craig, W.M. (1995). A peek behind the fence: Naturalistic observations of aggressive children. *Developmental Psycholology, 31,* 548–553. doi:10.1037/0012-1649.31.4.548

Nishina, A., & Juvonen, J. (2005). Daily reports of witnessing and experiencing peer harassment in middle school. *Child Development, 76,* 345–450.

Rivers, I. (2001). Retrospective reports of school bullying: Recall stability and its implications for research. *British Journal of Developmental Psychology, 19,* 129–142. doi:10.1348/026151001166001

Rivers, I. (2012). Morbidity among bystanders of bullying behavior at school: Concepts, concerns, and clinical/research issues. *International Journal of Adolescent Medicine and Health, 24,* 11–16.

Rivers, I., Chesney, T., & Coyne, I. (2011). Cyberbullying. In C.P. Monks & I. Coyne (Eds.), *Bullying in different contexts* (pp. 211–230). Cambridge: Cambridge University Press.

Rivers, I., Poteat, V.P., Noret, N., & Ashurst, N. (2009). Observing bullying at school: The mental health implications of witness status. *School Psychology Quarterly, 24,* 211–223. doi:10.1037/a0018164

Rivers, I., Poteat, V.P., Noret, N., & Ashurst, N. (2011, August). *Perpetration of bias-related victimization: Intersections with perceived sexual orientation at school.* Paper presented at a meeting of the American Psychological Association, Washington, DC.

Rivers, I., & Noret, N. (2010). "I h8 u": Findings from a five-year study of text and email bullying. *British Educational Research Journal, 36,* 643–671. doi:10.1080/01411920903071918

Salmivalli, K., Lagerspetz, K., Björkqvist, K., Österman, K., & Kaukiainen, A. (1996). Bullying as a group process: Participant roles and their relations to social status within the group. *Aggressive Behavior, 22,* 1–15.

Schäfer, M., Korn, S., Brodbeck, F., Wolke, D., & Schulz, H. (2005). Bullying role in changing contexts: The stability of victim and bully roles from primary to secondary school. *International Journal of Behavioral Development, 29,* 323–335. doi:10.1177/01650250544000107

Schoffstall, C.L., & Cohen, R. (2011). Cyber aggression: The relation between online offenders and offline social competence. *Social Development, 20,* 587–604. doi:10.1111/j.1467–9507.2011.00609.x

Smith, P.K., Mahdavi, J., Carvalho, M., Fisher, S., Russell, S., & Tippett, N. (2008).

Cyberbullying: Its nature and impact in secondary school pupils. *Journal of Child Psychology and Psychiatry, 49*, 376–385. doi:10.1111/j.1469–7610.2007.01846.x

Solberg, M., & Olweus, D. (2003). Prevalence estimation of school bullying with the Olweus Bully/Victim Questionnaire. *Aggressive Behavior, 29*, 239–268.

Twemlow, S. W., Fonagy, P., & Sacco. F. C. (2004). The role of the bystander in the social architecture of bullying and violence in schools and communities. *Annals of the New York Academy of Sciences, 1036*, 215–232. doi:10.1196/annals.1330.014

Williams, K. R., & Guerra, N. G. (2007). Prevalence and predictors of internet bullying. *Journal of Adolescent Health, 41*, 14–21. doi:10.1016/j.jadohealth.2007.08.018

Ybarra, M. L., & Mitchell, J. K. (2004). Online agressors/targets, aggressors and targets: A comparison of associated youth characteristics. *Journal of Child Psychology and Psychiatry, 47*, 1308–1316. doi:10.1111/j.1469–7610.2004.00328.x

APPENDIX SAMPLE QUESTIONS FOR PERPETRATORS

In the last week, how often have you *deliberately sent or posted messages or images electronically or tried to intimidate online** the same person or group of people with the intention of hurting or embarrassing them?

Response options: *never* (0), *once* (1), *twice* (2), *three times* (3), *four or more times* (4)

* This can include hurtful or embarrassing cell/mobile phone calls, SMS/text messages, e-mail messages, video messages or uploads, picture messages or uploads, Facebook entries, webpage entries including Bebo and Myspace, blog entries, app messages, instant messages, or intimidating others online including in online games.

> How well do you know this person or group of people?
> Response options: *not at all* (1), *a little* (2), *quite well* (3), *very well* (4)
> How do you know this person or group of people?
> Response options: *I don't* (1), *in my school* (2), *in my grade/year* (3), *in my class* (4), *other* (9)
> Did you do this alone?
> Response options: *no* (1), *yes* (2)
> Describe this person, or one of the people you tried to hurt or embarrass.
> Response items: *demographic data*
> How much did you intend to upset this person?
> Response items: *not at all* (0), *a little* (1), *moderately* (2), *quite a bit* (3), *extremely* (4)

SAMPLE QUESTIONS FOR TARGETS

In the last week, how often have you *received or seen posted messages or images electronically or been intimidated online** by one person or group of people who intended to hurt or embarrass you?

Response options: *never* (0), *once* (1), *twice* (2), *three times* (3), *four or more times* (4)

* This can include hurtful or embarrassing cell/mobile phone calls, SMS/ text messages, e-mail messages, video messages or uploads, picture messages or uploads, Facebook entries, webpage entries including Bebo and Myspace, blog entries, app messages, instant messages, or being intimidated by others online including in online games.

> How well do you know or think you know this person or group of people?
> Response options: *not at all* (1), *a little* (2) *quite well* (3), *very well* (4)
> How do you know or think you know this person or group of people?
> Response options: *I don't* (1), *in my school* (2), *in my grade/year* (3), *in my class* (4)
> Did you think more than one person was involved?
> Response options: *no* (1), *yes* (2)
> Describe this person, or one of the people who tried to hurt or embarrass you.
> Response items: *demographic data*
> How much did it upset you?
> Response items: *not at all* (0), *a little* (1), *moderately* (2), *quite a bit* (3), *extremely* (4)

SAMPLE QUESTIONS FOR BYSTANDERS

In the last week, how often have you seen someone or know someone *deliberately send or post messages or images electronically or try to intimidate online** one person or group of people with the intention of hurting or embarrassing them?

Response options: *never* (0), *once* (1), *twice* (2), *three times* (3), *four or more times* (4)

* This can include hurtful or embarrassing cell/mobile phone calls, SMS/text messages, e-mail messages, video messages or uploads, picture messages or uploads, Facebook entries, webpage entries including Bebo and Myspace, blog entries, app messages, instant messages, or intimidating others online including in online games.

> How well do you know the person or group of people who did this?
> Response options: *not at all* (1), *a little* (2), *quite well* (3), *very well* (4)
> How do you know the person or group of people who did this?
> Response options: *I don't* (1), *in my school* (2), *in my grade/year* (3), *in my class* (4), *other* (9)
> Did you become involved by passing on the message, post or image?

Response options: *no* (1), *yes* (2)

Describe this person, or one of the people who was targeted.

Response items: *demographic data*

How much did this upset you?

Response items: *not at all* (0), *a little* (1), *moderately* (2), *quite a bit* (3), *extremely* (4)

18 Qualitative Studies

Faye Mishna and Melissa Van Wert

Qualitative research represents a rich opportunity to explore the perspectives of young people and the environments in which they interact, including the cyber-environments. The voices of young people can be represented authentically through qualitative research and also contribute to knowledge building and theory development (Mishna, Antle, & Regehr, 2004). The knowledge generated through qualitative data complements the data gathered by quantitative methods (Cullingford & Morrison, 1995), and privileges individuals' "lived experience" (Van Manen, 1990). Qualitative research can expand and deepen our understanding of cyberbullying and provide directions for future research through generating new hypotheses.

Literature on cyberbullying is growing (see Smith and colleagues, this volume, Chapter 3). Most of this literature however, consists of quantitative research.[1] In contrast, there are relatively few studies that incorporate qualitative methods in the examination of cyberbullying. The purpose of this chapter is to explore the value of qualitative methodology in research on cyberbullying. We begin with a brief overview of available cyberbullying literature using a qualitative approach. We then discuss the value of qualitative research specifically in studying sensitive topic areas, enriching quantitative efforts, and understanding new technologies and social behavior in various contexts. We conclude with a discussion of qualitative techniques most suited to cyberbullying research and principles for the effective use of these techniques.

QUALITATIVE RESEARCH ON CYBERBULLYING

Currently, there is a small but valuable body of qualitative research on cyberbullying. Agatston, Kowalsi, and Limber (2007) conducted focus groups to gain a better understanding of the impact of cyberbullying in middle and high schools, and to recognize the possible need for prevention messages targeting students, educators, and parents. Single-sex focus groups were conducted with approximately 150 students at two middle and two high schools. The findings revealed that the students were very familiar with cyber technology. Most of the female students in this study felt cyberbullying was a problem in school, whereas the male students were less likely to identify cyberbullying as a problem. Importantly, students in the focus groups expressed reluctance to tell adults at school about cyberbullying, stating that they did not think adults could help them. Because cyberbullying incidents that occurred during school hours often involved text messaging, students did not want to report these incidents to school authorities as cellular phones were banned during school hours. Other than bullying by text, students reported that most incidents of cyberbullying occurred outside of school hours. Although students appeared more likely to report cyberbullying to parents, they were still reluctant to make this disclosure for fear of losing technological privileges. Students were able to suggest certain strategies for responding to cyberbullying, such as blocking or ignoring the perpetrator, but were less aware of strategies for responding as a bystander when witnessing cybervictimization and for requesting that questionable material be removed from websites.

Grigg (2010) used a qualitative, interpretative approach to studying cyberbullying with primary school, high school, and adult participants. The aims of this study were to determine what young people and adults perceived to be cyberbullying, to examine a spectrum of negative acts that occurred in cyberspace, and to test the knowledge of participants on cyberbullying. The researchers used purposive and convenience sampling to recruit youth participants who had received one or more unwanted communications during cellular phone or Internet use. Adult participants were recruited through social networking sites and were then interviewed through instant messenger. The researchers posited that this method of conducting the research provided participants the opportunity to be reminded of some of the negative acts that have taken place on the Internet. Through interviews and focus groups, Grigg (2010) discussed the definition and usefulness of the term *cyberbullying* with participants. Participants named a broad range of negative behaviors that occur through technology. Anger and frustration were apparent in the content of the interviews and focus groups, as participants felt their privacy had been invaded through the unwanted e-communications. There were no age or gender differences in the way participants perceived these negative behaviors. Younger participants were more familiar, however, with the term "cyberbullying." Participants discussed broadening the term cyberbullying to include a wide spectrum of aggressive communications that occur via technology.

Maher (2008) incorporated elements of ethnography, case study methods, and grounded theory to explore cyberbullying with a middle school class and their teachers over a one-year period. Data for this study were collected through observations, field notes, interviews, discussions with teachers, and recordings of online interactions. The class was selected because it contained computers with Internet capabilities, and the teacher wanted to explore the use of the Internet as a tool for communication. Both boys and girls in this study instigated cyberbullying, but boys were much more aggressive in the cyber world than girls and engaged in cyberbullying more frequently than girls. For boys, cyberbullying occurred during informal interactions outside of school hours as well as formal interactions during school. No instances of cyberbullying at home were recorded for girls. Boys also used aggressive communication techniques; for example, typing messages in all capital letters (e.g., "U SUCK," p. 55) and using intimidation tactics, such as consuming the chat room forum by sending a constant stream of empty messages. When using the class chat room from home, boys often engaged in cyberbullying focused on interest in girls, which elicited immediate and angry responses from the person subjected to the bullying. For instance, after receiving a message from another boy stating that he "liked" a girl, the message recipient responded with messages such as "shut up" and "bring it on" (p. 53). The individuals engaging in this behavior explained that they used these tactics to get the attention of others. Some instances of cyberbullying among girls involved masquerading, whereby one student posted messages under the name of another student. This research found that in some instances, bullying began face to face at school and then continued in the cyber world.

Mishna, McLuckie, and Saini (2009) used a phenomenological approach to understand the lived experiences of cyber abuse among children and youth. Over approximately 1.5 years, children and youth posted over 35,000 anonymous messages on a youth counseling website. The database of messages was systematically searched for posts related to cyber relationships and cyber abuse, resulting in a final sample of 346 posts from participants aged 6 to 24 years. The posts were read by multiple independent readers, followed by regular meetings for review and peer debriefing. The posts revealed that children and youth readily developed cyber relationships and had extensive involvement with online social networks. The children and youth reported encountering a range of cyber abusive experiences and discussed the detrimental effects of these experiences, which included bullying, stalking, sexual solicitation, and exposure to pornography. Cyberbullying was a frequent occurrence for this sample among real-life acquaintances and friends as well as among those with whom relationships had developed online. Cyberbullying was described as often related to sensitive issues such as sexual orientation, physical characteristics, and popularity. The children and youth often did not disclose the cyber abuse to adults. Similar to other research findings, the youth expressed fear that if their parents knew of their experiences, they would deny their computer privileges.

Mishna, Saini, and Solomon (2009) used a grounded theory framework to explore the perceptions and opinions of children and youth regarding cyberbullying. Seven mixed-gender focus groups were conducted in order to ask young people about their views on cyberbullying. Students were asked how often cyberbullying occurs, what forms it takes, who engages in cyberbullying, and questions regarding disclosure and awareness. Participants were not asked about their own experiences with cyberbullying to protect their confidentiality. Potentially sensitive questions about Internet use were not asked in order to promote openness in the group setting. After each focus group, the interview guide created for the study was updated, in order to ensure that the next focus group included questions based on previous participant responses. Some forms of traditional bullying and cyberbullying were considered by students to be similar, such as spreading rumors or making threats or derogatory comments. Students also discussed other forms unique to cyberbullying, such as coercion through webcams and masquerading as someone other than oneself. The young people in this study expressed that cyberbullying has made it possible for "non-stop bullying" (p. 1224) to occur, and that anonymity on the Internet fostered bullying in some children who would not otherwise engage in these behaviors. Although most of the students believed anonymity to be integral to cyberbullying, many incidents of cyberbullying appeared to take place in the context of the students' social groups and relationships and thus appeared to be perceived rather than actual anonymity. Young people did not feel that adults could help them cope with incidents of cyberbullying and feared losing their access to technology if they disclosed.

Nocentini and colleagues (2010) used structured focus groups to examine adolescent perceptions and definitions of the term *cyberbullying* in Italy, Spain, and Germany. Four scenarios were presented and discussed among participants, one presenting an incident of online written verbal aggression, one focusing on the use of pictures or images to bully, one involving impersonation using technology, and one presenting a case of online social exclusion. Participants were asked whether three traditional criteria for defining bullying (intentionality, imbalance of power, and repetition) and two nontraditional criteria (publicity and anonymity) were relevant in defining cyberbullying. The focus group transcripts were coded and main themes identified. Different words were used to describe bullying in the diverse cultures. Spanish participants considered all four scenarios to be cyberbullying, whereas Italian participants felt that the written verbal aggression and the use of images were representative of bullying. Participants across cultures felt that intention, power imbalance, repetition, publicity, and anonymity were all important and interrelated concepts in many ways. There appeared to be culturally specific terms used to describe similar experiences of cyberbullying, such as *cyber-mobbing* in Germany, *virtual* or *cyberbullying* in Italy, and *harassment via the Internet or mobile phone* in Spain.

Vandebosch and Van Cleemput (2008) used focus groups to gain detailed information about child and adolescent cyber practices as well as their individual and group norms with regard to electronic communication. These researchers involved male and female participants from 10 to 18 years old, all at various educational levels, in order to obtain a wide range of opinions on and experiences with cyberbullying. The focus groups elicited rich information about the positive and negative aspects of technology, and about individual experiences with cyberbullying. Most examples of cyberbullying involved instant messaging services, for instance, hacking into one's instant messenger account, or being contacted by unwelcome strangers through instant messaging. Several respondents reported negative experiences via mobile phones, such as receiving threatening calls. Cyberbullying appeared to be motivated by a wide range of factors; for instance, a desire for revenge against other bullies, or because they just did not like the person. In some cases, the perpetrator's intent to harm was very clear. It appeared that cyberbullying occurred within the context of existing offline or "actual" social groups.

These studies represent valuable contributions to our knowledge of cyberbullying. Insights from these studies can inform the design and interpretation of future research and can also inform prevention and intervention efforts. With this introduction to the available literature, we will now discuss the value of qualitative approaches to cyberbullying.

THE VALUE OF QUALITATIVE STUDIES
IN RESEARCH ON CYBERBULLYING

New Area of Research

Traditional bullying has long been documented and explored in social research. Cyberbullying, on the other hand, is a relatively recent phenomenon, with a correspondingly new yet growing body of knowledge. Given that technology-mediated communication and cyberbullying have emerged in recent history, qualitative research is a useful tool through which to explore these phenomena. Qualitative approaches can assist researchers in comprehending understudied topics holistically, as the evocative nature of the research process reveals the deep meaning of participant experiences (Black, 1994; Gilgun & Abrams, 2002). The holistic approach offered by qualitative research is also useful for developing theory and identifying directions for future research, which can assist in refining theoretical constructs related to cyberbullying (Black, 1994; Gilgun & Abrams, 2002).

Complexity of cyberbullying. When undertaking any research endeavor, the inherent complexities of individuals within their social and environmental contexts, including their cyber worlds, must be considered (Johnson & Puplampu, 2008; Mishna, Pepler, & Wiener, 2006). Bullying is incredibly complex and must be examined within the context it occurs and the larger social context (Cullingford & Morrison, 1995). Research focusing only on the individual typically seeks to control the influence of contextual variables, whereas an ecological systems framework (Bronfenbrenner, 1979) provides insight into the reciprocal relationships among all components and levels of an individual's world. All levels of the ecological system can be explored through qualitative research. Qualitative approaches provide an opportunity to engage with the richness of young people's thoughts and feelings about themselves and their worlds (Mishna et al., 2004) and allow for deep understanding of youth cultures and group processes from the perspectives of young people (Thornberg, 2011). Through qualitative approaches, researchers can understand the nuances, subtleties, and dynamics of cyberbullying, as well as the associated feelings and emotions (Cullingford & Morrison, 1995; Mishna, Saini et al., 2009; Smith & Brain, 2000; Spears, Slee, Owens, & Johnson, 2009). Although qualitative studies are generally self-contained within a particular period of time, participants bring their full life histories to the research encounter (Phoenix, Frosh, & Pattman, 2003). In this way, qualitative research can elicit a rich, holistic understanding of cyberbullying, taking into consideration individual, family, and systemic issues over time.

Qualitative Research and Social Change. Often invisible in social research, young people can be placed at the center of inquiry when using qualitative methods (Crivello, Camfield, & Woodhead, 2009). Conducting research *with* children rather than *on* children allows researchers to critically examine their assumptions about the nature of childhood and children's capacities, and also allows the previously unheard voices of children to be brought to the forefront (Camfield, Crivello, & Woodhead, 2009). Qualitative research provides children and youth the opportunity to name, define, and contextualize their experiences (Barter & Renold, 2000). Understanding these experiences is crucial for prevention and intervention efforts (Heary & Hennessy, 2002). We can only truly support young people if we position cyberbullying prevention and intervention in an intimate understanding of the everyday lives and perspectives of those actually involved in cyberbullying (Davidson, Ridgway, Kidd, Topor, & Borg, 2008). Conducting qualitative research with parents or teachers similarly elicits the understanding and views of adults who are most involved with the children and who will be instrumental to any strategies and interventions.

There are many ways in which qualitative research itself may actually both raise awareness and prevent future incidents of cyberbullying. In a unique research project that generated knowledge and raised consciousness of bullying, Dennis (2009) used "Theatre of the Oppressed" as a form of critical qualitative inquiry. This project began with ethnographic interviews and focus groups with high school students who had recently immigrated to the United States. Participating students were experiencing bullying at school but were uncomfortable discussing these negative experiences with their teachers and parents. The data collected from this work with newcomer students were then transformed into a dramatic reading by Dennis and her research team. "Theatre of the Oppressed" was then planned as part of a professional development day with teachers, at which time the researchers shared a bullying scene taken from the data. Teachers were asked to reenact the scene in various ways, and the scenes were collaboratively analyzed among the group. The research represented an opportunity for teachers to examine the bullying situations, recognize the roles they played during the interactions, and consider how the situations could be dealt with more effectively in the future (Dennis, 2009). The research team felt that "Theatre of the Oppressed" was one method of transforming oppressive conditions in the school under study.

Simply participating in qualitative research may enhance children's subjective sense of well-being and has long-term implications for improving social policy with authentic and accurate data (Camfield et al., 2009). Qualitative research encourages young people to share their experiences and places them in the position of expert. This may instill feelings of value and self-worth in young people, whose views and experiences are often discounted. It is rare for policy makers to actually interact with the children and youth about whom they design policy. Qualitative methods bring the voices of these children and youth to policy makers, ensuring that influential professionals learn about the real experiences of young people.

Qualitative Research: Addressing Sensitive Topics

Discussing experiences of victimization can be very difficult, and some individuals may prefer to stay silent. In daily life and in the research process, young people might avoid discussing sensitive issues such as harassment or bullying. As Mishna, McLuckie, and colleagues (2009) as well as Agatston and colleagues (2007) learned in their research, children and youth sometimes keep secrets about cyberbullying to avoid losing technological privileges. Keeping such secrets can create a very lonely world for young people and can make coping with victimization much more difficult. In qualitative studies, researchers are able to provide a venue to discuss sensitive issues, which creates opportunities for previously silenced voices to be heard (Dehue, Bolman, & Vollnik, 2008; Gilgun & Abrams, 2002; Slonje & Smith, 2008).

Qualitative approaches are sensitive and flexible and allow researchers to adapt elements of the research as it progresses based on participant responses (Cullingford & Morrison, 1995; Darbyshire, MacDougall, & Schiller, 2005; Mishna, Saini, et al., 2009). In this way, researchers have more control over the encounter and can make decisions in light of participants' comfort levels. Space is created for personal connections among researchers and participants, connections that may create a more comfortable and open research environment for young people (Davidson et al., 2008; Duncan, Drew, Hodgson, & Sawyer, 2009; Gilgun & Abrams, 2002). In an environment characterized by comfort, warmth, and openness, young people may feel better equipped to engage in difficult discussions regarding their experiences. Participants also may be more likely to trust researchers when a personal connection is established, leading to a more thorough understanding of young people's worlds as well as a more fulfilling experience for participants.

It is often easier to discuss other people instead of ourselves, especially when talking about sensitive or difficult issues. Commenting on a story about someone else's experiences of victimization rather than our own, is likely less stressful. For this reason, vignettes can be useful in both quantitative and qualitative research. Exploring sensitive topics through vignettes, young people can offer their perspectives on troubling scenarios and can utilize these scenarios as a platform through which to discuss their own experiences (Barter & Renold, 2000). In reading and responding to vignettes on cyberbullying, young people may feel more comfortable discussing their own similar experiences. Importantly, however, participants are able to refrain from bringing any of their own experiences into the research encounter. This is especially important for sensitive research areas such as cyberbullying.

VALUE OF INTEGRATING QUANTITATIVE
AND QUALITATIVE RESEARCH

There are unique advantages to utilizing multiple methods in conducting research on various topics including cyberbullying. Theoretical and methodological pluralism is helpful when engaging with complex phenomena (Thornberg, 2011) with different methods providing distinct insights into research questions (Camfield et al., 2009). Qualitative research can reveal important information about context for understudied constructs and underrepresented populations, and this contextual knowledge can enrich any quantitative data that are collected (Camfield et al., 2009; Cresswell, Shope, Plano Clark, & Green, 2006; Spears et al., 2009). When quantitative and qualitative research are used in combination, the full spectrum of young people's experiences can be appreciated, which increases the possibility of appropriately responding to the social service needs of children and adolescents (Darbyshire et al., 2005). In partnership, quantitative analysis can inform broad policy decisions, and the authentic narratives and human stories of qualitative research can influence the opinions of government officials and the public at large (Davidson et al., 2008).

Combining methodological approaches can allow researchers to obtain a deeper and more accurate understanding of a research topic. The quality of research findings is improved when researchers use multiple methods, because this means that the data are triangulated (Crivello et al., 2009). In other words, we can be sure of understanding cyberbullying correctly if information is collected in two or more ways. Triangulation of data sources and methods produces the most complete and detailed data possible, and also balances the strengths and weaknesses of each single source and method (Hall & Rist, 1999). The goal of triangulation is not to use different methods to come up with the same answers; rather, it is beneficial for knowledge generation regardless of whether different methods result in the same answers. Data generated through diverse research methods may both complement and contradict each other, offering an opportunity to better understand the complexities of cyberbullying (Hemming, 2008). Multi-method approaches also have pragmatic benefits. By providing children and youth with various opportunities and modalities of expression, researchers may be more likely to sustain participants' interest in the research and in turn obtain more accurate and complete data (Crivello et al., 2009; Darbyshire et al., 2005).

Quantitative instruments strive for objectivity by examining general concepts, such as cyberbullying, and parceling those concepts into specific, concrete, and understandable behaviors (Fevre, Robinson, Jones, & Lewis, 2010). The field of cyberbullying is relatively new and, as such, the conceptualization and operationalization of cyberbullying varies greatly in the literature. This body of literature does not offer a clear definition of cyberbullying (Vandebosch & Van Cleemput, 2008), implying that results from quantitative research may not be comparable across studies. Through the integration of qualitative and quantitative research methods, conceptual and operational clarity of ambiguous phenomena can emerge (Fevre et al., 2010).

Qualitative methods are a useful partner for quantitative methods, as they bring children's own subjective definitions, meanings, and experiences of cyberbullying to the forefront (Barter & Renold, 2000). Young people can partner with researchers to act as consultants to review potential instrument items and establish their relevance and utility (Vessey, Horowitz, & Carlson, 2008). Focus groups can be useful in informing the development of an instrument and in illuminating meaning behind responses in quantitative research (Heary & Hennessy, 2002). Through the use of focus groups, researchers can gain valuable insight into participants' ideas regarding content, design, format, and language of instruments (Heary & Hennessy, 2002). Recognizing that their views are but one component, it is nevertheless important to value the experiences and perceptions of young people as well as others in their lives such as teachers and parents, and align conceptualizations of cyberbullying with these experiences and perceptions (Vandebosch & Van Cleemput, 2008). In this way, qualitative research can be extremely useful in the development of instruments for quantitative research on cyberbullying (Leech & Onwuegbuzie, 2007).

NEW TECHNOLOGIES AND QUALITATIVE RESEARCH

Technology changes very rapidly, creating unique challenges for researchers, practitioners, and policy makers attempting to respond to cyberbullying (Jäger, Armado, Matos, & Possoa, 2010). In researching online environments, there is tension between fluidity and stability, and connection and exclusion (Dwyer & Davies, 2010). As technology continues to evolve dramatically and rapidly, the definition, measurement, and response to cyberbullying will also need to evolve (Spears et al., 2009). It is important for researchers to elicit the experiences and perspectives of young people, as these youth are at the forefront of technological advances (Mishna, Saini et al., 2009). Given the dramatic and ongoing increase in young people's use of technologies for social connections, paired with the relative lack of knowledge about cyberbullying, qualitative methods are helpful in allowing participant perspectives to emerge in all of their complexities (Mishna, Saini, et al., 2009).

New technologies can also assist in the advancement of qualitative methods. In an innovative approach to cyberbullying research, Spears and colleagues (2009) gathered digital audio recordings of stories related to covert bullying and cyberbullying and ultimately created an interactive website to continually gather these types of stories from around the globe. The ongoing nature of this project will allow the researchers to capture the changing nature of cyberbullying as it evolves across time and cultures, with consideration of the constant emergence of new technologies (Spears et al., 2009). In another example, Wright, Burnham, Inman, and Ogorchock (2009) employed a quantitative survey along with a focus group, the findings of which informed the development of a virtual environment in which a simulated cyberbullying incident was created. Wright and colleagues (2009) conducted this mixed methods research in order to gain a multifaceted understanding of cyberbullying. The virtual world allowed the researchers to create an authentic incident of cyberbullying in a relatively safe simulated environment. Data collected in each phase of this study provided insight into how, why, and when cyberbullying occurs, and were useful in informing the researchers about the types of scenarios that are helpful for education and awareness raising (Wright et al., 2009).

CONTEXTUALIZING SOCIAL BEHAVIOR
THROUGH QUALITATIVE RESEARCH

Qualitative paradigms have been central in exploring the complex behavior of social actors from various perspectives (Barter & Renold, 2000). A wide spectrum of content areas have been explored using qualitative research, including children's experiences with HIV (Blumenreich, 2004), child poverty and well-being (Crivello et al., 2009), pediatric health (Heary & Hennessy, 2002), health and exercise in primary schools (Hemming, 2008), marketing (Hall & Rist, 1999), breast cancer (Thomas, 2011), and psychiatric issues (Whitley & Crawford, 2005). Qualitative methods allow researchers to understand the complexity and range of young people's experiences, emphasizing the fluidity of their identities and the multiple aspects of their lives (Blumenreich, 2004). It is important for researchers, policy makers, teachers, parents, children, and adolescents to qualitatively consider the cultures and everyday contexts in which cyberbullying occurs (Thornberg, 2011). To illustrate the importance of understanding context, let us briefly consider a hypothetical incident of cyberbullying.

Case Example

Harry is a 15-year-old boy who presents to a school social worker because of skipping class frequently. When probed, Harry reluctantly, and with embarrassment, reveals that he misses class to avoid being ridiculed by his classmates. His classmates have been ridiculing him around the school ever since he sent a Facebook message to a female peer asking her on a date, and the female peer re-posted this message for the public to see on her Wall with the caption, "What a loser—never in a million years!"

How might we learn more about the causes and consequences of this incident of cyberbullying? The incident is likely much more complex than it first appears, and it is only through contextualizing this incident that we can begin to understand this complexity. We need to understand Harry as an individual in the context of his family, friendships, school, geographic location, and culture. Knowledge of these factors can help us understand Harry's strengths and vulnerabilities, and also can help us in planning whether and how to best intervene. It is necessary to know and understand Harry's reaction to the incident, and perhaps also the reactions of his parents, teachers, and school. In addition, it would be important to understand Harry's female peer in the context of her life. It is likewise important to consider the level of understanding of teachers, support staff, community professionals, and other adults interacting with Harry, in terms of the impact that technology and

Facebook has on young people. Qualitative research can include young people, parents, extended family members, teachers, and school administrators. Through understanding these diverse perspectives in their contexts, a rich understanding of cyberbullying can emerge.

METHODOLOGICAL CONSIDERATIONS
AND GUIDELINES FOR RESEARCH

Previous qualitative research with young people has used a wide spectrum of methods, including interviews, focus groups, observation, vignettes, photography, artwork, and examination of cultural artifacts. We will now summarize five qualitative research techniques that are best suited to cyberbullying research, as well as general principles for utilizing these and other qualitative approaches.

Qualitative Approaches Best Suited
to Cyberbullying Research

Focus groups. Focus groups can assist in deepening our understanding of youth cultures and group processes. Using methods such as focus groups, individuals with shared experiences are united (Peek & Forthergill, 2009). This may represent a first opportunity for participants to realize that they are not alone. Bringing vulnerable, stigmatized, or marginalized individuals into a group allows participants to examine the collective character of their experiences, put their knowledge together to promote social change, and both give and receive social support (Peek & Forthergill, 2009). When using focus groups, it is important to be mindful of confidentiality, and consider refraining from asking about personal experiences. Although some suggest that focus groups with children should include homogenous single-sex groups (Hoppe, Wells, Morrison, Gillmore, & Wilsdon, 1995), using mixed gender groups has resulted in some of the richest findings due to the differences in opinions and experiences of boys and girls (Davis & Jones, 1996; Heary & Hennessy, 2002). It is usually best to conduct focus groups with six to eight young people. The total number of focus groups conducted for any given research project will depend on the aims of study. It is best to record and transcribe verbatim the proceedings of focus groups, but it is critical to provide participants with the option to not be recorded. If focus groups occur via technology, for instance through chat groups, then a copy of these interactions can be saved for analysis. As noted however, youth must be offered the option to not save these records.

Interviews. Interviews can be conducted in numerous ways, and all bring the voices of youth to the forefront. Researchers may choose to conduct interviews face to face, or alternatively may choose to communicate through technology. Researchers may opt to communicate via e-mail or instant messenger, but must plan the interaction carefully to ensure that ethical safeguards are in place. Interviewers must be particularly attuned to the feelings of participants and be mindful that it might be more difficult to ascertain when participants are distressed when communicating via technology. Researchers should be aware of such issues as the length of time it takes participants to respond, the use of emoticons, and any changes in communication patterns of participants. It is also important to consider participant attention span, and set procedures in place to ensure that focus is maintained during the interview. Similar to focus group research, it is best to record and transcribe verbatim face-to-face interviews, although it is critical to provide the youth with the option to decline to have the interactions recorded.

Vignettes. Vignettes are particularly helpful for qualitative cyberbullying research as they allow children and youth to engage with a scenario of victimization without needing to discuss their own personal experiences. Vignettes can be used with individual participants or with a group of participants, and can be used as a self-contained method or as an adjunct to other research techniques (Barter & Renold, 2000). In responding to vignettes, young participants are able to discuss difficult experiences that they may or may not have directly encountered, while they can also explore and learn about the perspectives of different actors within the vignettes (Barter & Renold, 2000). The vignette technique thus allows researchers to elicit multiple interpretations of troubling scenarios, engage young people in discussion of sensitive topic areas, while at the same time allowing young participants to control the amount of their own personal disclosure in the research encounter (Barter & Renold, 2000).

Technology-Assisted Data Collection. With technology constantly advancing, we are now able to collect and analyze information in novel and innovative ways. When the subject under study is cyberbullying, it is particularly beneficial to consider utilizing technology in the collection of data. The phenomenon of cyberbullying occurs through technology-mediated communication, and therefore researchers should consider designing their studies to incorporate this evolving form of communication. Analyzing online interactions can provide great insight into cyberbullying. Researchers may choose, for example, to examine existing records from online forums and chat groups. Many public spaces on the Internet present opportunities for cyberbullying to occur, and researchers may look to these spaces in order to collect data and understand these forums for victimization. Consider, for instance, the comment boards that exist for each video posted on YouTube. Members of YouTube post comments in relation to the specific video, other videos, and other YouTube members. These comment boards can harbor negative interactions among YouTube members, and some of these interactions may constitute cyberbullying. Researchers may also have access to other online forums. Mishna and colleagues (2009) examined the concerns posted by children and youth to an anonymous, national, toll-free, 24-hour Web counseling, referral, and information service. These posts revealed important information about cyberbullying. Alternatively, participants may be asked to engage in technology-mediated communication specifically for research purposes. Some researchers may choose to create a website for the purposes of their research, which may include opportunities for both synchronous and asynchronous communication.

Opportunities for synchronous communication include chat rooms, where content is publicly visible to all members, as well as an instant messenger, where content is only visible to intended recipients. Researchers may choose to use asynchronous communication methods as well, such as e-mail or an electronic bulletin board. When creating opportunities for technology-mediated communication for research purposes, researchers should consider issues of privacy and confidentiality. It is important to consider protecting the information collected through techniques such as password protection and encryption. It is also important to have procedures in place in order to respond to any emergencies, distress, or safety concerns that arise from online interactions. Researchers must consider their physical proximity to the research participants, and emergency contacts in the area of the participants. If participants make disclosures about suicidal thoughts or intentions, abuse or neglect, or other forms of victimization, researchers must have standardized procedures in place for responding in a timely and appropriate manner. Researchers must also give careful consideration to how they will respond when incidents of cyberbullying do occur in the research process. Will researchers intervene? Will researchers observe for the purposes of data collection? These questions have serious ethical implications and must be given careful thought in the planning of the research.

Multiple/Combined Approaches. Using multiple methodological approaches for one research project is very useful. This balances the strengths and weaknesses of each single approach and produces a nuanced understanding of experiences.

Principles for Effective Use of Qualitative Approaches

Preparation and documentation. Significant preparation is required prior to undertaking qualitative research. Each decision related to the research process must be justified, and researchers should reflect on the motivations influencing these decisions (Jones, 2002). Pilot research with individuals similar to the intended participants will help to refine the organization, structure, and timing of the research process, and to enhance the rigor and trustworthiness of the findings (Jones, 2002; Mishna, 2004).

Unique ethical considerations. Researchers must consider the ethical issues unique to conducting qualitative research on cyberbullying among children and youth. Children and youth must be given the opportunity to give their consent and/ or assent to participate and to withdraw at any time. This is particularly salient when conducting research related to cyber technology, as it is one way in which children and youth can learn to set boundaries when communicating online. Some children and youth may provide too much information, too readily when communicating through technology, which can place them at risk for victimization. It is important for young people to be aware that they can and, in many cases, should, refuse to share information through technology. (Please see Mishna, Underwood, Milne, & Gibson, this volume, Chapter 12, for a more thorough discussion of ethical issues.)

Consideration of Research Space. It is important to consider the physical or cyber space in which research is conducted, as this will influence the interactions and communications that occur (Barker & Weller, 2003). When working with children and youth in the context of face-to-face interviews or focus groups, researchers should consider ways to promote an egalitarian research environment. Barker and Weller (2003) suggest, for example, allowing children to rearrange the seating space in a format that is comfortable. Researchers should also consider basic aspects of the physical space, such as the temperature of the room, the decorations on the walls, and whether or not the location is conveniently located and easy to find. When conducting research in cyber space, researchers should consider stating ground rules for interactions, and explicitly outlining how the research process will unfold. By providing young people with this information, they will be better prepared for the interactions that ensue and likely more comfortable throughout the research process.

Language and Norms. Qualitative research with young people requires an understanding of the languages and social norms of youth (Barker & Weller, 2003). This is particularly important for languages and social norms that have developed online, as adults typically do not have access to these cultures. The use of language evolves rapidly in cyber social worlds, and it is easy to become lost in the shorthand and informal vernacular prevalent at the moment of conducting research. Language may develop within unique groups of friends, schools, cities, or groups of individuals with common interests. Just as adult colleagues might write "FYI" in an e-mail to one another, young people may use acronyms such as "TTYS" (talk to you soon). Many adults are also adept at understanding the tone and character of electronic communications, whether in professional or personal settings. Similarly, young people have unique ways of conveying and interpreting the tone and character of their communications. It is important for researchers to commit time and resources to understanding the unique languages and norms that have developed within the group with whom they are conducting research.

Developmental Stage of Participants. Attention must be paid to the developmental and social abilities of participants (Heary & Hennessy, 2002). Researchers may need to tailor the format of interviews, focus groups, and other qualitative methods to meet the needs of young participants, and should consider children's abilities to communicate, attend to research interactions, and interact socially with others (Heary & Hennessy, 2002).

Reflexivity and Authenticity. When engaging in qualitative research with children and youth, researchers should aim to be reflexive, in order to ensure authentic representation of children's voices (Barker & Weller, 2003; Mishna et al., 2004). Reflexivity implies that researchers are at once looking both inward and outward, in order to understand how the self is represented in the research product (Jones, 2002). A theoretical understanding of reflexivity is at the core of any research study that is well planned and executed (Lloyd, 2009). The way researchers communicate and operate in the context of research on cyberbullying will depend on both their academic training and their personal histories (Davis, Watson, &

Cunningham-Burley, 2000). Since qualitative research is an interpretive process, it is necessary to consider the perspectives of the researcher(s) and the context of the research when interpreting findings (Blumenreich, 2004). The research process is impacted by the sense, intuition, creativity, and artistry of the researcher, and thus researchers must be clear with themselves and others about their place in composing the qualitative findings (Jones, 2002). Qualitative research allows for deep understanding of phenomena, which carries with it a significant responsibility. Researchers must tell the stories of participants in respectful and authentic ways (Jones, 2002). The story that is produced in the final research product should be recognizable to those who told it, meaning that it should emerge directly from their worlds and contexts (Jones, 2002). Reflexive thought facilitates an understanding of the opportunities and limitations created as a result of the researcher being situated within the research (Barker & Weller, 2003). Techniques such as journaling may assist researchers in becoming more self-aware of research actions and choices (Lloyd, 2009).

Attention to Feelings of Participants. The cyber world is crucially important to young people. Cyber technology often represents the link between children and youth and their social worlds, and it is thus all the more distressing when this link is marred by the trauma of cyberbullying. Researchers cannot neglect or underestimate the importance of the cyber world to children and youth, and must take particular care in understanding what technology means for their social lives. Researchers must also be aware that when using certain methodological techniques, such as vignettes or focus groups, young participants may be exposed to upsetting stories of other young people's experiences of cyberbullying (Barter & Renold, 2000). Children and adolescents may have difficulty anticipating the experiences that will be brought forth in qualitative research and may be unable to predict their reactions to this research (Mishna et al., 2004). It is important to remember that young participants have fewer life experiences, less familiarity with research, and less experience with articulating when they are uncomfortable (Duncan et al., 2009). For these reasons, researchers should be prepared to provide participants with resources that extend beyond the brief time of the research interaction. Researchers may opt to prepare a handout to give to all participants, listing helpful Web and other resources on cyberbullying. It also may be helpful to prepare a list of local social service agencies that are equipped to meet the needs of children and youth in distress.

CONCLUSION

The significant benefits of incorporating qualitative methods into research on cyberbullying have been reviewed for consideration and reflection. Qualitative research on understudied, complex and newly surfacing content areas such cyberbullying is valuable and viable. Moreover the utility of qualitative methods in combination with quantitative research is significant. Schools and social services can greatly benefit from an array of qualitative and quantitative research in order to keep pace with new social issues as they arise.

Note

1 Ang & Goh, 2010; Aricak et al., 2008; Calvete, Orue, Estevez, Villardon, & Padilla, 2010; Cassidy, Jackson, & Brown, 2009; Dehue, Bolman, & Vollink, 2008; Didden et al., 2009; Erdur-Baker, 2010; Hinduja & Patchin, 2007, 2008, 2009; Juvonen & Gross, 2008; Katzer, Fetchenhauer, & Belschak, 2009; Kowalski & Limber, 2007; Kowalski, Limber, & Agatston, 2008; Li, 2007; Livingstone & Haddon, 2008; Mesch, 2008; Mishna et al., 2010; Patchin & Hinduja, 2006; Pornari & Wood, 2010; Perren, Dooley, Shaw, & Cross, 2010; Raskauskas & Stoltz, 2007; Slonje & Smith, 2008; Sontag, Clemans, Graber, & Lyndon, 2011; Sourander et al., 2010; Vandebosch & Van Cleemput, 2009; Varjas, Henrich, & Meyers, 2009; Williams & Guerra, 2007.

References

Agatston, P. W., Kowalski, R., & Limber, S. (2007). Students' perspectives on cyber bullying. *Journal of Adolescent Health, 41*, S59–S60. doi:10.1016/j.jadohealth.2007.09.003

Ang, R. P., & Goh, D. H. (2010). Cyberbullying among adolescents: The role of affective and cognitive empathy, and gender. *Child Psychiatry and Human Development, 41*, 387–397. doi:10.1007/s10578–010–0176–3

Aricak, T., Siyahhan, S., Uzunhasanoglu, A., Saribeyoglu, S., Ciplak, S., Yilmaz, N., . . . Memmedov, C. (2008). Cyberbullying among Turkish adolescents. *Cyberpsychology & Behaviour, 11*(3), 253–263. doi:10.1089/cpb.2007.0016

Barker, J., & Weller, S. (2003). "Never work with children?": The geography of methodological issues in research with children. *Qualitative Research, 3*(2), 207–227. doi:10.1177/14687941030032004

Barter, C., & Renold, E. (2000). "I wanna tell you a story": Exploring the application of vignettes in qualitative research with children and young people. *International Journal of Social Research Methodology, 3*(4), 307–323. doi:10.1080/13645570050178594

Black, N. (1994). Why we need qualitative research. *Journal of Epidemiology and Community Health, 48*, 425–426. doi:10.1136/jech.48.5.425-a

Blumenreich, M. (2004). Avoiding the pitfalls of "conventional" narrative research: Using poststructural theory to guide the creation of narratives of children with HIV. *Qualitative Research, 4*(1), 77–90. doi:10.1177/1468794104041108

Bronfenbrenner, U. (1979). *The ecology of human development: Experiments by nature and design*. Cambridge, MA: Harvard University Press.

Calvete, E., Orue, I., Estevez, A., Villardon, L., & Padilla, P. (2010). Cyberbullying in adolescents: Modalities and aggressors' profile. *Computers in Human Behavior, 26*, 1128–1135. doi:10.1016/j.chb.2010.03.017

Camfield, L., Crivello, G., & Woodhead, M. (2009). Wellbeing research in developing countries: Reviewing the role of qualitative methods. *Social Indices Research, 90*, 5–31. doi:10.1007/s11205–008–9310-z

Cassidy, W., Jackson, M., & Brown, K. N. (2009). Sticks and stones can break my bones, but how can pixels hurt me? Student's experiences with cyber-bullying. *School Psychology International, 30*(4), 383–402. doi:10.1177/0143034309106948

Cresswell, J. W., Shope, R., Plano Clark, V. L., & Green, D. O. (2006). How interpretive qualitative research extends mixed methods research. *Research in the Schools, 13*(1), 1–11.

Crivello, G., Camfield, L., & Woodhead, M. (2009). How can children tell us about their wellbeing? Exploring the potential of participatory research approaches within young lives. *Social Indicators Research, 90*, 51–72. doi:10.1007/s11205–008–9312-x

Cullingford, C., & Morrison, J. (1995). Bullying as a formative influence: The relationship between the experience of school and criminality. *British Educational Research Journal, 21*(5), 547–561. doi:10.1080/0141192950210501

Darbyshire, P., MacDougall, C., & Schiller, W. (2005). Multiple methods in qualitative research with children: More insight or just more? *Qualitative Research, 5*(4), 417–436. doi:10.1177/1468794105056921

Davidson, L., Ridgway, P., Kidd, S., Topor, A., & Borg, M. (2008). Using qualitative research to inform mental health policy. *Canadian Journal of Psychiatry, 53*(3), 137–145.

Davis, A., & Jones, L. (1996). Environmental constraints on health: Listening to children's views. *Health Education Journal, 55*, 363–374. doi:10.1177/001789699605500402

Davis, J., Watson, N., & Cunningham-Burley, S. (2000). Learning the lives of disabled children: Developing a reflexive approach. In P. Christensen & A. James (Eds.), *Research with children: Perspectives and practices* (pp. 201–224). London: Falmer Press.

Dehue, F., Bolman, C., & Vollink, T. (2008). Cyberbullying: Youngsters' experiences and parental perception. *Cyberpsychology & Behavior, 11*(2), 217–225. doi:10.1089/cpb.2007.0008

Dennis, B. (2009). Acting up: Theatre of the oppressed as critical ethnography. *International Journal of Qualitative Methods, 8*(2), 65–97.

Didden, R. Scholte, R.H.J., Korzilius, H., De Moor, J.M.H., Vermeulen, A., O'Reilly, M., . . . Lancioni, G. (2009). Cyberbullying among students with intellectual and developmental disability in special education settings. *Developmental Neurorehabilitation, 12*(3), 146–151. doi:10.1080/17518420902971356

Duncan, R.E., Drew, S.E., Hodgson, J. & Sawyer, S.M. (2009). Is my mum going to hear this? Methodological and ethical challenges in qualitative health research with young people. *Social Science & Medicine, 69*, 1691–1699. doi:10.1016/j.socscimed.2009.09.001

Dwyer, C., & Davies, G. (2010). Qualitative methods III: Animating archives, artful interventions and online environments. *Progress in Human Geography, 34*(1), 88–97. doi:10.1177/0309132508105005

Erdur-Baker, O. (2010). Cyberbullying and its correlation to traditional bullying, gender and frequent and risky usage of Internet-mediated communication tools. *New Media & Society, 12*(1), 109–125. doi:10.1177/1461444809341260

Fevre, R., Robinson, A., Jones, T., & Lewis, D. (2010). Researching workplace bullying: The benefits of taking an integrated approach. *International Journal of Social Research Methodology, 13*(1), 71–85. doi:10.1080/13645570802648671

Gilgun, J.F., & Abrams, L.S. (2002). The nature and usefulness of qualitative social work research: Some thoughts and an invitation to dialogue. *Qualitative Social Work, 1*(1), 39–55. doi:10.1177/1473325002001001743

Grigg, D.W. (2010). Cyber-aggression: Definition and concept of cyberbullying. *Australian Journal of Guidance & Counselling, 20*(2), 143–156. doi:10.1375/ajgc.20.2.143

Hall, A.L., & Rist, R .C. (1999). Integrating multiple qualitative research methods or avoiding the precariousness of a one-legged stool. *Psychology & Marketing, 16*(4), 291–305. doi:10.1002/(SICI)1520–6793(199907)16:4<291::AID-MAR2>3.3.CO;2-R

Heary, C.M., & Hennessy, E. (2002). The use of focus group interviews in pediatric health care research. *Journal of Pediatric Psychology, 27*(1), 47–57. doi:10.1093/jpepsy/27.1.47

Hemming, P. J. (2008). Mixing qualitative research methods in children's geographies. *Area, 40*(2), 152–162. doi:10.1111/j.1475–4762.2008.00798.x

Hinduja, S., & Patchin, J. W. (2007). Offline consequences of online victimization. *Journal of School Violence, 6*(3), 89–112. doi:10.1300/J202v06n03_06

Hinduja, S., & Patchin, J. W. (2008). Cyberbullying: An exploratory analysis of factors related to offending and victimization. *Deviant Behaviour, 29*(2), 129–156. doi:10.1080/01639620701457816

Hinduja, S., & Patchin, J. W. (2009). *Bullying beyond the schoolyard: Preventing and responding to cyberbullying.* Thousand Oaks, CA: Sage.

Hoppe, M. J., Wells, E., Morrison, D. M., Gillmore, M. R., & Wilsdon, A. (1995). Using focus groups to discuss sensitive topics with children. *Evaluation Review, 19*(1), 102–114. doi:10.1177/0193841X9501900105

Jäger, T., Amado, J., Matos, A., & Possoa, T. (2010). Analysis of experts' and trainers' views on cyberbullying. *Australian Journal of Guidance & Counselling, 20*(2), 169–181. doi:10.1375/ajgc.20.2.169

Johnson, G. M., & Puplampu, K. P. (2008). Internet use during childhood and the ecological techno-subsystem. *Canadian Journal of Learning and Technology, 34*(1), 19–28.

Jones, S. R. (2002). (Re)Writing the word: Methodological strategies and issues in qualitative research. *Journal of College Student Development, 43*(4), 461–474.

Juvonen, J., & Gross, E. F. (2008). Extending the school grounds? Bullying experiences in cyberspace. *Journal of School Health, 78*(9), 496–506. doi:10.1111/j.1746–1561.2008.00335.x

Katzer, C., Fetchenhauer, D., & Belschak, F. (2009). Cyberbullying: Who are the victims? *Journal of Media Psychology, 21*(1), 25–36. doi:10.1027/1864–1105.21.1.25

Kowalski, R. M., & Limber, S. P. (2007). Electronic bullying among middle school students. *Journal of Adolescent Health, 41*, S22–S30. doi:10.1016/j.jadohealth.2007.08.017

Kowalski, R., Limber, S., & Agatston, P. W. (2008). *Cyber bullying.* Malden MA: Blackwell Publishing. doi:10.1002/9780470694176

Leech, N. L., & Onwuegbuzie, A. J. (2007). An array of qualitative data analysis tools: A call for data analysis triangulation. *School Psychology Quarterly, 22*(4), 557–584. doi:10.1037/1045–3830.22.4.557

Li, Q. (2007). Bullying in the new playground: Research into cyberbullying and cyber victimisation. *Australasian Journal of Educational Technology, 23*(4), 435–454.

Livingstone, S., & Haddon, L. (2008). Risky experiences for children online: Charting European research on children and the Internet. *Children & Society, 22*, 314–323. doi:10.1111/j.1099–0860.2008.00157.x

Lloyd, C. (2009). Reflexivity and reflection in an Australian mobile phone study: A methodological discussion. *Australian Journal of Communication, 36*(1), 37–50.

Maher, D. (2008). Cyberbullying: An ethnographic case study of one Australian upper primary school class. *Youth Studies Australia, 27*(4), 49–57.

Mesch, G. S. (2006). Family relations and the Internet: Exploring a family boundaries approach. *Journal of Family Communication, 6*(2), 119–138. doi:10.1207/s15327698jfc0602_2

Mishna, F. (2004). A qualitative study of bullying from multiple perspectives. *Children & Schools, 26*(4), 234–247. doi:10.1093/cs/26.4.234

Mishna, F., Antle, B. J., & Regehr, C. (2004). Tapping the perspectives of children: Emerging ethical issues in qualitative research. *Qualitative Social Work, 3*(4), 449–468. doi:10.1177/1473325004048025

Mishna, F., Cook, C., Gadalla, T., Daciuk, J., & Solomon, S. (2010). Cyber bullying behaviors among middle and high school students. *American Journal of Orthopsychiatry, 80*(3), 362–374. doi:10.1111/j.1939-

Mishna, F., McLuckie, A., & Saini, M. (2009). Real-world dangers in an online reality: A qualitative study examining online relationships and cyber abuse. *Social Work Research, 33*(2), 107–119. doi:10.1093/swr/33.2.107

Mishna, F., Pepler, D., & Wiener, J. (2006). Factors associated with perceptions and responses to bullying situations by children, parents, teachers, and principals. *Victims & Offenders, 1*(3), 255–288. doi:10.1080/15564880600626163

Mishna, F., Saini, M., & Solomon, S. (2009). Ongoing and online: Children and youth's perceptions of cyber bullying. *Children and Youth Services Review, 31*, 1222–1228. doi:10.1016/j.childyouth.2009.05.004

Nocentini, A., Calmaestra, J., Schultze-Krumbholz, A., Scheithauer, H., Ortega, R., & Menesini, E. (2010). Cyberbullying: Labels, behaviours and definitions in three European countries. *Australian Journal of Guidance & Counselling, 20*(2), 129–142. doi:10.1375/ajgc.20.2.129

Patchin, J. W., & Hinduja, S. (2006). Bullies move beyond the schoolyard: A preliminary look at cyberbullying. *Youth Violence and Juvenile Justice, 4*(2), 148–169. doi:10.1177/1541204006286288

Peek, L., & Forthergill, A. (2009). Using focus groups: Lessons from studying daycare centers, 9/11, and Hurricane Katrina. *Qualitative Research, 9*(1), 31–59. doi:10.1177/ 1468794108098029

Perren, S., Dooley, J., Shaw, T., & Cross, D. (2010). Bullying in school and cyberspace: Associations with depressive symptoms in Swiss and Australian adolescents. *Child & Adolescent Psychiatry & Mental Health, 4*(28), 1–10. doi:10.1186/1753-2000-4-28

Phoenix, A., Frosh, S., & Pattman, R. (2003). Producing contradictory masculine subject positions: Narratives of threat, homophobia and bullying in 11–14 year old boys. *Journal of Social Issues, 59*(1), 179–195. doi:10.1111/1540-4560.t01-1-00011

Pornari, C. D., & Wood, J. (2010). Peer and cyber aggression in secondary school students: The role of moral disengagement, hostile attribution bias, and outcome expectancies. *Aggressive Behavior, 36*, 81–94. doi:10.1002/ab.20336

Raskauskas, J., & Stoltz A. D. (2007). Involvement in traditional and electronic bullying among adolescents. *Developmental Psychology, 43*(3), 564–575. doi:10.1037/0012-1649.43.3.564

Slonje, R., & Smith, P. K. (2008). Cyberbullying: Another main type of bullying? *Scandinavian Journal of Psychology, 49*, 147–154.

Smith, P. K., & Brain, P. (2000). Bullying in schools: Lessons from two decades of research. *Aggressive Behavior, 26*, 1–9. doi:10.1002/(SICI)1098–2337(2000)26:1<1::AID-AB1>3.0.CO;2-7

Sontag, L. M., Clemans, K. H., Graber, J. A., & Lyndon, S. T. (2011). Traditional and cyber aggressors and victims: A comparison of psychosocial characteristics. *Journal of Youth and Adolescence, 40*(4), 392–404. doi:10.1007/s10964–010–9575–9

Sourander, A., Brunstein Klomek, A., Ikonen, M., Lindroos, J., Luntamo, T., Koskelainen, M., . . . Helenius, H. (2010). Psychosocial risk factors associated with cyberbullying among adolescents: A population based study. *Archives of General Psychiatry, 67*(7), 720–729. doi:10.1001/archgenpsychiatry.2010.79

Spears, B., Slee, P., Owens, L., & Johnson, B. (2009). Behind the scenes and screens: Insights into the human dimension of covert and cyberbullying. *Journal of Psychology, 217*(4), 189–196. doi:10.1027/0044–3409.217.4.189

Thomas, E. (2011). From qualitative data to instrument development: The Women's Breast Conflict Scale. *The Qualitative Report, 16*(4), 908–932.

Thornberg, R. (2011). "She's weird!"—The social construction of bullying in school: A review of qualitative research. *Children & Society, 25*, 258–267. doi:10.1111/j.1099–0860.2011.00374.x

Van Manen, M. (1990). *Researching lived experience: Human science for an action sensitive pedagogy.* London: Althouse Press; New York: SUNY Press.

Vandebosch, H., & Van Cleemput, K. (2008). Defining cyberbullying: A qualitative research into the perceptions of youngsters. *Cyberpsychology & Behavior, 11*(4), 499–505. doi:10.1089/cpb.2007.0042

Vandebosch, H., & Van Cleemput, K. (2009). Cyberbullying among youngsters: Profiles of bullies and victims. *New Media & Society, 11*(8), 1349–1371.

Varjas, K., Henrich, C.C., & Meyers, J. (2009). Urban middle school students' perceptions of bullying, cyberbullying, and school safety. *Journal of School Violence, 8*(2), 159–176. doi:10.1080/15388220802074165

Vessey, J.A., Horowitz, J.A., & Carlson, K.L. (2008). Psychometric evaluation of the Child-Adolescent Teasing Scale. *The Journal of School Health, 78*(6), 344–351. doi:10.1111/j.1746–1561.2008.00312.x

Whitley, R., & Crawford, M. (2005). Qualitative research in psychiatry. *Canadian Journal of Psychiatry, 50*(2), 108–115. doi:10.1080/10673220590956474

Williams, K., & Guerra, N. (2007). Prevalence and predictors of Internet bullying. *Journal of Adolescent Health*, S14–S21. doi:10.1016/j.jadohealth.2007.08.018

Wright, V.H., Burnham, J.J., Inman, C.T., & Ogorchock, H.N. (2009). Cyberbullying: Using virtual scenarios to educate and raise awareness. *Journal of Computing in Teacher Education, 26*(1), 35–43.

Part VI

Implications

19 How Research Findings Can Inform Legislation and School Policy on Cyberbullying

Marilyn Campbell

Recent empirical research has found that the psychological consequences for young people involved in cyberbullying are more severe than in the case of traditional bullying (Campbell, Spears, Slee, Butler, & Kift, 2012; Perren, Dooley, Shaw, & Cross, 2010). Cybervictimization has been found to be a significant predictor of depressive symptoms over and above that of being victimized by traditional bullying (Perren et al., 2010). Targets of cyberbullying also have reported higher anxiety scores and social difficulties than traditional victims, with those students who had been bullied by both forms showing similar anxiety and depression scores to targets of cyberbullying (Campbell et al., 2012). This is supported by the subjective views of many young people, not involved in bullying, who believed that cyberbullying is far more harmful than traditional bullying (Cross et al., 2009). However, students who were traditionally bullied thought the consequences of this kind of bullying were harsher than did those students who were cyberbullied (Campbell, et al., 2012). In Slonje and Smith's study (2008), students reported that text messaging and e-mail bullying had less of an impact than traditional bullying, but that bullying by pictures or video clips had more negative impact than traditional bullying.

Depending on the particular circumstances, a number of reasons for the more severe impact of cyberbullying on victims have been suggested: a wider audience, anonymity of the perpetrator, the more enduring nature of the written word, and the ability to reach the target at any time and in any place, including the target's home. Furthermore, cyberbullies may feel emboldened because they cannot see their targets or their immediate responses and believe that, because of their anonymity, they will not be detected. It has been suggested that this anonymity may increase the intensity of the attacks and encourage them to continue for longer than they would in face-to-face interactions (Conn, 2004). While it is true that cyberbullying can only threaten physical violence rather than inflict it, research has shown that verbal and psychological bullying may have more negative long-term effects (Reid, Monsen, & Rivers, 2004).

Cyberbullying has been shown to be a problem in most countries where technology is widely available (Cross et al., 2009; Patchin & Hinduja, 2010; Smith,

Mahdavi et al., 2008). Bullying in all its forms is a complex social relationship problem that is deeply embedded in our societies. Nevertheless, solutions to this problem are often considered the school's responsibility, as this is where most young people spend a significant amount of their time and conduct social relationships. Parents also turn to schools to prevent and to intervene in bullying cases. This is so even when the behavior is conducted out of school hours and outside of school grounds, as is the case in cyberbullying (Cross et al., 2009; Smith, Mahdavi et al., 2008). However, schools by themselves are not able to deal with what is a societal problem. Research has shown that all forms of bullying are not just a dyadic relationship problem between a student who bullies and a target (Salmivalli, 1999), but bullying is firmly embedded in the surrounding social milieu. From Bronfenbrenner's (1979) theoretical framework on ecological systems theory, we know that students who are involved in bullying are influenced by their peers, families, schools, communities, and countries in which they live (Espelage & Swearer, 2003). Therefore, strategies to combat this must involve not only individuals and schools but also governments in the form of legislation, and national and state/provincial stakeholders in the form of policies to prevent and intervene in cyberbullying.

CYBERBULLYING AND THE LAW

There is a common perception that the "law" provides a clear rule that exists to punish/regulate behavior that is obviously wrong (there being a clear distinction between right and wrong), and that therefore the enactment of a law will provide a quick and easy fix to the problem of cyberbullying. This perception is based on the misunderstanding that the law is only used for adversarial and punitive purposes. However, there are many purposes the law can serve: deterrent, administer punishment, mechanism for determining reasonable compensation to victims, mark of societal norms, and an influence on policy making. There are also many different areas or types of law that could apply to cyberbullying: criminal, vilification, law of torts, defamation, privacy and discrimination, to name a few (Kift, 1999). Furthermore, the situation is made more complex by the fact that different laws exist in different countries and states/regions. Given this complexity, a better understanding of legal and policy issues related to cyberbullying in schools appears to be an important part of prevention and intervention efforts. The following sections describe the ways in which criminal law and civil law relate to cyberbullying. The role of the law is then discussed as reflecting societal norms and influencing policies on cyberbullying.

Criminal Law

The three roles the criminal justice system may serve in relation to cyberbullying are remedial, retributive, and a deterrent for young people (Chan, 2009).

In Australian and New Zealand law, with the exception of Division 8B *Crimes Act 1900* (N.S.W.), bullying, and therefore cyberbullying, is not a criminal offense per se (Campbell, Butler, & Kift, 2008). This is similar to the situation in the United Kingdom (Marczak & Coyne, 2010) and in the United States. The law in these countries, however, names criminal offenses most associated with bullying as assault, threats, extortion, stalking, or harassment. However, bullying by students is usually seen more as a disciplinary matter in schools than as a crime; the police are rarely involved and prosecutions are uncommon (Campbell et al., 2008). Nevertheless, in many instances, cyberbullying can constitute criminal conduct, especially when the behavior is seriously threatening, harassing, or intimidating. While there may be a natural tendency to seek to avoid the criminalization of young people in this context, criminal sanctions are likely appropriate to more cases than are prosecuted, and very few young people seem to appreciate their potential for attracting criminal liability. This is demonstrated by a case of cyberbullying by 8th grade children in the United States who were found guilty of threatening classmates online and sentenced to community service and probation. However, the children said, "I didn't know any of this was going to happen . . . [we] believe[d] [instant messaging] IM is private and fleeting" (Kift, Campbell, & Butler, 2010). In fact, most students who cyberbully believe there is little risk of being identified, as cyberspace is unsupervised by adults. Consequently, cyberbullies seem not to fear punishment (Dempsey, Sulkowski, Nichols, & Storch, 2009).

In the United States, there are 47 states that have legislation that addresses school bullying (Snakenborg, Van Acker, & Gable, 2011; Stuart-Cassell, Bell, & Singer, 2011). Of these, 36 specify that cyberbullying is prohibited, and in 13 state laws, schools are given jurisdiction over off-campus cyber actions that interfere with the learning environment of the school. As most of the laws have been enacted since 2001, many believe they were motivated by the shootings at several high schools in the United States in the late 1990s and the subsequent reports that many of the perpetrators of these shootings had felt bullied by their peers (Limber & Small, 2003). Some states have also already enacted legislation where cyberbullying is a crime, or at least a misdemeanor (Snakenborg et al., 2011). Notwithstanding, the law has struggled to keep pace with advances in technology, and cyberbullying is no exception. As Nicholson (2006) argued, using laws that were not designed for bullying means legal solutions for bullying are rarely satisfactory. These laws were often drafted before the advent of the current technology, and prosecutors have to shoe-horn cyberbullying into the existing laws. For example, in the United States, the challenge of attempting to force existing criminal laws clearly beyond their original remit to fit emerging cyberbullying conduct was starkly highlighted in the "Lori Drew Myspace case." In this case, a student's mother, Lori Drew, created a fake Myspace account in the name of a teenage boy to first befriend and then harass and taunt 13-year-old Megan Meier, who subsequently committed suicide. Drew was initially convicted of three misdemeanor counts of intentionally accessing computers without authorization, on the basis she had violated Myspace's terms of service (by creating a false profile). Her conviction was overturned on appeal, with the court holding that such an outcome set a dangerous precedent by potentially criminalizing breaches of contract and a multitude of quite innocent and common terms of service violations (Kift et al., 2010).

Civil Law

The other system of law that is applicable to schools and cyberbullying is civil law. This type of law is invoked to pay damages or compensation to a target. For example, under Australian law, parents are not responsible for their children's behavior, and children do not usually have the large amounts of money required to pay compensation. Consequently, it is usually the school or the school system that is sued for being negligent in their duty of care. This kind of lawsuit is decided more on the balance of probabilities rather than strict proof, within the criteria of reasonableness. Therefore, a plaintiff needs to prove that (1) there was a duty of care, (2) that the duty of care was breached, and (3) this breach caused the injury, either physical or psychological (Butler, Kift, & Campbell, 2009). This duty of care extends to protecting a student from the conduct of other students. However, the resulting psychiatric injury or recognized psychiatric illness must be distinguished from transitory emotional or mental distress.

For example, in Australian law, there is precedent where the school's duty of care is not limited to incidents occurring on school grounds or during official school hours. In *Geyer v Downs* (1977, 138CLR 91), a school was held to have owed a duty of care to a student who had arrived at school early and was injured when struck by a softball bat. As the principal had instructed the students to sit quietly and not play as there were no teachers available for supervision, the court ruled these instructions constituted a relationship of school teacher and pupil, which is necessary to invoke the relevant duty of care, which was deemed to be breached. Similarly, in *Trustees of the Roman Catholic Church for the Diocese of Bathurst v Koffman* (Australian Torts Reports 81–399, 1996), a 12-year-old school boy injured in an incident involving older students successfully sued his school for breach of duty of care despite the incident occurring 20 minutes after the end of the school day and 400 meters from school grounds. Judge J.A. Shellar went on to say that, depending on the circumstances, the duty of care could extend to pupils bullied on the journey on the bus or while they were walking to or from school (Butler, et al., 2009).

Civil liability is usually invoked because schools failed to act in their duty of care (Hinduja & Patchin, 2011). Schools have abundant information that shows that cyberbullying has negative consequences; therefore, as part of their duty of care, they should reasonably foresee that students could be damaged from this activity and take reasonable preventative steps to stop cyberbullying from harming a student. One way to do this is to provide both pre-service and in-service education for teachers where new research findings can be disseminated to inform school practice.

Socially Normative Function of the Law

Another purpose of the law is to convey to the population information about what is normative behavior. Although the legislation might not be enforced, it can carry the role of "symbolically announcing what society deems good and valuable" (Limber & Small, 2003, p. 448). Evan (1965) went further, advocating that the law can become an instrument of social change. He states that "law emerges not only to codify existing customs, morals or mores, but also to *modify* the behavior and the values presently existing in a particular society" (p. 286). Legislation with these purposes in mind could be useful for the prevention and intervention of cyberbullying. For example, for community education purposes, legislation against cyberbullying could be enacted with no real will to prosecute, similar to anti-spanking children legislation in New Zealand and Scandinavia (Campbell et al., 2008).

To influence policies. Legislation can enshrine the notion that all forms of bullying are unacceptable behavior and could require all schools in a country or state to develop and keep active an appropriate school policy around bullying (Ananiadou & Smith, 2002). Since 1999, schools in England have been legally required to have an antibullying policy (Samara & Smith, 2008). Many states in America have enacted formal legislation to direct school districts to update bullying policies to include electronic forms (Surdin, 2009). If governments mandate or even encourage such policies with the requisite resources and funding, this political commitment may make a difference to the prevalence of cyberbullying (Limber & Small, 2003). However, when mandates are legislated without funding, school districts are likely to use boilerplate documents to satisfy requirements, rather than crafting carefully developed policies and involving all stakeholders in the process.

Cyberbullying policies in schools. A school's antibullying policy can be viewed as a framework to show commitment to the prevention and intervention of bullying, including cyberbullying, and to demonstrate and communicate its procedural response to the whole-school community (Smith, Smith, Osborn, & Samara, 2008). The requirements for antibullying policies fall into two components: the contents or coverage of the policy and the process components. That is, what is in the actual written policy; and how the policy was written, implemented, reviewed, and evaluated.

Policy Content. There have been several studies that have examined the content of antibullying policies, and each has used a different coding system. Smith, Smith, et al. (2008) in their content analysis of 142 antibullying policies from one English county coded policy content into definitions of bullying behavior, reporting and responding to bullying incidents, recording incidents, and strategies for prevention. The analysis found there was a great range of scores in the adequacy and coverage of school antibullying policies according to the authors' criteria. While two thirds of schools gave some kind of definition of bullying and said parents would be informed, there was generally no guidance for response to bullying incidents for anyone other than teaching staff (i.e., other school staff, parents, or student bystanders), not many statements of how records would be kept, and very few policies mentioned cyberbullying. Woods and Wolke (2003) based their analysis of 34 primary schools' policies on Olweus's whole-school intervention program. This consisted of four key principles: awareness of adults, involvement of both home and school, firm limits of unacceptable behavior, and application of nonhostile sanctions. They found that 44% of these schools stressed the importance of having serious talks with parents about bullying incidents in their policies, but only 26% of these schools involved parents in the planning of preventative bullying strategies.

A recent study of legislation and policies in the United States (Stuart-Cassell et al., 2011) determined that antibullying legislation in 45 states include requirements that school districts adopt bullying policies. Model policies have been developed in 41 states, although in only 29 states was such a policy required by the legislation. Interestingly, three states that do not have antibullying laws also created model policies. In 20 states, districts must have their policies reviewed at the state level.

In general, there are calls for strong and detailed policies with language that can be easily understood by both students and adults, outlining what bullying behaviors are, that they are unacceptable, the penalties involved, and how bullying is reported (Hinduja & Patchin, 2011). However, there is concern over the definitions of bullying and cyberbullying (see Chapter 2). One problem with school policies is that they may not define cyberbullying with sufficient precision. The nuances of words are important for effective prevention and deterrence, with policy enforcement requiring clarity and precision in language. School policies may be practically and legally ineffectual if the language used is too vague and does not address the foreseeable risk. A clear, precise, and unambiguous definition is needed. However, in an effort to accomplish this, one must ensure that the complexities and subtleties of cyberbullying are not lost, and simplistic solutions may not be appropriate in response to a simple definition (Campbell, Cross, Spears, & Slee, 2010).

Antibullying policies should also encourage reporting of cyberbullying. This is difficult as there are many reasons why students do not report such incidents to adults, including the fear of retaliation and the fear of having the technology taken away from them (Campbell, 2005a; Rigby, 1997). Thus, there should be some kind of provision to protect reporters of cyberbullying. One strategy some schools have applied to overcome this has been the training of peers to refer bullied students to teachers (Soutter & Mckenzie, 2000). In addition, there should be clear and transparent steps describing what will happen after the reporting. An explicit process for investigating complaints needs to be articulated, and all parties need to be confident that it will be followed.

Although sanctions should be part of a school's anti-cyberbullying policy, the policy will only serve as a reactionary measure to unwanted behavior if sanctions are the main emphasis. These types of policies alone will not be as successful as those which also include preventative strategies such as promoting a positive school climate, fostering students' connectedness to school, and educating them about cyberbullying (Shariff, 2008). Unfortunately, in developing anti-cyberbullying policies, many schools seem to take a punitive view to the problem, similar to how the law is regarded in curbing cyberbullying. Reactive measures were found to be much higher on the agenda for primary schools' antibullying policies than those that are preventative (Woods & Wolke, 2003).

Policy processes. Consideration of who should contribute to antibullying policies is an issue that has not received much attention. Given that there will be conflicting values and opinions about the content of the policy, it is imperative that the policy is crafted collaboratively within each school. To ensure a shared value system and consistency in administering the policy, this should include the whole-school community (Brown, Jackson, & Cassidy, 2006). However, the voices of parents and especially young people are often silent in this process (Woods & Wolke, 2003). This is despite research findings that schools demonstrate more ownership of the policy if they develop it themselves, including all stakeholders in the process (Glover, Cartwright, Gough, & Johnson, 1998). One way to allow schools to comply with legislation while maintaining their individuality may be the use of a model policy or detailed framework that provides information to promote in-depth discussion for each content area in the antibullying policy for schools (Limber & Small, 2003).

Policies need to be known and implemented consistently by the whole-school community and not just gather dust once they have been written. This can be accomplished by disseminating the policy on the school website, in a school handbook, or in student diaries/planners. Some schools remind students of the policy by the use of posters in classrooms, articles in school newsletters, talks at assembly, curriculum modules, and staff and parent in-service (Butler, Kift, Campbell, Slee, & Spears, 2011).

Policies also need to be evaluated to determine if they are actually achieving their policy intent (Farrington, 2001). Surveys or interviews with students, staff and parents could be used to assess their knowledge of the policy and the perceived effectiveness of the policy. Regular review of policies after evaluation could lead to revisions, keeping the policy up-to-date and relevant, and thus ensuring its intended purposes.

There is disagreement about where an antibullying policy should be situated in schools. Some schools have a stand-alone policy, some include a section in their general behavior policy, and some prefer to put an anti-cyberbullying policy in an Information and Communication Technology acceptable use policy. The last option is probably the least desirable as it implies cyberbullying is a technological problem, rather than a social one. It is interesting to note in the United Kingdom that after compulsory antibullying policy legislation was introduced, there was a steady trend for schools to have a separate antibullying policy rather than as part of a behavior management policy (Samara & Smith, 2008). However, regardless of where the policy is located, it should be: clearly written comprehensive; morally, educationally, and legally defensible; enforceable; and, enforced.

How Do School Policies Reflect the Expectations of the Law? While legislation can mandate or encourage schools to develop antibullying policies, policy makers must also be cognizant of the relevant criminal and civil laws when designing such policies. Both legislation and policies need precise definitions regarding the behavior to which they refer. A definition ensures objectivity and removes doubts that may result from different subjective views or opinions on a topic. Although examples of the behavior should be provided, they should be inclusive; that is, the definition should not be restricted to a named set of types of behaviors as this could cause doubt if a particular behavior is not included (Butler et al., 2012). As Shariff (2008) writes, "to understand legal power, it is important to look at the language of law, for in law, language is power" (p. 190).

As Chapter 2 has stated, definitions of cyberbullying usually start with the three concepts from traditional bullying: intent to hurt, imbalance of power, and a usually repeated action. Smith, Smith, et al. (2008) found that while most school policies in England gave a definition of bullying, they did not make it clear that it is different from other forms of aggression. In an examination of Australian school policies, Butler et al. (2012) also found that while all schools surveyed included a definition of bullying, not all included all three concepts. Some definitions did not include an imbalance of power, therefore widening the type of conduct covered. Some only listed the ways bullying could occur (e.g., "A bully is someone who tries to build their own sense of worth by picking on others"). Cyberbullying was only mentioned by 8.5% of schools in 2004 (Smith, Smith, et al., 2008), and by 2010, still less than half the schools surveyed made any explicit reference to cyberbullying (Butler et al., 2011).

Notwithstanding, it is important to recognize that in law "there is no magic in the term bullying." For example, depending on the circumstances, a school authority may be held responsible for having breached its duty of care to a student by a failure to take reasonable care to prevent harm from even one instance of objectionable behavior (Butler et al., 2011). Policies, as mentioned previously, should be legally defensible. That is, if challenged in a court of law, the policy could be defended by the school by the fact that they knew and understood that their actions were within the parameters of the law and court decisions (Shariff, 2008).

IMPORTANCE OF RESEARCH FOR LEGISLATION AND POLICY MAKING

Research has been shown to contribute to the framing of legislation and policy. The following are two examples that illustrate how crucial research is for the development of such laws and policies.

The first example is a debate that began in schools when cyberbullying was an emerging problem. At first, it was thought that this first form of bullying could be the tactic of a new breed of students who bullied their victims from outside the school, and therefore the school had no moral or legal jurisdiction to prevent or intervene. Early reports, however, advocated that when the consequences of cyberbullying were manifested in school grounds, schools therefore had a responsibility to act (Brown et al., 2006). Research has now confirmed that most cyberbullying does occur outside of school grounds and outside of school hours (Cross et al., 2009; Smith, Mahdavi, et al., 2008). In addition, research has also shown that the majority of students who cyberbully are known peers rather than strangers (Kowalski & Limber, 2007). Furthermore, many studies have shown that there is a definite overlap of students who are involved in both traditional and cyber forms of bullying (Campbell, Spears, Slee, Butler, & Kift, 2011; Cross et al., 2009). This knowledge and understanding of relevant empirical research is therefore critical for legislation and policy making within schools, so that policies do not have separate sections for traditional and cyberbullying, as many students are involved in both forms of bullying.

A second example is the issue of banning mobile/cell phones from schools. One of the ways young people cyberbully is through their mobile/cell phone, which often has Internet connectivity. There have been many calls to ban the use of these phones during school hours on school property as a precaution against their misuse. In a study in Germany, Pfetsch, Steffgen, and Konig (2009) measured the rate of cyberbullying in schools after a six-month trial, comparing the rates of cyberbullying in those schools that had banned mobile/cell phones from school grounds with a matched number of control schools that had not banned cell phones. No differences were found in the prevalence of cyberbullying during this time. As it has been shown that both parents and young people themselves want students to have their phones with them at all times (Campbell, 2005b), there seems to be no basis as yet to bring such tension between the school and parents for the purpose of reducing cyberbullying.

There is, however, a paucity of legal research, not just on cyberbullying legislation but on legislation against bullying in general (Chan, 2009). There are scant empirical examinations of legislation on bullying to show what is effective (Shariff, 2008), although research is underway (Stuart-Cassell et al., 2010). For example, we assume that if young people are educated that certain behaviors in cyberbullying have criminal penalties, it could act as a deterrent. However, with the impulsive nature of students, perhaps this is not as successful a deterrent as we could wish. Most students know that creating graffiti is a criminal offense, but this does not seem to deter some young people. It would seem likely that any law on cyberbullying probably would not stop most 14-year-olds from ostracizing one another online. Another difficulty is that many young people believe that if they bully anonymously, they are invisible and cannot be traced and punished, and thus the application of the law as a deterrent is lost on them.

Unfortunately, there is also scarce research on the effectiveness of school antibullying policies. In secondary schools with detailed and consistently applied antibullying policies, rates of bullying have been shown to have slightly lower (Glover et al., 1998). However, primary schools in England with detailed antibullying policies were compared to schools with low-scoring policies (Woods & Wolke, 2003), and no relationship was found between direct bullying and antibullying policies. However, a higher incidence of relational bullying was found in those schools with detailed antibullying policies. The authors give several explanations for this finding but conclude that antibullying polices are not well implemented and could be addressing general aggression and antisocial behavior rather than bullying (Woods & Wolke, 2003). The findings may also indicate that there is a vast gap between what was written in the policies and their daily integration in the life of the school.

It is difficult to measure the effectiveness of legislation and policies on cyberbullying. Even if they are in place, it is difficult to measure their degree of dissemination and the fidelity of implementation and, more important, whether they reduce cyberbullying. This involves the measurement difficulties associated with determining baseline data, consistency of measurement approaches, global or specific questions, time periods asked, and frequency of response (see Chapter 8), as well as comparability between countries. However, without reliable, comprehensive data collected over time, the effectiveness of these measures cannot be judged.

CONCLUSION

Cyberbullying has been shown to be an international problem involving young people, with emerging research showing it has more negative consequences than traditional bullying. Society has often therefore invoked both legislative and policy solutions in an effort to reduce the harm from bullying. Research has already established that cyberbullying is prevalent, harmful, and crosses the geographical boundaries of school, home, and countries. The serious harm that may result from cyberbullying could mean the intervention of criminal and/or civil law is appropriate. What is needed is more informed debate on the need for different kinds of legislation. More education should be provided for parliamentarians, judges, and lawyers about the complexities of cyberbullying among young people so informed decisions can be made on the basis of research. However, although the law can make a contribution to the reduction of cyberbullying, it is not sufficient on its own. In addition, more research is needed to assess the effectiveness of antibullying policies, both as to the processes of collaborative construction, dissemination, evaluation and review as well as the content. Technology is ever changing and as electronic communication changes, gaining more features and functionality, the law and school policies need to be routinely updated.

References

Ananiadou, K., & Smith, P. (2002). Legal requirements and nationally circulated materials against school bullying in European countries. *Criminal Justice, 2,* 471–491. doi:10.1177/17488958020020040501

Australian Torts Reports. (1996). 81–399, 63,597.

Bronfenbrenner, U. (1979). *The ecology of human development.* Cambridge, MA: Harvard University Press.

Brown, K., Jackson, M., & Cassidy, W. (2006). Cyber-bullying: Developing policy to direct responses that are equitable and effective in addressing this special form of bullying. *Canadian Journal of Educational Administration and Policy, 57,* 1–35.

Butler, D., Kift, S., & Campbell, M. A. (2009). Cyber bullying in schools and the law: Is there an effective means of addressing the power imbalance? *eLaw Journal: Murdoch Electronic Journal of Law, 16,* 84–114.

Butler, D., Kift, S., Campbell, M. A., Spears, B., & Slee, P. (2011). School policy responses to cyberbullying: An Australian legal perspective. *International Journal of Law and Education, 16*(2), 7–28.

Campbell, M. A. (2005a). Cyberbullying: An old problem in a new guise? *Australian Journal of Guidance and Counselling, 15,* 68–76. doi:10.1375/ajgc.15.1.68

Campbell, M. A. (2005b, October). *The impact of the mobile phone on young people's social life.* Paper presented at the Social Change in the 21st Century Conference, Brisbane, Australia.

Campbell, M. A., Butler, D., & Kift, S. (2008). A school's duty to provide a safe learning environment: Does this include cyberbullying? *Australia and New Zealand Journal of Law and Education, 13*(2), 21–32.

Campbell, M. A., Cross, D., Spears, B., & Slee, P. (2010). *Cyberbullying—Legal implications for schools.* Occasional paper 118. Melbourne: Centre for Strategic Education.

Campbell, M. A., Spears, B., Slee, P., Butler, D., & Kift, S. (2011). *The prevalence of cyberbullying in Australia.* Paper presented at the International Observatory of Violence in Schools Conference, Mendoza, Argentina, April 2011.

Campbell, M. A., Spears, B., Slee, P., Butler D., & Kift, S. (2012). Victims' perceptions of traditional and cyberbullying, and the psychosocial correlates of their victimisation. *Emotional and Behavioural Difficulties, 17,* 389–401.

Chan, P. C. (2009). Psychosocial implications of homophobic bullying in schools. A review and directions for legal research and the legal process. *The International Journal of Human Rights, 13,* 143–175. doi:10.1080/13642980902789403

Conn, K. (2004). *Bullying and harassment: A legal guide for educators.* Alexandria, VA: ASCD.

Cross, D., Shaw, T., Hearn, L., Epstein, M., Monks, H., Lester, L., . . . Thomas, L. (2009). *Australian covert bullying prevalence study (ACBPS).* Western Australia: Report prepared for the Department of Education, Employment and Workplace Relations (DEEWR).

Dempsey, A. G., Sulkowski, M. L., Nichols, R., & Storch, E. (2009). Differences between peer victimization in cyber and physical settings and associated adjustment in early adolescence. *Psychology in the Schools, 46,* 962–972. doi:10.1002/pits.20437

Espelage, D. L., & Swearer, S. M. (2003). Research on school bullying and victimization: What have we learned and where do we go from here? *School Psychology Review, 32,* 365–383.

Evan, W. M. (1965). Law as an instrument of social change. In A. W. Gouldner & S. M. Miller (Eds.), *Applied sociology: Opportunities and problems* (pp. 285–293). New York: Free Press.

Farrington, D. (2001). *Evidence-based policy on crime and justice.* Paper presented at the 3rd International Inter-disciplinary Evidence-Based Policies and Indicators Conference, University of Durham, July 2001.

Glover, D., Cartwright, N., Gough, G., & Johnson, M. (1998). The introduction of anti-bullying policies: Do policies help in the management of change? *School Leadership and Management, 18,* 89–105. doi:10.1080/13632439869790

Hinduja, S., & Patchin, J. (2011). Cyberbullying: A review of the legal issues facing educators. *Preventing School Failure: Alternative Education for Children and Youth, 55*(2), 71–78. doi:10.1080/1045988X.2011.539433

Kift, S. (1999). Stalking in Queensland: From the nineties to Y2K. *Bond Law Review, 11*(1), 144.

Kift, S., Campbell, M. A., & Butler, D. (2010). Cyberbullying in social networking sites and blogs: Legal issues for young people and schools. *Journal of Law Information and Science, 20*(2), 61–99.

Kowalski, R., & Limber, S. (2007). Electronic bullying among middle school students. *Journal of Adolescent Health, 41,* 22–30. doi:10.1016/j.jadohealth.2007.08.017

Limber, S. P., & Small, M. A. (2003). State laws and policies to address bullying in schools. *School Psychology Review, 32,* 445–455.

Marczak, M., & Coyne, I. (2010). Cyberbullying at school: Good practice and legal aspects in the United Kingdom. *Australian Journal of Guidance and Counselling, 20,* 182–193. doi:10.1375/ajgc.20.2.182

Nicholson, A. (2006). Legal perspective on bullying. *Teacher, 2,* 22–37.

Patchin, J. W., & Hinduja, S. (2010). Cyberbullying and self-esteem. *Journal of School Health, 80,* 614–621. doi:10.1111/j.1746–1561.2010.00548.x

Perren, S., Dooley, J., Shaw, T., & Cross, D. (2010). Bullying in school and cyberspace: Associations with depressive symptoms in Swiss and Australian adolescents. *Child and Adolescent Psychiatry and Mental Health, 4*(28), 1–10. doi:10.1186/1753–2000–4-28

Pfetsch, J., Steffgen, G., & Konig, A. (2009, November). *Banning solves the problem? Effect of banning mobile phone use in schools on cyberbullying.* Poster presented at XIV Workshop on Aggression, Berlin.

Reid, P., Monsen, J., & Rivers, I. (2004). Psychology's contribution to understanding and managing bullying within schools. *Educational Psychology in Practice, 20,* 241–244.

Rigby, K. (1997). What children tell us about bullying in schools. *Children Australia, 22*(2), 18–28.

Salmivalli, C. (1999). Participant role approach to school bullying: Implications for intervention. *Journal of Adolescence, 22,* 453–459. doi:10.1006/jado.1999.0239

Samara, M., & Smith, P. K. (2008). How schools tackle bullying, and the use of whole school policies: Changes over the last decade. *Educational Psychology, 28,* 663–676. doi:10.1080/01443410802191910

Shariff, S. (2008). *Cyber-bullying: Issues and solutions for the school, the classroom and the home.* London: Routledge.

Slonje, R., & Smith, P. K. (2008). Cyberbullying: Another main type of bullying. *Scandinavian Journal of Psychology, 49,* 147–154. doi:10.1111/j.1467–9450.2007.00611.x

Smith, P. K., Mahdavi, J., Carvalho, M., Fisher, S., Russell, S., & Tippett, N. (2008).

Cyberbullying: Its nature and impact in secondary school pupils. *Journal of Counselling Psychology and Psychiatry, 49,* 376–385.

Smith, P. K., Smith, C., Osborn, R., & Samara, M. (2008). A content analysis of school anti-bullying policies: Progress and limitations. *Educational Psychology in Practice, 24,* 1–12. doi:10.1080/02667360701661165

Snakenborg, J., Van Acker, R., & Gable, R. A. (2011). Cyberbullying: Prevention and intervention to protect our children and youth. *Preventing School Failure: Alternative Education for Children and Youth, 55*(2), 88–95. doi:10.1080/1045988X.2011.539454

Stuart-Cassell, V., Bell, A., & Springer, J. F. (2011). *Analysis of state bullying laws and policies.* Report submitted to the U.S. Department of Education. Retrieved from http://www.ed.gov/about/offices/list/opepd/ppss/index.html

Surdin, A. (2009, January 1). In several states, a push to stem cyber-bullying: Most of the laws focus on schools. *The Washington Post.*

Woods, S., & Wolke, D. (2003). Does the content of anti-bullying policies inform us about the prevalence of direct and relational bullying behaviour in primary schools? *Educational Psychology, 23,* 381–401. doi:10.1080/01443410303215

20 Using Research to Inform Cyberbullying Prevention and Intervention

Donna Cross and Jenny Walker

While bullying and victimization among school-age children continues to be a major public health problem, it is also becoming more predictable and preventable. Extensive observational and experimental research, especially that conducted since the early 1990's, has identified many potential causes and consequences of bullying behaviors. While further research is still needed to understand this phenomenon better, these advances in bullying-related research have contributed to the development of some effective interventions. Even large-scale programs, such as the Finnish *KiVa* program, have demonstrated that it is possible to reduce the prevalence and impact of bullying, including cyberbullying, among school students (Kärnä et al., 2011; Salmivalli, Kärnä, & Poskiparta, 2011; Salmivalli, Kaukiainen, & Voeten, 2005).

In contrast to traditional bullying research, limited quality evidence is available to understand the social context and to identify the temporal sequence of factors and consequences associated with cyberbullying behaviors (Smith et al., 2008). Moreover, this research has not kept pace with the rapidly increasing rate of young people's access to information and communication technology. Analogous to traditional (non-cyber) bullying, and perhaps predictably, cyberbullying seems to be conducted in the presence of peers and is associated with numerous social, emotional, physical, and academic negative outcomes among those who are targeted and those who perpetrate these behaviors (Beran & Li, 2007; Hinduja & Patchin, 2010; Li, 2010; Sourander et al., 2010; Ybarra, Mitchell, Wolak, & Finkelhor, 2006).

Consequently, to understand how to best address this new behavior when planning for cyberbullying prevention and intervention, an important first step is to consider the similarities and differences between traditional bullying and cyberbullying, as both these behaviors manifest within a similar social context. Second, given the ubiquitous nature of social media and other technology use by young people in particular, it is essential that the limited explanatory research conducted to date be used effectively to develop ways to address negative online behaviors. This is especially critical given that policies and interventions/programs, *regardless of the state of evidence related to cyberbullying*, are (perhaps opportunistically) currently being disseminated and implemented in most countries throughout the world because of the need for schools, families, and other community members to do something to address this problem (European Cooperation in Science and Technology (COST, 2011). Hence, the challenge for cyberbullying researchers is to judiciously synthesize (and continue to expand) what qualitative and quantitative evidence is available about possible ways to reduce cyberbullying: to help schools, families, and other community organizations to make decisions and enhance the actions they are taking *now* to help young people, *not necessarily when researchers say they are ready.*

Accordingly, this chapter first discusses how traditional bullying prevention and intervention research can inform ways to reduce cyberbullying behavior, and then proposes a conceptual model (PRECEDE/PROCEED) that can use the current evidence-based understanding to plan and implement prevention and intervention strategies. This conceptual model is then operationalized via a case study describing the formative research undertaken for the *Cyber Friendly Schools* intervention research project conducted in Australia. The chapter concludes with a discussion of what further research is required to support policy and practice to reduce cyberbullying among young people.

What Contribution Can Traditional Bullying Intervention Research Make to Interventions to Reduce Cyberbullying in Young People?

Several studies (mostly cross-sectional) have shown a coexistence of face-to-face and cyberbullying behaviors (e.g. Beran & Li, 2007; Cross et al., 2009; Hinduja & Patchin, 2008; Raskauskas & Stoltz, 2007; Smith et al., 2008; Vandebosch & Van Cleemput, 2009). Young people who are cyberbullied are likely to report being traditionally bullied also, and those who cyberbully others are also more likely to report traditionally bullying others (Cross et al., 2009b; Salmivalli et al., 2011; Smith et al., 2008; Vandebosch & Van Cleemput, 2009). Data from the Australian Covert Bullying Prevalence Study, for example, suggests that 87% of students who were cyberbullied were also bullied in non-cyber ways, and 77% of students who reported they cyberbullied others also reported bullying others in other ways (Cross et al., 2009b).

The overlap between cyber and other types of bullying has some important implications for interventions and suggests that strategies to address non-cyber bullying behaviors may also be beneficial in reducing cyberbullying behaviors. An interesting starting point for cyberbullying intervention research is provided by longitudinal data from the *KiVa* Project in Finland. These data suggest that much of what the whole-school community—educators, parents, and students—are currently doing to prevent and/or reduce traditional bullying may also have some benefit in reducing cyberbullying (Salmivalli et al., 2011). Although the program did not directly address cyberbullying, that behavior decreased along with traditional bullying in schools that implemented the KiVa program.

Various proactive and reactive strategies have been suggested to address traditional bullying, ranging from individual skills-based approaches to class and peer group initiatives. Growing evidence suggests that whole-school interventions that incorporate both preventive and response elements in a complementary manner may be the most effective, nonstigmatizing means to prevent and manage bullying behavior (Cross et al., 2010; Rigby & Slee, 2008; Smith, Ananiadou, & Cowie, 2003; Stevens, Bourdeaudhuij, & Van Oost, 2001; Vreeman & Carroll, 2007). A whole-school approach is collaborative and systematic, targeting bullying and other social behavior at all levels of a school's ecology, including students, parents, teachers, and other school staff, as well as the wider community (Rigby & Slee, 2008).

Some reviews of the effectiveness of traditional bullying interventions have found school-based programs to be modestly successful (Rigby & Slee, 2008; Vreeman & Carroll, 2007). Farrington and Ttofi's (2009b) analyses of 44 of the highest-quality evaluations of school-based bullying programs implemented from 1983 to May 2009 concluded that school-based bullying prevention programs, especially those that provide a comprehensive (whole-school) approach, are the most effective in reducing bullying perpetration and victimization, achieving on average a 20–23% reduction in rates of perpetration, and a 17–20% reduction in rates of victimization.

In their meta-analysis, Farrington and Ttofi (2009a) identified the components of effective school-based traditional bullying programs by correlating program components with weighted mean effect sizes for being bullied and bullying others. The most effective school intervention components found to be associated with a decrease in victimization were the use of videos, disciplinary methods, work with peers, parent training, and cooperative group work. The program components found to be associated with a decrease in bullying perpetration were parent training, improved playground supervision, disciplinary methods, school assemblies, videos, information for parents, classroom rules, and classroom management. Consequently, while classroom activities seem necessary, they may not be sufficient to achieve positive behavior change without other structural and social supports. It will be important to determine which of these components, and what other proactive and reactive strategies unique to cyberbullying behavior, are needed.

The issues that characterize the relationship between technology use and behavior are likely to impact the nature of young people's engagement in and the consequences associated with exposure to cyberbullying in different ways. Interventions to specifically address cyberbullying also need to consider factors such as the increased anonymity and breadth of audience provided by mobile phones and the Internet, as well as young people's potentially unlimited access to their social contacts and technology, and the lack of authority in cyberspace to support students who may be bullied (Falconer, 2010). Moreover, the public anxieties about the detrimental outcomes of cyberbullying, particularly among adolescents, including publicized cases of suicide (Livingstone, 2008), have served to "blame" technology for the problem. This media-fanned panic may encourage technology solutions, such as parental and school-enforced restrictions, when this behavior appears more deeply embedded in relational issues. Inappropriate, imprudent, or poorly planned interventions may lead to iatrogenic outcomes, exacerbating the problem for adolescents.

A planning model such as the social ecological framework (Bronfenbrenner, 1977) provides a structure for educational and ecological supports for actions and conditions needed to address cyberbullying. This multisetting model assumes that bullying behavior is a group phenomenon determined by multiple factors interacting over time (not single factors like technology), and related to factors in the neighborhood, family, school, and/or peers (Urbis Proprietary Limited, 2011). Bullying prevention and intervention strategies organized within this model include the interactions and relationships in a child's life at school (policy, classroom and school climate, behavior support, peer support, school yard improvements); in the classroom (curriculum); in the community; and at home (engaging and involving parents and the wider community); and with peers (Cross, Monks et al., 2010). These combined actions are also called a *whole-school approach* and include proactive and reactive responses generally targeting the following groups of students (Kutash, Duchnowski, & Lynn, 2006; Miller, Eckert, & Mazza, 2009; Urbis Proprietary Limited, 2011):

- Universal or primary prevention interventions *engaging the whole school, families, and the community*. This level of nonstigmatizing intervention can reach a broad range of children and adolescents and can enhance peer support (Barrett, Farrell, Ollendick, & Dadds, 2006; Sawyer et al., 2010; Urbis Proprietary Limited, 2011). At this level, curricular activities can be incorporated into the school program so that all students receive basic information.
- Selective or secondary *interventions engaging students who are identified as being at risk of being victimized or perpetrators of bullying behavior* due to personal, familial, or environmental conditions (Miller et al., 2009; Urbis Proprietary Limited, 2011). These interventions address specific risk factors and are individualized, but the need to screen students for participation may stigmatize students (Anderson & Doyle, 2005).
- Indicated or targeted (tertiary) interventions engaging *students who are experiencing or perpetrating bullying behaviors* to prevent further problems (Jordan, Hindes, & Saklofske, 2009) with highly individualized and specialized programs such as individual intervention plans (Stephens, 2011) and case management (Wyman et al., 2010).

While there is evidence to suggest whole-school programs may be more effective than piecemeal strategies to reduce bullying, their success is often related to the rigor of planning and development, including drawing on quality existing evidence, consulting with the target audience(s) throughout the development process, conducting targeted and systematic pilot tests, maximizing target audience engagement and ownership and providing quality training, and then actively monitoring the delivery and uptake of the intervention (Green & Kreuter, 1991). These planning and pilot phases help to determine the feasibility, appropriateness, and efficaciousness (i.e., achieves short-term cognitive, affective, behavioral, and/ or psychosocial outcomes) of the intervention.

The following section describes how empirical research (such as that currently available for cyberbullying among young people) can be used to plan and develop an intervention within an ecological framework, the organizational context for planning, the planning network and the step-by-step process of developing the intervention, and its implementation and evaluation. This framework, known as PRECEDE-PROCEED (Green & Kreuter, 1991; Windsor, Clark, Boyd, & Goodman, 2004), was the (formative research) planning mechanism used to develop the whole-school intervention tested as part of the Australian *Cyber Friendly School* project (Child Health Promotion Research Centre, 2011).

The three-year Cyber Friendly School project (CFSP) was a group randomized controlled intervention trial conducted in Western Australia from 2010–2012. The study assessed the effectiveness of an innovative student-led universal and targeted school cyberbullying intervention. Thirty-six nongovernment secondary schools (3,382 Grade 8 students—mean age 13 years) were randomly recruited to participate in the project, and then randomly assigned to the intervention and control conditions. The CFSP intervention developed using the PRECEDE-PROCEED model, provided whole-school (including family, peers, and school staff) policy and practice to ameliorate the harms associated with cyberbullying. The intervention was implemented with the assistance of a trained group of Grade 10 Cyber Student Leaders/catalysts (two years older than the study cohort) in cooperation with the trained pastoral care staff and classroom teachers within schools. The online and written educational and environmental strategies were implemented by student leaders, parents/carers, and school staff who were supported with professional learning and training.

Planning Interventions to Address Cyberbullying: The PRECEDE-PROCEED Model

There is consensus that if intervention strategies are based on a careful understanding of relevant theory and systematic approaches to their design, targeting, implementation, and evaluation, there is a greater likelihood that programs will be effective (e.g., Glanz, Lewis, & Rimmer, 1997; Nutbeam & Harris, 1999; World Health Organization, 1996). To successfully reduce cyberbullying, an intervention needs to be grounded, where possible, in theoretical and empirical evidence. Historically, for traditional bullying this evidence has been largely reductionist, focusing on the individual or victim blaming. It typically included understanding the target behavior's:

- magnitude and distribution in the population;
- determinants; and
- the risk and protective factors that may affect intervention opportunities.

Alternatively, ecological approaches view the behavior as a product of the individual and the systems in which they interact (e.g., culture, family, community, and the physical and social environment—online and offline; Bunton & Macdonald, 1992). In an ecological model, these environments need to provide knowledge and skills to enable the target audience to make decisions to engage in positive behavior, and encourage these positive behaviors, while making these behaviors accessible and available. These determinants of behavior provide support for positive behavior change (Minkler, 1989).

This transactional view of behavior posits that behavior is largely controlled or limited by the environment in which it occurs and that to modify behavior, it is necessary to change environmental variables (Green & Kreuter, 1991). Hence, cyberbullying interventions, for example, should seek to empower young people to control the determinants of their online (and offline) behavior. To do so effectively, it needs to fit with the needs of the target audience and the environments to which it is applied. With school-age cyberbullying, for example, this argues strongly for the involvement of young people as co-researchers and major contributors to an intervention's development (Wong, Zimmerman, & Parker, 2010).

An ecological approach for cyberbullying behavior, which is less understood than most behaviors, would require specifying which ecologies can potentially provide the best outcomes. To first "do no harm" and be accountable for possible iatrogenic effects, it may be necessary initially to restrict cyberbullying interventions to selected levels of complex systems (such as delivery through families, peers, and schools); and then second, intervene where actions can with some certainty be appropriately matched with identified needs. These requirements are well served by thorough intervention planning using conceptual frameworks such as the PRECEDE-PROCEED model (Green & Kreuter, 1991; Windsor et al., 2004).

One of the most rigorous data-driven intervention research planning frameworks is the PRECEDE-PROCEED model (Green & Kreuter, 1991; Windsor et al., 2004). This model recognizes that behaviors like cyberbullying are caused by multiple factors; and, as such, these causes must be systematically evaluated to identify the necessary intervention components. The PRECEDE component of the framework (Predisposing, Reinforcing, Enabling Constructs in Educational Diagnosis and Evaluation; Green, 1970) provides a systematic assessment of antecedents or underlying causes of a behavior such as cyberbullying, while the PROCEED or Policy, Regulatory and Organisational Constructs in Educational and Environmental Development recognizes the need for interventions to go beyond traditional educational approaches to change health behaviors. PRECEDE and PROCEED together provide a nine-step planning process (Green & Kreuter, 1991). This chapter addresses only the PRECEDE component of the planning model, Phases one to five, to generate a highly focused set of factors as targets for intervention (for further information, see Green & Kreuter, 1991).

The model below shows a broad representation of the PRECEDE-PROCEED model for planning and evaluation and shows the continuous series of steps in planning, implementation, and evaluation and how this model "begins with the end in mind" (Green & Kreuter, 1991, p. 35).

- Phase 1—Social assessment and situational analysis
- Phase 2—Epidemiological assessment
- Phase 3—Behavioral and environmental assessment
- Phase 4—Educational assessment
- Phase 5—Administrative and policy assessment
- Phases 6 to 9—Implementation and evaluation assessment

As is fundamental for the development of cyberbullying interventions (Spears, Slee, Owens, & Johnson, 2009), the PRECEDE-PROCEED model is based on the principle of participation, such that the target audience—young people for example—are highly involved in identifying and prioritizing problems and developing and implementing intervention components. This is particularly important in cyberbullying intervention development because of young people's technological expertise relative to adults and their knowledge of how other young people are using these technologies (Spears, Slee, Campbell, & Cross, 2011; Third, Richardson, Collin, Rahilly, & Bolzan, 2011). During the *Cyber Friendly Schools Project* (CFSP) young people (and to a lesser extent other members of the target audience: parents and teachers) were empowered as co-researchers to be major contributors to the CFSP intervention planning and development.

Case Study: The Cyber Friendly Schools Project

To illustrate how the PRECEDE-PROCEED intervention research planning model has been applied to develop a cyberbullying intervention, a brief description of its application to the formative development of the Cyber Friendly Schools Project (CFSP) intervention follows. This formative research for the CFSP was conducted from 2007–2010, prior to the project beginning in 2011.

Planning for Cyberbullying Interventions

Phase 1—Social Assessment and Situational Analysis

The Phase 1 social assessment provides an understanding of the needs of the target group and, in the case of the CFSP, determining if cyberbullying is sufficiently problematic to young people (among other quality of life concerns) to warrant further investigation. Qualitative research methods (as discussed in Chapter 10) recommended for the social assessment phase include the use of discussion groups, nominal group process (Delbecq, Van de Ven, & Gustafson, 1986), the Delphi technique (Van de Ven & Delbecq, 1974), focus groups (Basch, 1987), and surveys.

The CFSP social assessment involved two levels of data collection:

1. The Delphi technique was conducted with 22 youth, education, and technology stakeholders to assess their understanding of the reach, impact, and underlying contextual issues associated with cyberbullying among school-age students in Australia.
2. Nineteen focus groups were conducted involving 198 students aged 11 to 15 years. These focus groups were segmented by age and gender, which resulted in diversity across groups rather than within groups (Krueger, 1998).

Findings from the CFSP formative social assessment found cyberbullying to be a significant impairment to young people's quality of life, especially given the large amount of time they spend socializing online. Consistent with other research the CFSP social assessment found:

- Students who are targets of cyberbullying and those who cyberbully others appear to experience considerable mental, emotional, social, physical and conduct and academic problems (e.g., Aoyama, Saxon, & Fearon, 2011; Erdur-Baker & Kavsut, 2007; Hinduja & Patchin, 2010; Kowalski & Limber, 2007; Li, 2010; Sourander et al., 2010; Wang, Nansel, & Iannotti, 2011).
- Students who are targets of cyberbullying experience a high effect-to-danger ratio, such that it contributes great harm, or effect, to the target while minimizing the risk that the perpetrator will be caught, put in danger, or reported for bullying (Bjorkqvist, 1994).
- Greater harm appears to come from being bullied in an online environment related to greater perpetrator anonymity, an unlimited audience, lack of non-verbal communication, 24/7 potential access to target, and because negative online behavior is less able to be noticed by authority figures like parents and/ or teachers (Heirman & Walrave, 2008).
- Picture/video clip cyberbullying appears to have a greater negative impact on students who are bullied in this way (Slonje & Smith, 2008).
- Targets of cyberbullying are less likely to report the bullying to adults and seek necessary help (Dooley, Gradinger, Strohmeier, Cross, & Spiel, 2010; Juvonen & Gross, 2008; Li, 2007; Smith et al., 2008).
- Adults are perceived to be less informed and less helpful about the issues around cyberbullying (Agatston & Limber, 2007; Smith et al., 2008).

- Students fear their computers or mobile phones will be taken away from them if they report cyberbullying to adults, and therefore suffer longer with this behavior before seeking help (National Children's Home, 2002; Patchin & Hinduja, 2006).

Phase 2—Epidemiological Assessment

This phase uses epidemiological data to identify the magnitude and distribution of the behavior (e.g., cyberbullying) in the target audience. An epidemiological assessment is usually conducted using existing data sets. These data show which subgroups are most affected and who is at greatest risk.

The epidemiological assessment for the CFSP involved:

1. The interrogation of prevalence data from other Australian and international research;
2. The secondary analyses of previously collected longitudinal data comprising 13,330 8- to 14-year-old students (Cross et al., 2009b);
3. The collection of additional nationally representative cross-sectional data from over 7,000 Australian students aged 10 to 14 as part of the Australian Covert Bullying Prevalence Study (Cross et al., 2009b);
4. The collection of additional prospective longitudinal data from over 3,000 students in the local community (Cross, Brown, Epstein, & Shaw, 2010).

The Epidemiological Assessment found:

- Estimates of the prevalence of cyberbullying vary considerably across different studies internationally, ranging from 1–62% of students reporting cyber-victimization and 0.8–53% cyber perpetration, largely due to use of different definitions of cyberbullying, the types of media studied, and the reference time period, for example, never, during the last year, last term, etc. (see Smith & Slonje, 2009, for a review).
- Cyberbullying occurs with less frequency than traditional bullying in Australia, but its prevalence is still significant and possibly increasing (e.g., Cross et al., 2009b; Smith, Mahdavi, Carvalho, & Tippett, 2006).
- In Australia, cyberbullying prevalence ranges from approximately 10% to 25% according to students' "global cyberbullying" responses (e.g., how often were you cyberbullied) versus questions addressing specific cyberbullying behaviors (e.g., how often were you sent a nasty text message?) (e.g., Cross et al., 2009b).
- Cyberbullying behavior increases with age, with the most significant increase at transition to secondary school, and the target is slightly more likely to be girls than boys in Australian schools (e.g., Cross et al., 2009b).

- Cyberbullying is more likely to be experienced by students outside of school hours than during school hours (Smith et al., 2008).

Phase 3—Behavioral and Environmental Assessment

This stage identifies the behavioral and environmental risk and protective factors that contribute to the prevalence and the severity of cyberbullying behavior, and investigates why some students bully others and why victims of bullying may be targeted. This phase provides an inventory of influential behavioral and environmental (e.g., organizational and regulatory) factors that are then rated in terms of changeability and importance (e.g., contribute significantly to cyberbullying) to choose the targets for intervention. This stage usually also involves a significant review of the literature via meta-analyses or meta-evaluation.

Given the nascent state of cyberbullying research, the behavioral and environmental assessment for the CFSP involved:

1. A meta-evaluation, where published research was assessed using a multi-method narrative literature review that synthesized cyberbullying-related evidence (Harden et al., 2004; Mays, Pope, & Popay, 2005; Thomas et al., 2004) from primary studies and other gray literature sources to identify risk and protective factors (e.g., Cross et al., 2009b);
2. Reviewing behavioral and environmental data collected previously in longitudinal data sets (Cross et al., 2009b) and the prospective longitudinal data collected from over 3,000 students across Western Australia (Cross, Brown, et al., 2010);
3. Conducting focus groups with 10-15-year-old students;
4. Interviewing teachers and parents via central intercept and focus groups.

The environmental and behavioral assessment identified the following factors as the most changeable and important to address cyberbullying among young Australians aged 11 to 15 years:

For young people who cyberbully: traditionally bullying others (e.g., Cross et al., 2009b); lacking empathic responsiveness (Steffgen & König, 2009); moral approval of cyberbullying (Williams & Guerra, 2007); not feeling safe at school (Sourander et al., 2010); greater access to, more frequent use of, greater dependency on, more positive beliefs about and greater proficiency with technology (Hinduja & Patchin, 2008; Smith et al., 2008); parents who are less involved with monitoring/understanding children's computer and Internet use (Vandebosch & Van Cleemput, 2009); perceptions of their friends as not trustworthy, or caring and helpful (Williams & Guerra, 2007).

For young people who are cyberbullied by others: feeling less popular (Vandebosch & Van Cleemput, 2009); being a target of traditional bullying (König, Gollwitzer, & Steffgen, 2010); not feeling safe at school (Sourander et al., 2010); a lack of knowledge of cyber safety (Agatston & Limber, 2007); transition from primary to secondary school (Cross et al., 2009b; Pellegrini et al., 2009; Rigby, 1997); emotional and peer problems; lack of cyber safety skills such as maintaining privacy, for example, not sharing passwords, inadequate knowledge of how to use the Internet safely such as settings in Facebook, poor help-seeking behavior (Avery, 1974; Sandels, 1974; Schieber & Thompson, 1996); bystanders not providing support (Gini, Pozzoli, Borghi, & Franzoni, 2008).

Phase 4—Educational Assessment

Using the social, health, behavioral, and environmental factors associated with cyberbullying among students aged 10 to 15 years collected in phases 1–3, Phase 4 assesses three levels of the antecedents of the behaviors and environmental factors that affect the target population: namely, predisposing, reinforcing, and enabling factors.

1. Predisposing factors are mostly psych-social factors that occur prior to the (cyberbullying) behavior and provide motivation to engage in the behavior (e.g., knowledge, feelings, beliefs, values, and self-confidence and self efficacy; plus age, gender, SES, ethnicity, personality, etc.);
2. Reinforcing factors occur after the (cyberbullying) behavior is performed (e.g., positive or negative consequences, reactions or feedback from peers, and other significant others) that encourages or discourages the behavior from being repeated;
3. Enabling factors also occur prior to the (cyberbullying) behavior and support a student's motivation to act. These include skills or actions by an individual, and organizational factors such as availability and affordability.

The educational assessment for the CFSP involved:

Focus groups and interviews conducted with students, teachers, and parents, as described previously, to identify which predisposing, enabling, and reinforcing factors should be addressed in the intervention. Also, a student leaders' day-long summit involving over 200 15-year-old students was conducted to determine what young people believe other young people, adults, schools, Government and Industry should do to reduce cyberbullying. The Summit gave students the opportunity to identify predisposing, enabling, and reinforcing factors relating to cyberbullying prevention and intervention via group interviews and electronic voting technology (Cross et al., 2010).

The educational assessment for CFSP identified the following predisposing, reinforcing, and enabling factors as needing to be addressed for cyberbullying prevention and intervention: *Predisposing factors included* children's and parents' lack of knowledge about cyber safety behavior and a perception of low risk of harm while using ICT; lacking empathic responsiveness; moral approval of cyberbullying; not feeling safe at school.

Enabling factors included young people and parents' (and other adults') inability to identify the safest ways to use the Internet and mobile phones; adults' poorly developed ICT skills; young people's lack of confidence (social and due to poor adult efficacy) to talk to trusted adults for help; greater access to, more frequent use of, greater dependency on, and greater proficiency with technology; less frequent involvement and monitoring by parents/caregivers generally and with regard to young people's computer and Internet use.

Reinforcing factors included parents allowing children to use the Internet and mobile phones with low levels of monitoring, and their perception that their children have adequate abilities to use the Internet and mobile phones safely; having friends who cyberbully/bully others/are bullied/cyberbullied; traditionally bullying others/being a target of traditional bullying; feeling less popular; peers supporting cyberbullying and not acting to support students who are victimized.

Phase 5—Administrative and Policy Assessment

This stage identifies the policies, time, staffing support, and other resources and circumstances in schools, homes, and communities that could most significantly hinder or facilitate implementation of the intervention. This phase for CFSP identified factors such as the crowded/competing curriculum; school priorities other than cyberbullying; and limited school resources, including time, staff commitment to the intervention, staff capacity to implement cyberbullying programs, and busy parents.

Planning Implications for the CFSP Intervention

These PRECEDE findings were applied to the CFSP intervention by:

- Targeting students from age 12 onward, immediately following their transition to secondary school;
- Encouraging a whole-school action to develop a positive social environment and ethos that encourages and empowers students to take positive action to help when they see bullying online and offline;
- Explicitly linking cyberbullying with the schools' traditional bullying policies and programs;
- Helping schools to develop or review their school policy/ies addressing cyberbullying, including how students can report cyberbullying and clear, consistent steps for staff to respond to cyberbullying reports;

- Ensuring cyberbullying prevention knowledge and skills were addressed explicitly in classroom and home intervention programs;
- Providing selective and indicated (Miller, Eckert, & Mazza, 2009) intervention strategies for both students who are victimized and those who cyberbully others;
- Training and education for school staff to raise awareness of and skills to prevent and respond to cyberbullying (including cyber safety education);
- Providing 8–10 hours/year of online curriculum and self-paced support for students to develop their social competency online, including social decision making to help them deal with relational difficulties;
- Encouraging students to develop and practice specific online skills in contexts relevant to the students' online experiences, where judgments and responses are best learned in the situations in which they occur, or close re-creations of these;
- Including curriculum that addressed empathy building, moral development, digital citizenship and respecting the privacy of self and others, and the use of pictures/videos online;
- Addressing help-seeking and help-provision strategies, including providing skill to peers to provide positive support to others online and offline;
- Providing opportunities for students to learn about safer and positive social uses of technology;
- Increasing parents' understanding of the developmental and behavioral characteristics of children that increase their vulnerability when online, and providing parents with strategies to monitor, model, and teach cyber safety skills to their children;
- Helping students to communicate with their parents and other family members about cyberbullying; and
- Linking participants to government cyber safety initiatives.

FUTURE RESEARCH DIRECTIONS

Despite young people's increasing access to ICT, there is still much to learn about how to intervene to reduce and prevent cyberbullying. Consistently in research to-date, there is negligible discussion concerning the theoretical structure of cyberbullying and the relative importance of the factors unique to this behavior. For example, during cyberbullying the social goals for the aggressor may be less tangible and delayed, whereas in traditional bullying situations the effect is often immediately observable to the aggressor, such as in the facial expressions of the target of the bullying (Dooley, Pyalski, & Cross, 2009).

Reviews of traditional bullying interventions have generally found them to be more effective among younger age groups (Rigby & Slee, 2008), although Farrington and Ttofi (2009b) found that interventions were more effective with the increasing age of the students. Further research is needed to understand what ages are critical developmental and behavioral windows to prevent and/or intervene to reduce cyberbullying. Are cyberbullying interventions, for example, best delivered prior to the secondary school transition that is associated with a spike in traditional bullying rates (Cross et al., 2009a; Pellegrini et al., 2009; Rigby, 1997), and when students are also likely to be adjusting to new accessibility to technology (i.e., first phone, laptop for schoolwork, SNS profile etc.)?

When considering who to target, cyberbullying research has to-date been largely limited to mainstream populations. Future research needs to consider other population groups, such as special needs students, students who are geographically isolated, or cultural groups who may be more vulnerable.

Given that cyberbullying appears to occur in the context of social groups and relationships (Mishna, Saini, & Solomon, 2009), bystanders represent a critical group to consider in prevention and intervention strategies. Further research is required to investigate bystander (participant) roles and ways to engage bystanders to help cyberbullying targets, ways in which bystanders can best intervene in cyberbullying incidents, and what is likely to increase the odds of cyber bystanders intervening. There may be, for example, many more opportunities for bystander intervention given cyberbullying often involves a greater breadth of audience than traditional bullying.

Given even fewer young people seem willing to talk with an adult about cyberbullying than the proportion who report talking to adults about traditional bullying, more in-depth qualitative research is needed to understand why students are less willing to tell adults and what types of support young people need from peers, family, and other trusted adults. For instance, because adults may be less proficient with the technology, would students report cyberbullying to adults more for emotional support than practical help? Would students' likelihood of reporting cyberbullying differ according to the type of teacher—whether the teacher is younger and technologically savvy, for example?

Although some research is available (Campbell, Butler, & Kift, 2008), a deeper understanding is required of the impact of regulatory actions such as new laws, school policies, and procedures to prevent and respond to cyberbullying. Schools need significantly more guidance in developing appropriate targeted case management procedures to respond to cyberbullying incidents because of the technical challenges posed by cyberbullying, its distribution, location, and the possible lack of access to the perpetrator (due to anonymity, for example).

Last, process-based research is critically needed to understand the best ways to engage young people in this intervention research development process. During the formative evaluation process conducted for the CFSP, students genuinely wanted to contribute. They felt they had much to offer, saw their role in addressing cyberbullying as important, and were surprised that they weren't asked to do this more often.

"It surprised me that parents and adults now need and trust us kids to make a difference." Student Participant, Cyber Friendly Student Summit 2008

SUMMARY

While there is an urgent need to investigate ways to effectively prevent and respond to cyberbullying behaviors, evidence from traditional bullying intervention research may be an important first response to cyberbullying until more specific and in-depth evidence becomes available. The new and emerging cyberbullying evidence, however, is beginning to help distinguish some important understandings about behavioral and environmental factors that may help to reduce cyberbullying and its harms.

Synthesizing and applying the available evidence in a rigorous and systematic way using an intervention planning framework, such as provided with the PRECEDE-PROCEED model, can help to distinguish the most changeable and important developmental and behavioral targets for cyberbullying prevention and intervention. The advanced technological knowledge among young people, compared to earlier generations, means it is imperative to partner with young people in the research and intervention delivery process, including their understandings and perceptions of cyberbullying as well as their recommendations for effective strategies to address this behavior and its consequences.

Nonetheless, further research is needed without delay to investigate issues such as the theoretical nature and structure of cyberbullying and the relative importance of the factors unique to this behavior; the critical developmental and behavioral windows to prevent and/or intervene to reduce cyberbullying, especially with non-mainstream and other potentially vulnerable populations; as well as ways to encourage help-seeking and help-provision, especially from bystanders. Moreover, as communication technology and its use continues to flourish exponentially, and young people become even more cyber immersed for communication and relationships and recreation, intervention research will need to be anticipatory and nimble to provide relevant prevention and intervention strategies to support young people's decision making and positive social action.

References

Agatston, P. W., & Limber, S. (2007). Students' perspectives on cyber bullying. *Journal of Adolescent Health, 41*, S59–S60. doi:10.1016/j.jadohealth.2007.09.003

Anderson, S., & Doyle, M. (2005). Intervention and prevention programs to support student mental health: The literature and examples from the MindMatters Plus initiative. *Australian Journal of Guidance and Counselling, 15*(2), 220–227. doi:10.1375/ajgc.15.2.220

Aoyama, I., Saxon, T. F., & Fearon, D. D. (2011). Internalizing problems among cyberbullying victims and moderator effects of friendship quality. *Multicultural Education & Technology Journal, 5*(2), 92–105. doi:10.1108/17504971111142637

Avery, G. (1974). The capacity of young children to cope with the traffic system: A review. New South Wales, Australia: Traffic Accident Research Unit, Department of Motor Transport.

Barrett, P. M., Farrell, L. J., Ollendick, T. H., & Dadds, M. (2006). Long-term outcomes of an Australian universal prevention trial of anxiety and depression symptoms in children and youth: An evaluation of the friends program. *Journal of Clinical Child and Adolescent Psychology, 35*(3), 403–411.

Basch, C.E. (1987). Focus group interview: An underutilized research technique for improving theory and practice in health education. *Health Education & Behavior, 14*(4), 411. doi:10.1177/109019818701400404

Beran, T.T., & Li, Q. (2007). The relationship between cyberbullying and school bullying. *Journal of Student Wellbeing, 1*(2), 15–33.

Bjorkqvist, K. (1994). Sex differences in physical, verbal and indirect aggression: A review of recent research. *Sex Roles, 30*, 177–188. doi:10.1007/BF01420988

Bronfenbrenner, U. (1977). Towards an experimental ecology of human development. *American Psychologist, 32*, 513–530. doi:10.1037/0003–066X.32.7.513

Bunton, R., & Macdonald, G. (1992). *Health promotion: Disciplines and diversity.* London: Routledge. doi:10.4324/9780203412848

Campbell, M., Butler, D., & Kift, S. (2008). A school's duty to provide a safe learning environment: Does this include cyberbullying? *Australia and New Zealand Journal of Law and Education, 13*(2), 21–32.

Child Health Promotion Research Centre. (2011). An empirical intervention to reduce cyberbullying in adolescents. Annual report to Healthway. Perth, Western Australia: Edith Cowan University, Child Health Promotion Research Centre.

Cross, D., Brown, D., Epstein, M., & Shaw, T. (2010). Cyber friendly schools project: Strengthening school and families' capacity to reduce the academic, social, and emotional harms secondary students' experience from cyber bullying (CFSP (PEET)). Perth, Western Australia: Child Health Promotion Research Centre, Edith Cowan University.

Cross, D., Monks, H., Hall, M., Shaw, T., Pintabona, Y., Erceg, E., . . . Lester, L. (2011). Three year results of the Friendly Schools whole-of-school intervention on Children's bullying behavior. *British Educational Research Journal, 37*(1), 105–129.

Cross, D., Shaw, T., Hearn, L., Epstein, M., Monks, H., Lester, L, & Thomas, L. (2009). Australian Covert Bullying Prevalence Study (ACBPS). Western Australia: Report prepared for the Department of Education, Employment and Workplace Relations (DEEWR).

Delbecq, A.L., Van de Ven, A.H., & Gustafson, D.H. (1986). *Group techniques for program planning: A guide to nominal group and Delphi processes.* Middleton, WI: Green Briar Press.

Dooley, J.J., Gradinger, P., Strohmeier, D., Cross, D., & Spiel, C. (2010). Cyber-victimization: The association between help-seeking behaviors and self-reported emotional symptoms in Australia and Austria. *Australian Journal of Guidance and Counselling, 20*(2), 194–209. doi:10.1375/ajgc.20.2.194

Dooley, J.J., Pyalski, J., & Cross, D. (2009). Cyberbullying versus face-to-face bullying. *Zeitschrift für Psychologie/Journal of Psychology, 217*(4), 182–188. doi:10.1027/0044–3409.217.4.182

Erdur-Baker, O., & Kavsut, F. (2007). Cyber bullying: A new face of peer bullying. *Eğitim Araştırmaları—Eurasian Journal of Educational Research, 7*(26), 31–42.

European Cooperation in Science and Technology (COST). COST ACTION IS0801—Cyber bullying: Coping with negative and enhancing positive uses of technologies, in relationships in educational settings, 2009–2012. Retrieved from http://sites.google.com/site/costis0801/

Falconer, S. (2010). *Reality bytes: Characteristics of bullying in the cyber and non-cyber environments.* Unpublished Thesis, Edith Cowan University, Perth.

Farrington, D.P., & Ttofi, M.M. (2009a). Reducing school bullying: Evidence-based implications for policy. *Crime and Justice, 38*(1), 281–345.

Farrington, D.P., & Ttofi, M.M. (2009b). School-based programs to reduce bullying and victimization. *Campbell Systematic Reviews*. Oslo: The Campbell Collaboration.

Gini, G., Pozzoli, T., Borghi, F., & Franzoni, L. (2008). The role of bystanders in students' perception of bullying and sense of safety. *Journal of School Psychology, 46*, 617–638. doi:10.1064/jsp.2008.02.001

Glanz, K., Lewis, F.M., & Rimmer, B.K. (1997). *Health behavior and health education: Theory, research and practice* (2nd ed.). San Francisco: Jossey-Bass Inc.

Green, L.W. (1970). Identifying and overcoming barriers to the diffusion of knowledge about family planning. *Advances in Fertility Control, 5*(2), 21–29.

Green, L., & Kreuter, M. (1991). *Health promotion planning: An educational and environmental approach*. Mountain View, CA: Mayfield Publishing Company.

Harden, A., Garcia, J., Oliver, S., Rees, R., Shepherd, J., Brunton, G., & Oakley, A. (2004). Applying systemetic review methods to study people's views: An example from public health. *Journal of Epidemiology and Community Health, 58*(9), 794–800. doi:10.1136/jech.2003.014829

Heirman, W., & Walrave, M. (2008). Assessing concerns and issues about the mediation of technology in cyberbullying. *Cyberpsychology: Journal of Psychosocial Research on Cyberspace, 2*(2), 1–12.

Hinduja, S., & Patchin, J.W. (2008). Cyberbullying: An exploratory analysis of factors related to offending and victimization. *Deviant Behavior, 29*(2), 129–156. doi:10.1080/01639620701457816

Hinduja, S., & Patchin, J.W. (2010). Bullying, cyberbullying, and suicide. *Archives of Suicide Research, 14*(3), 206–221. doi:10.1080/13811118.2010.494133

Jordan, J.J., Hindes, Y.L., & Saklofske, D.H. (2009). School psychology in Canada: A survey of roles and functions, challenges and aspirations. *Canadian Journal of School Psychology, 24*(3), 20. doi:10.1177/0829573509338614

Juvonen, J., & Gross, E.F. (2008). Extending the school grounds?: Bullying experiences in cyber space. *Journal of School Health, 78*(9), 496–505. doi:10.1111/j.1746-1561.2008.00335.x

Kärnä, A., Voeten, M., Little, T.D., Poskiparta, E., Kaljonen, A., & Salmivalli, C. (2011). A large-scale evaluation of the KiVa antibullying program: Grades 4–6. *Child development, 82*(1), 311–330. doi:10.1111/j.1467-8624.2010.01557.x

König, A., Gollwitzer, M., & Steffgen, G. (2010). Cyberbullying as an act of revenge? *Australian Journal of Guidance and Counselling, 20*(2), 210–224. doi:10.1375/ajgc.20.2.210

Kowalski, R.M., & Limber, S.P. (2007). Electronic bullying among middle school students. *Journal of Adolescent Health, 41*, S22–S30. doi:10.1016/j.jadohealth.2007.08.017

Krueger, R.A. (1998). *Moderating focus groups* (Vol. 4). London: Sage Publications.

Kutash, K., Duchnowski, A.J., & Lynn, N. (2006). *School-based mental health: An empirical guide for decision-makers*. The Research & Training Center for Children's Mental Health, Louis de la Parte Florida Mental Health Institute, University of Florida.

Li, Q. (2007). New bottle but old wine: A research of cyberbullying in schools. *Computers in Human Behavior, 23*(4), 1777–1791. doi:10.1016/j.chb.2005.10.005

Li, Q. (2010). Cyberbullying in high schools: A study of students' behaviors and beliefs about this new phenomenon. *Journal of Aggression, Maltreatment & Trauma, 19*(4), 372–392. doi:10.1080/10926771003788979

Livingstone, S. (2008). Taking risky opportunities in youthful content creation: Teenagers' use of social networking sites for intimacy, privacy and self-expression. *New Media & Society, 10*(3), 393. doi:10.1177/1461444808089415

Mays, N., Pope, C., & Popay, J. (2005). Systematically reviewing qualitative and quantitative evidence to inform management and policy making in the health field. *Journal of Health Services Research and Policy, 10*(Suppl. 1), 6–20. doi:10.1258/1355819054308576

Miller, D. N., Eckert, T. L., & Mazza, J. J. (2009). Suicide prevention programs in the schools: A review and public health perspective. *School Psychology Review, 38*(2), 168–188.

Minkler, M. (1989). Health education, health promotion and the open society: A historical perspective. *Health Education & Behavior, 16*(1), 17–30. doi:10.1177/109019818901600105

National Children's Home. (2002). 1 in 4 children are the victims of "on-line bullying." Retrieved from http://www.nch.org.uk/information/index.php?i=237

Nutbeam, D., & Harris, E. (1999). *Theory in a nutshell: A guide to health promotion theory*. Sydney, NSW: McGraw-Hill.

Patchin, J. W., & Hinduja, S. (2006). Bullies move beyond the schoolyard: A preliminary look at cyberbullying. *Youth Violence and Juvenile Justice, 4*(2), 148–169.

Pellegrini, A. D., Long, J. D., Solberg, D., Roseth, C., Dupuis, D., Bohn, C., & Hickey, M. (2009). Bullying and social status during school transitions. In S. Jimerson, S. Swearer, & D. Espelage (Eds.), *Handbook of bullying in schools: An international perspective*. Hoboken, NJ: Routledge.

Raskauskas, J., & Stoltz, A. D. (2007). Involvement in traditional and electronic bullying among adolescents. *Developmental Psychology, 43*, 564–575. doi:10.1037/0012-1649.43.3.564

Rigby, K. (1997). What children tell us about bullying in schools. *Children Australia, 22*(2), 28–34.

Rigby, K., & Slee, P. (2008). Interventions to reduce bullying. *International Journal of Adolescent Medicine and Health, 20*(2), 165–183. doi:10.1515/IJAMH.2008.20.2.165

Salmivalli, C., Kärnä, A., & Poskiparta, E. (2011). Counteracting bullying in Finland: The KiVa program and its effects on different forms of being bullied. *International Journal of Behavioral Development, 35*(5), 405–411. doi:10.1177/0165025411407457

Salmivalli, C., Kaukiainen, A., & Voeten, M. (2005). Anti-bullying intervention: Implementation and outcome. *British Journal of Educational Psychology, 75*(3), 465–487. doi:10.1348/000709905X26011

Sandels, S. (1974). Why are children injured in traffic? The Skandia Report 2. Stockholm: Skandia Insurance Company.

Sawyer, M. G., Pfeiffer, S., Spence, S. H., Bond, L., Graetz, B., Kay, D., . . . Sheffield, J. (2010). School-based prevention of depression: A randomised controlled study of the Beyondblue schools research initiative. *Journal of Child Psychology and Psychiatry, 51*(2), 199–209. doi:10.1111/j.1469–7610.2009.02136.x

Schieber, R., & Thompson, N. (1996). Developmental risk factors for childhood pedestrian injuries. *Injury Prevention Journal, 2*, 228–236.

Slonje, R., & Smith, P. K. (2008). Cyberbullying: Another main type of bullying? *Scandinavian Journal of Psychology, 49*(2), 147–154. doi:10.1111/j.1467–9450.2007.00611.x

Smith, P. K., Ananiadou, K., & Cowie, H. (2003). Interventions to reduce school bullying. *Canadian Journal of Psychiatry, 48*, 591–599.

Smith, P. K., Mahdavi, J., Carvalho, M., Fisher, S., Russell, S., & Tippett, N. (2008). Cyberbullying: Its nature and impact in secondary school pupils. *Journal of Child Psychology and Psychiatry, 49*(4), 376–385. doi:10.1111/j.1469–7610.2007.01846.x

Smith, P. K., Mahdavi, J., Carvalho, M., & Tippett, N. (2006). An investigation into cyberbullying, its forms, awareness and impact, and the relationship between age and gender in cyberbullying. Research Brief No. RBX03–06. London: Department for Education and Skills.

Smith, P. K., & Slonje, R. (2009). Cyberbullying: The nature and extent of a new kind of bullying, in and out of school. In S. Jimerson, S. Swearer, & D. Espelage (Eds.), *Handbook of bullying in schools: An international perspective*. Hoboken, NJ: Routledge.

Sourander, A., Klomek, A. B., Ikonen, M., Lindroos, J., Luntamo, T., Koskelainen, M., . . . Helenius, H. (2010). Psychosocial risk factors associated with cyberbullying among adolescents. *Archives of General Psychiatry, 67*(7), 720–728. doi:10.1001/archgenpsychiatry.2010.79

Spears, B., Slee, P., Campbell, M. A., & Cross, D. (2011). Education change and youth voice: Informing school action on cyberbullying. Centre for Strategic Education, Occasional Paper 208.

Spears, B., Slee, P., Owens, L., & Johnson, B. (2009). Behind the scenes and screens: Insights into the human dimension of covert and cyberbullying. *Zeitschrift für Psychologie/Journal of Psychology, 217*(4), 189. doi:10.1027/0044–3409.217.4.189

Steffgen, G., & König, A. (2009, 13th–15th May). *Cyber bullying: The role of traditional bullying and empathy*. Paper presented at The Good, the Bad, and the Challenging: The User and the Future of Information and Communication Technologies (COST Action 298), Copenhagen, Denmark.

Stephens, P. (2011). Preventing and confronting school bullying: A comparative study of two national programmes in Norway. *British Educational Research Journal, 37*(3), 381–404. doi:10.1080/01411921003692868

Stevens, V., Bourdeaudhuij, I. D., & Van Oost, P. (2001). Anti-bullying interventions at school aspects of programme adaptation and critical issues for further programme development. *Health Promotion International, 16*(2), 155–167. doi:10.1093/heapro/16.2.155

Third, A., Richardson, I., Collin, P., Rahilly, K., & Bolzan, N. (2011). Intergenerational attitudes towards social networking and cybersafety: A living lab. Melbourne, AUS: Cooperative Research Centre for Young People, Technology and Wellbeing.

Thomas, J., Harden, A., Oakley, A., Oliver, S., Sutcliffe, K., Rees, R. . . . Kavanagh, J. (2004). Integrating qualitative research with trials in systematic reviews. *British Medical Journal, 328*(7446), 1010–1018. doi:10.1136/bmj.328.7446.1010

Urbis Proprietary Limited. (2011). The psychological and emotional wellbeing needs of children and young people: Models of effective practice—Final Report Prepared for the Department of Education and Communities. Canberra, AUS: Department of Education and Communities.

Vandebosch, H., & Van Cleemput, K. (2009). Cyberbullying among youngsters: Profiles of bullies and victims. *New Media and Society, 11*, 1349–1371.

Van de Ven, A. H., & Delbecq, A. L. (1974). The effectiveness of nominal, Delphi, and interacting group decision making processes. *Academy of Management Journal*, 605–621.

Vreeman, R. C., & Carroll, A. E. (2007). A systematic review of school-based interventions to prevent bullying. *Archives of Pediatric and Adolescent Medicine, 161*, 78–88. doi:10.1001/archpedi.161.1.78

Wang, J., Nansel, T. R., & Iannotti, R. J. (2011). Cyber and traditional bullying: Differential association with depression. *Journal of Adolescent Health, 48*(4), 415–417. doi:10.1016/j.jadohealth.2010.07.012

Williams, K.R., & Guerra, N.G. (2007). Prevalence and predictors of Internet bullying. *Journal of Adolescent Health, 41*, S14–S21. doi:10.1016/j.jadohealth.2007.08.018

Windsor, R., Clark, N., Boyd, N., & Goodman, R. (2004). *Evaluation of health promotion, health education and disease prevention programs* (3rd ed.). Boston: McGraw Hill Humanities.

Wong, N.T., Zimmerman, M.A., & Parker, E.A. (2010). A typology of youth participation and empowerment for child and adolescent health promotion. *American Journal of Community Psychology*, 1–15.

World Health Organization. (1996). Promoting health through schools. The World Health Organization's global school health initiative. Geneva: World Health Organization.

Wyman, P.A., Brown, C.H., LoMurray, M., Schmeelk-Cone, K., Petrova, M., Yu, Q. . . . Wang, W. (2010). An outcome evaluation of the Sources of Strength suicide prevention program delivered by adolescent peer leaders in high schools. *American Journal of Public Health, 100*(9), 1653. doi:10.2105/AJPH.2009.190025

Ybarra, M.L., Mitchell, K.J., Wolak, J., & Finkelhor, D. (2006). Examining characteristics and associated distress related to internet harassment: Findings from the second youth internet survey. *Pediatrics, 118*(4), e1169–e1177. doi:10.1542/peds.2006–0815

Part VII
Going Forward

21 Future Research Questions in Cyberbullying

Jina Yoon

In the last decade, research on cyberbullying has provided much needed knowledge about this relatively new form of bullying. Earlier studies documented prevalence and developmental patterns (e.g., age and gender) of cyberbullying among children (Kowalski & Limber, 2007; Williams & Guerra, 2007; Ybarra & Mitchell, 2004). Research findings also identified a number of correlates of cybervictimization, including depression (Patchin & Hinduja, 2006; Perren, Dooley, Shaw, & Cross, 2010), anxiety (Dempsey, Sulkowski, & Nichols, 2009), and suicidal ideation (Hinduja & Patchin, 2010). Along with cyberbullying cases that have been widely publicized by the popular media, these studies have alerted us to the significance of hostile, aggressive behaviors using communication technology among children and adolescents. As the field pushes this research area forward, researchers must address the many challenges in studying cyberbullying, as have been outlined throughout the other chapters of this book. This chapter explores possible research questions that would stimulate future research efforts and thus contribute to ongoing theory building and intervention/prevention efforts against cyberbullying.

CONCEPTUAL UNDERSTANDING SHAPED BY EMPIRICAL DATA

Conceptually, we do not distinguish bullying and victimization experiences by the location of its occurrence (e.g., hallway, playground, etc.). We know that the pattern of peer interactions is stable across settings, and thus expect the power imbalance and hostile and hurtful behaviors to be exhibited in a similar way in cyberspace, just as we expect bullying behaviors to be consistent across other locations: hallways, the playgrounds and the cafeteria, the school bus, the classroom. The question is whether cyberbullying is an extension of traditional bullying that surfaces as children gradually gain access to communication technology, or whether it is a unique form of bullying that involves distinct processes and dynamics, requiring a different conceptualization from how we view traditional bullying.

A number of studies suggested that those who bully others face to face also engage in cyberbullying, and that traditional victims are also victimized by others in cyberspace (Hinduja & Patchin, 2009; Raskauskas & Stoltz, 2007). These findings seem to support the idea that cyberbullying is an extension of traditional bullying. In contrast, Ybarra, Diener-West, and Leaf (2007) found that most adolescents who reported online harassment were not bullied at school, suggesting that there might be a group of youth who are victimized online only. Furthermore, it has been argued that some cyberbullies are victims of traditional bullying (Hinduja & Patchin, 2010) who use electronic means to retaliate against their traditional perpetrators. Current research relies heavily on cross-sectional studies and correlational designs, and is therefore limited in explaining the ways that cyberbullying and traditional bullying may emerge over time and interact across different contexts (e.g., classroom and texts). Longitudinal studies that examine a pattern of online and traditional bullying and victimization are needed to shed light on the relation between cyberbullying and traditional bullying.

PATTERN OF TRADITIONAL BULLYING AND CYBERBULLYING: PERSON-CENTERED APPROACH

As indicated above, one of the consistent findings is a significant overlap between cyberbullying and traditional, face-to-face bullying (e.g., $r = .54$ in Taiariol, Yoon, Hillman, & Markman, 2010). However, we know little about the pattern of experiences involving different types of bullying (physical, verbal, social, and cyber) among students at different ages. To date, the dominant analysis in bullying research has been the variable-centered approach, measuring physical, verbal, social, and cyberbullying independently.

Using a cluster analysis, Dollar, Yoon, Taiariol, Hillman, and Markman (2011) identified three groups of students who are engaged in different levels of bullying and victimization: "noninvolved," those who are not involved in any bullying experiences; "occasional victims," those who are occasional victims of social and verbal bullying once or twice during the school year; and "bully-victims," those who are victims of physical, verbal, and social bullying once a week and of cyberbullying once or twice during the school year as well as bullying others using all types (physical, verbal, social, and cyber) once or twice during the school year. This study involved a small sample of 7th and 8th grade students, and the level of reported cyberbullying was low. However, an important point is that there seems to be a group of students who share the similar levels of bullying and victimization across different types, and that cyberbullying was reported along with other forms of bullying. There might be other subgroups of children who represent different a combination of bullying and victimization experiences. For example, is there a group of children who engage in verbal bullying and cyberbullying? Do these children differ in their characteristics from those children who engage in physical bullying? In the traditional bullying literature, the perpetrator-target group has been described as possessing a set of characteristics (e.g. impulsive, reactive, and aggressive) compared to the perpetrator group and target group (See Sekol & Farrington, 2010, for a review). Future research is warranted to investigate different groups of children who are involved in traditional bullying and cyberbullying and to examine characteristics that describe each group. If there are distinctive features associated with those who bully others across different settings including cyberspace versus those who are limited to traditional bullying or cyberbullying, these features could be quite informative in developing more targeted intervention and prevention programs. For example, empirically identified groups may differ in outcomes and adjustments after bullying incidents, allowing us to identify those students who are more prone to depressive symptoms and exhibit low coping and impulsivity, and further allowing us to predict those who are more vulnerable for suicide.

It has been suggested that the effects of cyberbullying are more harmful than traditional bullying (Campbell, 2005; Raskauskas & Stoltz, 2007). Based on the potential to reach wide audiences and the speed of circulation, it certainly makes sense that cyberbullying has potentially devastating impacts on youth, but the existing studies do not provide a clear answer as to whether cyberbullying is more harmful than traditional bullying. Studies that directly compare cyberbullying and traditional bullying would address this question. Given a correlation between these two bullying types, negative adjustment indicators associated with cyberbullying do not provide a clear picture of a unique contribution of cyberbullying and cybervictimization. As seen in perpetrator-target groups, the greatest adjustment difficulties are expected among those students who are involved in bullying and victimization across different contexts (traditional and cyber).

CYBERBULLYING IN DEVELOPMENTAL PERSPECTIVE

According to the Internet and American Life Project, Parent-Teen Survey (Pew Research Center, 2009), 93% of teens use the Internet, 78% are on Facebook and other social network sites, and 72% text. These numbers simply attest that cyberspace and online communication have become a major context of adolescents' social life. Only a few studies have examined the effects of online communication on different aspects of adolescent development (see Valkenburg & Peter, 2011, for a review), and we are beginning to get a glimpse of how adolescents socialize in cyberspace. Valkenburg and Peter (2011) argue that online communication provides opportunities for adolescents to accomplish three important developmental tasks: identity, intimacy, and sexuality. Their review of the current literature suggests that online communication is related to positive outcomes, including self-esteem (Schmitt, Dayanim, Matthias, 2008), quality of existing friendships (Valkenburg & Peter, 2007), and sexual self-exploration (Subrahmanyam, Greenfield, & Tynes, 2004). These studies suggest that many adolescents take advantage of online communication and demonstrate healthy social interactions in cyberspace, despite the digital world often being characterized as challenging and dangerous. This is an important point to remember as we investigate cyberbullying and try to identify ways to prevent and intervene. We have a lot to learn about adolescents' normal behaviors and social interactions in cyberspace and online communication in our understanding of cyberbullying. For example, how do adolescents use technology in their socialization? What is the role of Facebook and other social network sites on peer reputations and peer groups? How do adolescents negotiate online conflicts? In particular, we need to know how adolescents exercise self-control and moral reasoning in cyberspace where additional challenges such as immediacy and anonymity are expected. With these understandings of normal online behaviors, we could identify specific risks for cyberbullying, and thus find ways to target the risks in our prevention and intervention efforts.

Another interesting issue is a developmental pattern of cyberbullying and cybervictimization over time. It is possible that the pattern of bullying experiences is different depending on the developmental stage. As children get older and increase their engagement with technology, cyberspace becomes another context within which bullying perpetration occurs, and many questions arise. Do they change their forms of cyberbullying over the course of a developmental period (e.g., middle childhood vs. early adolescence vs. late adolescence)? As different communication technology tools become available to them, how do children's individual characteristics interact with these tools over time? Are there any risk factors for cyberbullying specific for certain developmental stages? For example, it is possible that a context of a clique in early adolescence serves as a risk factor for cyberbullying whereas romantic relationships at a later adolescence present challenges. As we explore these questions, we will gain insight as to how children's experiences in cyberbullying shape and change, leading to better understanding of a developmental pattern of bullying experiences in the context of peer relationships over time.

Cyberspace is a unique social context for interpersonal exchange that requires a level of social sophistication, social awareness, and social skills as well as technological knowledge. Online communication often involves truncated or limited information and lacks cues and feedback that may be available in face-to-face interactions, such as facial expressions, gestures, and emotional tones. One area of research that warrants attention is how children and adolescents perceive, problem solve, and respond to social situations in this challenging context, and how these ways of interaction sometimes lead to cyberbullying and cybervictimization. An extensive body of literature suggests that aggressive children and adolescents tend to behave aggressively in a variety of situations, in part due to biased or deficient patterns of processing social cues, and/or the presence of a set of beliefs that support use of aggression (for a review, see Crick & Dodge, 1994; Dodge, 2006). Specifically, these aggressive children are known to have difficulties in encoding social information, to make hostile attributions when interpreting others' intent, to generate more aggressive solutions in problem solving, and to expect tangible rewards from aggressive behaviors. Given these difficulties and beliefs in face-to-face interactions, online communication would be particularly challenging for some children, particularly those who lack social knowledge and have peer problems in face-to-face interactions. For example, lack of contextual details (e.g., nonverbal cues) may increase encoding errors in their processing of texts or e-mails with a peer and facilitate attributional biases in interpreting the peer's intent. Negative interpersonal representations/schema about peers may be a particularly salient factor in social information processing in cyberspace. As children try to appraise a situation in a series of e-mail or text exchanges, missing information or ambiguous cues may be filtered through this negative schema, fueling their hostile attributions and emotional responses. This process may be one mechanism that explains a pattern of bullying behaviors in both face-to-face interactions and cyberspace. It will be also interesting to examine the role of heightened disinhibition and reduced empathy in processing social information in cyberspace and online communication. Future studies should explore cognitive and emotional processes that are involved in cyberbullying and cybervictimization. Better understanding of these cognitive and emotional processes would help us assess the extent to which individual vulnerability interacts with the unique aspects of cyberspace context, and help us identify those children who are at a greater risk for cyberbullying.

Research That Informs Prevention and Intervention Efforts

Extant studies on cyberbullying and online communication highlight the tremendous needs for identifying effective prevention and intervention strategies. Those approaches that have been proven to be effective for traditional bullying could be used to address cyberbullying, but their applicability to cyberspace would need to be carefully examined. Grounded in socioecological framework (Espelage & Swearer, 2004), prevention and intervention programs for traditional bullying often utilize peers, parents, and teachers with a primary goal of creating positive environments in which bullying behaviors are not tolerated and pro-social behaviors are encouraged. As in traditional bullying, parents and teachers play a critical role in identifying and addressing cyberbullying and cybervictimization. Because of the challenges children face in the cyberspace and online communication, adult guidance and monitoring may be particularly important for cyberbullying. However, a number of obstacles seem to hamper parents' and teachers' involvement in cyberbullying incidents. Smith et al. (2005) indicated that one third to over one half of students who were cyberbullied did not report the incident to a parent or adult, while Juvonen and Gross (2008) reported that 90% did not tell an adult. These numbers are much higher than those in traditional bullying, and highlight a significant challenge we face in addressing cyberbullying. Furthermore, adults are less familiar with online communication technology, so that they may not fully understand many aspects of cyber activities and feel inadequate and not knowledgeable to talk to students. In addition, cyberbullying often takes place outside school, making teachers and school administrators reluctant to address it. Given these challenges, it is critical to develop training programs for parents and teachers. Recommended school-level prevention efforts include specific designation of cyberbullying as an inappropriate behavior in school policy and creating a positive school climate (Hinduja & Patchin, 2009). Equally important is a systematic evaluation of these approaches and programs that would inform us of their efficacy and effectiveness in preventing and reducing cyberbullying.

One of the interesting questions in prevention efforts is what protects children from cyberbullying. A few studies have examined parental variables such as overall parental monitoring and parental control via software (Taiariol et al., 2010). Other studies investigated contextual variables such as location of computer. However, Mesch (2009) found that parents using software and recording online activities had no effect on cyberbullying and neither did the location of the computer. The prevalent use of smart phones and laptop computers has made texting, instant messaging, and e-mails available beyond the boundary of a physical space, making parental monitoring and control further limited. Parental monitoring and parental control may be an index of overall parent involvement associated with positive social adjustment, and thus lead to less cyberbullying in their children. Using monitors and limiting technology use may be the same as putting metal detectors in school, and may not be effective in preventing cyberbullying. Future studies should investigate specific aspects of parental involvement in cyberspace and online communication, such as parents' guidance and limit setting before a cell phone or Facebook is introduced to a child, or ongoing monitoring of the child's technology use so that prevention efforts could target those areas.

The roles of bystanders and peer relations also need to be better understood in cyberbullying. Studies on traditional bullying have highlighted the significant effects of the peer ecology on peer victimization and bullying (e.g., Hodges, Boivin, Vitaro, & Bukowski, 1999; Salmivalli, Lagerspetz, Björkqvist, & Osterman, 1996). Hodges et al. (1999) found that individual risk factors are predictive of peer victimization when the peer ecology is characterized by low peer support (e.g., not having protective friends and actively rejected by peers). Kärnä, Voeten, Poskiparta, and Salmivalli (2010) reported that the relation between individual risk factors and victimization was strongest in classrooms where bullies are supported and targets are not defended. Sainio, Veentra, Huitsing, and Salmivalli (2011) found defended targets are less likely to show depression and anxiety and to be rejected by peers. These peer contexts may be particularly unique in cyberbullying. The definition and effects of bystanders may be different in the context of cyberbullying. When it involves personal communications between bullies and victims, such as in e-mails and texts, the presence of bystanders may be minimal compared to school grounds. Even when a student becomes aware that his or her friend is being tormented via a series of texts, his or her responses to defend the friend may be difficult. Furthermore, a passive bystander could quickly become an active participant of harmful exchanges when an embarrassing picture is forwarded to others. If the recipients of the pictures are not known to the target, the unknown size of bystanders (and potential perpetrators) may be particularly distressing. The fact that cyberbullying takes place beyond physical space and boundaries requires us to expand the concept of bystanders, and broaden our understanding of bystander behaviors. Having peer support is important in dealing with emotional distress of traditional bullying (Davidson & Demaray, 2007; Sainio et al., 2011) and would be also critical for those who experience cybervictimization. However, the challenging question is how we reduce negative bystander effects in cyberspace where disinhibition is promoted and empathic responses are reduced. Specific mechanisms that facilitate empathic and sensitive responses in cyberspace should be identified in future studies, and should be integrated into universal prevention programs.

With respect to prevention of cyberbullying, universal prevention that targets the general student population may be particularly beneficial to promote healthy online communication and prevent cyberbullying. Topics such as digital citizenship and Internet safety have been suggested as areas that we need to address with students (Collier, 2011). This is an important prevention approach in that the focus is not so much on responding to cyberbullying, but rather on promoting competence in cyberspace and online communication. This could be in a form of a public campaign, school-based program, or community-based initiatives. However, the potential impact of these approaches on cyberbullying awaits rigorous empirical investigations. Also, given that more and more young children gain access to online communication tools, of a particular interest is identifying when the universal prevention programs are most effective, so that the timing of these programs could be considered for implementation. For school-based universal prevention, one important issue is the feasibility of these programs in current school climates, with limited funding, focus on academic achievement, and multiple demands on teachers. Thus, innovative ways to educate students about digital citizenship and Internet safety need to be identified. One of the ways to enhance feasibility is to integrate innovative approaches into existing programs or routines (Adelman & Taylor, 2003). For example, instead of rolling out a new program, integrating topics of digital citizenship and Internet safety into existing programs (e.g., social emotional learning, anti-bullying programs), or existing curriculum (e.g., social studies) may be a possibility.

CONCLUSION

What we know about cyberbullying so far presents a complex picture of peer interactions that involve different forms and methods (e.g., text messaging, chat rooms, and social networking websites) in the complicated dynamics of peer relations. A few publicized cyberbullying cases with devastating outcomes have produced much public attention and outcry. Much work is needed to identify research-based strategies to combat cyberbullying. As we have learned from studies on traditional bullying, a better understanding of intrapersonal and contextual risk and protective factors is much needed in our effort to develop effective prevention and intervention strategies for cyberbullying. Converging knowledge from future studies on these risk and protective factors of cyberbullying and cybervictimization will lead to specific recommendations in universal and targeted prevention programs.

References

Adelman, H. S., & Taylor, L. (2003). On sustainability of project innovations as systemic change. *Journal of Educational & Psychological Consultation, 14*(1), 1–25. doi:10.1207/S1532768XJEPC1401_01

Campbell, M. A. (2005). Cyberbullying: An old problem in a new guise? *Australian Journal of Guidance and Counselling, 15*, 68–76.

Collier, A. (2011). Digital literacy, digital citizenship. Retrieved from http://www.slideshare.net/ConnectSafely/digital-literacy-digital-citizenship

Crick, N. C., & Dodge, K. A. (1994). A review and reformulation of social information processing mechanisms in children's social adjustment. *Psychological Bulletin, 115*, 74–101. doi:10.1037/0033–2909.115.1.74

Davidson, L. M., & Demaray, M. (2007). Social support as a moderator between victimization and internalizing-externalizing distress from bullying. *School Psychology Review, 36*(3), 383–405.

Dollar, T., Yoon, J., Taiariol, J., Hillman, S., & Markman, B. (2011). Bullying experiences in middle school: A person centered approach. Paper presented at an annual Graduate Exhibition, Wayne State University, Detroit.

Dempsey, A. G., Sulkowski, M. L., & Nichols, R. (2009). Differences between peer victimization in cyber and physical settings and associated psychosocial adjustment in early adolescence. *Psychology in the Schools, 46*(10), 962–972. doi:10.1002/pits.20437

Dodge, K. A. (2006). Translational science in action: Hostile attributional style and the development of aggressive behavior problems. *Development and Psychopathology, 18*, 791–814. doi:10.1017/S0954579406060391

Espelage, D., & Swearer, S. (Eds.). (2004). *Bullying in American schools: A social-ecological perspective on prevention and intervention*. Mahwah, NJ: Lawrence Erlbaum Associates Publishers.

Hinduja, S., & Patchin, J. W. (2009a). *Bullying beyond the schoolyard: Preventing and responding to cyberbullying*. Thousand Oaks, CA: Corwin Press.

Hinduja, S., & Patchin, J. (2009b). Preventing cyberbullying: Top ten tips for educators. Cyberbullying Research Center. Retrieved from http://www.cyberbullying.us/Top_Ten_Tips_Educators_Cyberbullying_Prevention.pdf

Hinduja, S., & Patchin, J. W. (2010). Bullying, cyberbullying, and suicide. *Archives of Suicide Research, 14*(3), 206–221. doi:10.1080/13811118.2010.494133

Hodges, E., Boivin, M., Vitaro, F., & Bukowski, W. (1999). The power of friendship: Protection against an escalating cycle of peer victimization. *Developmental Psychology, 35*, 94–10. doi:10.1037/0012–1649.35.1.94

Juvonen, J., & Gross, E. (2008). Extending the school grounds? Bullying experiences in cyberspace. *Journal of School Health, 78*, 496–505. doi:10.1111/j.1746–1561.2008.00335.x

Kärnä, A., Voeten, M., Poskiparta, E., & Salmivalli, C. (2010). Vulnerable children in varying classroom contexts: Bystanders' behaviors moderate the effects of risk factors on victimization. *Merrill-Palmer Quarterly: Journal of Developmental Psychology, 56*(3), 261–282.

Kowalski, R. M., & Limber, S. P. (2007). Electronic bullying among middle school students. *Journal of Adolescent Health, 41*, S22–S30. doi:10.1016/j.jadohealth.2007.08.017

Mesch, G. S. (2009). Parental mediation, online activities, and cyberbullying. *CyberPsychology & Behavior, 12*(4), 387–393. doi:10.1089/cpb.2009.0068

Patchin, J. W., & Hinduja, S. (2006). Bullies move beyond the schoolyard: A preliminary look at cyberbullying. *Youth Violence and Juvenile Justice, 4*(2), 148–169. doi:10.1177/1541204006286288

Perren, S., Dooley, J., Shaw, T., & Cross, D. (2010). Bullying in school and cyberspace: Associations with depressive symptoms in Swiss and Australian adolescents. *Child and Adolescent Psychiatry and Mental Health, 4*(28), 1–10. doi:10.1186/1753-2000-4-28

Pew Internet & American Life Project (2009). Retrieved from http://www.pewinternet.org/Reports/2005/Teens-and-Technology.aspx

Raskauskas, J., & Stoltz, A. D. (2007). Involvement in traditional and electronic bullying among adolescents. *Developmental Psychology, 43*(3), 564–575.doi:10.1037/0012-1649.43.3.564

Sainio, M., Veenstra, R., Huitsing, G., & Salmivalli, C. (2011). Victims and their defenders: A dyadic approach. *International Journal of Behavioral Development, 35*(2), 144–151. doi:10.1177/0165025410378068

Salmivalli, C., Lagerspetz, K., Björkqvist, K., & Österman, K. (1996). Bullying as a group process: Participant roles and their relations to social status within the group. *Aggressive Behavior, 22*(1), 1–15.

Schmitt, K. L., Dayanim, S., & Matthias, S. (2008). Personal homepage construction as an expression of social development. *Developmental Psychology, 44*, 496–506. doi:10.1037/0012-1649.44.2.496

Sekol, I., & Farrington, D. P. (2010). The overlap between bullying and victimization in adolescent residential care: Are bully/victims a special category? *Children and Youth Services Review, 32*(12), 1758–1769. doi:10.1016/j.childyouth.2010.07.020

Smith, P. K., Mahdavi, J., Carvalho, M., Fisher, S., Russell, S., & Tippett, N. (2008). Cyberbullying: Its nature and impact in secondary school pupils. *Journal of Child Psychology and Psychiatry, 49*, 376–385. doi:10.1111/j.1469-7610.2007.01846.x

Subrahmanyam, K., Greenfield, P. M., & Tynes, B. (2004). Constructing sexuality and identity in an online teen chat room. *Journal Applied Developmental Psychology, 25*, 651–666.

Taiariol, J., Yoon, J., Hillman, S., & Markman, B. (2011, April). Cyberbullying: Associations with other forms of bullying, family factors, and school adjustment. Presented at New directions in cyberbullying research: Beyond prevalence. Symposium conducted at the biennial meeting of the Society for Research in Child Development, Montreal, Canada.

Valkenburg, P. M., & Peter, J. (2007). Online communication and adolescent well-being: Testing the stimulation versus the displacement hypothesis. *Journal of Computer-Mediated Communication, 12*(4), 1169. doi:10.1111/j.1083-6101.2007.00368.x

Valkenburg, P. M., & Peter, J. (2011). Online communication among adolescents: An integrated model of its attraction, opportunities, and risks. *Journal of Adolescent Health, 48*, 121–127. doi:10.1016/j.jadohealth.2010.08.020

Williams, K.R., & Guerra, N.G. (2007). Prevalence and predictors of internet bullying. *Journal of Adolescent Health, 41*, S14–S21. doi:10.1016/j.jadohealth.2007.08.018

Ybarra, M.L., Diener-West, M., & Leaf, P.J. (2007). Examining the overlap in Internet harassment and school bullying: Implications for school interventions. *Journal of Adolescent Health, 41*, S42–S50. doi:10.1016/j.jadohealth.2007.09.004

Ybarra, M.L., & Mitchell, J.K. (2004). Youth engaging in online harassment: Associations with caregiver-child relationships, Internet use, and personal characteristics. *Journal of Adolescence, 27*(3), 319–336. doi:10.1016/j.adolescence.2004.03.007

22 Summary and Conclusions

Donna Cross, Sheri Bauman,
and Jenny Walker

This book provides a comprehensive understanding of the major issues related to conducting quality cyberbullying research—from carefully defining cyberbullying and cyberbullying theory development, to the development of cyberbullying measures and research methodology and the implications of this research for policy and practice. Each chapter provides a unique perspective encouraging the development of new cyberbullying research knowledge, and suggests actions that will enable researchers to conduct more effective research in this area. This chapter synthesizes and reflects on the understandings and converging recommendations provided by the authors of the preceding chapters and invites readers to share their cyberbullying research with this group via the website.

To submit papers for the think tank website, contact sherib@u.arizona.edu, who will then post to the www.icbtt.arizona.edu website.

PART I—INTRODUCTION

Chapter 1 provides an overview of the key findings from the scholarly literature to contextualize the remaining chapters. Walker, Craven, and Tokunaga contend that while there is a growing body of cyberbullying research, consensus is still lacking in many areas of study. Areas of agreement do, however, include the main differences between cyberbullying and non-cyberbullying (e.g., related to disinhibition, perceived anonymity, and unique power and control issues afforded by the virtual world), and that some young people use both their online and offline worlds to bully others. It seems that most cyber targets/perpetrators are likely also to be traditional targets/perpetrators, but it is not yet clear whether the virtual world provides more or less opportunity for friends to provide immediate support for each other. Limited consensus exists related to prevalence rates, largely due to how differently cyberbullying behavior is defined within and between countries. Some researchers concur that cyberbullying behavior appears to be more pronounced among middle school-aged youth, but is not limited to this age group and continues, albeit at decreased rates, into adulthood.

No consistency of findings appears evident across studies to understand which gender, if either, is most likely to be involved as a perpetrator, target, dual perpetrator/target, or as a witness to cyberbullying, and the degree of that involvement. A more nuanced picture is emerging, however, of the ways in which young people are motivated to use cyberbullying to navigate their relationships, especially around issues of popularity and sexuality.

Research has also not yet reliably shown whether or not the consequences of different types of cyberbullying are more severe and long term than those of non-cyberbullying. Longitudinal research is needed to increase knowledge of the long-term effects of cyberbullying. Current understandings suggest that specific forms and features of cyberbullying may have differential effects on the target, the perpetrator, and the dual perpetrator/target, but clarification is needed.

Walker et al. also present a summary of current challenges in cyberbullying research, including the use of consistent definitions and the lack of studies grounded in theory. As discussed in Part III of this book, the lack of a consistent definition poses serious problems in measurement, not the least of which is the difficulty in making cross-study comparisons, and ultimately undermining the quality of research in the field. The weakness of cyberbullying measurement is further exacerbated by researchers' use of global- and specific-item measures. The authors recommend that these issues need to be carefully addressed to ensure cyberbullying incidents are measured correctly and include not only the details of the incidents, but also the broader picture in which the events take place.

Chapter 1 concludes by examining what is working in traditional bullying research and how it can inform cyberbullying research. The authors illustrate how the use of theory-driven research using robust methodological designs and measurement techniques has led to a strong body of research and empirically tested anti-bullying programs in the field of traditional bullying. Meta-analyses have been conducted to identify key findings and new directions for research, and cross-cultural, international research projects are underway. Drawing upon what has been learned in the field of traditional bullying, the authors present 10 key recommendations that can be used to avoid previous research pitfalls and to minimize limitations when conducting cyberbullying research.

PART II—DEFINITION

Part II of this book examines issues associated with having a universal definition of cyberbullying. The authors suggest that to increase our understanding of cyberbullying and build a solid, *coherent* body of research findings, it is vital that researchers work from a commonly agreed definition.

Why a Definition for Cyberbullying Matters

In Chapter 2, Bauman provides a brief background to the term *cyberbullying*, emphasizing the need for a clear, precise, and universal definition of cyberbullying, and outlining the conceptual, theoretical, and methodological challenges that can arise when this is not the case. The usefulness of applying the widely accepted components of the definition of traditional bullying (intentional harm, repetition, and power imbalance) to the definition of cyberbullying is reviewed by the authors, who then pose questions for researchers to consider as they work toward a universal definition. For example, do we determine the power differential in cyberbullying by offline indicators such as social status, popularity, etc., or by proficiency with the technology itself?

Defining Cyberbullying

In Chapter 3, Smith, del Barrio, and Tokunaga address in greater depth the questions introduced in Chapter 2. First, they present an overview of bullying as a subset of aggression, which embraces indirect aggression, relational aggression, and social aggression. The authors review the *general* agreement among researchers that bullying is an intentional aggressive act, perpetrated via any of the forms of aggression (physical, verbal, cyber, direct, or indirect) that includes an imbalance of power between the perpetrator and target, and which has some element of repetition. They also provide a review of the term "bullying" in different languages (English, Italian, Spanish, and Japanese) to make the case that bullying can be thought of as a "natural category" (Rosch & Mervis, 1975), a concept that is readily understood regardless of whether not there is a term for it in the lexicon.

The authors of this chapter then examine in some detail the three main criteria associated with bullying:

1. Intent to harm. (Noting the difficulties inherent in determining intent, and using the perspective of the target, perpetrator, and informed outsider, the authors present three criteria to help make a judgment of intent to harm. Did the target experience harm? Did the perpetrator intend not only the behavior but also the harm? Would a reasonable person judge that the action could be foreseen as likely to cause harm to the target?)
2. Imbalance of power. (Indicative criteria include being physically weaker, verbally less fluent, lacking confidence or self-esteem, being outnumbered, lacking friends or social support, and being in a low status or rejected position in the peer group. Oftentimes, imbalance of power can be thought of as being somehow different from the group and thus having less power in the social hierarchy; for example, the new student in a classroom.)
3. Repetition. (Although repetition often is thought of as central to bullying, the authors suggest that it is not an *essential* criterion and should be thought of as more of a *probabilistic* indicator.)

The authors next review the definition of cyberbullying as "an aggressive act carried out by a group or individual, *using electronic forms of contact*, repeatedly and over time against a victim who cannot easily defend him or herself" (Smith, Mahdavi, Carvalho, Fisher, Russell, & Tippett, 2008, p. 376). In trying to determine if this definition is useful, the authors consider what is meant by electronic forms of contact, how power imbalance plays out in cyberbullying, and what is meant by repetition in cyberbullying.

- What is meant by electronic forms of contact? With the advent of smart phones, it now may be more useful to distinguish among the different *kinds* of communication exchange rather than the different communication *devices.*
- Power imbalance in relation to cyberbullying: In the virtual world, this may mean being more tech-savvy than the target. The anonymity afforded may also contribute to power imbalance; it is difficult to respond to an unknown perpetrator who now can follow you into the safety of your own home.
- Repetition: Due to the difficulties of determining what repetition means in the virtual world, Smith et al. suggest that the perspective of an outsider should be the "ultimate" consideration (p. 16).

Similar to the recommendations in numerous other chapters in this book, Chapter 3 closes by reminding researchers to include the perspective of young people while working toward a consensus on defining cyberbullying.

Alternative Views—Cyberaggression or Cyberbullying?

The authors of Chapter 4 present an alternative perspective in defining cyberbullying behavior, proposing the term cyberaggression. While Bauman, Underwood, and Card encourage researchers to continue to work toward a universal definition of cyberbullying, they remind us that there is not yet a consensus on the exact nature of cyberbullying, and that current definitions are untested and may be restrictive. They propose that, at least in the short term, researchers focus on and label the behaviors we are studying as *cyberaggression.* They argue this would allow researchers to continue to study cyberbullying while grappling with the challenge of what bullying means in the virtual world.

Similar to Smith et al. in Chapter 2, the authors argue that it is imperative that this definitional research include the thoughts of young people. This process, they suggest, will allow for the continuing empirical evaluation and assessment (as opposed to assumption) of whether elements of traditional bullying, such as repetition, make sense and should be retained in the context of electronic communication.

Bauman et al. conclude Part II of the book by challenging researchers to develop more precise and valid measures of cyberaggression that keep the perspectives of young people center stage while systematically continuing to work toward determining what bullying means in the virtual world.

PART III—THEORIES

Part III examines why a theoretical framework is critical for cyberbullying researchers, arguing it guides the research endeavor, and provides a structure that helps researchers identify important research questions and links those to existing knowledge. Lester (2005) suggests that theoretical frameworks are not unequivocally helpful in research, especially when subscribers to a theory make efforts to have data fit a theory, and may omit or ignore important information that is not consistent with the theory. Moreover, in efforts to think within theoretical boundaries, researchers may neglect or overlook the contextual information that helps explain the results (Lester, 2005).

Theoretical Framework for Cyberbullying Research

In Chapter 5, Espelage, Rao, and Craven take the position that a theoretical framework is not only useful but essential to research in any field. The authors argue that given cyberbullying is a new area of research, it will be important to review existing theories (most often of bullying, but also of aggression and victimization) and test their application to this new phenomenon. They encourage researchers to examine related theories that offer potential as components of theory of cyberbullying. The authors examine numerous theories including Social Ecological Theory, Social Information Processing Theory, General Strain Theory, Social Norms Theory, Social Learning Theory, and Self Concept Theory and make the following observations:

- *Social Ecological Theory* situates bullying in the context of several nested and interrelated systems, so that studies of bullying need to consider the individual participants (perpetrators, targets, bystanders) in the context of families, schools, communities, and society, and the interactions among those systems. This framework appears useful to a theory of cyberbullying because cyberspace can be conceptualized as a system (perhaps even a microsystem, given the role of technology in the lives of young people), that interacts with the other systems.
- *Social Information Processing* (SIP) theory is often used to explain other forms of aggression and may have much to offer a theory of cyberbullying. This theory considers aggressive behavior to be the result of ineffective cognitive processing of social information, which could include interactions in the world of electronic communication. One of the often-cited features of electronic communication is the reduction in social cues, which can lead to misunderstandings and aggressive responses to mistakenly attributed content. It would be useful to empirically test whether the absence of visual cues online exacerbates social information processing deficits, and whether cognitive biases such as hostile attribution and self-blame biases explain some cyberbullying behaviors.

- *General Strain Theory* may be helpful to explain cyberbullying behavior, perpetrated by those who are targeted in face-to-face situations. In Chapter 5 a test of this theory in the context of cyberbullying is provided, and the results indicate that perpetration of bullying in a face-to-face context was predictive of later cyberbullying perpetration. This suggests that cyberbullying may be an extension of other bullying behaviors and that existing theory, such as General Strain Theory, might be applicable.
- *Social Norms Theory* was also tested empirically, to determine whether the function of victimizing others in cyberspace is the same as that in traditional settings: that is, to establish and maintain the social hierarchy. From this perspective, cyberbullying others, particularly to elevate one's social status, would be grounds for further victimization to preserve the existing hierarchy.
- *Social Learning Theory* suggests the strong correlations between traditional and cyberbullying behaviors reported in numerous studies are best explained by vicarious learning and modeling. Self-concept theory was also hypothesized to play a major role in bullying behavior; whether that will be found in the cyberbullying context remains to be seen.

Where existing explanatory theories are insufficient, as suggested by the authors in Chapter 5, it behooves researchers to use applicable components from existing theories to revise, extend, and blend those theories as needed and then design empirical studies that contribute to the development of a sound theory of cyberbullying.

In Chapter 6, Craven and her colleagues provide an example of how to develop and test a theory-based model using Exploratory Structural Equation Modeling (ESEM). They found evidence for a model that includes traditional bullying, victimization, and four bystander roles. They extended the model to include cyberbullying, with the same four bystander roles. They propose hypotheses based on the hypothetical structure they developed, and invited testing of the model. The authors argue that this kind of theory testing is essential to develop an integrated and empirically based theory of cyberbullying. Having such theory to guide future research would add credibility and provide a mechanism for integrating findings from a variety of disciplines and planning future research.

PART IV—METHODS

Given cyberbullying behavior is relatively new compared to traditional bullying behavior, the research methodology used to understand this phenomenon is developing quickly. Many authors in this book suggest researchers should avoid relying on methodological practices that have become the norm for traditional bullying research, and instead explore a diverse range of potential methodologies. Bauman, in Chapter 7, suggests that to research cyberbullying well, it may be necessary, but not sufficient, to only use the best techniques from existing bullying research. However, she and others also recommend being creative in developing new methods to effectively understand the complexity and nuances unique to cyberbullying behavior.

Sampling for Cyberbullying Research

In Chapter 8, Bauman discusses the importance of careful sample selection to ensure the validity and applicability of research findings, particularly as current cyberbullying research is often innovative and exploratory in nature. She strongly encourages researchers to acknowledge possible sampling bias in their publications, and to be attentive to sampling bias, critically reviewing the methodology before citing publications. Bauman argues that neglecting to do this may erroneously imply the research findings are valid and applicable.

Bauman highlights that the potential for sampling bias must also be carefully considered in researchers' own studies, as the findings may vary according to the sampling method selected. She encourages cyberbullying researchers to consider using previous research or conducting small pilot studies to ascertain appropriate sample sizes and confidence intervals, and to consider:

1) sampling designs that meet the purpose of the study (for instance, sampling requirements may be least stringent for exploratory studies and most stringent for longitudinal intervention studies);
2) the important variables in their study;
3) their target population;
4) the required consent procedures;
5) the likelihood of nonresponse and attrition; and
6) the intended methods of data collection and analysis.

Bauman concludes by highlighting how sampling planning will become increasingly important as the field of cyberbullying research advances. Studies examining the efficacy of intervention strategies, for example, will need to randomly assign groups (e.g., schools) rather than individuals to experimental and control conditions. The resulting intraclass correlations among data from individuals in the same group may result in reduced power and increased error. As sampling strategies can either increase or reduce sampling bias and total error, Bauman strongly recommends that researchers carefully plan and provide rationales for sampling decisions that, in turn, will allow readers and other researchers to accurately judge the validity of the findings.

Methods Used for Cyberbullying Research

Espinoza and Juvonen in Chapter 9 argue that while largely descriptive quantitative (self-report survey) methodology has been conducted to date to investigate cyberbullying, other methods need to be considered. They review the strengths and weaknesses of online survey administration and telephone surveys and recommend the use of cross-method comparisons to provide information about the benefits of different survey techniques and to help explain discrepant findings.

The authors also discuss the value of using qualitative data collected via interviews and focus groups to investigate cyberbullying experiences, attitudes, and perceptions. They explain how these methods enable the in-depth exploration of cyberbullying issues and highlight important nuances of cyberbullying behaviors that may not be readily observed using quantitative methodology.

Espinoza and Juvonen also prompt readers to consider how increasingly complex cyberbullying research questions will require more diverse methodology and suggest that methods that have been useful in the broader fields of school bullying and electronic communication—such as daily assessments of events and feelings to reveal the day-to-day association of variables of interest (increasingly possible with mobile technologies), the use of peers as informants for data collection, and observational methods in online contexts such as chat rooms and social networking sites—are currently underutilized in cyberbullying research. The authors conclude by suggesting that the use of a wide range of methods will enrich cyberbullying research and maximize the insights that can be gained and will help to understand the robustness of particular findings.

Guiding Principles for Cyberbullying Research

In Chapter 10, Bauman and Cross provide five principles that serve as useful guidelines for cyberbullying research methods. First, they recommend that researchers *actively engage multiple disciplinary teams* and their methodologies in the design and conduct of cyberbullying research. While such collaboration may bring challenges and will require careful team composition, a multidisciplinary approach encourages an innovative, comprehensive approach to a complex phenomenon requiring knowledge to be drawn from various fields including communication, psychology, and technology.

Second, Bauman and Cross suggest researchers *use quality methods from traditional bullying and other relevant research* as a foundation to study the phenomenon of cyberbullying. Novel methods used in small studies may be identified from "gray literature" (for instance, non-peer-reviewed articles, reports, and unpublished theses). Testing theories to determine their applicability to cyberbullying behavior, and the development of new theories, are also to be encouraged.

Third, researchers should *develop a set of procedures that are intentionally inclusive of the target population's voice* to identify key language, behaviors, and perspectives, to inform cyberbullying research methods. Advice should be obtained from reference and advisory groups to ensure comprehensive knowledge about the complex social norms and expectations in particular environments, and to guide the development of measures. Similar to the recommendations of other authors, the recruitment of youth as advisors and collaborators in cyberbullying research may enhance the design, delivery, and evaluation of anti-cyberbullying interventions.

Fourth, the authors recommend researchers *promote and conduct formative research* to ensure that research methodology captures the nuances of studying cyberbullying behavior. They suggest qualitative studies will be particularly useful in developing theory and providing a basis for quantitative analysis.

Finally, consistent with the recommendations from Mishna (Chapter 12), Bauman and Cross encourage researchers to *adhere to accepted ethical protocol* that shows respect and care, and considers unique challenges associated with cyberbullying research. Researchers collecting data online must ensure consent and privacy rights are protected, particularly for young participants.

Recommendations Regarding Cyberbullying Research Methodology

In Chapter 10, Underwood and Card identify the important methodological questions emerging as the field of cyberbullying research advances. They explain that while most studies rely on self-reported measures of cyberbullying, investigations of the validity of these data indicate the potential for under- or overreporting of cyberbullying behaviors in comparison to peer reports. They encourage the use of alternatives to self-report measures, including the direct observation of cyber behaviors made possible by electronic communication technologies, which while bringing their own challenges, would enable the development of improved measurement procedures.

Further, the authors suggest cyberbullying may be better conceptualized as a continuous rather than categorical variable, to avoid the assumption that cyberbullying others or being cyberbullied are invariant behaviors, and that encourage the investigation of risk factors predicting differential levels of cyberbullying. The authors also discuss the relative advantages and limitations of variable- and person-centered analyses and suggest cyberbullying research would benefit from using a dyadic approach to studying aggressive behavior. For example, stable aggressor-victim relationships may develop if individuals who cyberbully are drawn to specific behaviors among those they target.

Finally, the authors suggest longitudinal studies (or adding measures of cyberbullying to longitudinal assessments of other aggressive behaviors) would greatly enhance new knowledge about the developmental trends, stability, and consequences for adolescent adjustment of cyberbullying.

Ethical Issues in Cyberbullying Research

In Chapter 12, Mishna and colleagues examine how children and adolescents' familiarity with and frequent use of continually developing technologies may present challenges for researchers with relatively less knowledge of these technologies, and create significant ethical dilemmas when conducting cyberbullying research. For instance, direct access to young people's online communications and information provides accurate data but may raise ethical challenges for researchers. Young people may disguise or unknowingly provide information about risky or illegal behaviors. Mishna et al. suggest decisions about whether to intervene on the basis of such data can be difficult, and are complicated by limited definitional clarity of "intent" and "harm" in relation to cyberbullying and other behaviors.

The authors also suggest that when conducting cyberbullying research, there may be tension between the ethical responsibilities to prevent harm to young people while also protecting their privacy and confidentiality. Ethical dilemmas can also arise when schools or families desire access to data in response to concern for young people's well-being. They recommend researchers clearly and consistently communicate to participants the extent of confidentiality in cyberbullying research, as respondents may have concerns about reporting bullying behaviors.

The authors also highlight that ethical guidelines may vary according to the country or region where the research takes place, especially given legislation relating to illegal behavior in cyber settings is continually developing. They suggest the necessity of obtaining informed consent is made challenging by differential requirements regarding the age at which parent/guardian consent is required and the manner in which it should be obtained, all of which must be carefully navigated by cyberbullying researchers.

Strong recommendations are made by Mishna et al. about the need to constantly reexamine ethical issues in a collaborative and flexible manner—even beyond the ethical review process of the intended research. Cyberbullying researchers need to be especially respectful of the agency, capacity, and knowledge of young people, while also working to address mistaken beliefs about technology and relationships. Last, the authors remind researchers they have an ethical responsibility to disseminate findings that may enhance young people's well-being and capacity to deal with cyberbullying.

Innovative Methodological Strategies to Address Cyberbullying

In Chapter 13, Spears and Zeederberg highlight how the relatively recent emergence of cyberbullying behavior provides an opportunity to reflect on emerging methods that are relevant to cyber settings. They reason that researchers face the challenge of adapting to cyber environments using research and knowledge initially derived from offline contexts. Cyberbullying researchers need to consider how, with advanced information technology, young people increasingly interact and congregate online in "publically networked spaces" (e.g., social networking sites, online games), which overlap with and interact with offline spaces, including schools and homes. Hence, the authors maintain that offline locations are not necessarily the only nor the most appropriate settings to target cyberbullying behaviors; instead, they recommend the use of online spaces to address these behaviors.

Spears and Zeederberg describe, using the example of a successful marketing campaign *Smart Online: Safe Offline (SOSO)* project targeting bystander behavior, how online social marketing can develop, deliver, and evaluate cyberbullying messages to young people in the "places" they choose to frequent, such as Facebook and YouTube. They advise that messages delivered in these online environments are more relevant, targeted, and meaningful, especially if they are guided and designed by young people. When young people are involved as "co-researchers," Spears contends that their preferences and expertise in cyber communication are acknowledged and utilized.

To conclude, Spears and Zeederberg recommend that interventions and preventative approaches to cyberbullying need to extend beyond the school environment to incorporate online publically networked places frequented by young people to disseminate anti-cyberbullying messages to large proportions of the population, in forms that are acceptable and suitable for children and adolescents.

PART V—MEASURES

In addition to the need for a strong theoretical foundation, as discussed in Part III, cyberbullying research must be based on accurate measurement. To date, cyberbullying researchers have used mostly self-constructed measures, with few providing the psychometric properties of those measures. Some cyberbullying measures borrow from existing bullying measures and add some additional items, while others are new measures entirely. Ybarra in Chapter 14 clearly demonstrates how differences in findings can be attributed to the way survey items are constructed and worded.

Beginning with Good Measures

An essential step in developing measures is to determine and report the psychometric properties (reliability and validity) of those measures. In Chapter 15, Noel Card uses the domain representation framework to conceptualize measurement of cyberbullying or cyberaggression. Reliability, or repeatability, is described and illustrated graphically to provide a visual representation of what internal consistency means. Card reminds us that reliability is a property of the measure within a population, not a feature of the measure itself, and he proposes that cyberbullying researchers always report the reliability of a measure for their population. Contrary to conventional beliefs, Card explains that validity (the degree to which a scale measures what it is intended to measure) is not dependent on reliability, and that latent variable Confirmatory Factor Analysis is a method for researchers to evaluate construct validity even for measures that have low reliability.

Card suggests that to date, cyberbullying researchers are better at reporting reliability than validity data, possibly due to the lack of clarity on definitions and delineation of the boundaries of cyberbullying behavior. A further complication suggested by Card is the lack of clear expectations for relations among constructs, which he indicates may become clearer as theoretical foundations are clarified.

Last, Card advises that the absence of measurement invariance in the cyberbullying literature is a weakness that needs to be addressed. This issue is also discussed by Strohmeier, Aoyama, Gradinger, and Toda in Chapter 16 with respect to translation, with few researchers evaluating measurement invariance across gender, age, school setting, etc. Many researchers concur this testing must be done to ensure the measures used in cyberbullying research are well-studied and to ensure the findings using these measures are relevant.

Translating Cyberbullying Measures for Cross-Cultural Studies

In Chapter 16, the question of translating measures is discussed by Strohmeier, Aoyama, Gradinger, and Toda. The authors suggest that one of the first challenges for cross-cultural studies is translating key terms that may not have exact equivalents in other languages. This lack of corresponding terms clearly makes comparative studies difficult to conduct.

To respond to this challenge, Strohmeier and Gradinger recommend that prior to developing measures, the domain representations need to be described in such a way that the manifestations of the behavior in both cultures are included. Next, they suggest researchers consider the response options that will minimize bias due to cultural patterns. Finally, they describe the importance of empirically testing measurement invariance, and illustrate this by describing a study where the same measure was used with participants from Austria and Japan. The authors used multiple-group Confirmatory Factor Analysis to test for factor-form invariance, factor loading invariance, intercept invariance, and residual invariance in a three-factor model. They were able to achieve some invariance on two of the factors between the two countries, but concluded they were unable to demonstrate that their scale was valid cross-culturally, which means comparisons between the two countries using this measure should not be made. The authors conclude it is essential to complete this kind of measurement testing in cross-cultural cyberbullying research. In this case, the authors examined invariance across countries, but this level of instrument evaluation also needs to be conducted for gender, race/ethnicity, etc., to ensure the measures can be confidently used with identified groups.

What about Cyberbullying Should Be Measured?

One of the factors that make it difficult to accumulate a body of knowledge is the variety of ways in which researchers measure the construct of cyberbullying, particularly if the measures don't accurately reflect the components of a common definition. In Chapter 17, Rivers argues that cyberbullying criteria have not been included in measures to date. He suggests that if researchers adopt the cyberbullying definition, more refined questions need to inquire about power imbalance, repetition, and intent, while also considering the unique aspects of the cyber-environment.

Rivers also suggests that since cyberbullying, along with traditional bullying, is a relationship problem, a way to assess aspects of the relationship is to include questions about the parties involved in the most recent incident. He also comments that the many timescales used in current scales (e.g., last two weeks, last year, last school term) again makes it difficult to compare findings of studies. Rivers suggests the longer time frames may be asking respondents to invoke memories that may have been distorted by time, and recommends that a shorter time frame (five days or a week) would be more accurate. He also recommends the use of daily diaries or reporting on the last five days, as data collection strategies to reduce the problems associated with longer time frames.

While frequency is often equated with severity, Rivers argues that frequency is not the best way to measure the impact of the cyberbullying on the target. He recommends a more informative approach such as asking follow-up questions when a respondent indicates that she or he has experienced cyberbullying (such as "How much did this upset you?"). The need to study the potential moderators and mediators of distress caused by cyberbullying is also recommended.

Qualitative Cyberbullying Research Measures

Mishna and VanWert (Chapter 18) describe the valuable ways in which qualitative studies can provide a broader and deeper understanding of cyberbullying, taking systems into account. Similar to Spears et al., they suggest qualitative approaches are particularly useful if they involve youth, not just as participants but as co-investigators, utilizing their intimate knowledge of the cyber-environment to influence the design of studies and interpretation of data.

The authors also provide a sound rationale to encourage cyberbullying researchers to use quantitative and qualitative—mixed methods—to take advantages of the strengths of each and to benefit from the richness of qualitative data and the statistical data in quantitative research. They conclude that as technology continues to advance, qualitative processes can help cyberbullying researchers to remain current by listening to the voices of young people.

PART VI—IMPLICATIONS OF RESEARCH

Part VI in this book highlights how cyberbullying researchers must continually synthesize and extend the qualitative and quantitative evidence the inform methods to prevent cyberbullying, and assist families, schools, and communities to implement policy and practices.

Legislation and School Policy

In Chapter 19, Campbell contends that strategies to combat cyberbullying should involve not only individuals and schools but also governments and communities at local and national levels, through the development of legislation and policies. She describes the importance of understanding the relationship between criminal and civil law in the context of cyberbullying. For example, Campbell discusses how cyberbullying behavior is often seen as a disciplinary matter for schools, but also how especially serious and threatening behaviors can constitute a criminal offense. In addition, she suggests that while civil lawsuits can be raised against schools for failing to protect a student from other students, this depends upon proof of serious injury or subsequent psychiatric illness.

Campbell recommends that schools show their commitment to preventing all forms of bullying behavior through their anti-bullying policies and by providing professional learning that helps members of the school community to effectively respond to these behaviors. She suggests that the content of these school policies is often variable, but they typically include definitions of bullying behaviors, procedures for reporting these behaviors, and potential consequences for bullying. She recommends that care be taken to ensure definitions are precise and in accordance with criminal and civil legislation, and that the policies explicitly encourage the reporting of cyberbullying. She encourages schools to ensure the policies are collaboratively developed by students, parents, school staff, and other members of the school community and written in language that is easily understood by both students and adults. She also recommends the wide dissemination and consistent implementation of policies, complemented by whole-school strategies to prevent cyberbullying.

The importance of quality research to inform legislation and policy development is specified by Campbell as key to ensure there is evidence of their effectiveness in preventing cyberbullying. She provides an example of how many school mobile phone policies ban mobile phone use during school time, yet research indicates that this policy does not impact the prevalence of cyberbullying. She recommends cyberbullying researchers need to further explore the relationship between legislation, policies, and bullying behavior.

Campbell closes this chapter by describing how criminal legislation often struggles to keep pace with the speed of technological change and cyber communication. She concludes nevertheless, that anti-bullying legislation is still a powerful means for communicating to the population that bullying behaviors should not be tolerated.

Prevention and Intervention

In Chapter 20, Cross and Walker suggest that given the apparent overlap between cyberbullying and other bullying behaviors, traditional bullying intervention research may be an important starting point when considering prevention and intervention to reduce cyberbullying. In particular, they discuss how whole-school approaches to address traditional bullying, such as the Finish KiVa program, have demonstrated effectiveness in reducing bullying behaviors, including cyberbullying, in schools.

The authors state that interventions to prevent cyberbullying must be grounded in theoretical and empirical evidence and contend that researchers synthesize and apply this evidence rigorously and systematically using an intervention planning framework such as the PRECEDE-PROCEED model. This model provides, for example, a comprehensive nine-step process for planning, implementing, and evaluating an intervention. Importantly, the authors show how researchers involved with the Australian Cyber Friendly Schools Project used this model to assess the:

1) needs of young people in relation to cyberbullying behavior;
2) magnitude and distribution of cyberbullying behaviors; and
3) behavioral, environmental, educational, administrative, and policy-based factors that contribute to these behaviors.

Cross and Walker conclude that further research is needed to establish the theoretical basis of cyberbullying, to determine the developmental and behavioral windows for prevention and intervention, and to develop methods for improving young people's help-seeking and help-provision behaviors. They also argue that consideration of how cyberbullying affects non-mainstream population groups is also required. They suggest the use of communication technology is advancing so rapidly that cyberbullying research must be anticipatory and flexible to provide prevention and intervention strategies in a timely manner. Similar to other authors, the authors conclude it is imperative to partner with young people, to ensure their understandings and perceptions of cyberbullying guide the development, dissemination, and delivery of interventions and strategies.

CONCLUSIONS

On the basis of recommendations made in this book it seems important for researchers to consider the follow key issues when conducting cyberbullying research.

* Intentionally and actively engage young people as co-researchers in all aspects of cyberbullying research to better understand their complex social norms and expectations, language, and perspectives. Their involvement will help to increase the relevancy of research processes, impact and outcomes, including defining and measuring cyberbullying, and implementing research methods and prevention and intervention policy and practice.
* Determine a universal and accepted definition for cyberbullying behavior that considers the three criteria associated with traditional bullying: intent to harm, imbalance of power, and repetition.
* Use the term cyberaggression to refer to an intentional harmful behavior against another person using electronic technology, while determining how to define bullying in a cyber-environment.

- Engage multidisciplinary teams drawn from diverse fields such as psychology, communication, technology, biostatistics, health promotion, and education to conduct cyberbullying research.
- Consider the need to determine equivalent corresponding cyberbullying terminology in other languages and empirically test the measurement invariance of this translation to increase the validity of cross-cultural studies.
- Design empirical studies to test explanatory theories for cyberbullying behavior, taking into account possible components from theories related to aggression and bullying behavior.
- Develop valid and reliable measures of cyberbullying behavior (and cyberaggression), and assess and provide the psychometric properties of these measures for the population being studied.
- Consider using shorter time frames in questions assessing cyberbullying behaviors (such as in the last week or using daily diaries) to increase the validity and accuracy of reporting.
- Use qualitative and quantitative—mixed methods—to increase the richness and usefulness of cyberbullying data.
- Study the potential moderators and mediators of distress caused by cyberbullying rather than associate only the frequency of cyberbullying behavior with severity.
- Use quality, emerging, and innovative methods relevant to cyber settings, such as publically networked spaces frequented by young people, instead of only traditionally used offline methods.
- Conduct pilot studies to help determine sample size, given so little research is available in this area, and consider how sampling decisions will become more complex as cyberbullying research advances.
- Consider alternative or more innovative methods to collect cyberbullying data than self-report behavioral measures, such as observational methods in online contexts, and online daily assessments of events and feelings to understand, for example, the real-time association of variables of interest.
- Examine the many ethical challenges associated with studying cyberbullying (such as obtaining informed consent online, observing risky or illegal behaviors online, the tension of protecting privacy and confidentiality, and ethical responsibilities to prevent harm), being especially respectful of the agency, capacity, and knowledge of young people.
- Conduct longitudinal studies to build new knowledge related to developmental trends, and the consequences and correlates of cyberbullying behavior.
- Ground individual and institutional intervention research in theoretical and empirical evidence to inform, develop, and then empirically evaluate cyberbullying-related legislation, policy, and practice.
- Critically review the quality of published cyberbullying research to discern valid studies and results.

References

Lester, F. K. (2005). On the theoretical, conceptual, and philosophical foundations for research in mathematics education. *ZDM, 37*, 457–467.

Rosch, E., & Mervis, C. G. (1975). Family resemblances: Studies in the internal structure of categories. *Cognitive Psychology, 7*, 573–605.

Smith, P. K., Mahdavi, J., Carvalho, M., Fisher, S., Russell, S., & Tippett, N. (2008). Cyberbullying: Its nature and impact in secondary school pupils. *Journal of Child Psychology & Psychiatry, 49*, 376–385.

Appendix

Existing Measures
Bullying/Cyberbullying Measure

Michele Ybarra, Ph.D.

In the last 12 months, how often have you been *bullied* . . . ?

	Every day or almost every day	A few times a week	A few times a month	Once or a few times in the past year	Never	Decline to answer
In person	O	O	O	O	O	O
By phone call (on a cell phone or land line)	O	O	O	O	O	O
By text message	O	O	O	O	O	O
Online (such as through e-mail, on a social networking site, or through instant messenger)	O	O	O	O	O	O
By written word (e.g., notes)						

In the last 12 months, how often have you been *bullied* . . . ?

	Every day or almost every day	A few times a week	A few times a month	Once or a few times in the past year	Never	Decline to answer
At school	O	O	O	O	O	O
At home	O	O	O	O	O	O
On the way to and from school	O	O	O	O	O	O
Somewhere else	O	O	O	O	O	O

In the last 12 months, how often has someone *bullied* you by . . . ?

	Every day or almost every day	A few times a week	A few times a month	Once or a few times in the past year	Never	Decline to answer
Hitting, kicking, pushing, or shoving you	O	O	O	O	O	O
Making threatening or aggressive comments to you	O	O	O	O	O	O
Calling you mean names	O	O	O	O	O	O
Making fun of you or teasing you in a nasty way	O	O .	O	O	O	O
Leaving you out or not letting you into a group because they were mad at you or were trying to make you upset						
Spreading rumors about you, whether they were true or not						

Thinking just about the past 12 months, when you were *bullied* . . . ?

	Yes	No	Decline to answer
Was it by someone who had more power or strength than you? This could be because the person was bigger than you, had more friends, was more popular, or had more power than you in another way.	O	O	O
Was it repeated, so that it happened again and again?	O	O	O
Did it happen over a long period of time? We mean more than a week or so?	O	O	O

The Adolescent Virtual Behaviors Instrument

Rhonda Craven

To what extent have you experienced the following when you are talking to other people using a computer online or when using a mobile phone to send and receive messages? *Please circle your response.*

		Never	Less than yearly	Every 6 months	Monthly	Fort-nightly	Weekly	Daily
1	I have seen nasty comments written about me on public websites	1	2	3	4	5	6	7
2	Individuals have tried to gather private information about me	1	2	3	4	5	6	7
3	Individuals have digitally altered my photo(s) without my permission	1	2	3	4	5	6	7
4	I have been inappropriately questioned about my sexual identity	1	2	3	4	5	6	7
5	Other users have teased me on public websites	1	2	3	4	5	6	7
6	Individuals have sent me intimidating messages	1	2	3	4	5	6	7
7	I have been asked to send inappropriate pictures/video of myself	1	2	3	4	5	6	7

(Continued)

	Never	Less than yearly	Every 6 months	Monthly	Fort-nightly	Weekly	Daily
8 Individuals have been spiteful to me on public websites	1	2	3	4	5	6	7
9 My online messages were deliberately ignored by other individuals	1	2	3	4	5	6	7
10 Friends have betrayed me by leaking untrue information about me to others	1	2	3	4	5	6	7
11 I have received inappropriate pictures/videos of someone I knew that was not meant to be shared	1	2	3	4	5	6	7
12 Individuals have misinterpreted the truth in order to spread gossip	1	2	3	4	5	6	7
13 When using some public websites there have been users who have been hostile toward me	1	2	3	4	5	6	7
14 Individuals have threatened to harm me	1	2	3	4	5	6	7
15 I have been inappropriately questioned about my sexual identity	1	2	3	4	5	6	7

AVBI BREAK DOWN

Flaming

1 I have seen nasty comments written about me on public websites
5 Other users have teased me on public websites
8 Individuals have been spiteful to me on public websites
13 When using some public websites, there have been users who have been hostile toward me

Cyber Stalking

2 Individuals have tried to gather private information about me
6 Individuals have sent me intimidating messages
9 My online messages were deliberately ignored by other individuals
14 Individuals have threatened to harm me
16 Individuals have viewed messages on my phone to find private information

Misinformation

3 Individuals have digitally altered my photo(s) without my permission
10 Friends have betrayed me by leaking untrue information about me to others
12 Individuals have misinterpreted the truth in order to spread gossip

Indecent Harassment

4 I have been inappropriately questioned about my sexual identity
7 I have been asked to send inappropriate pictures/video of myself
11 I have received inappropriate pictures/videos of someone I knew that was not meant to be shared
15 I have been inappropriately questioned about my sexual identity

PSYCHOMETRIC PROPERTIES

The new AVBI cyber bullying instrument is designed to measure four distinct factors for targets of cyberbullying (flaming, misinformation, indecent harassment, and cyber stalking). A total of ($N = 116$) first-year psychology students and adult users of social networking site Facebook participated in a study to test its psychometric properties (see Newey, Craven, Denson, Yeung, & Finger, 2011). A confirmatory factor analysis (CFA) demonstrated support for the reliability and validity of this new measure (see Newey et al., 2011). The hypothesized model demonstrated sound psychometric properties and excellent goodness of fit indices with a CFI .93, TFI .92, and a RMSEA of .082. The factor loadings for each

Table A.1 Factor Loadings for the Subscales of the ABVI-Target Scale

	Misinformation	Indecent Harassment	Flaming	Harassment
Items		Factor Loadings		
1	.72	.63	.85	.62
2	.78	.81	.78	.85
3	.93	.62	.87	.76
4		.81	.69	.91
5				.71

individual item indicated that all four factors are within acceptable ranges .62 to .93. This indicates that the factors were well defined by their corresponding items. The correlations between the factors were significant ($p < .001$) and ranged from .85–.37 (see Table A.1) although some of the correlations are slightly higher than expected.

Confirmed Factors

1. *Misinformation* refers to the spreading of untrue and damaging information about another through posts on webpages, slam books, e-mails, text messages, or via instant messaging. Examples include students posting untrue and hurtful information about their targets (Hinduja & Patchin, 2009; Kowalski et al., 2008; Willard, 2006).
2. *Indecent Harassment or Sexting* is the practice of sending sexual images such as nude or partially nude photos of the targets through mobile phone picture messaging to other students to view (ABC, 2009; Battersby, 2008).
3. *Flaming refers* to a type of cyberbullying that typically occurs in public online forums (e.g., discussion rooms and chat rooms) when individuals or groups become the targets of angry and rude messages via electronic means. If continual argument persists, usually including rude and vulgar language, then a "flame war" has begun (Kowalski et al., 2008; Willard, 2006).
4. *Cyber Stalking* is related to harassment, except cyber stalking takes harassment to another level and usually involves repetitive threats, lurking, and intimidation. For example, a student may receive an anonymous e-mail of threats to physically hurt or spy on that student, for example, I've been watching you (Li; 2007; Willard, 2006).

References

ABC News. (2009, May 3). NSW schools to get "sexting" fact sheets. Retrieved from http://www.abc.net.au/news/2009–05–03/nsw-schools-to-get-sexting-fact-sheets/1670886.

Battersby, L. (2008, July 10). Sexting: Fears as teens targeted. *The Sydney Morning Herald.* Retrieved from http://www.smh.com.au/technology/sexting-fears-as-teens-targeted-20090616-cfp1.html.

Hinduja, S., & Patchin, J. W. (2009). *Bullying beyond the schoolyard: Preventing and responding to cyberbullying.* Thousand Oaks, CA: Sage Publications.

Kowalski, R. M., Limber, S. P., & Agatston, P. W. (2008). *Cyber bullying: Bullying in the digital age.* Oxford, UK: Blackwell Publishing.

Li, Q. (2007). New bottle but old wine: A research of cyberbullying in schools. *Computers in Human Behavior, 23*(4), 1–15. doi:10.1016/j.chb.2005.10.005.

Newey, K. A., Craven, R C., Denson, N., Yeung, A. S, and Finger, L. (2011, June). *The adolescent behaviours instrument: The development of a psychometrically sound measure of cyber bullying.* Poster presented at the Sixth Self Biennial International Conference: the Centrality of Self Theory and Research for Enabling Human Potential, Quebec City, Canada.

Willard, N. (2006). *Cyber bullying and cyber threats: Responding to the challenge of online social cruelty, threats and distress.* Eugene, OR: Centre for Safe and Responsible Internet Use.

Note: The Parent Survey is available in Spanish. The psychometric properties of these measures are currently being determined. This series of surveys was developed by Sheri Bauman, Noel Card, Alexandra Barre, and John Kozlowski for use in their prospective longitudinal survey.

Parent Survey

ID # _____

> In this survey, we want to ask about the use of technology in your home and about your child's experiences. When we ask about your child, we want you to specifically think of the child who is participating in this study.
>
> There are items in the survey that ask about cyberbullying. **Cyberbullying means using technology (the Internet, cell phones) to threaten or harass someone, or to damage their reputation or their friendships (by spreading rumors, excluding them from groups, embarrassing or humiliating them).**

Part A: Please tell us the following about you:

Gender: ☐ Male ☐ Female

Age Group: ☐ younger than 30 ☐ 30–39 ☐ 40–49 ☐ 50–59

Race/Ethnicity: ☐ African American ☐ Asian American ☐ Caucasian
  ☐ Latino/Hispanic

☐ Native American ☐ Biracial ☐ Other ☐ Prefer not to answer

1. Do you have the Internet at home? ☐ Yes ☐ No (If no, please skip to 2 below)

a. If yes, do you have all your children's passwords, screen names, and e-mail addresses?
  ☐ Yes ☐ No ☐ Unsure

b. If yes, where is the computer used by your child located?
  ☐ in a public room (living room, family room, etc.)
  ☐ in the child's bedroom
  ☐ in a sibling's bedroom
  ☐ other

c. If yes, do you have a Block or filter program on your home computer?
  ☐ Yes ☐ No

d. If yes, do you view the history of websites visited by your child?
  ☐ Yes ☐ No

2. Do you have a cell phone? ☐ Yes ☐ No

3. Does the child in this study have a personal cell phone? ☐ Yes ☐ No

Part B: Your use of technology

How would you rate your overall skills using technology (Internet, cell phones)?

☐ a novice (just learning)   ☐ minimally competent (I can do the essentials, but need lots of help)

☐ proficient   ☐ expert (I'm really a whiz)

Please mark the column that corresponds to how often YOU:

	Never	Monthly	Weekly	Daily
Send or receive e-mails				
Send or receive text messages				
Play online games				
Use the Internet to find information				
Visit social networking sites (e.g., MySpace, Facebook)				
Shop online				
Keep a blog				
Comment on other blogs				
Instant Message (IM)				
Visit chat rooms				
Go to Internet dating sites				

How often do you do the following:

	Never	Monthly	Weekly	Daily
Restrict the amount of time your child spends on the computer				
Review the history of websites your child visits				
Install filters or protective software on your home computer				
Talk with your child about right and wrong behaviors using technology				

About how often do you **communicate with your child by:**

	Never	Monthly	Weekly	Daily
E-mail				
Text message				
Cell phone calls				

For each activity, indicate about how often you believe YOUR CHILD does these things:

	Never	Monthly	Weekly	Daily
Sends or receive e-mails				
Sends or receive text messages				
Plays online games (e.g., Kidzworld, Club Penguin, Runescape, etc.)				
Looks up things online for school (homework, reports, clubs)				
Visits social networking sites (e.g., MySpace, Facebook,)				
Shops online				
Designs websites or web pages				
Keeps a blog				
Comments on other blogs				
Uses Instant Messaging (IM)				
Visits chat rooms online				

Please respond to the next group of questions about **your child's school:**

At my child's school:	Strongly Disagree	Dis-agree	Not sure	Agree	Strongly Agree
There is a clear policy about cyberbullying					
Teachers are well-informed about cyberbullying					
Teachers take steps to stop cyberbullying					
The school keeps parents informed about cyberbullying					
Cyberbullying is a big problem.					

Please indicate how often you believe the following things have happened *to your child* **DURING THE CURRENT SCHOOL YEAR:**

	Never	Once or twice	Three – five times	More than 5 times	I don't know
Talked with you about your online activities					
Showed their online profile (on MySpace, for example) to you					
Changed or added to their online profile					
Gave a friend one of their passwords					
Gotten more than one e-mail address or screen name					
Been in an online fight					
Received online messages that made them feel afraid					
Received mean or nasty e-mail messages					
Received mean or nasty text messages					
Sent mean or nasty messages online					
Sent mean or nasty text messages					
Sent a text message to scare someone					
Received a scary text message					
Had someone post bad or embarrassing things about them online					
Had someone send text messages about them that were not true					
Sent an embarrassing photo of someone via cell phone					
Found out someone had sent an embarrassing photo of them to their friends					
Had someone pretend to be your child and send an e-mail or text message that damaged his or her reputation or friendships					
Pretended to be someone else online					
Had his or her secrets shared online or by cell phone without your permission					

(Continued)

	Never	Once or twice	Three – five times	More than 5 times	I don't know
Shared someone else's secrets online or by cell phone without that person's permission					
Forwarded an e-mail, IM, or text message without the person's permission					
Had an e-mail, IM, or text message he or she sent to someone forwarded to others without his or her permission					
Had someone spread a rumor about him or her online					
Spread a rumor about someone online					
Been excluded (left out) of an online group					
Excluded someone else from an online group					
Seen mean things about a teacher online					
Posted mean things about a teacher online					
Read something online or in a text message in which someone said they were going to kill someone else or commit suicide					

In your opinion, how often do you think the following things happen **at your child's school?**

	Never	Monthly	Weekly	Daily	I don't know
People at school cyberbully others by computer					
People at school cyberbully others by cell phone					
Students get around school district Internet filters and visit sites they are not supposed to visit					

How often have the following things happened to **your child DURING THE CURRENT SCHOOL YEAR?**

	Never	Once or Twice	3–5 times	More than 5 times	I don't know
He/she stayed home from school because of something that happened online or by cell phone					
He/she confronted someone at school because of something that happened online or by cell phone					
He/she had trouble concentrating because of something that happened online or by cell phone					
He/she got in trouble at school for something that happened online or by cell phone					

Has your child ever been cyberbullied? If so, who was the bully? **Check all that apply.**

☐ I do not know
☐ He/she has never been cyberbullied
☐ I don't know who did it
☐ Someone in one of his/her classes
☐ A close friend
☐ Someone at school that he/she does not know at all
☐ A peer or classmate that your child dislikes

Which of the following would advise your child to do if he or she were cyberbullied?

☐ I don't know
☐ Retaliate or get even with the bully
☐ Just ignore it
☐ Tell the bully to stop
☐ Tell an adult at school about it
☐ Tell me (parent)
☐ Tell their friends
☐ Print the offending material to show to an adult

What would you advise your child to do if he/she saw someone else being cyberbullied?

☐ I do not know
☐ Join in

☐ Tell the bully(ies) to stop
☐ Leave the situation (chat room, website, hang up phone)
☐ Tell their friends about it
☐ Talk to the victim privately about it
☐ Report the situation to an adult at school
☐ Report the situation to me

What would advise your child to do if he/she discovered a hate page about a student at his or her school?

☐ I don't know
☐ Post their opinion on it
☐ Leave the page
☐ Tell their friends
☐ Tell the "victim"
☐ Tell an adult at school
☐ Tell me

What would advise your child to do if he/she discovered a hate page about a teacher at his or her school?

☐ I don't know
☐ Post their opinion on it
☐ Leave the page
☐ Tell their friends
☐ Tell the teacher
☐ Tell another adult at school
☐ Tell me

Which of the following do you think would help reduce cyberbulling? (Mark all that apply)

☐ Teach lessons in school about the effects of cyberbullying
☐ Have an anonymous phone line for students to report cyberbullying
☐ Have a clear policy saying the school does not tolerate cyberbullying
☐ Call the police to arrest students who cyberbully
☐ Punish students who participate in cyberbullying
☐ Notify parents when cyberbullying happens
☐ Use non-punitive strategies to address each incident
☐ Provide a list of resources (websites, books, etc.) that have tips for parents and teachers

☺ **THANK YOU FOR COMPLETING THE SURVEY!!** ☺

Teacher Survey

Please answer the following questions honestly. There are no right or wrong answers.

Please indicate your level of agreement with each statement about **this school**.

	Strongly Disagree	Disagree	Not sure	Agree	Strongly Agree
There is a specific policy about cyberbullying at this school.					
Teachers and staff are well-informed about cyberbullying.					
Teachers and staff take steps to stop cyberbullying.					
The school keeps parents informed about cyberbullying.					
Cyberbullying is a big problem.					
There is a specific policy about bullying.					
All staff consistently intervene when bullying occurs.					
Students report bullying incidents to adults at this school.					
Teachers and staff are knowledgeable about the technology their students use.					

How familiar are you with the following technologies?

	Not at all familiar	A little familiar	Fairly familiar	Very familiar
Text messaging				
E-mail				
Instant Messaging				
Chat rooms				
YouTube				
Social networking sites (e.g., Myspace, Facebook, Twitter)				
Sending photos or videos by cell phone				
Posting photos or videos on the Internet				

In your opinion, how often do you think the following things happen at this school?

	Never	Sometimes	Often	I don't know
Kids at school cyberbully others by computer				
Kids at school cyberbully others by cell phone				
Students get around school Internet filters and visit sites they are not supposed to visit				
Students use social networking sites to cyberbully others				

Please indicate how often you have personally experienced the following:

	Never	Sometimes	Often	I don't know
Harassment by e-mail				
Receiving mean or threatening text messages				
Had negative things posted about you on rateyourteacher.com or another website				
Harassment by cell phone				
Being harassed via e-mail or text messages by parents of students				
Had photos or video of you posted online without your consent				

Which of the following would advise a student to do if he or she were cyberbullied?

☐ I don't know
☐ Fight back/retaliate
☐ Just ignore it
☐ Tell the bully to stop
☐ Tell an adult at school about it
☐ Tell their parents
☐ Tell their friends
☐ Print the offending material to show to an adult
☐ Print the full header of an offending e-mail
☐ Other _____

Which of the following would you advise a student to do if he or she saw someone else being cyberbullied?

☐ I do not know
☐ Join in
☐ Tell the bully(ies) to stop
☐ Leave the situation (chat room, website, hang up phone)
☐ Tell their friends about it
☐ Talk to the victim privately about it
☐ Report the situation to an adult at school
☐ Tell their parents

What would you advise A STUDENT to do if he/she discovered a hate page about a student at his or her school?

☐ I don't know
☐ Post their opinion on it
☐ Leave the page
☐ Tell their friends
☐ Tell the "victim"
☐ Tell an adult at school
☐ Tell their parents

What would you advise a student to do if he/she discovered a hate page about a teacher at his or her school?

☐ I don't know
☐ Post their opinion on it
☐ Leave the page
☐ Tell the principal
☐ Tell that teacher
☐ Tell another teacher at school
☐ Tell their parents

What would you do if you discovered a hate page about another teacher at your school?

☐ I don't know
☐ Tell the teacher
☐ Tell the principal
☐ Contact the website host and demand it be taken down
☐ Call the police

For the following questions, please tell us how frequently each of these students has done/experienced the following **during this school year**.

(Overt Aggression 1)

This kid hits or kicks others . . .	Never	Once or twice	Three– five times	More than 5 times	I don't know
Name 1					
Name 2					
Name 3					
Name 4					
Name 5					
Name 6					

(Overt Aggression 2)[1]

This kid pushes others around . . .	Never	Once or twice	Three– five times	More than 5 times	I don't know
Name 1					
Name 2					

[1] To conserve space, we list only two names for each section, but the actual survey contains lines for 10 names.

Source: Pilot form of survey developed by Sheri Bauman and Noel A. Card.

(Overt Aggression 3)

This kid says mean things to others or calls them names . . .	Never	Once or twice	Three– five times	More than 5 times	I don't know
Name 1					
Name 2					

(Relational Aggression 1)

This kid spreads rumors about others . . .	Never	Once or twice	Three– five times	More than 5 times	I don't know
Name 1					
Name 2					

(Relational Aggression 2)

This kid tries to keep others from being part of activities or groups ...	Never	Once or twice	Three–five times	More than 5 times	I don't know
Name 1					
Name 2					

(Relational Aggression 3)

This kid tries to make others ignore or not talk to certain children ...	Never	Once or twice	Three–five times	More than 5 times	I don't know
Name 1					
Name 2					

(Cyber Aggression 1)

This kid sends mean text messages ...	Never	Once or twice	Three–five times	More than 5 times	I don't know
Name 1					
Name 2					

(Cyber Aggression 2)

This kid says mean things in online chats ...	Never	Once or twice	Three–five times	More than 5 times	I don't know
Name 1					
Name 2					

(Cyber Aggression 3)

This kid posts mean things about others online ...	Never	Once or twice	Three–five times	More than 5 times	I don't know
Name 1					
Name 2					

(Overt Victimization 1)

This kid gets hit or kicked by others . . .	Never	Once or twice	Three–five times	More than 5 times	I don't know
Name 1					
Name 2					

(Overt Victimization 2)

This kid gets pushed around by others . . .	Never	Once or twice	Three–five times	More than 5 times	I don't know
Name 1					
Name 2					

(Overt Victimization 3)

Others say mean things to or call this kid names . . .	Never	Once or twice	Three–five times	More than 5 times	I don't know
Name 1					
Name 2					

(Relational Victimization 1)

Others spread rumors about this kid . . .	Never	Once or twice	Three– five times	More than 5 times	I don't know
Name 1					
Name 2					

(Relational Victimization 2)

Others keep this kid from being part of activities or groups . . .	Never	Once or twice	Three– five times	More than 5 times	I don't know
Name 1					
Name 2					

(Relational Victimization 3)

Others get kids to ignore or not talk to this kid . . .	Never	Once or twice	Three–five times	More than 5 times	I don't know
Name 1					
Name 2					

(Cyber Victimization 1)

This kid gets mean text messages from others . . .	Never	Once or twice	Three– five times	More than 5 times	I don't know
Name 1					
Name 2					

(Cyber Victimization 2)

This kid gets picked on in online chats . . .	Never	Once or twice	Three– five times	More than 5 times	I don't know
Name 1					
Name 2					

(Cyber Victimization 3)

Others post mean things about this kid online . . .	Never	Once or twice	Three– five times	More than 5 times	I don't know
Name 1					
Name 2					

Index

Printed in Great Britain
by Amazon